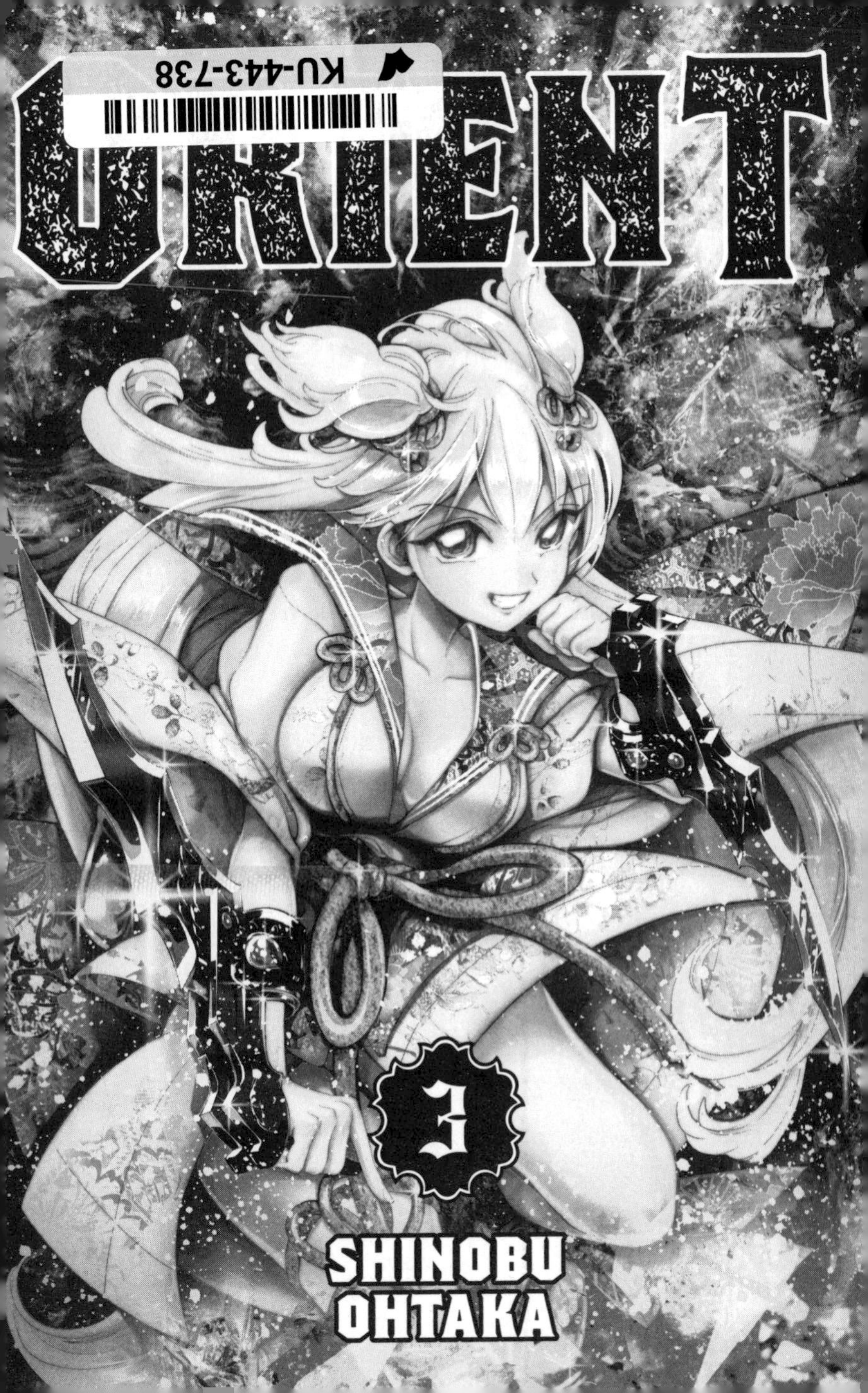
ORIENT
3
SHINOBU
OHTAKA

ORIENT

3

SHINOBU OHTAKA

ORIENT

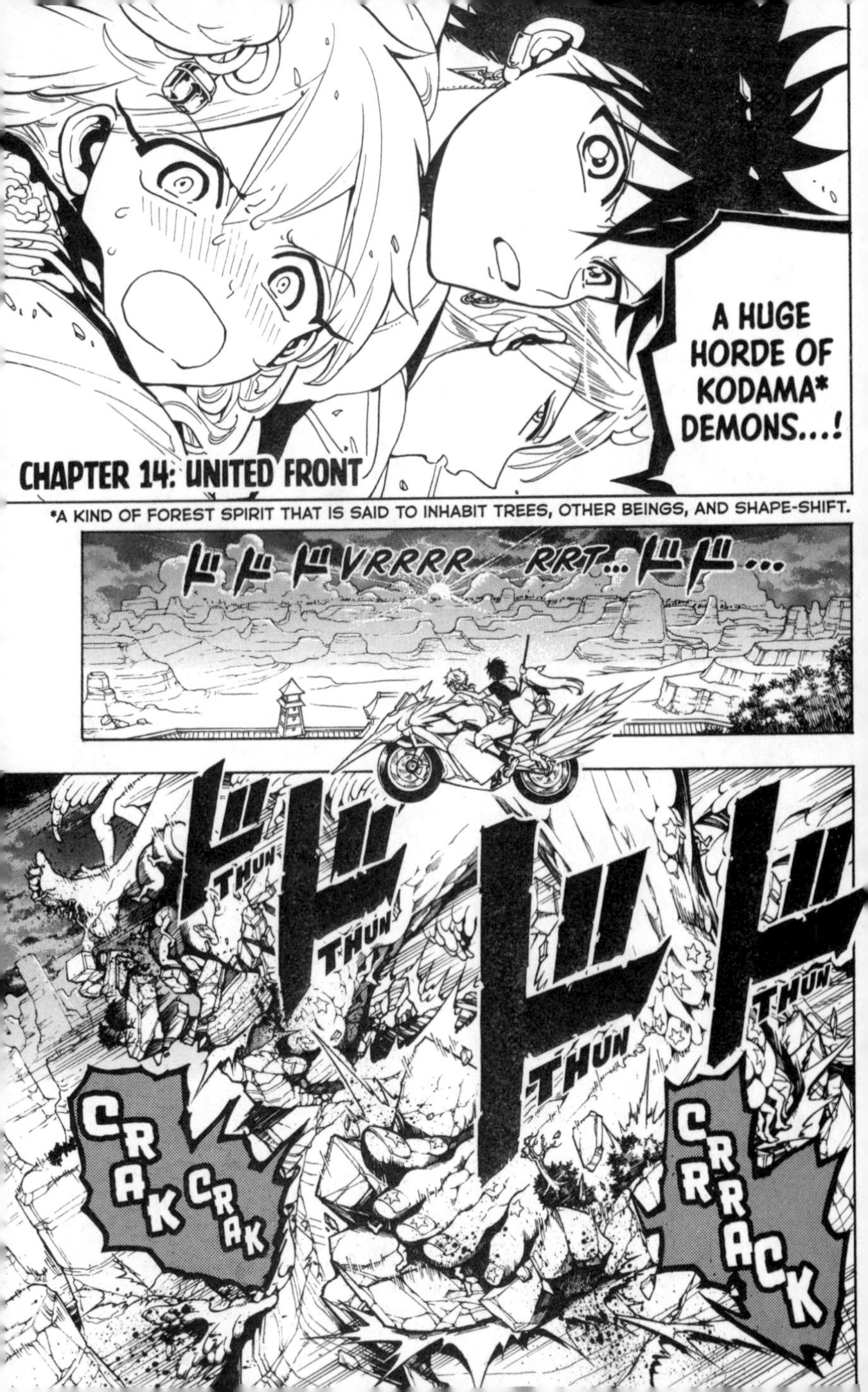
A HUGE HORDE OF KODAMA* DEMONS...!
CHAPTER 14: UNITED FRONT
*A KIND OF FOREST SPIRIT THAT IS SAID TO INHABIT TREES, OTHER BEINGS, AND SHAPE-SHIFT.
ドドドVRRRR RRT...ドド...
THUN
THUN
THUN
THUN
CRRRRACK
CRAK CRAK

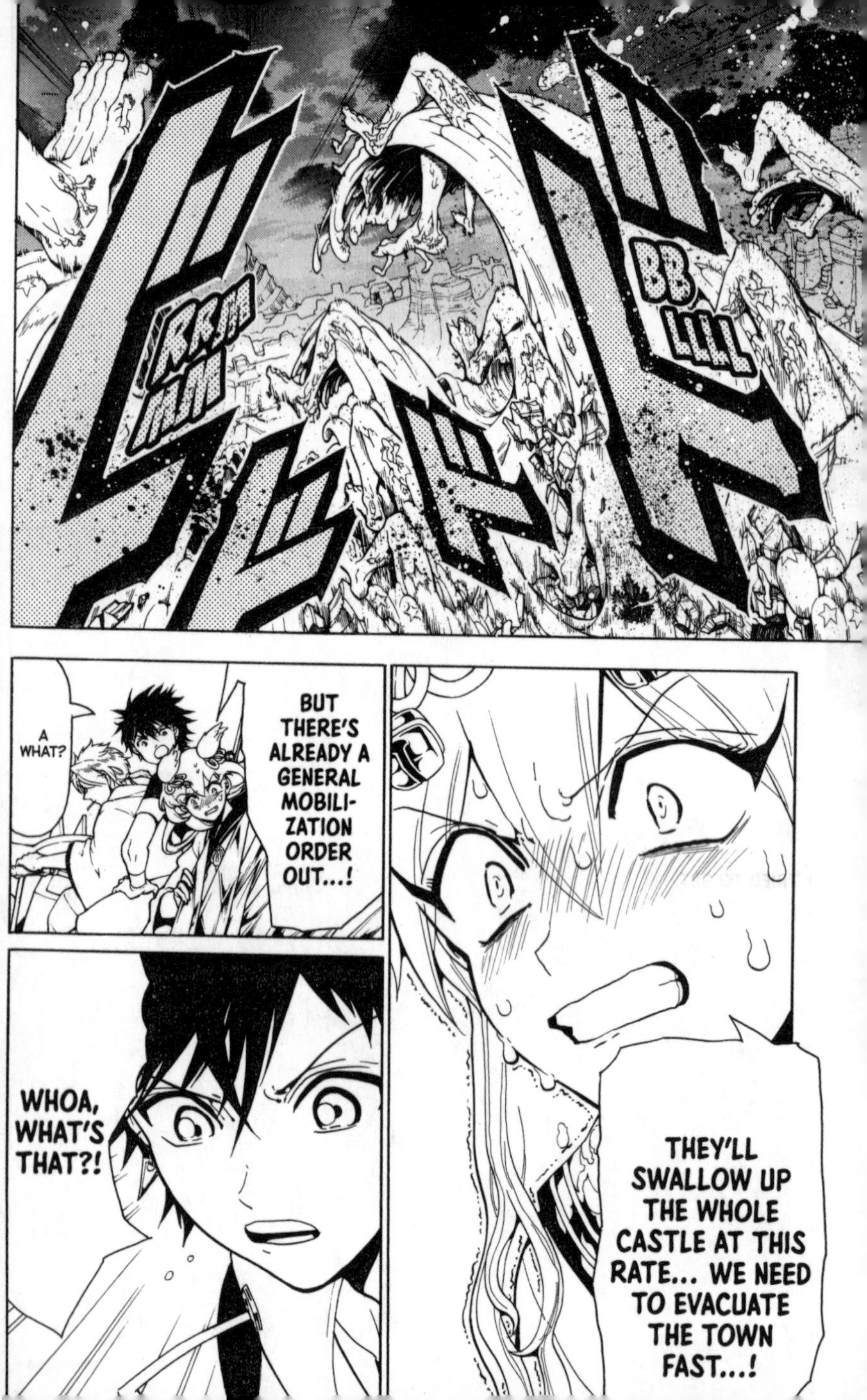
BBLLLL
THEY'LL SWALLOW UP THE WHOLE CASTLE AT THIS RATE... WE NEED TO EVACUATE THE TOWN FAST...!
BUT THERE'S ALREADY A GENERAL MOBILIZATION ORDER OUT...!
A WHAT?
WHOA, WHAT'S THAT?!

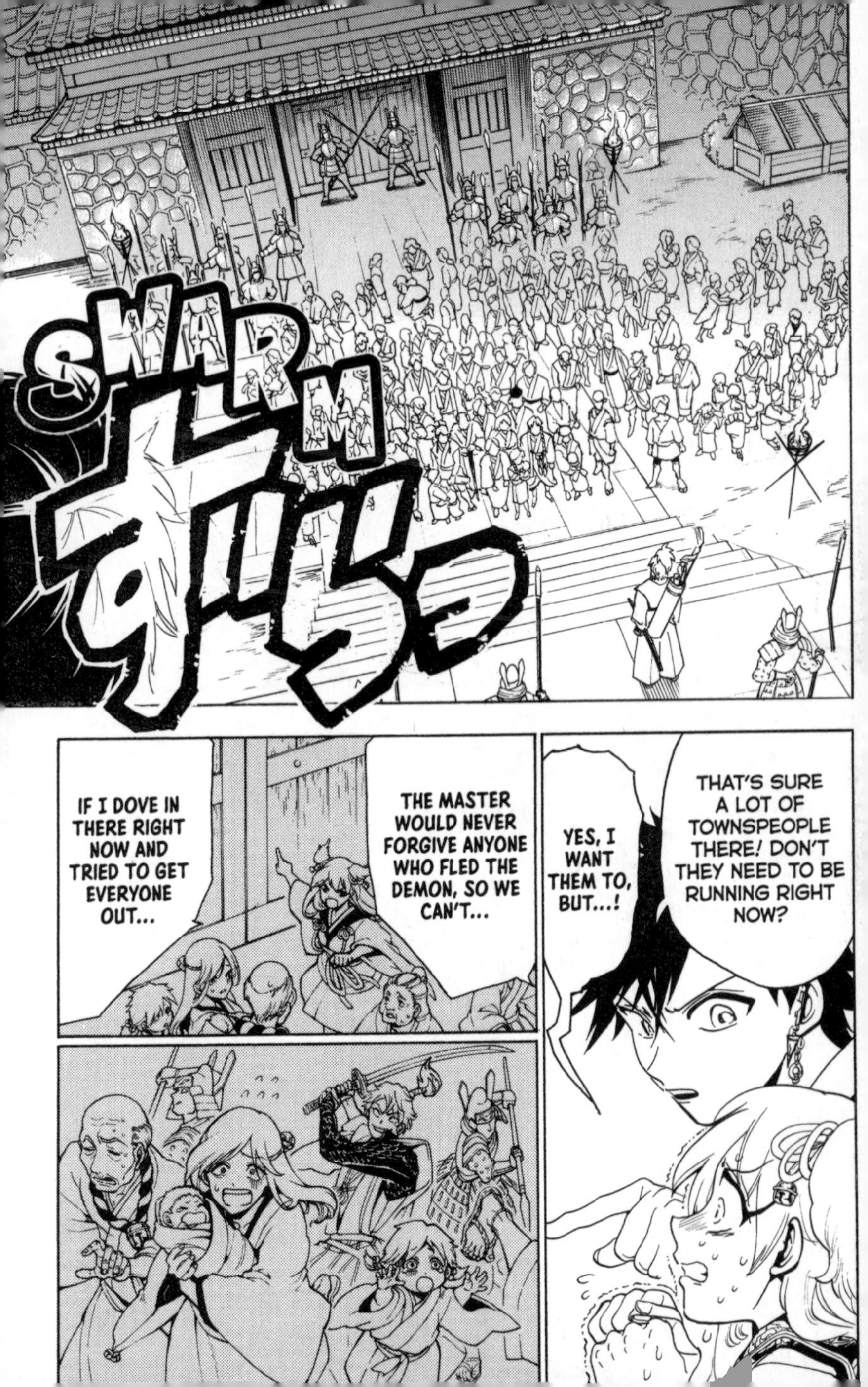
SWARM
THAT'S SURE A LOT OF TOWNSPEOPLE THERE! DON'T THEY NEED TO BE RUNNING RIGHT NOW?
YES, I WANT THEM TO, BUT...!
THE MASTER WOULD NEVER FORGIVE ANYONE WHO FLED THE DEMON, SO WE CAN'T...
IF I DOVE IN THERE RIGHT NOW AND TRIED TO GET EVERYONE OUT...

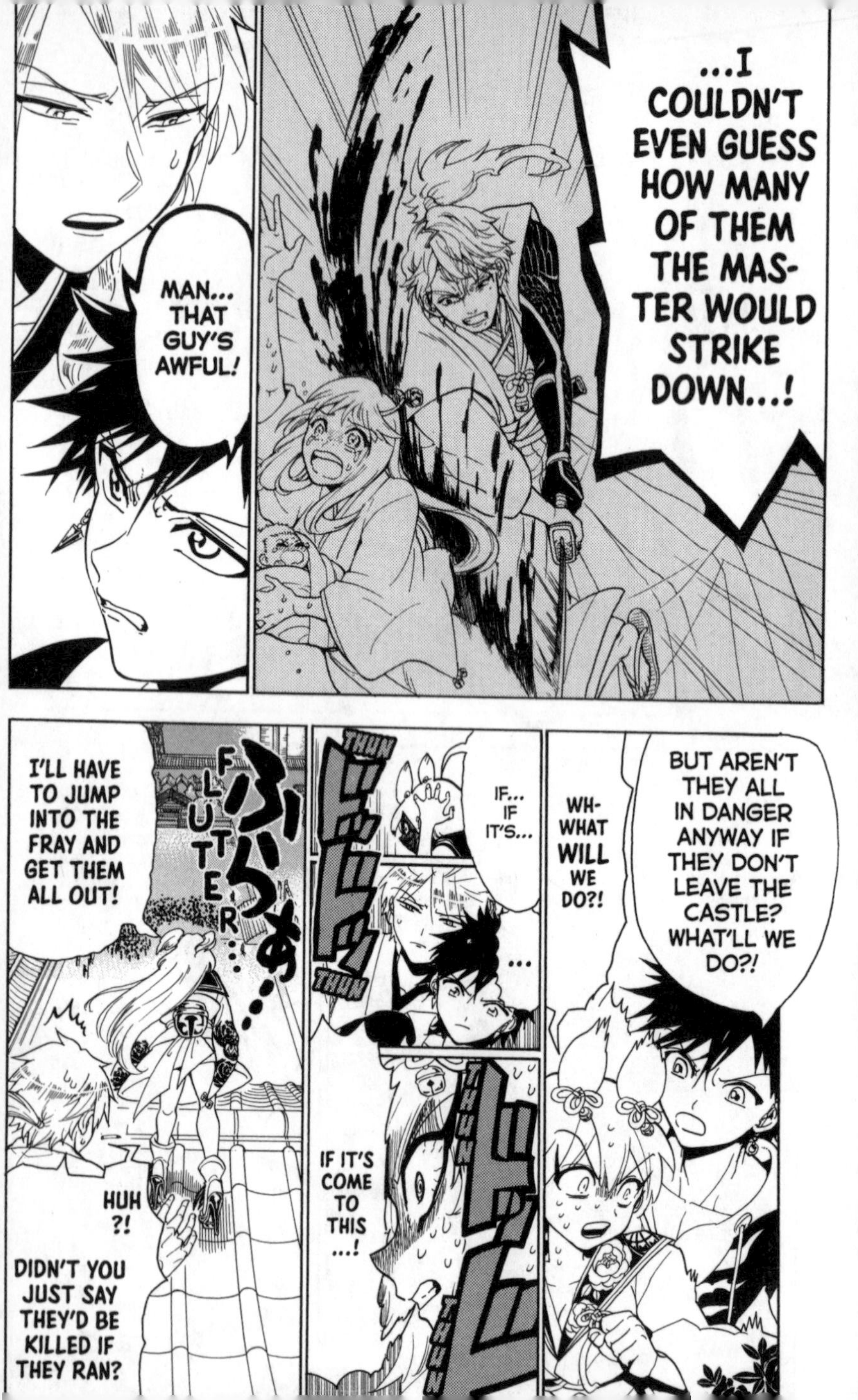
...I COULDN'T EVEN GUESS HOW MANY OF THEM THE MASTER WOULD STRIKE DOWN...!
MAN... THAT GUY'S AWFUL!
BUT AREN'T THEY ALL IN DANGER ANYWAY IF THEY DON'T LEAVE THE CASTLE? WHAT'LL WE DO?!
WH-WHAT WILL WE DO?!
THUN
IF... IF IT'S...
THUN
...
THUN
IF IT'S COME TO THIS...!
FLUTTER...
I'LL HAVE TO JUMP INTO THE FRAY AND GET THEM ALL OUT!
HUH?!
DIDN'T YOU JUST SAY THEY'D BE KILLED IF THEY RAN?

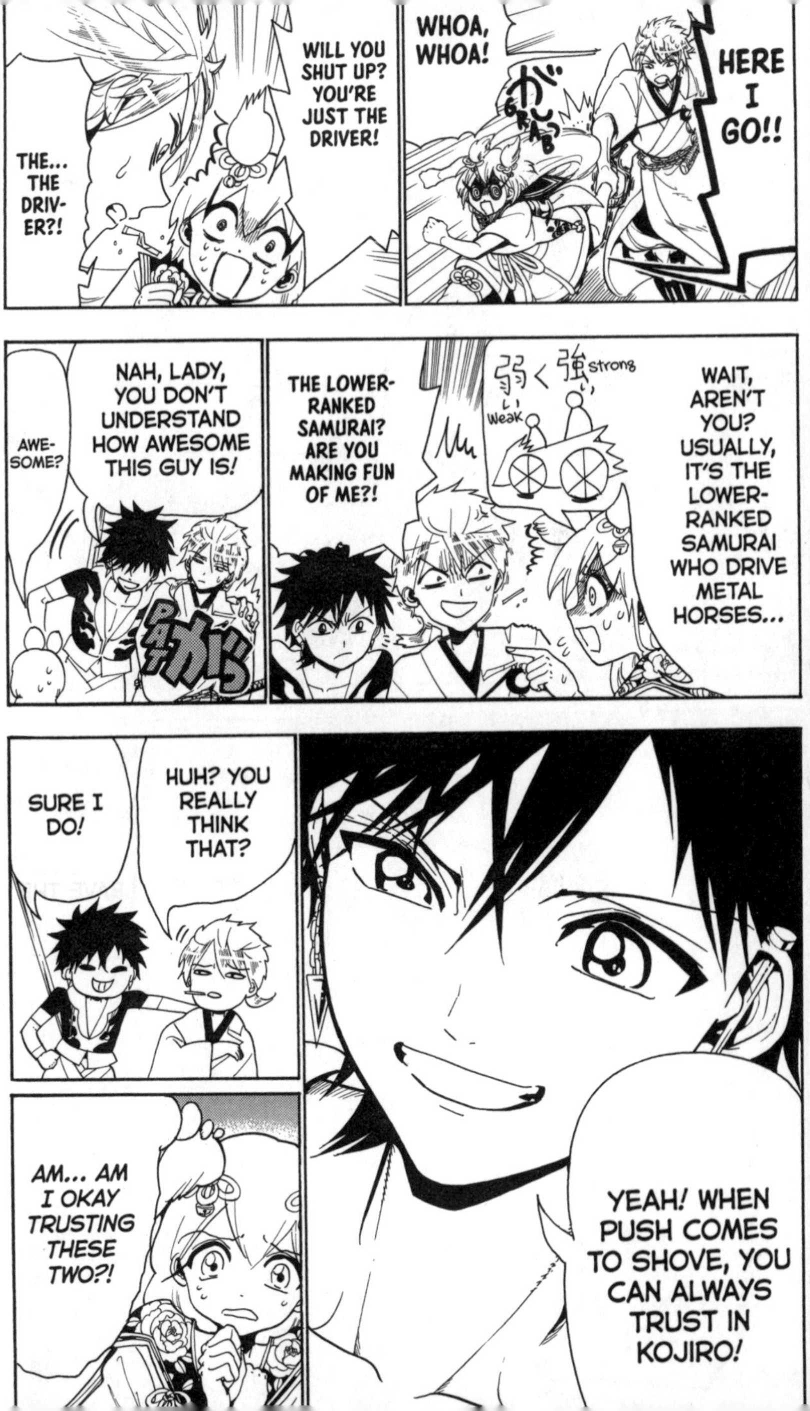
HERE I GO!!
WHOA, WHOA!
GRAB
WILL YOU SHUT UP? YOU'RE JUST THE DRIVER!
THE... THE DRIV-ER?!
WAIT, AREN'T YOU? USUALLY, IT'S THE LOWER-RANKED SAMURAI WHO DRIVE METAL HORSES...
強 strong
弱く weak
THE LOWER-RANKED SAMURAI? ARE YOU MAKING FUN OF ME?!
NAH, LADY, YOU DON'T UNDERSTAND HOW AWESOME THIS GUY IS!
AWE-SOME?
YEAH! WHEN PUSH COMES TO SHOVE, YOU CAN ALWAYS TRUST IN KOJIRO!
HUH? YOU REALLY THINK THAT?
SURE I DO!
AM... AM I OKAY TRUSTING THESE TWO?!

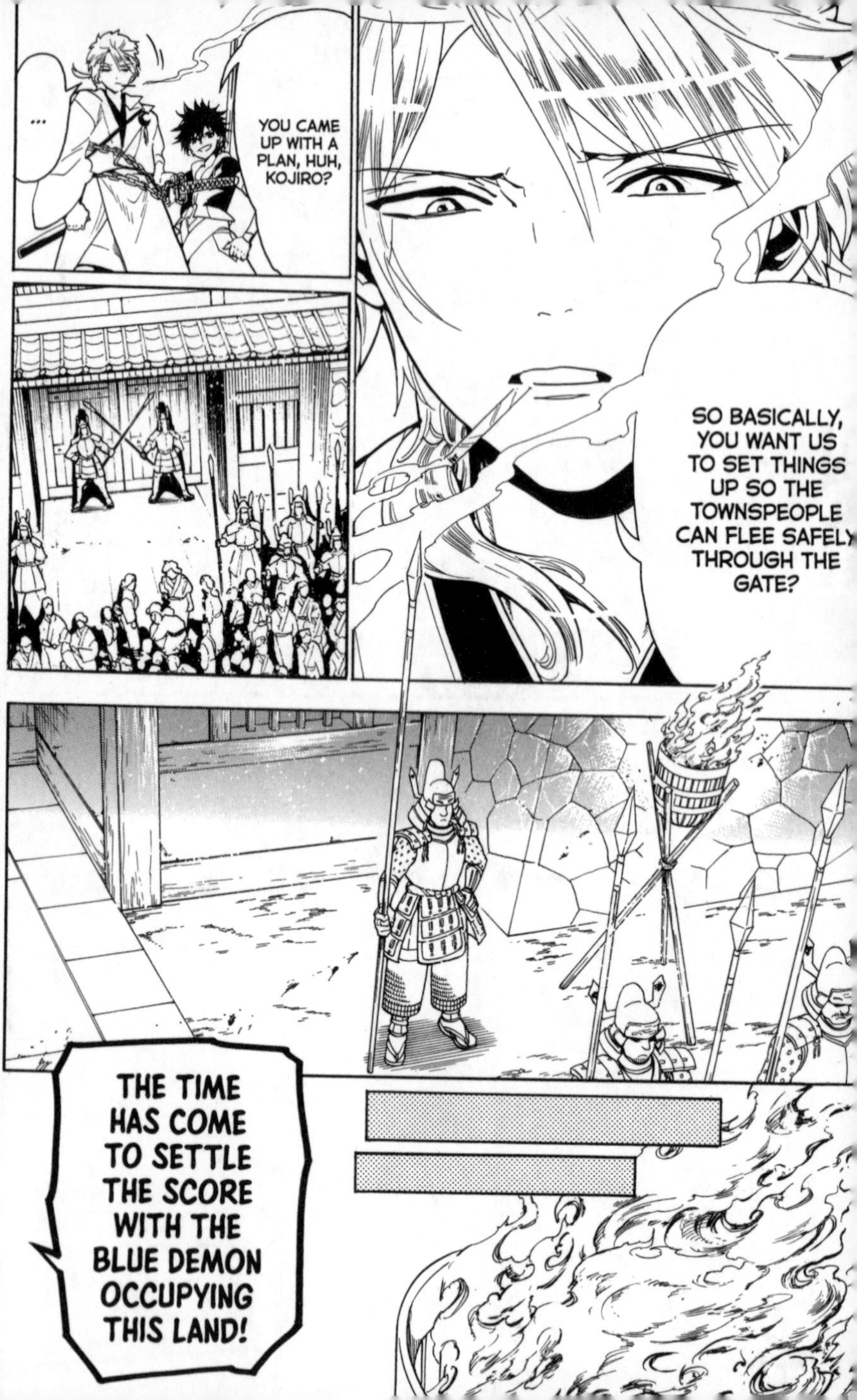
SO BASICALLY, YOU WANT US TO SET THINGS UP SO THE TOWNSPEOPLE CAN FLEE SAFELY THROUGH THE GATE?
YOU CAME UP WITH A PLAN, HUH, KOJIRO?
...
THE TIME HAS COME TO SETTLE THE SCORE WITH THE BLUE DEMON OCCUPYING THIS LAND!

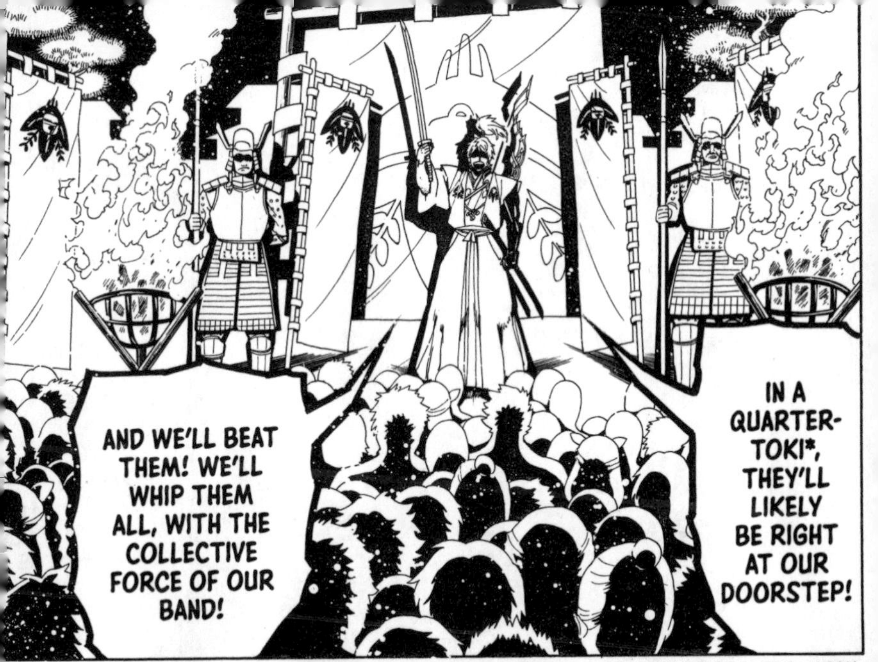
IN A QUARTER-TOKI*, THEY'LL LIKELY BE RIGHT AT OUR DOORSTEP!
AND WE'LL BEAT THEM! WE'LL WHIP THEM ALL, WITH THE COLLECTIVE FORCE OF OUR BAND!

*THE DAY WAS DIVIDED INTO SIX "TOKI" IN EDO JAPAN.

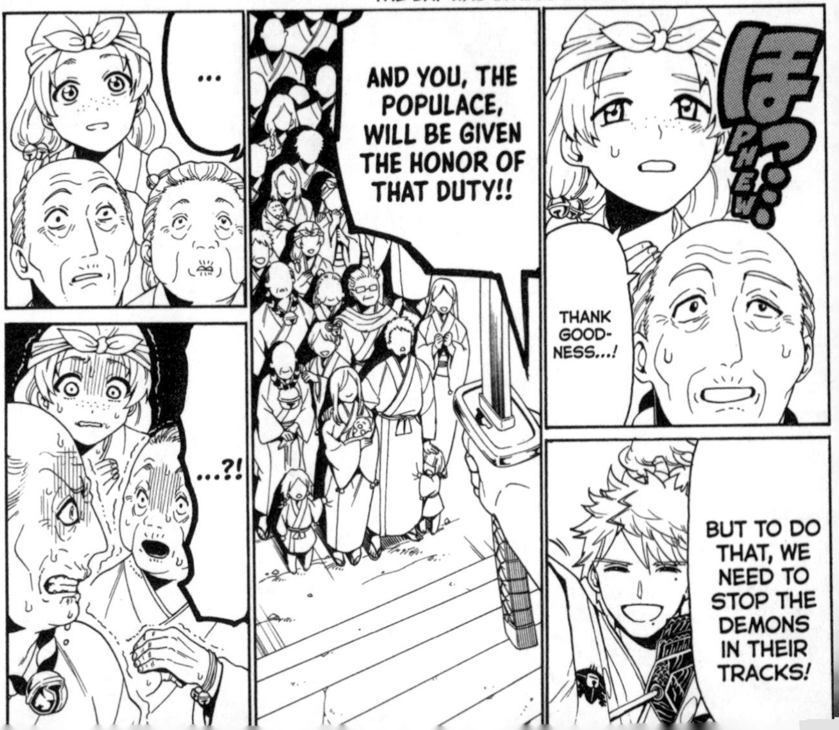
ほっ
PHEW
THANK GOOD-NESS...!
BUT TO DO THAT, WE NEED TO STOP THE DEMONS IN THEIR TRACKS!
AND YOU, THE POPULACE, WILL BE GIVEN THE HONOR OF THAT DUTY!!
...
...?!

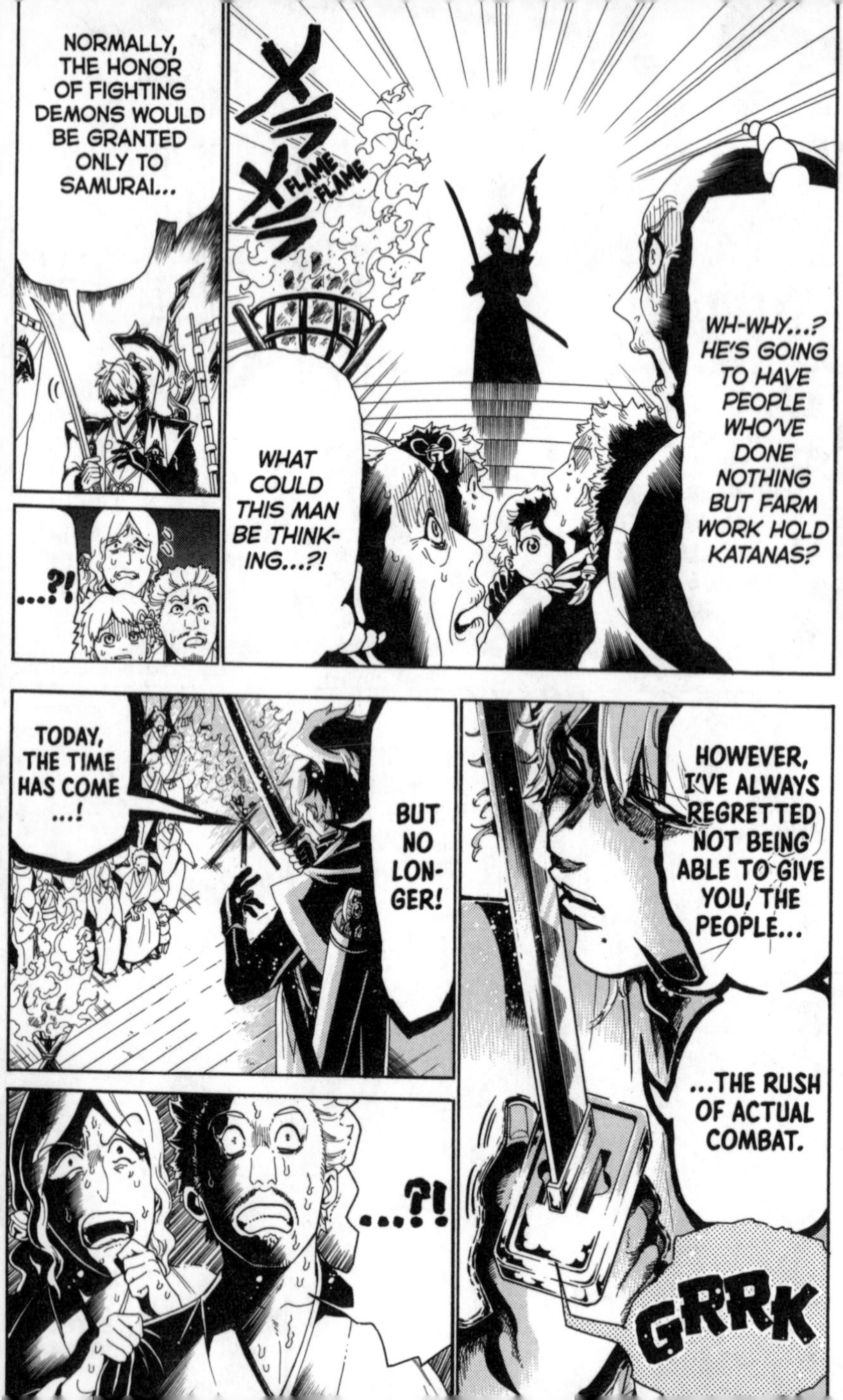
FLAME FLAME
WH-WHY...? HE'S GOING TO HAVE PEOPLE WHO'VE DONE NOTHING BUT FARM WORK HOLD KATANAS?
WHAT COULD THIS MAN BE THINK-ING...?!
NORMALLY, THE HONOR OF FIGHTING DEMONS WOULD BE GRANTED ONLY TO SAMURAI...
...?!
HOWEVER, I'VE ALWAYS REGRETTED NOT BEING ABLE TO GIVE YOU, THE PEOPLE...
...THE RUSH OF ACTUAL COMBAT.
GRRK
BUT NO LON-GER!
TODAY, THE TIME HAS COME ...!
...?!

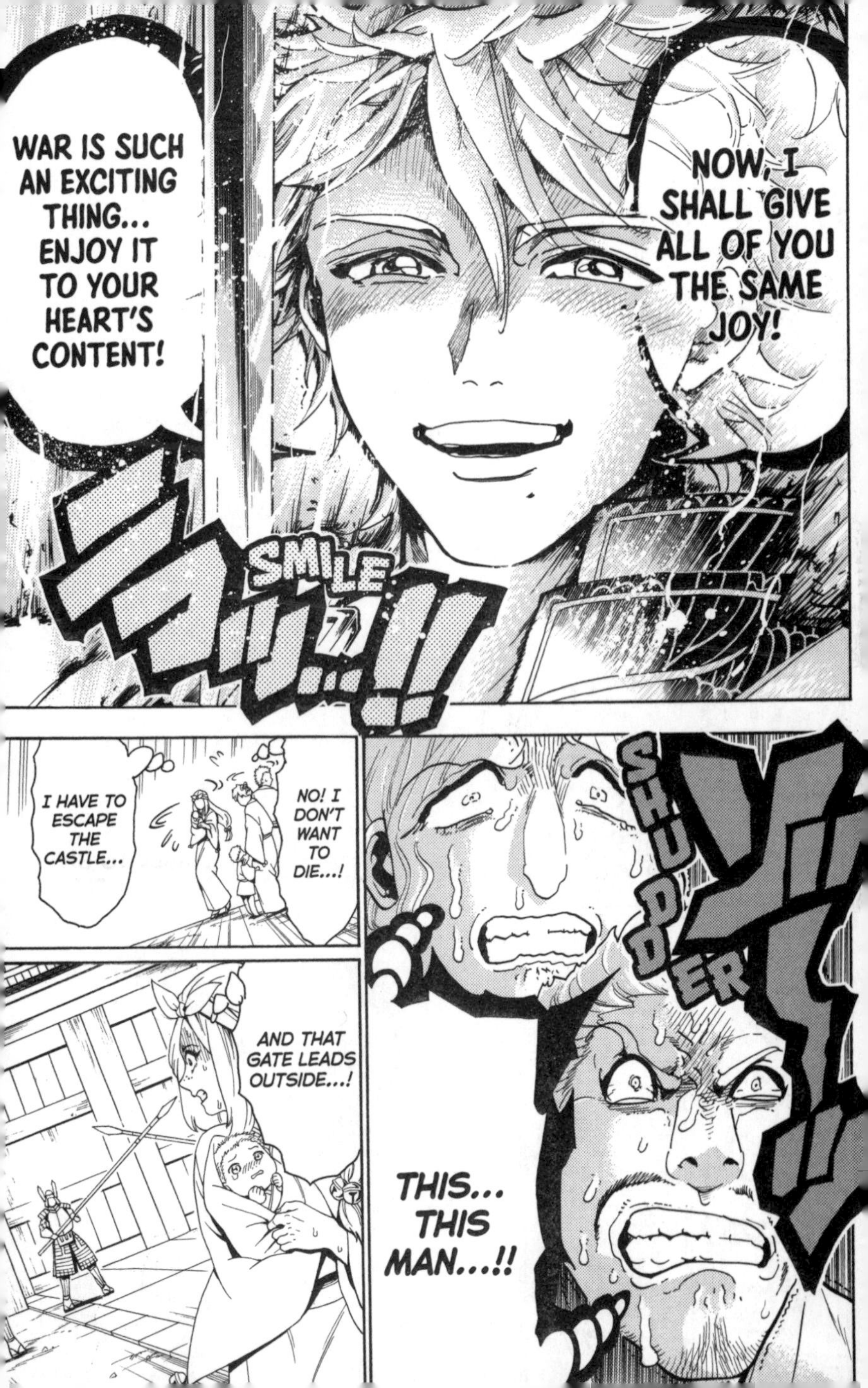
NOW, I SHALL GIVE ALL OF YOU THE SAME JOY!
WAR IS SUCH AN EXCITING THING... ENJOY IT TO YOUR HEART'S CONTENT!
SMILE
SHUDDER
THIS... THIS MAN...!!
NO! I DON'T WANT TO DIE...!
I HAVE TO ESCAPE THE CASTLE...
AND THAT GATE LEADS OUTSIDE...!

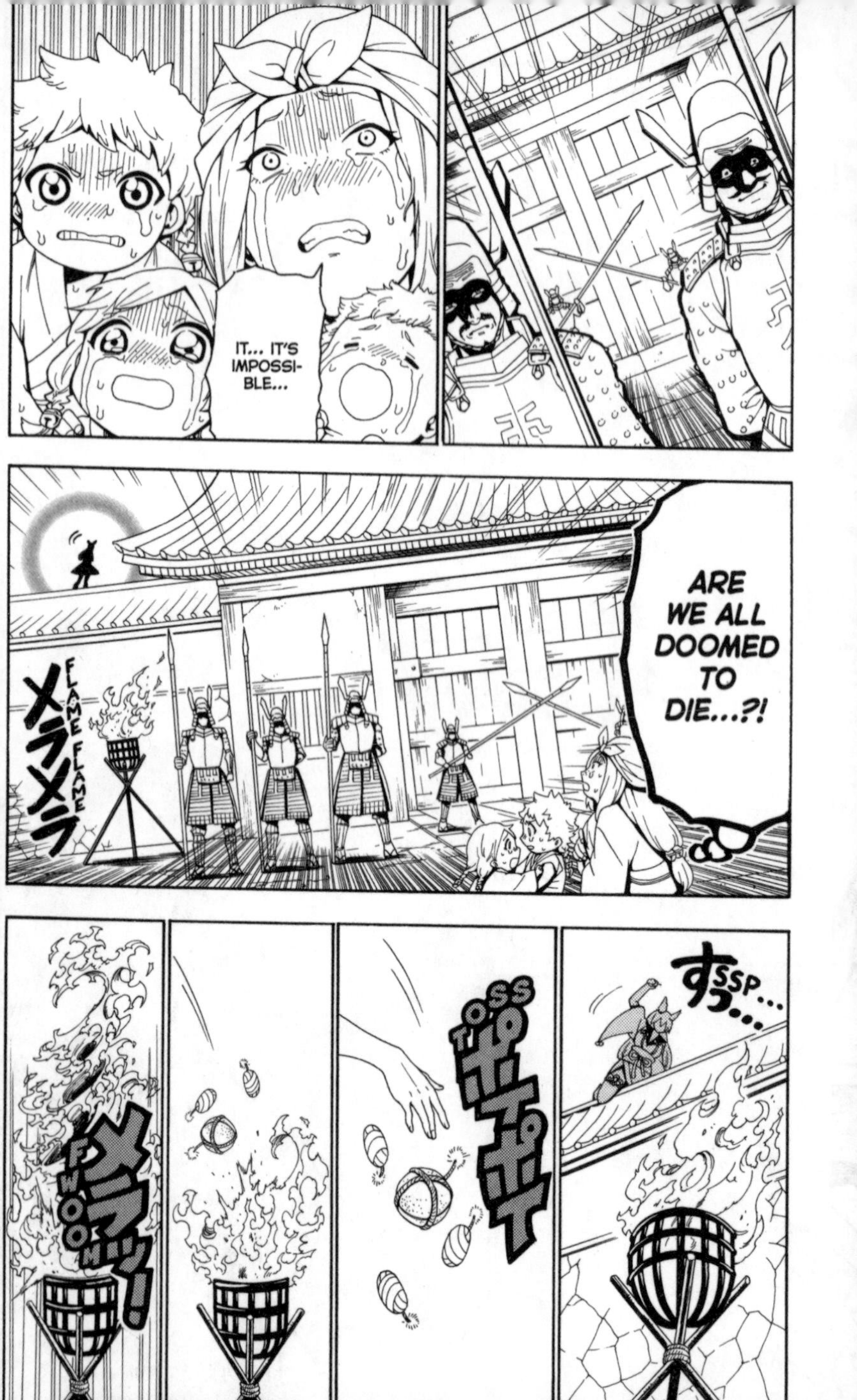
IT... IT'S IMPOSSIBLE...
ARE WE ALL DOOMED TO DIE...?!
メラメラ FLAME FLAME
すっ... SSP...
ポイポイ TOSS TOSS
メラッ FWOOM!

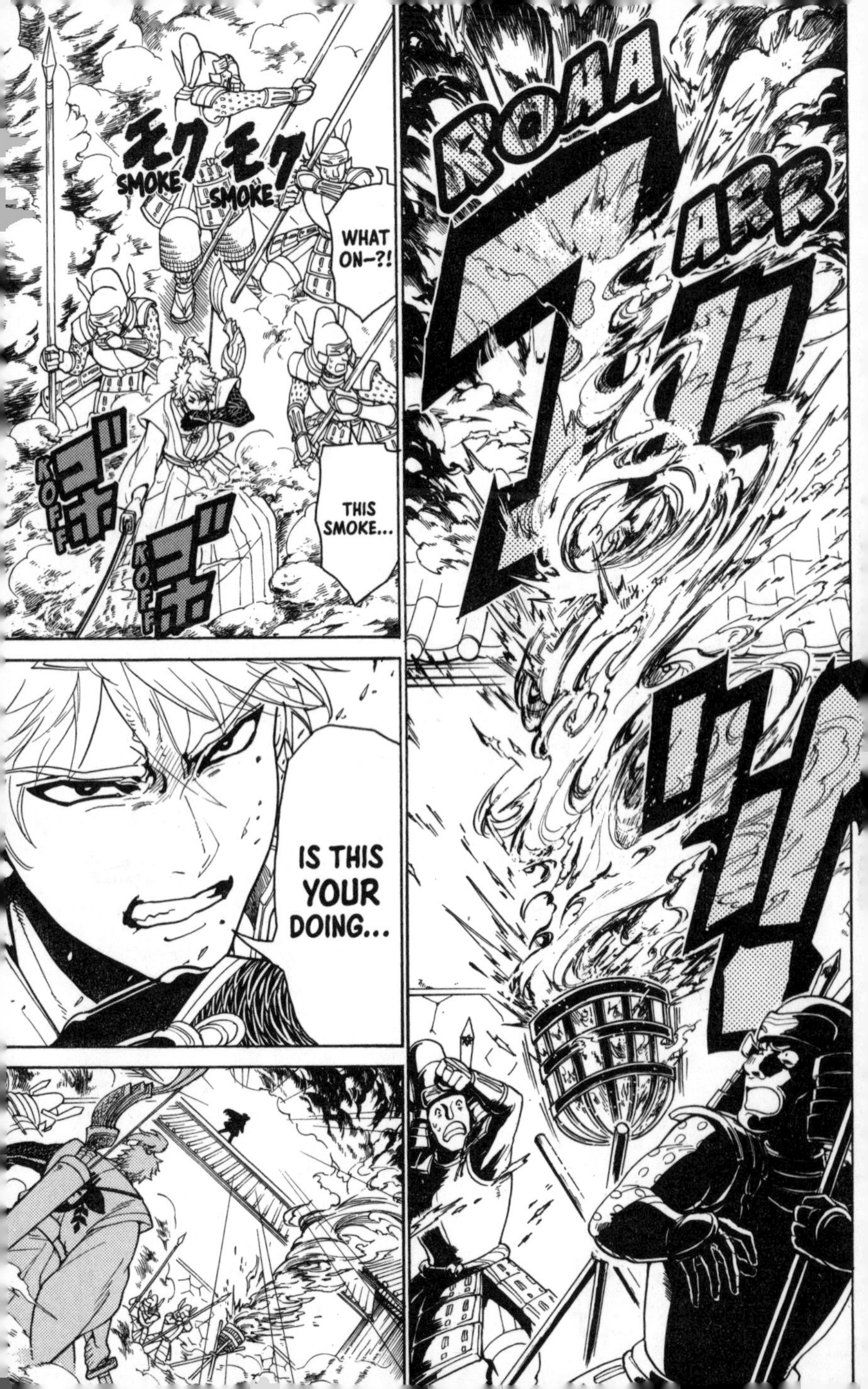
ROAAARR
モクモク
SMOKE SMOKE
WHAT ON-?!
ゴホゴホ
KOFF KOFF
THIS SMOKE...
IS THIS YOUR DOING...

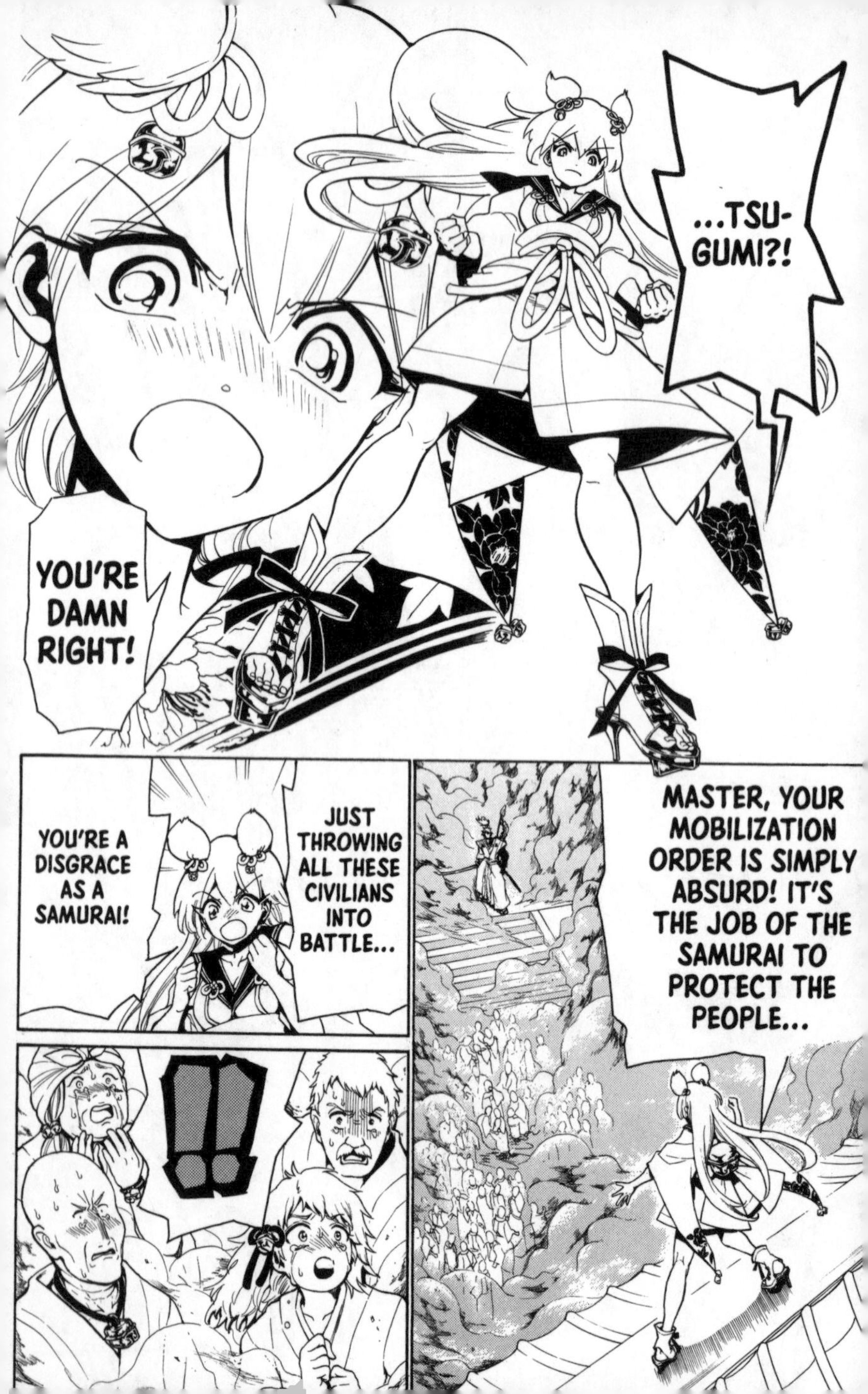
...TSU-GUMI?!
YOU'RE DAMN RIGHT!
MASTER, YOUR MOBILIZATION ORDER IS SIMPLY ABSURD! IT'S THE JOB OF THE SAMURAI TO PROTECT THE PEOPLE...
JUST THROWING ALL THESE CIVILIANS INTO BATTLE...
YOU'RE A DISGRACE AS A SAMURAI!
!!

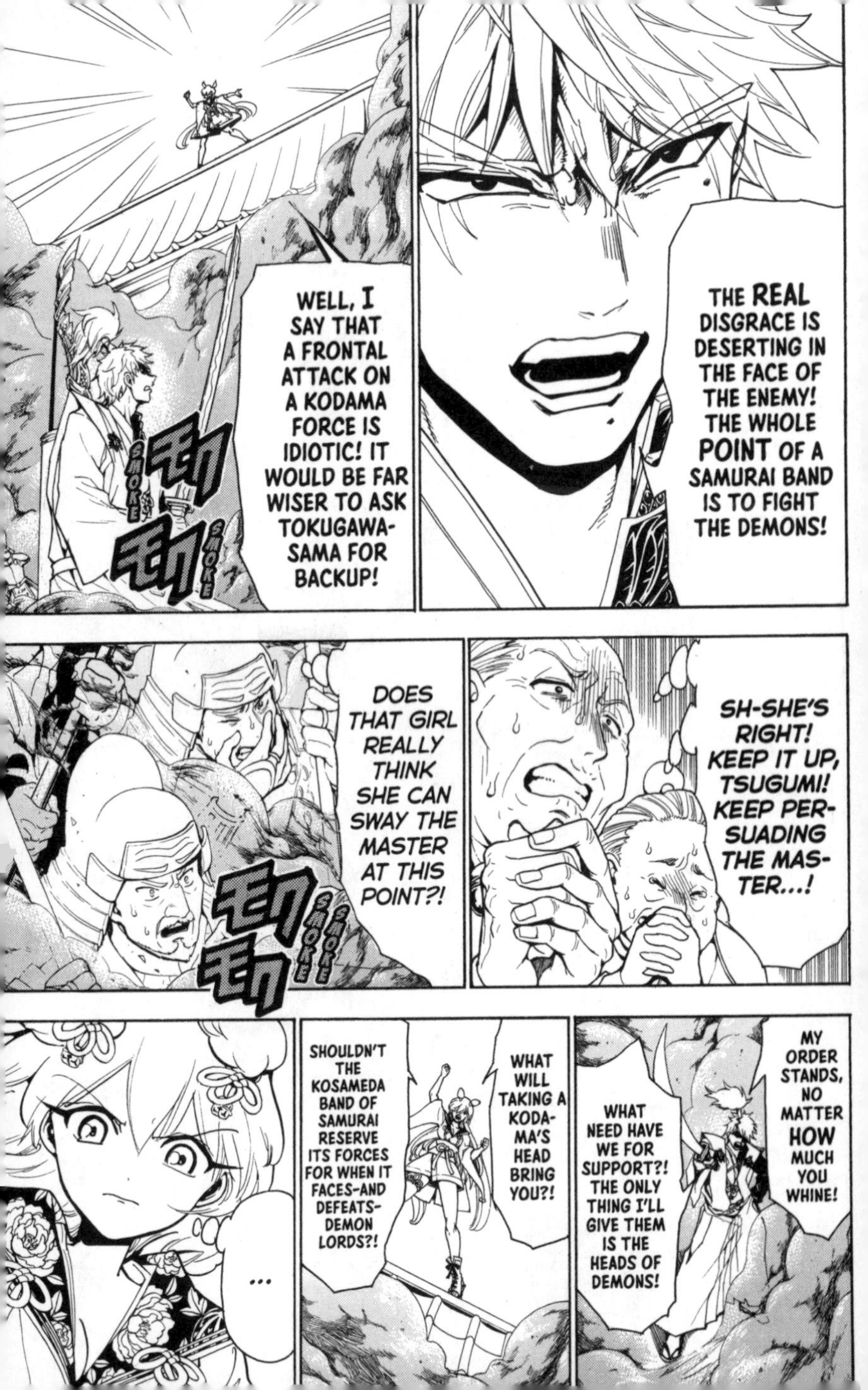
THE REAL DISGRACE IS DESERTING IN THE FACE OF THE ENEMY! THE WHOLE POINT OF A SAMURAI BAND IS TO FIGHT THE DEMONS!
WELL, I SAY THAT A FRONTAL ATTACK ON A KODAMA FORCE IS IDIOTIC! IT WOULD BE FAR WISER TO ASK TOKUGAWA-SAMA FOR BACKUP!
モク SMOKE
モク SMOKE
SH-SHE'S RIGHT! KEEP IT UP, TSUGUMI! KEEP PER-SUADING THE MAS-TER...!
DOES THAT GIRL REALLY THINK SHE CAN SWAY THE MASTER AT THIS POINT?!
モク SMOKE
モク SMOKE
MY ORDER STANDS, NO MATTER HOW MUCH YOU WHINE!
WHAT NEED HAVE WE FOR SUPPORT?! THE ONLY THING I'LL GIVE THEM IS THE HEADS OF DEMONS!
WHAT WILL TAKING A KODA-MA'S HEAD BRING YOU?!
SHOULDN'T THE KOSAMEDA BAND OF SAMURAI RESERVE ITS FORCES FOR WHEN IT FACES-AND DEFEATS-DEMON LORDS?!
...

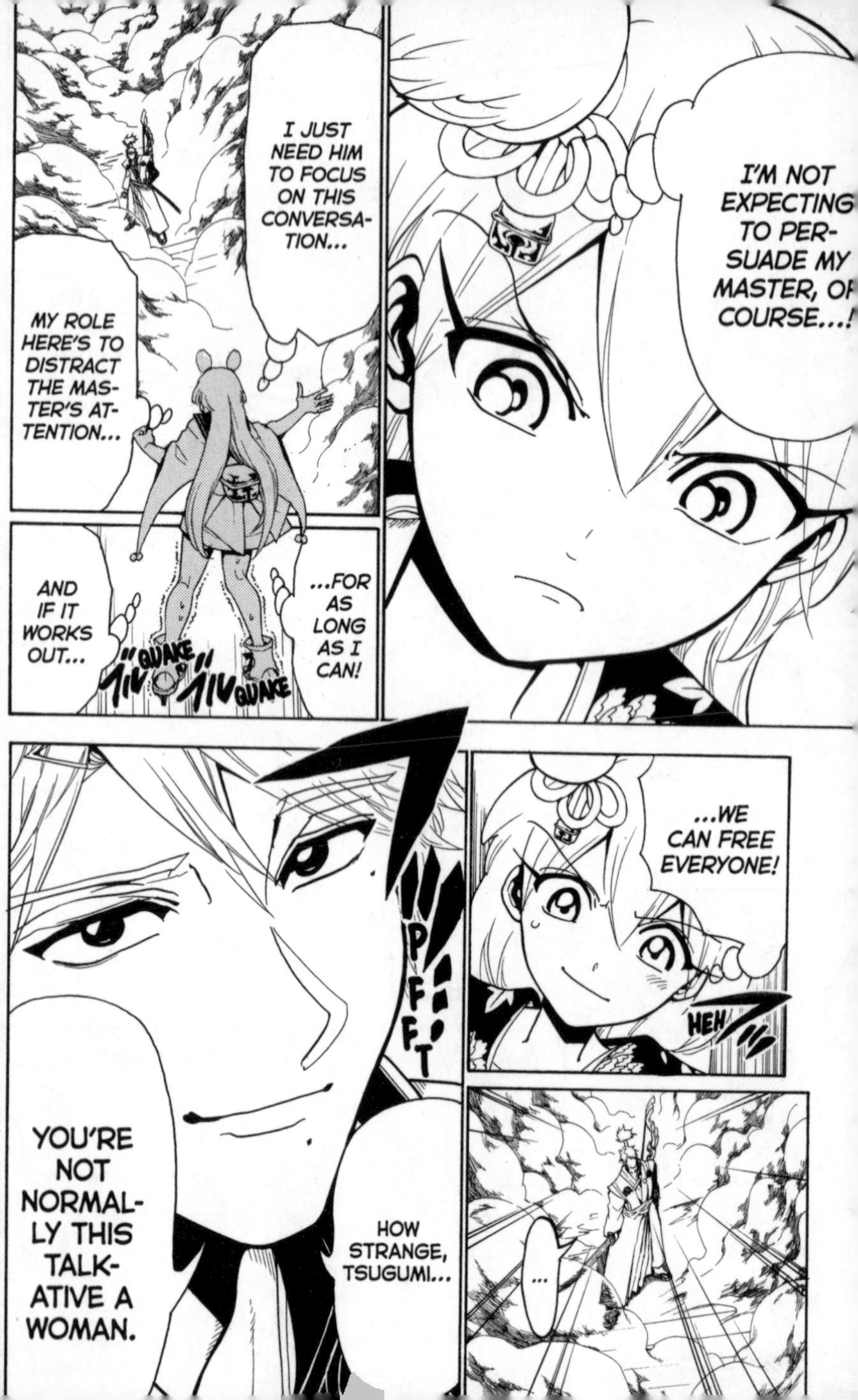
I'M NOT EXPECTING TO PERSUADE MY MASTER, OF COURSE...!
I JUST NEED HIM TO FOCUS ON THIS CONVERSATION...
MY ROLE HERE'S TO DISTRACT THE MASTER'S ATTENTION...
...FOR AS LONG AS I CAN!
AND IF IT WORKS OUT...
QUAKE
QUAKE
...WE CAN FREE EVERYONE!
HEH
...
PFFFT
HOW STRANGE, TSUGUMI...
YOU'RE NOT NORMALLY THIS TALKATIVE A WOMAN.

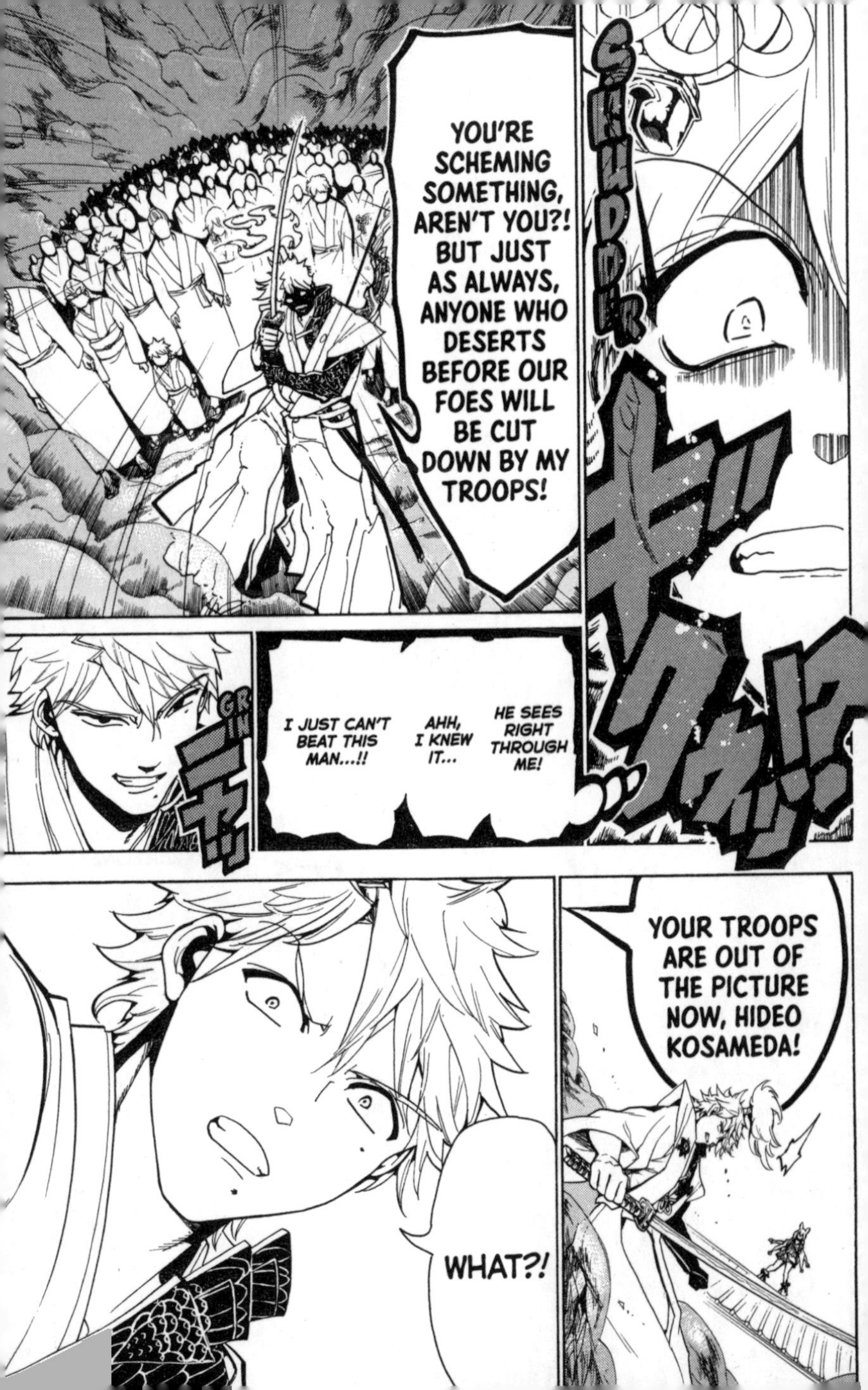
SHUDDER
YOU'RE SCHEMING SOMETHING, AREN'T YOU?! BUT JUST AS ALWAYS, ANYONE WHO DESERTS BEFORE OUR FOES WILL BE CUT DOWN BY MY TROOPS!
HE SEES RIGHT THROUGH ME!
AHH, I KNEW IT...
I JUST CAN'T BEAT THIS MAN...!!
GRIN
YOUR TROOPS ARE OUT OF THE PICTURE NOW, HIDEO KOSAMEDA!
WHAT?!

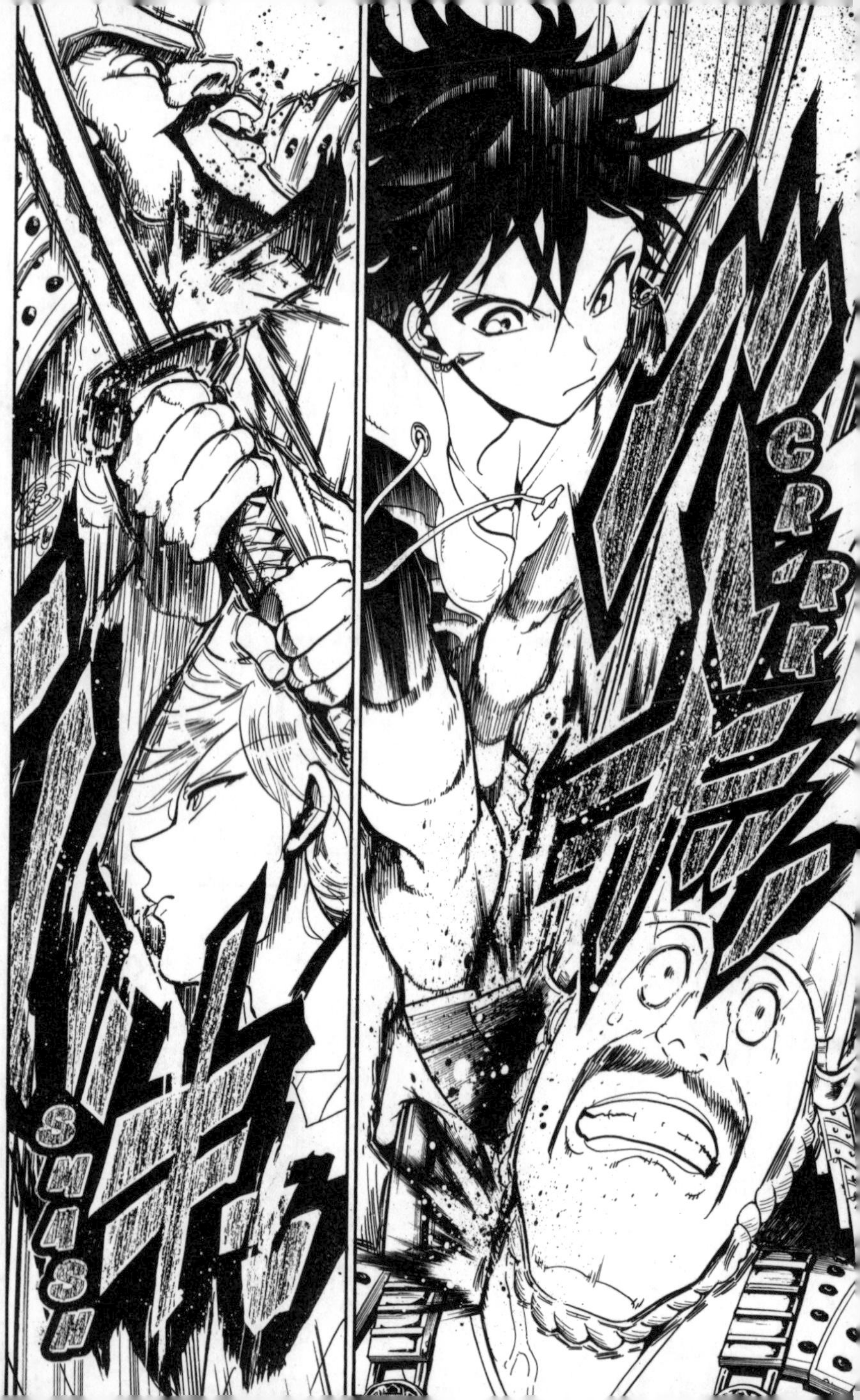
CRRK
SMASH

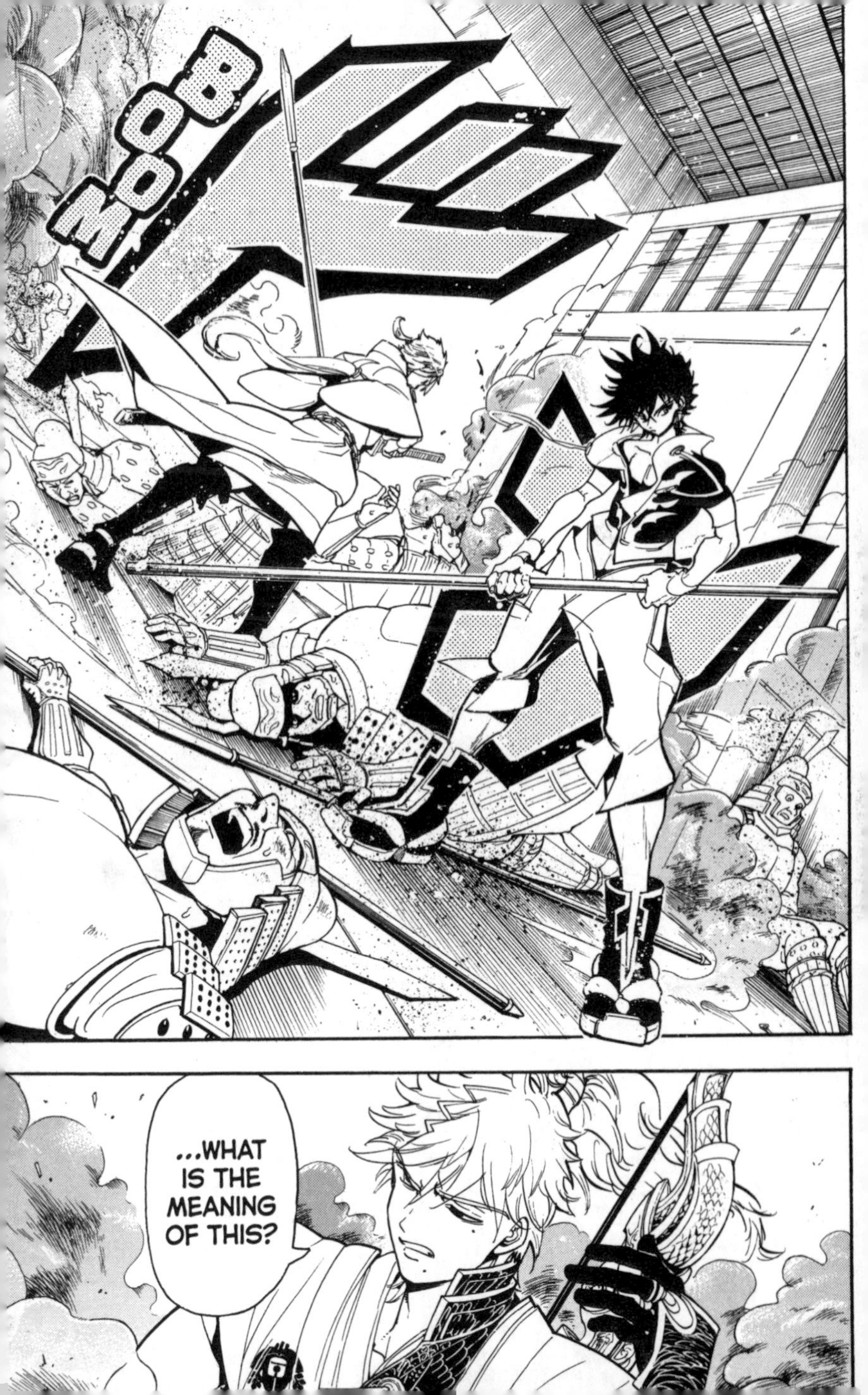
BOOM
...WHAT IS THE MEANING OF THIS?

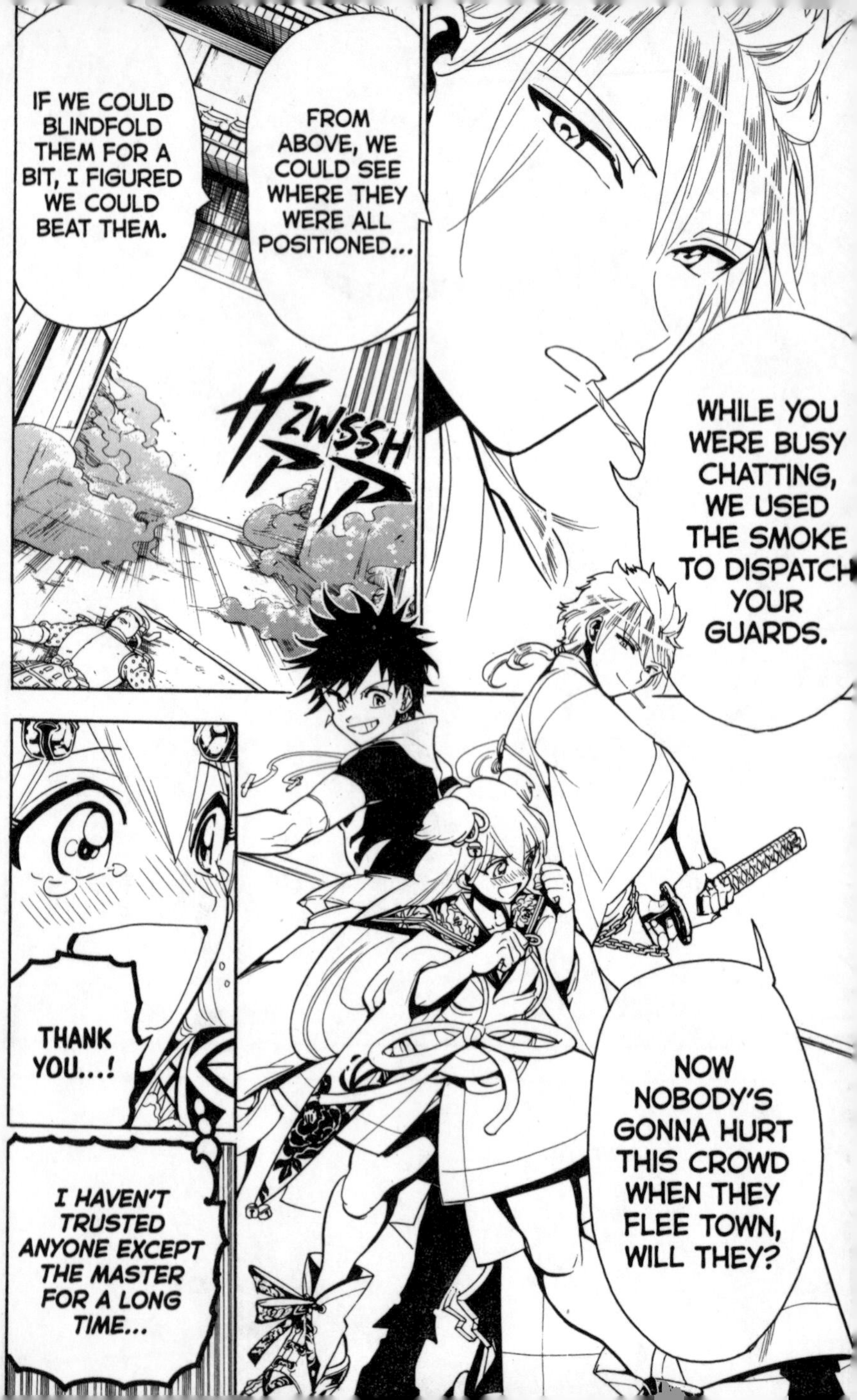
FROM ABOVE, WE COULD SEE WHERE THEY WERE ALL POSITIONED...
IF WE COULD BLINDFOLD THEM FOR A BIT, I FIGURED WE COULD BEAT THEM.
HZWSSH
WHILE YOU WERE BUSY CHATTING, WE USED THE SMOKE TO DISPATCH YOUR GUARDS.
NOW NOBODY'S GONNA HURT THIS CROWD WHEN THEY FLEE TOWN, WILL THEY?
THANK YOU...!
I HAVEN'T TRUSTED ANYONE EXCEPT THE MASTER FOR A LONG TIME...

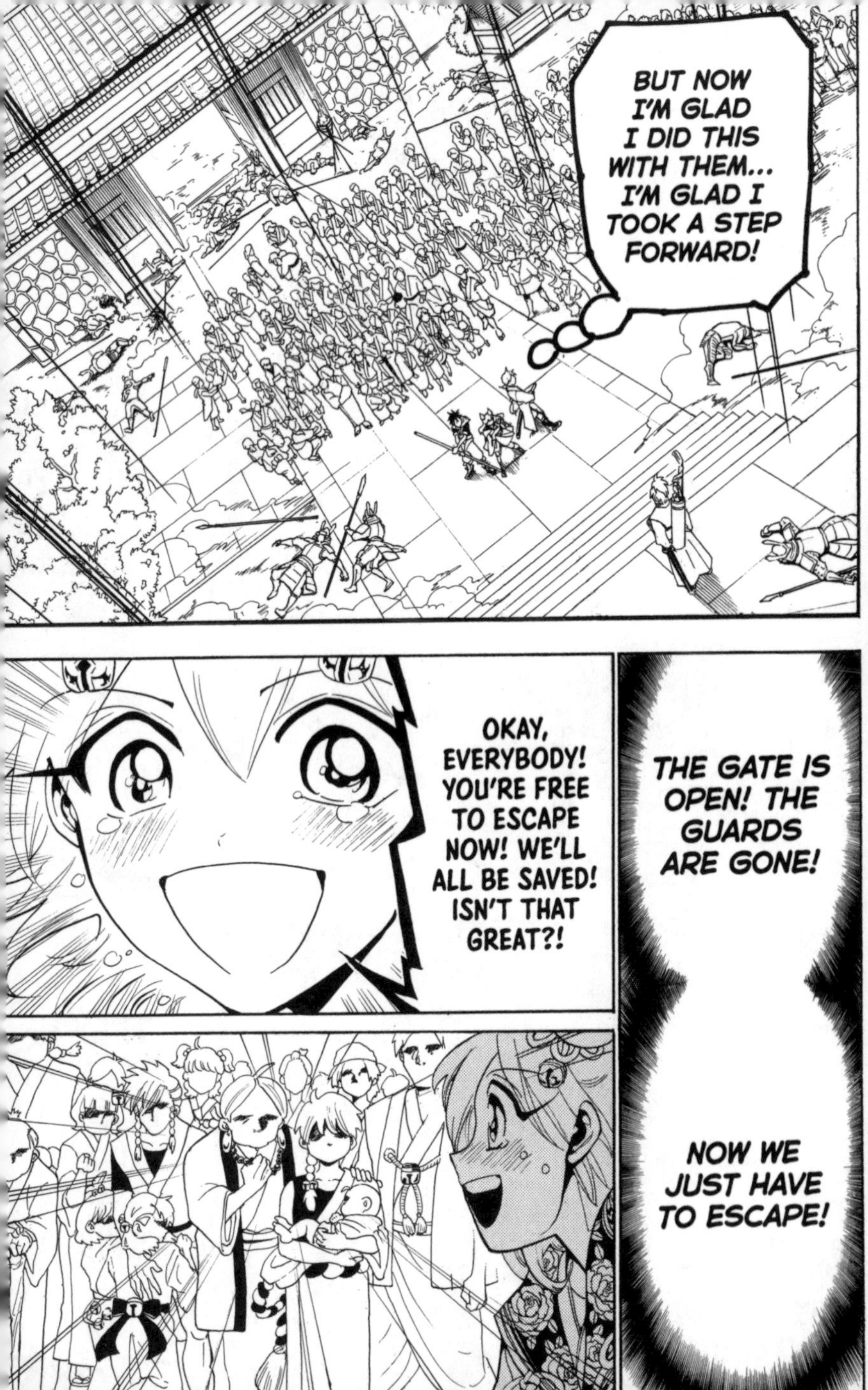
BUT NOW I'M GLAD I DID THIS WITH THEM... I'M GLAD I TOOK A STEP FORWARD!
THE GATE IS OPEN! THE GUARDS ARE GONE!
NOW WE JUST HAVE TO ESCAPE!
OKAY, EVERYBODY! YOU'RE FREE TO ESCAPE NOW! WE'LL ALL BE SAVED! ISN'T THAT GREAT?!

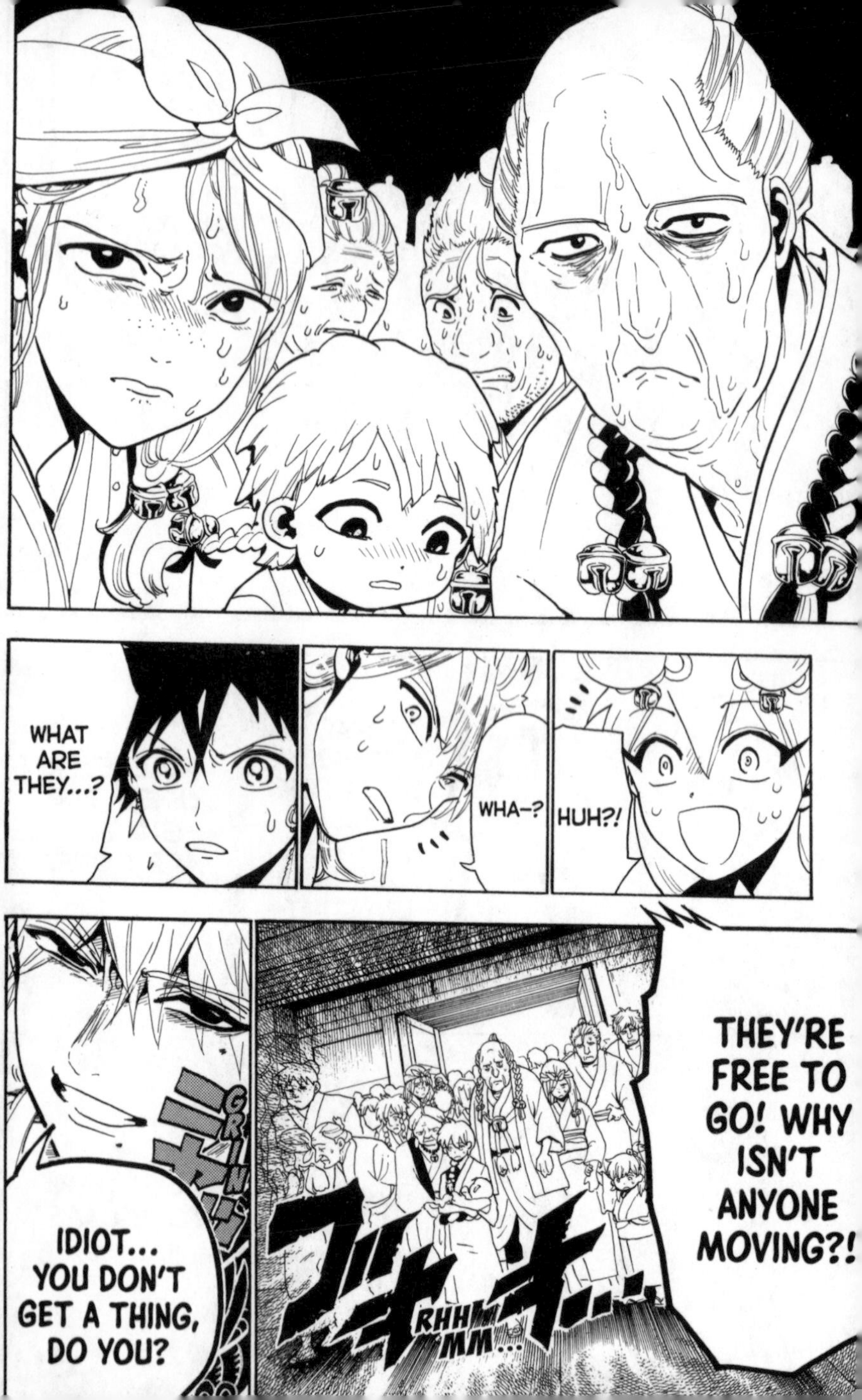
HUH?!
WHA-?
WHAT ARE THEY...?
THEY'RE FREE TO GO! WHY ISN'T ANYONE MOVING?!
RHHMM...
GRIN
IDIOT... YOU DON'T GET A THING, DO YOU?

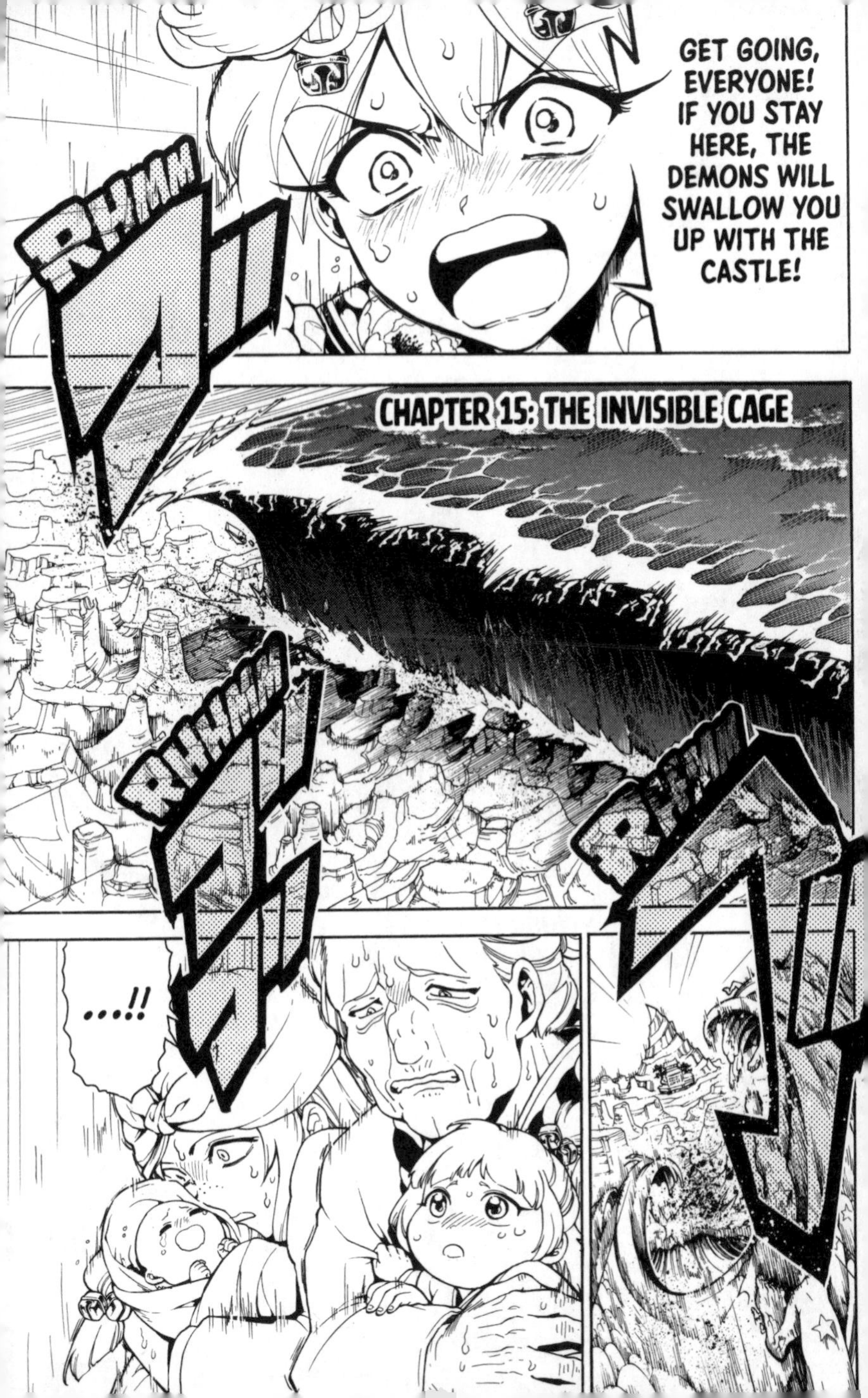
GET GOING, EVERYONE! IF YOU STAY HERE, THE DEMONS WILL SWALLOW YOU UP WITH THE CASTLE!
RHMM
CHAPTER 15: THE INVISIBLE CAGE
RHMMM
RHM
...!!

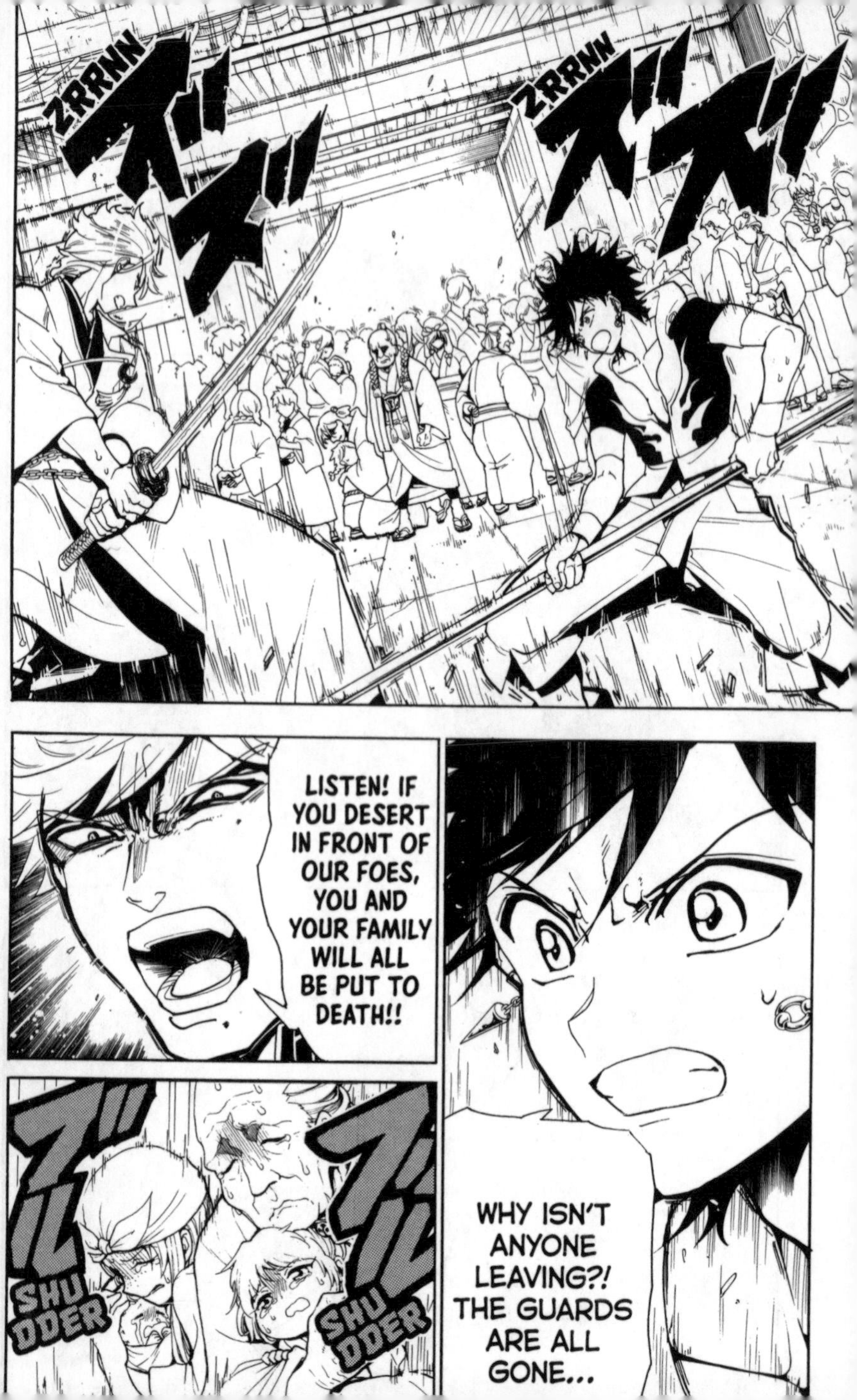
ZRRNN
ZRRNN
WHY ISN'T ANYONE LEAVING?! THE GUARDS ARE ALL GONE...
LISTEN! IF YOU DESERT IN FRONT OF OUR FOES, YOU AND YOUR FAMILY WILL ALL BE PUT TO DEATH!!
SHUDDER
SHUDDER

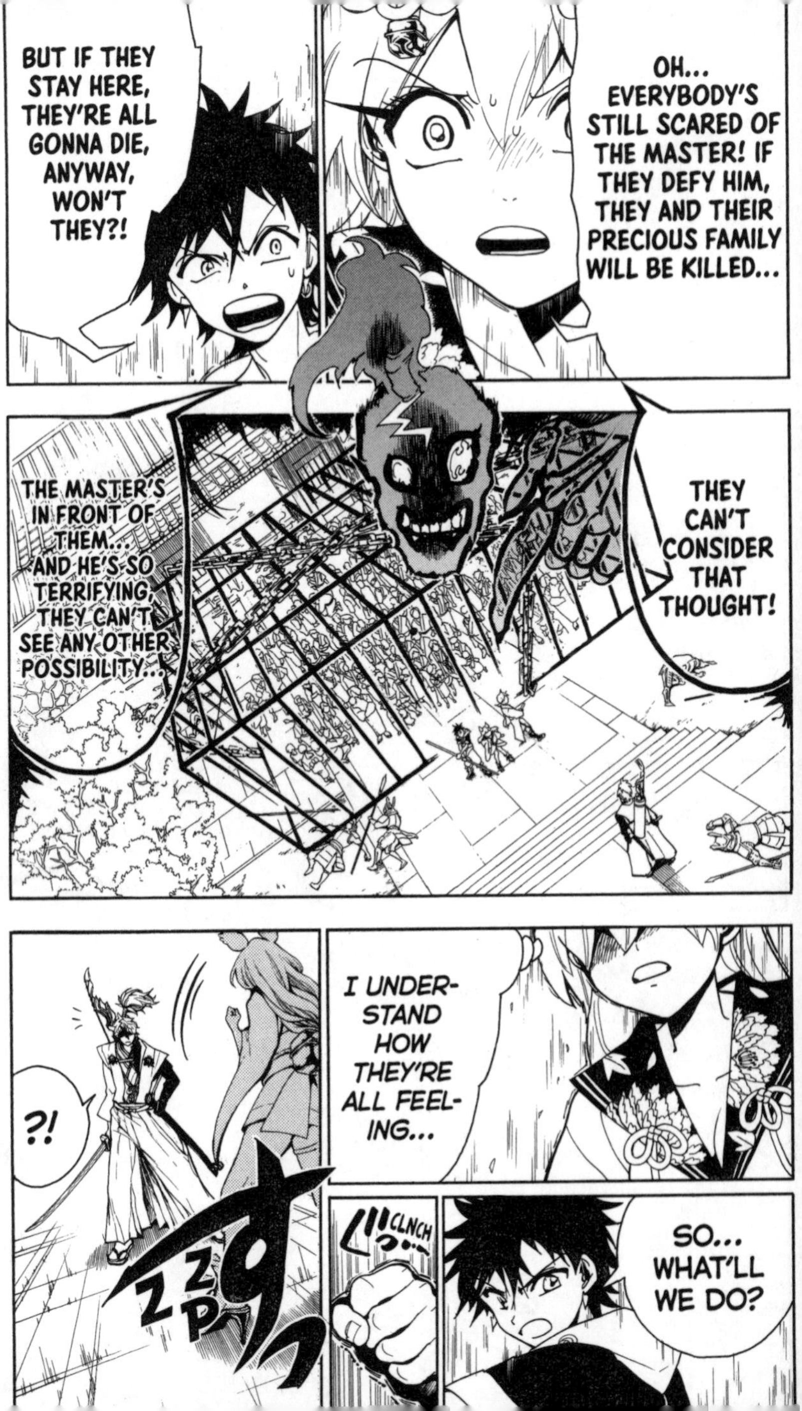
OH... EVERYBODY'S STILL SCARED OF THE MASTER! IF THEY DEFY HIM, THEY AND THEIR PRECIOUS FAMILY WILL BE KILLED...
BUT IF THEY STAY HERE, THEY'RE ALL GONNA DIE, ANYWAY, WON'T THEY?!
THEY CAN'T CONSIDER THAT THOUGHT!
THE MASTER'S IN FRONT OF THEM... AND HE'S SO TERRIFYING, THEY CAN'T SEE ANY OTHER POSSIBILITY...
I UNDER-STAND HOW THEY'RE ALL FEEL-ING...
SO... WHAT'LL WE DO?
CLNCH
?!
ZZP

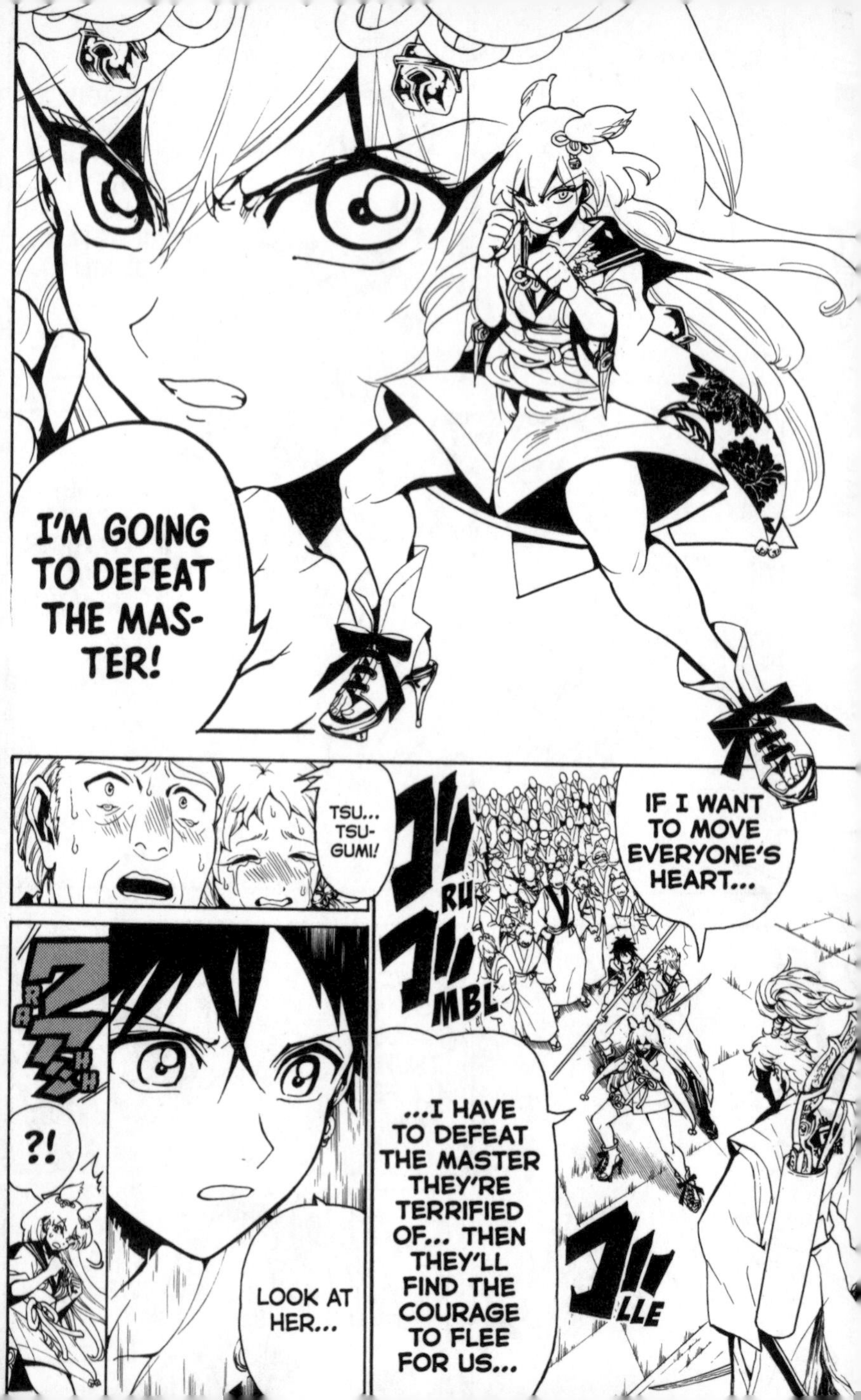
I'M GOING TO DEFEAT THE MASTER!
IF I WANT TO MOVE EVERYONE'S HEART...
RUMBL
...I HAVE TO DEFEAT THE MASTER THEY'RE TERRIFIED OF... THEN THEY'LL FIND THE COURAGE TO FLEE FOR US...
LLE
TSU... TSU-GUMI!
RAHH
LOOK AT HER...
?!

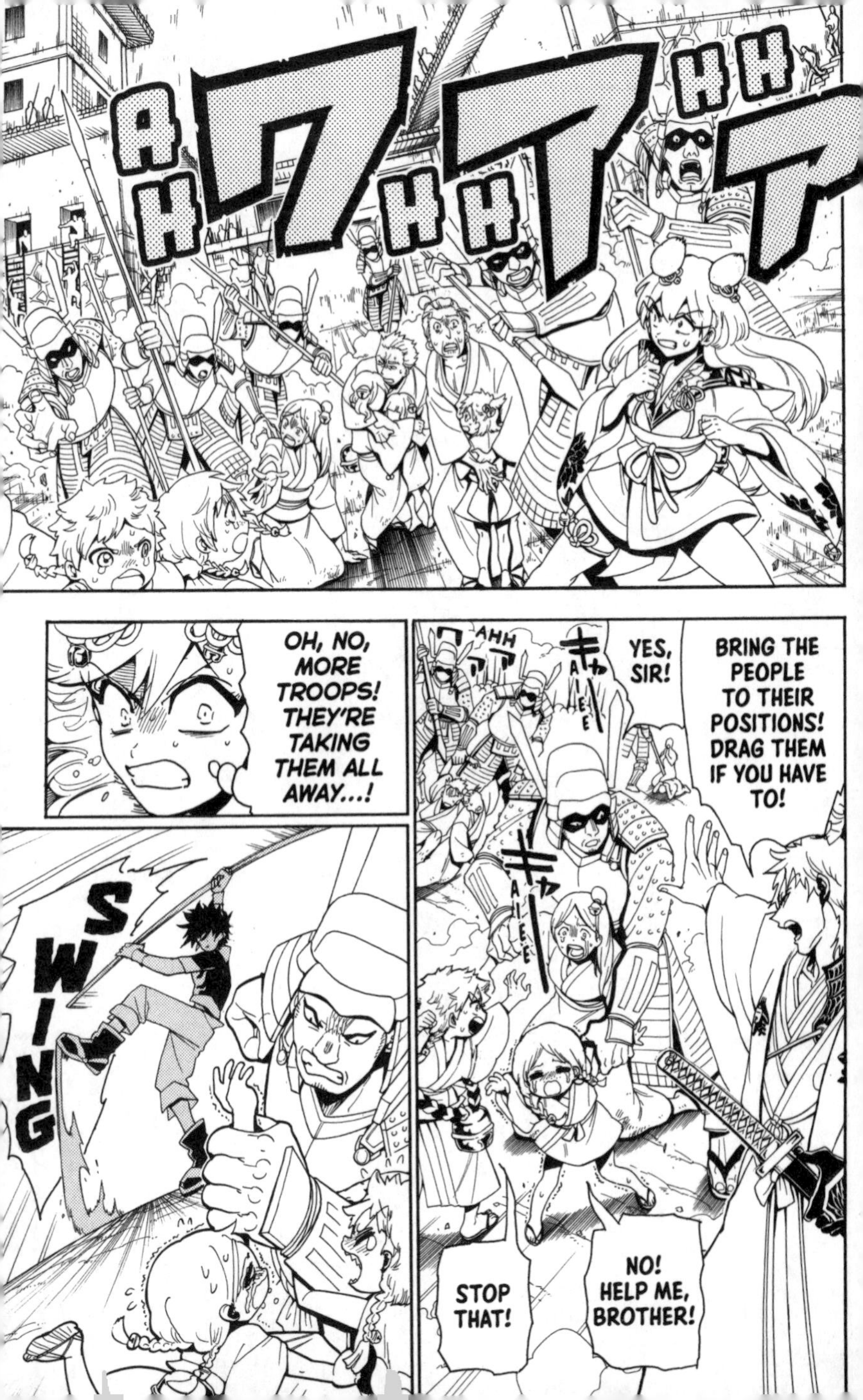
AHHHHHHH
BRING THE PEOPLE TO THEIR POSITIONS! DRAG THEM IF YOU HAVE TO!
YES, SIR!
AIEEE
AHH
AIEEE
NO! HELP ME, BROTHER!
STOP THAT!
OH, NO, MORE TROOPS! THEY'RE TAKING THEM ALL AWAY...!
SWING

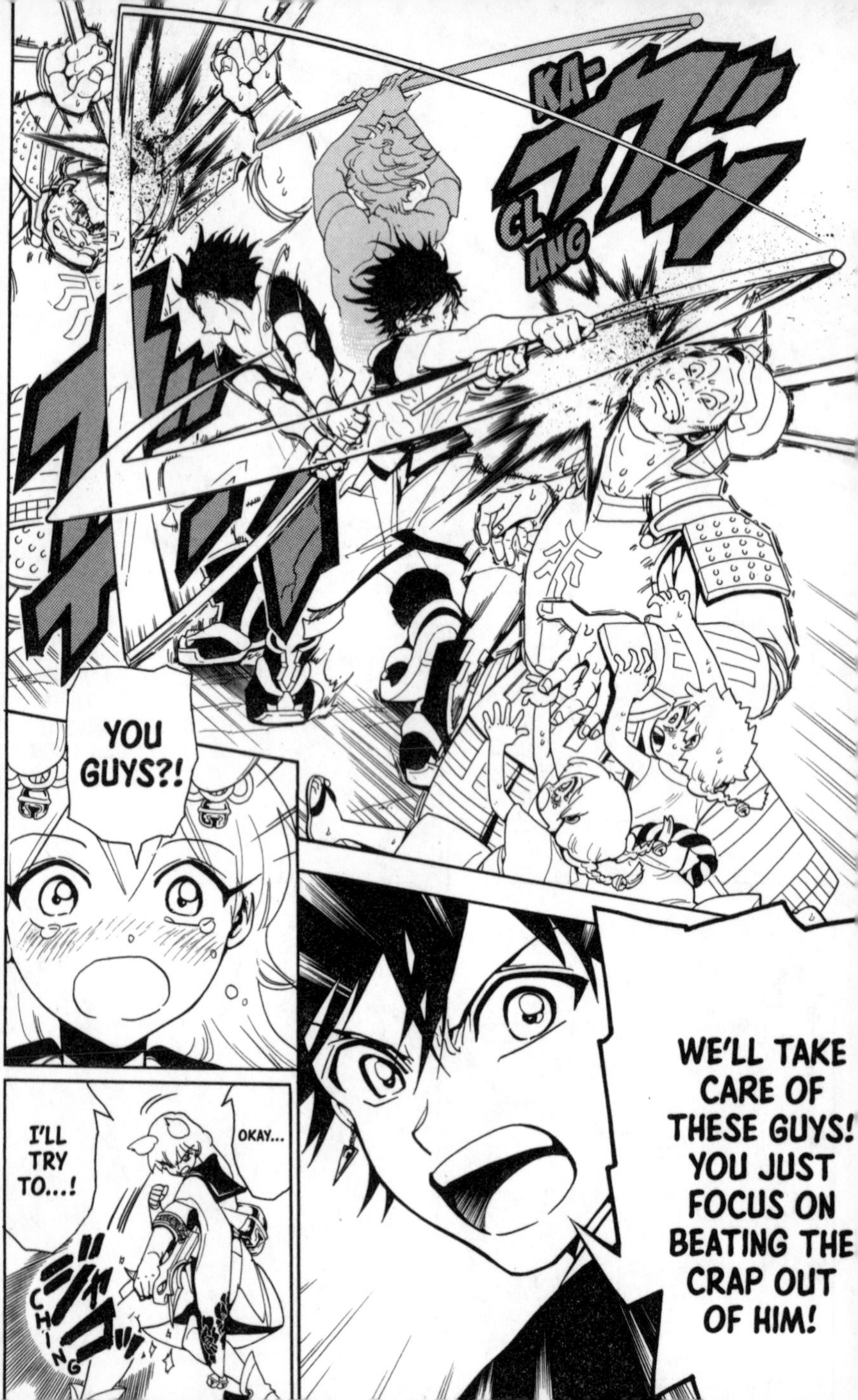
KA-
CL ANG
WE'LL TAKE CARE OF THESE GUYS! YOU JUST FOCUS ON BEATING THE CRAP OUT OF HIM!
YOU GUYS?!
OKAY...
I'LL TRY TO...!
CHING

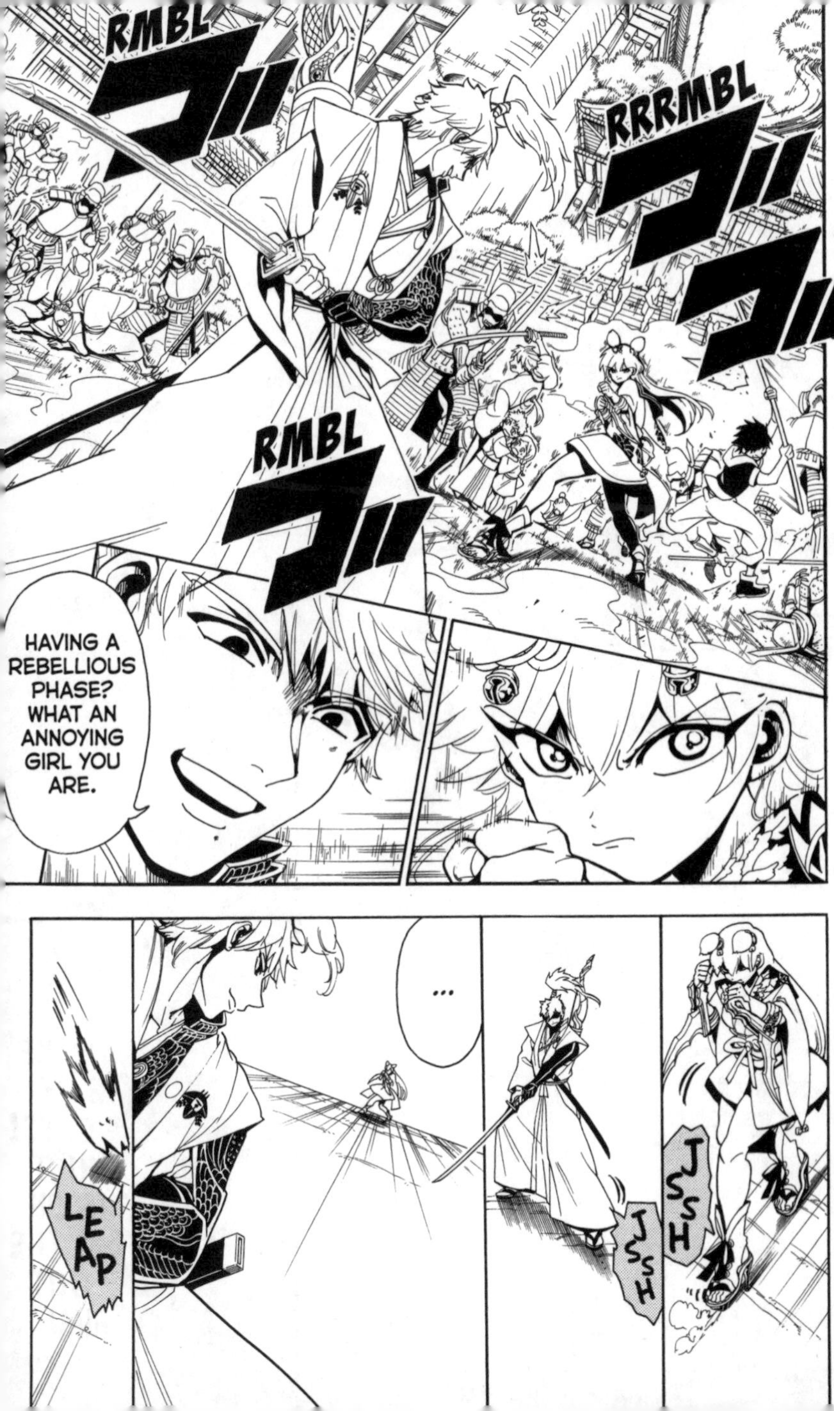
RRRMBL
RMBL
RMBL
HAVING A REBELLIOUS PHASE? WHAT AN ANNOYING GIRL YOU ARE.
JSSH
JSSH
...
LEAP

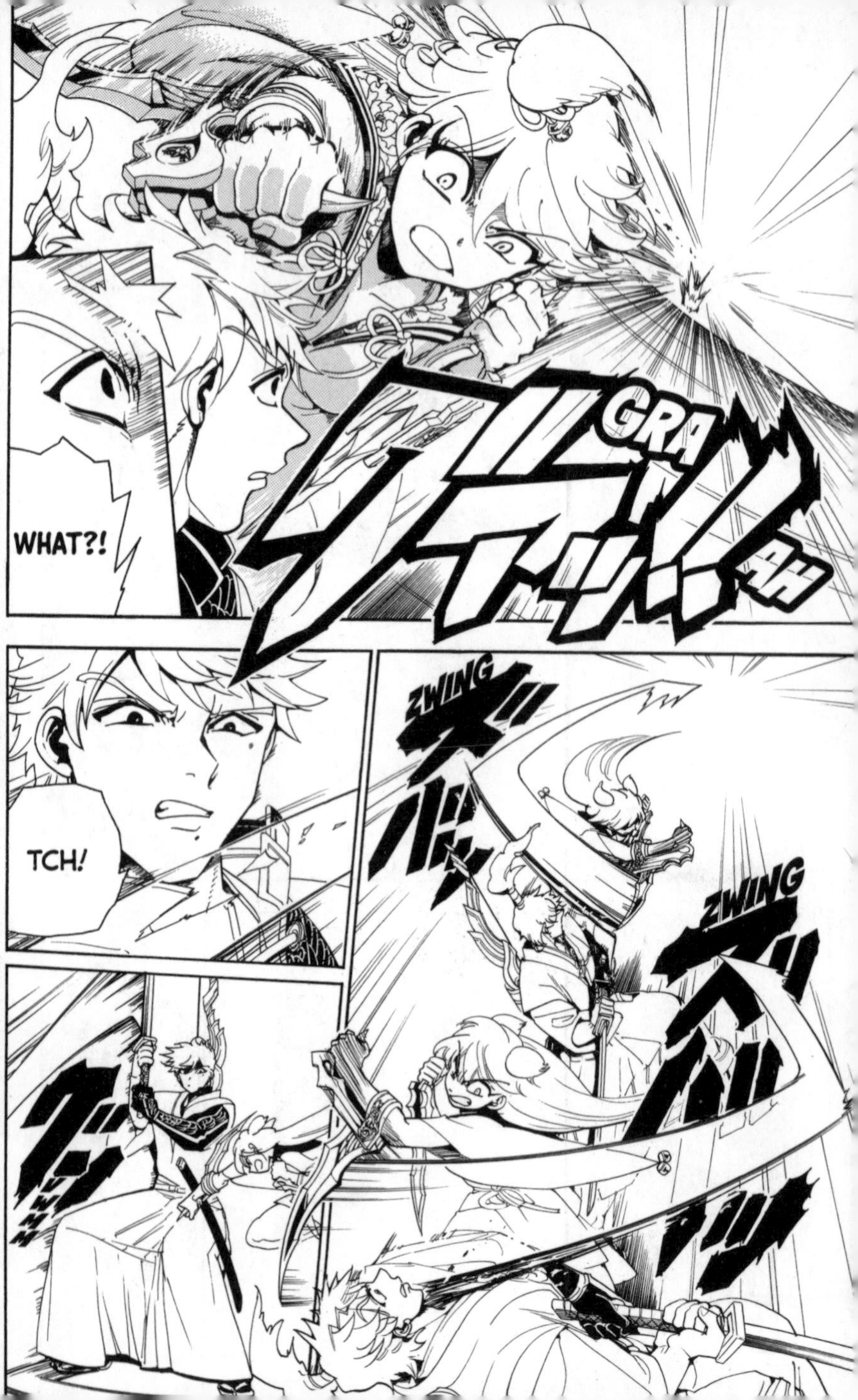
GRA
AH
WHAT?!
ZWING
ZWING
TCH!
VWMM

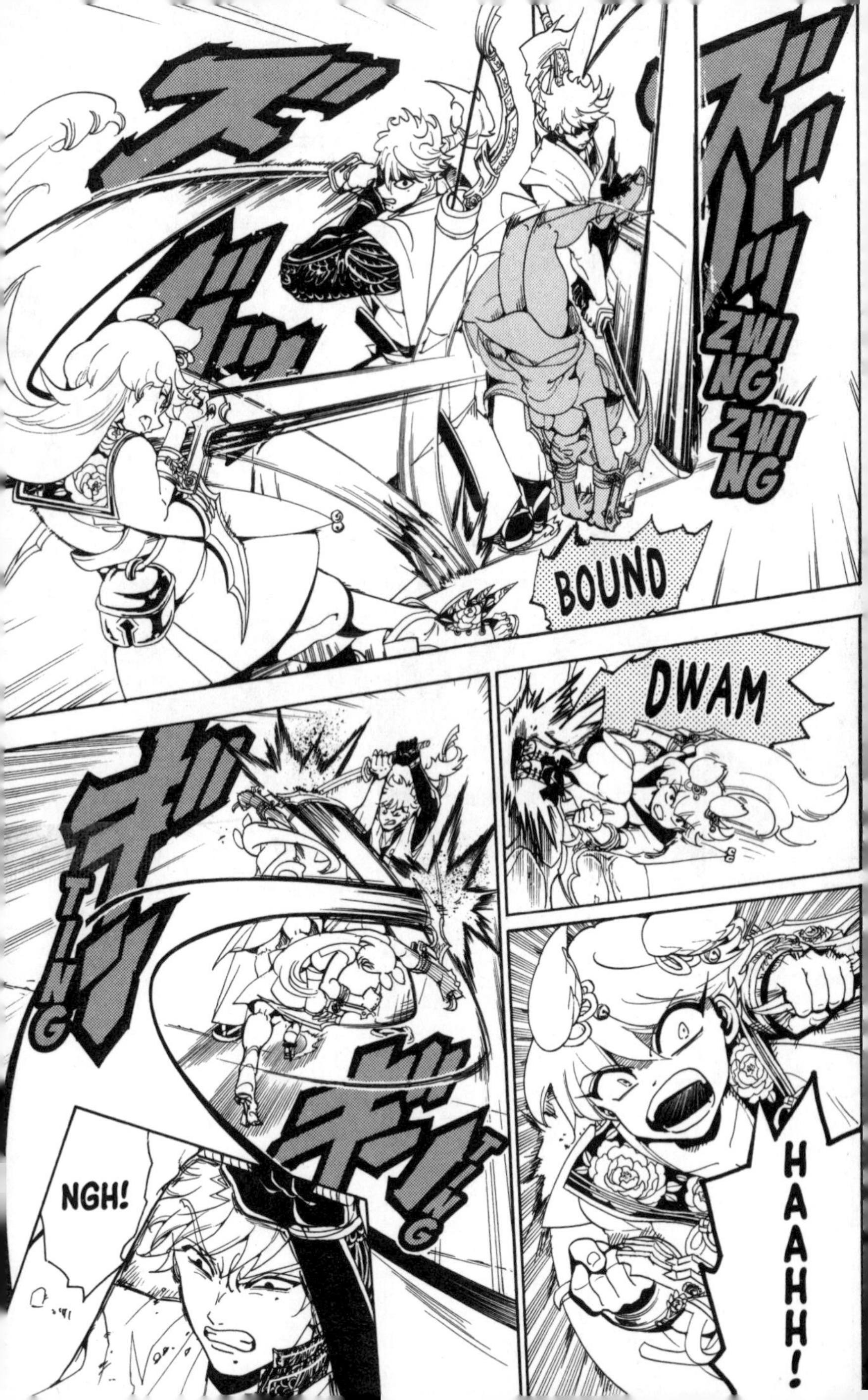
ZWING ZWING
BOUND
DWAM
TING
HAAHH!
NGH!

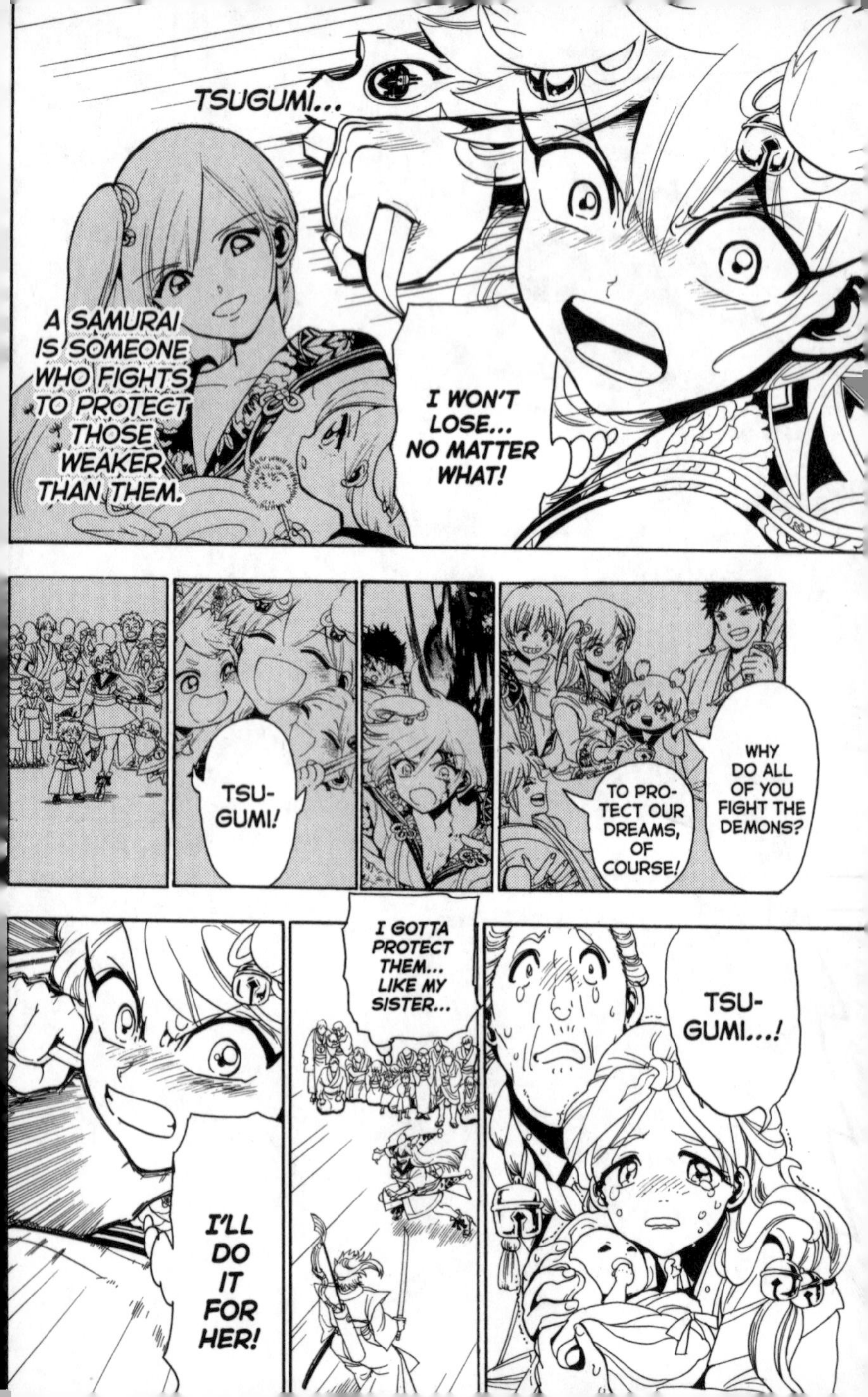
TSUGUMI...
I WON'T LOSE... NO MATTER WHAT!
A SAMURAI IS SOMEONE WHO FIGHTS TO PROTECT THOSE WEAKER THAN THEM.
WHY DO ALL OF YOU FIGHT THE DEMONS?
TO PROTECT OUR DREAMS, OF COURSE!
TSU-GUMI!
TSU-GUMI...!
I GOTTA PROTECT THEM... LIKE MY SISTER...
I'LL DO IT FOR HER!

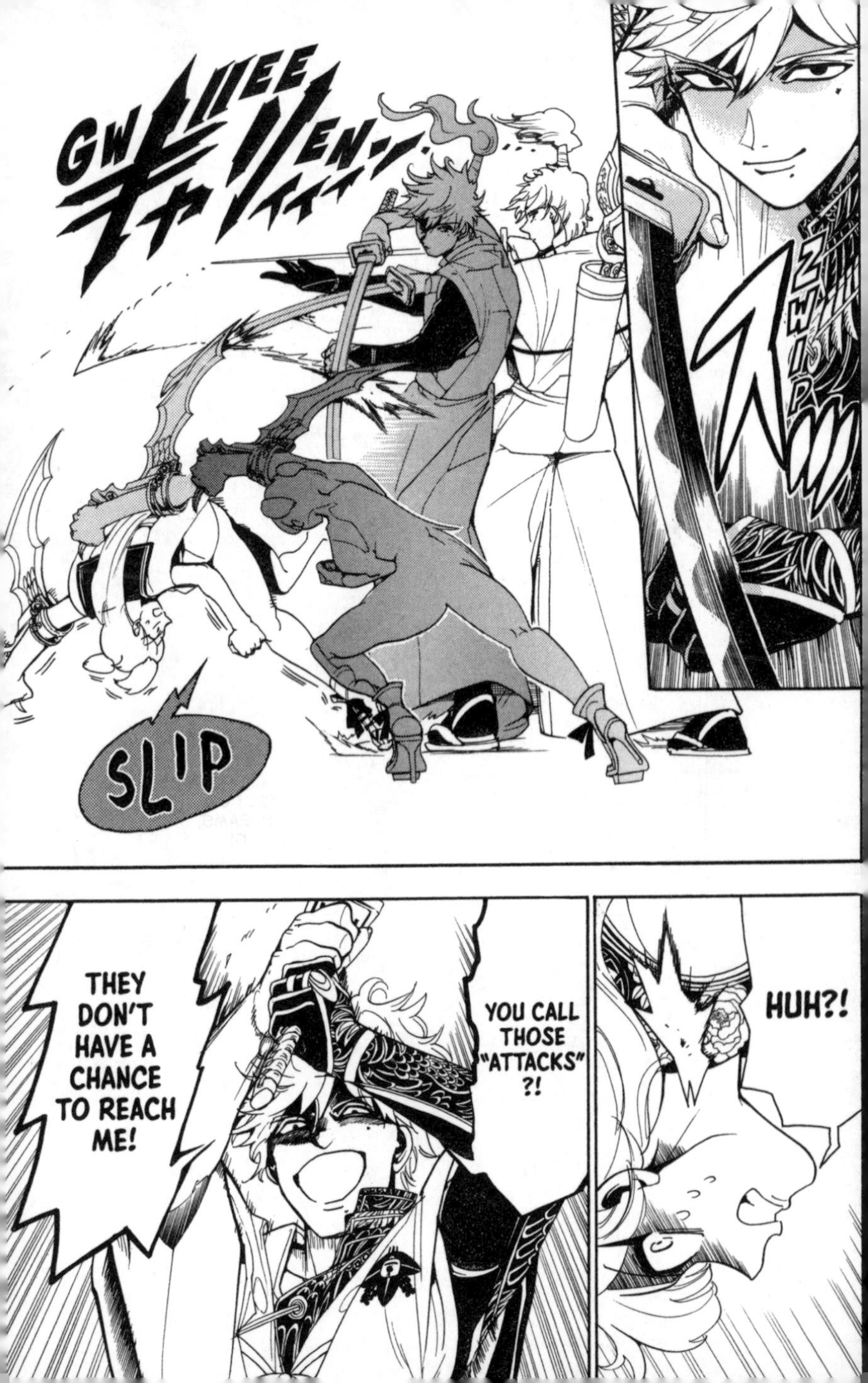
ZWIP
GWIIIEEEN--
SLIP
HUH?!
YOU CALL THOSE "ATTACKS" ?!
THEY DON'T HAVE A CHANCE TO REACH ME!

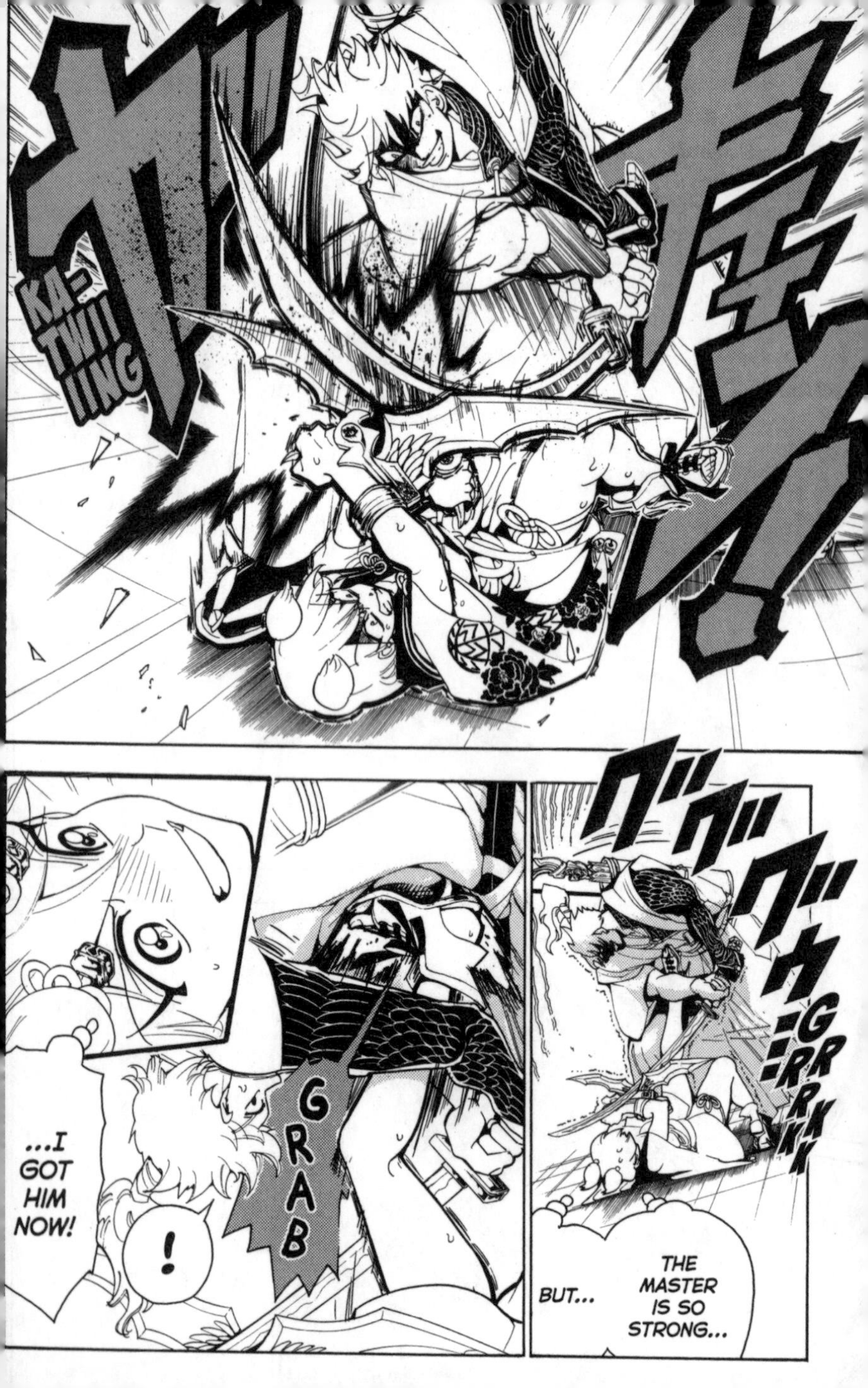
KA-TWIIIING
GRRRKKK
BUT...
THE MASTER IS SO STRONG...
GRAB
...I GOT HIM NOW!
!

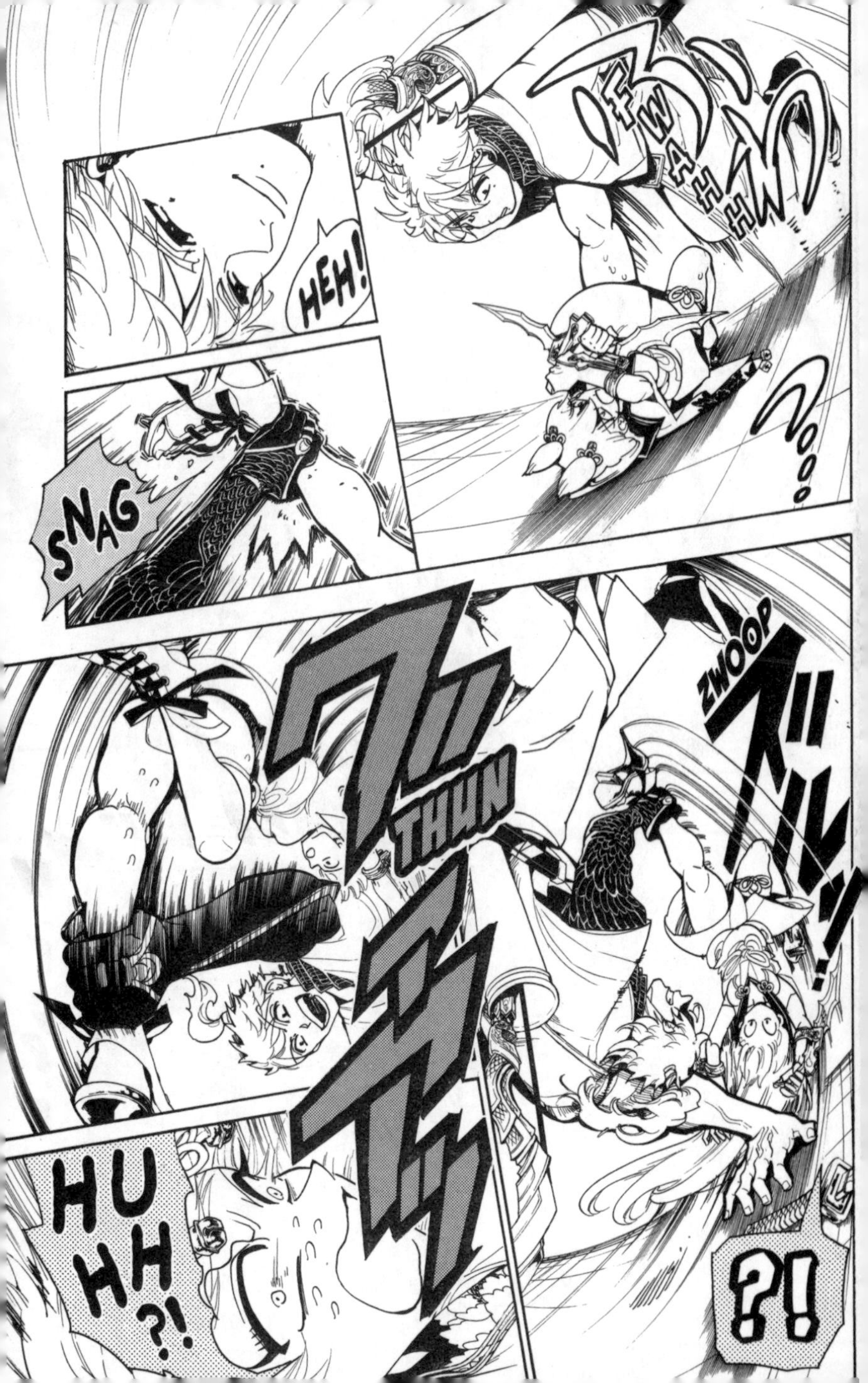
FWAHHH
HEH!
SNAG
ZWOOP
THUN
?!
HUHH?!

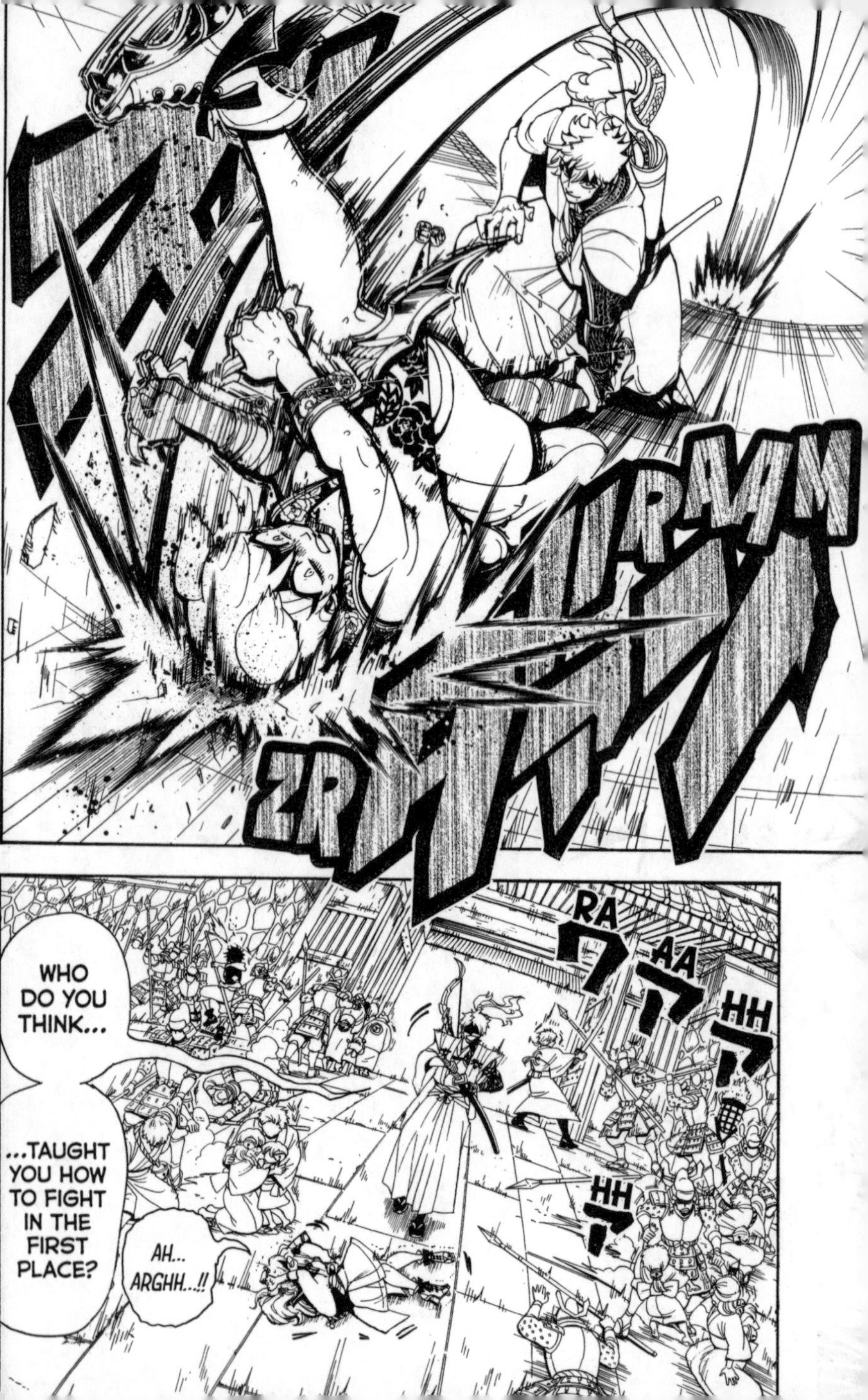

ZR
RAMN
RA
AA
HH
HH
WHO DO YOU THINK...
...TAUGHT YOU HOW TO FIGHT IN THE FIRST PLACE?
AH... ARGHH...!!

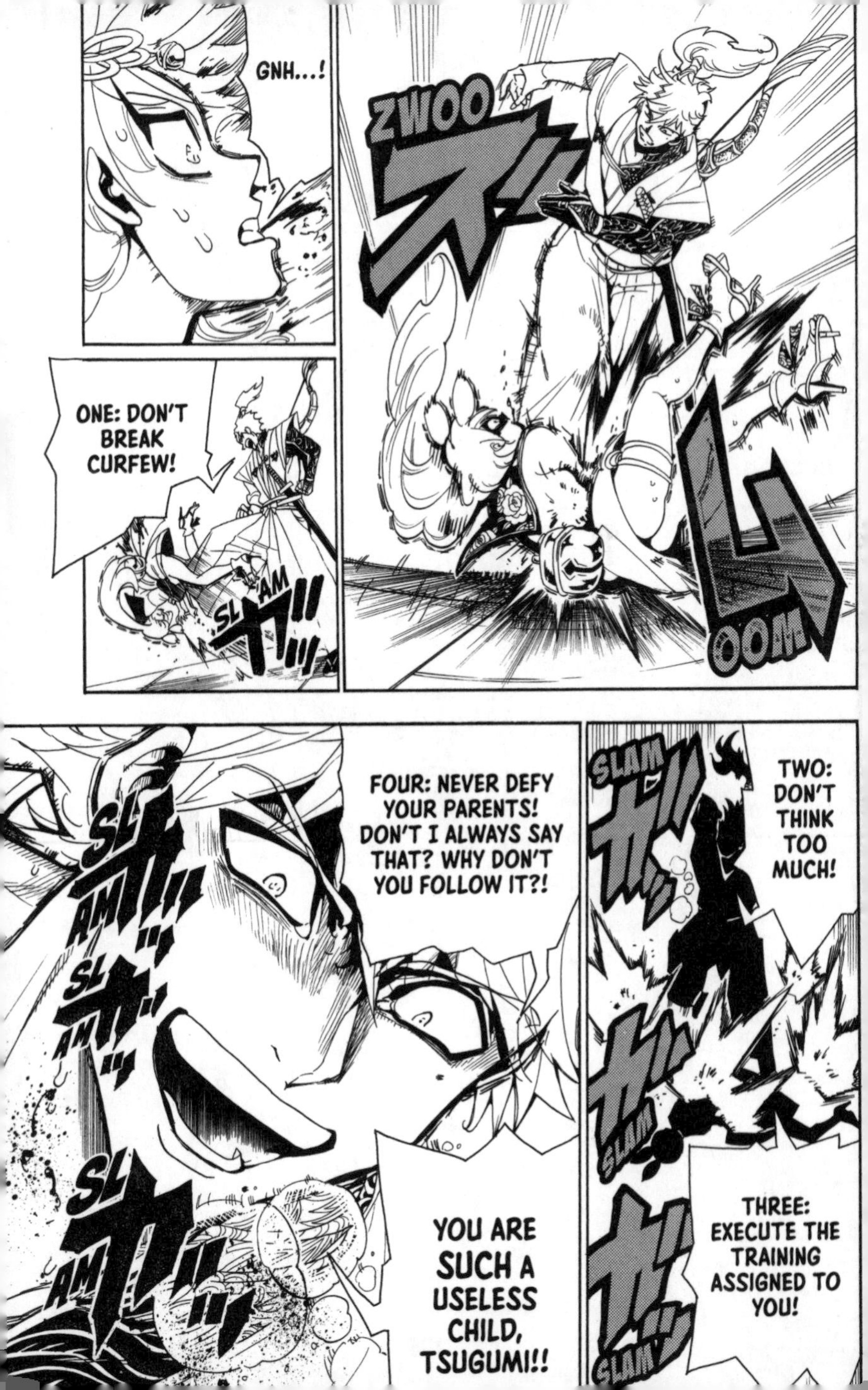
ZWOO
OOM
GNH...!
ONE: DON'T BREAK CURFEW!
SLAM
SLAM
TWO: DON'T THINK TOO MUCH!
SLAM
SLAM
THREE: EXECUTE THE TRAINING ASSIGNED TO YOU!
FOUR: NEVER DEFY YOUR PARENTS! DON'T I ALWAYS SAY THAT? WHY DON'T YOU FOLLOW IT?!
SLAM
SLAM
SLAM
YOU ARE SUCH A USELESS CHILD, TSUGUMI!!

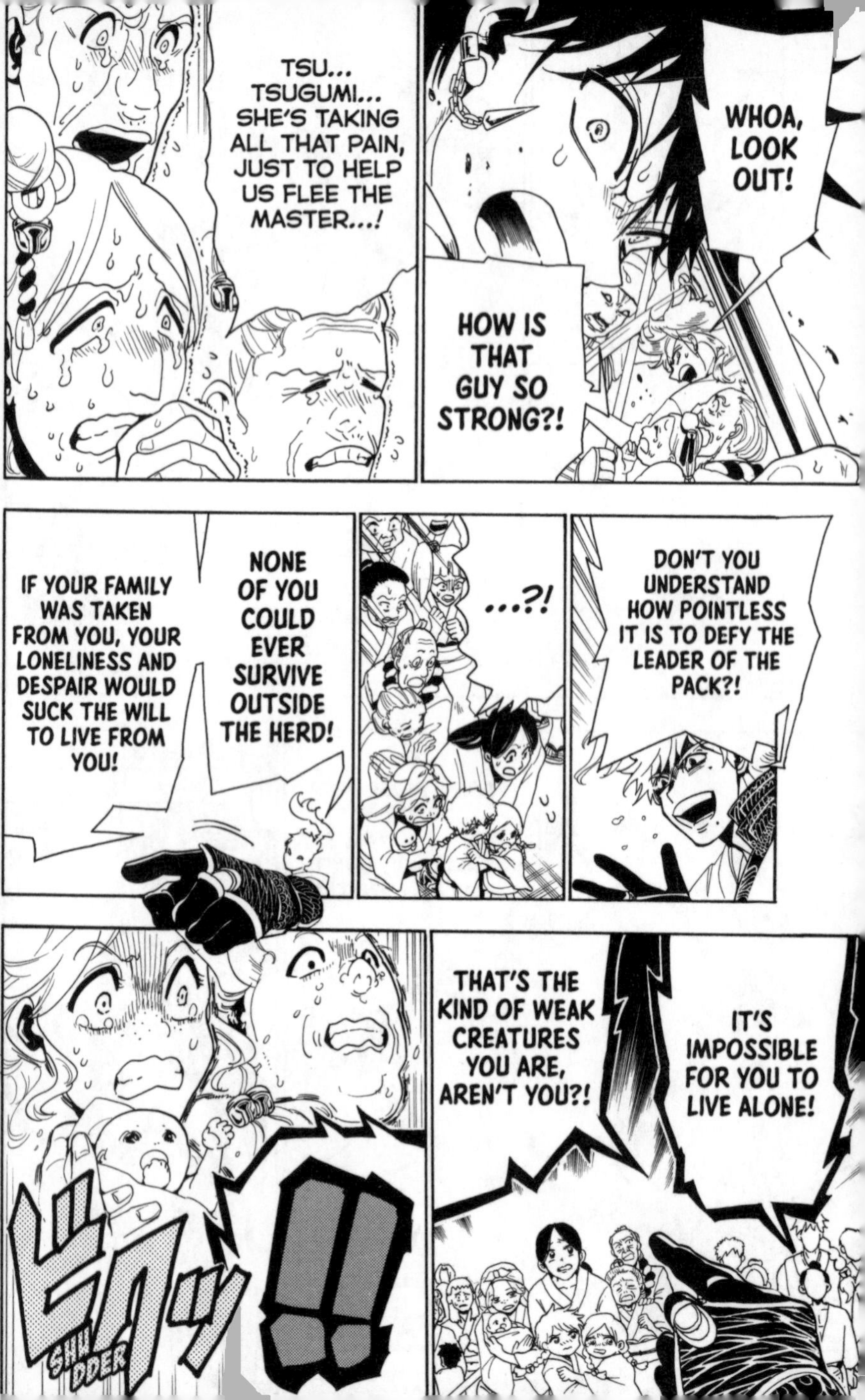
WHOA, LOOK OUT!
HOW IS THAT GUY SO STRONG?!
TSU... TSUGUMI... SHE'S TAKING ALL THAT PAIN, JUST TO HELP US FLEE THE MASTER...!
DON'T YOU UNDERSTAND HOW POINTLESS IT IS TO DEFY THE LEADER OF THE PACK?!
...?!
NONE OF YOU COULD EVER SURVIVE OUTSIDE THE HERD!
IF YOUR FAMILY WAS TAKEN FROM YOU, YOUR LONELINESS AND DESPAIR WOULD SUCK THE WILL TO LIVE FROM YOU!
IT'S IMPOSSIBLE FOR YOU TO LIVE ALONE!
THAT'S THE KIND OF WEAK CREATURES YOU ARE, AREN'T YOU?!
!!
ビクッ
SHUDDER

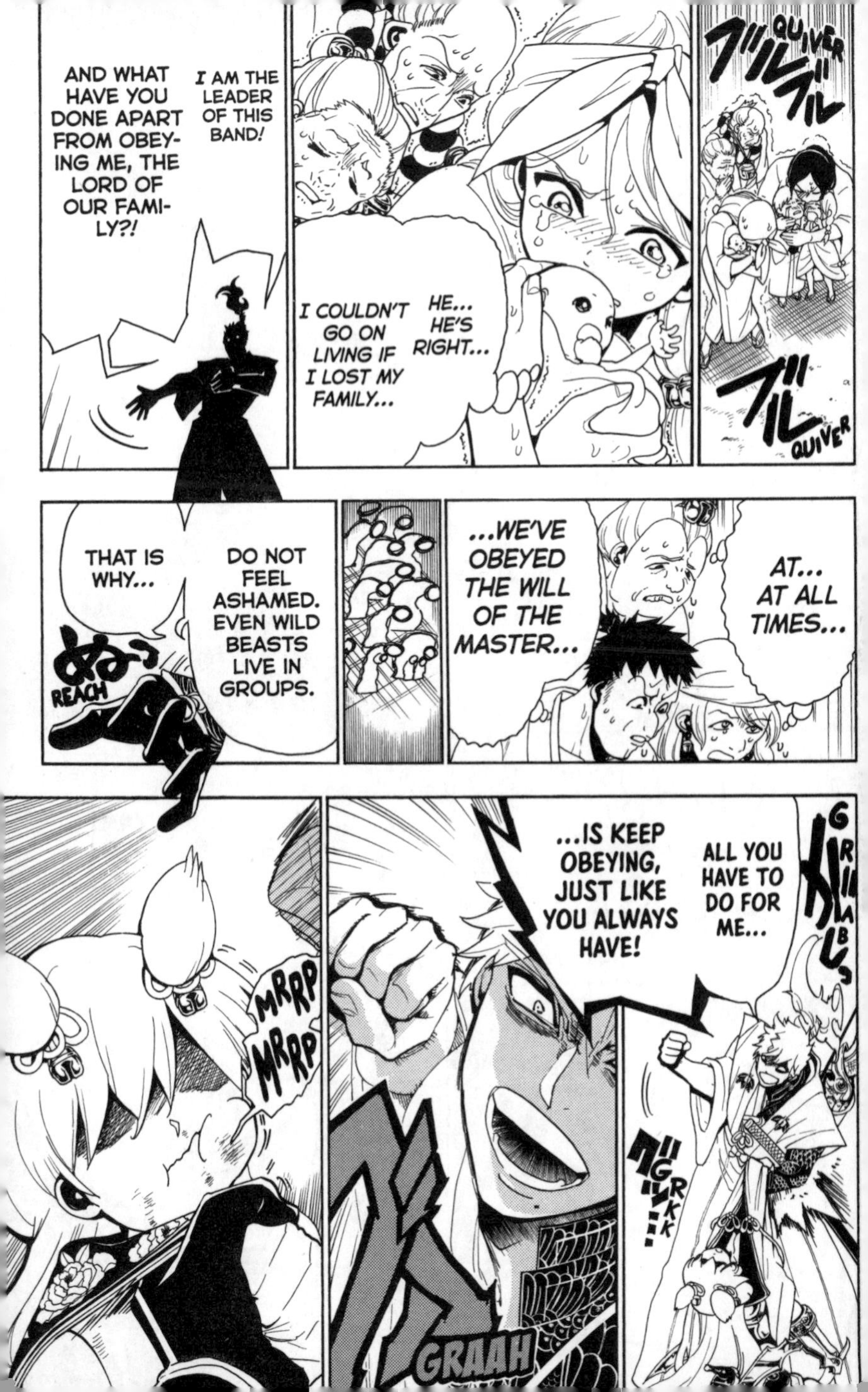
ブルブル
QUIVER
ブル
QUIVER
HE... HE'S RIGHT...
I COULDN'T GO ON LIVING IF I LOST MY FAMILY...
I AM THE LEADER OF THIS BAND!
AND WHAT HAVE YOU DONE APART FROM OBEYING ME, THE LORD OF OUR FAMILY?!
AT... AT ALL TIMES...
...WE'VE OBEYED THE WILL OF THE MASTER...
DO NOT FEEL ASHAMED. EVEN WILD BEASTS LIVE IN GROUPS.
THAT IS WHY...
ぬっ
REACH
ALL YOU HAVE TO DO FOR ME...
...IS KEEP OBEYING, JUST LIKE YOU ALWAYS HAVE!
GRAB
GRRK!!
GRAAH
MRRP MRRP

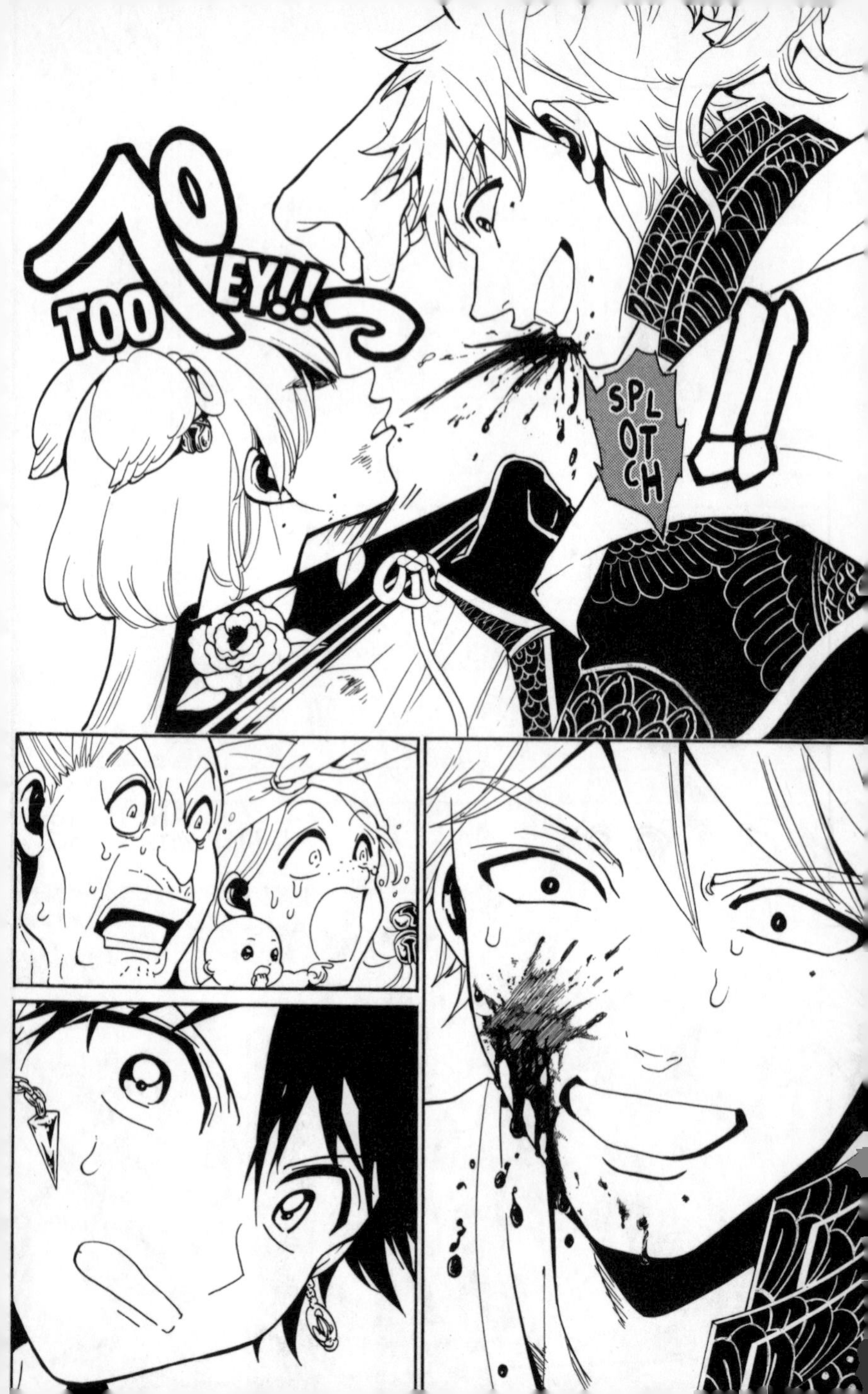
TOOPEY!!
SPLOTCH
!!

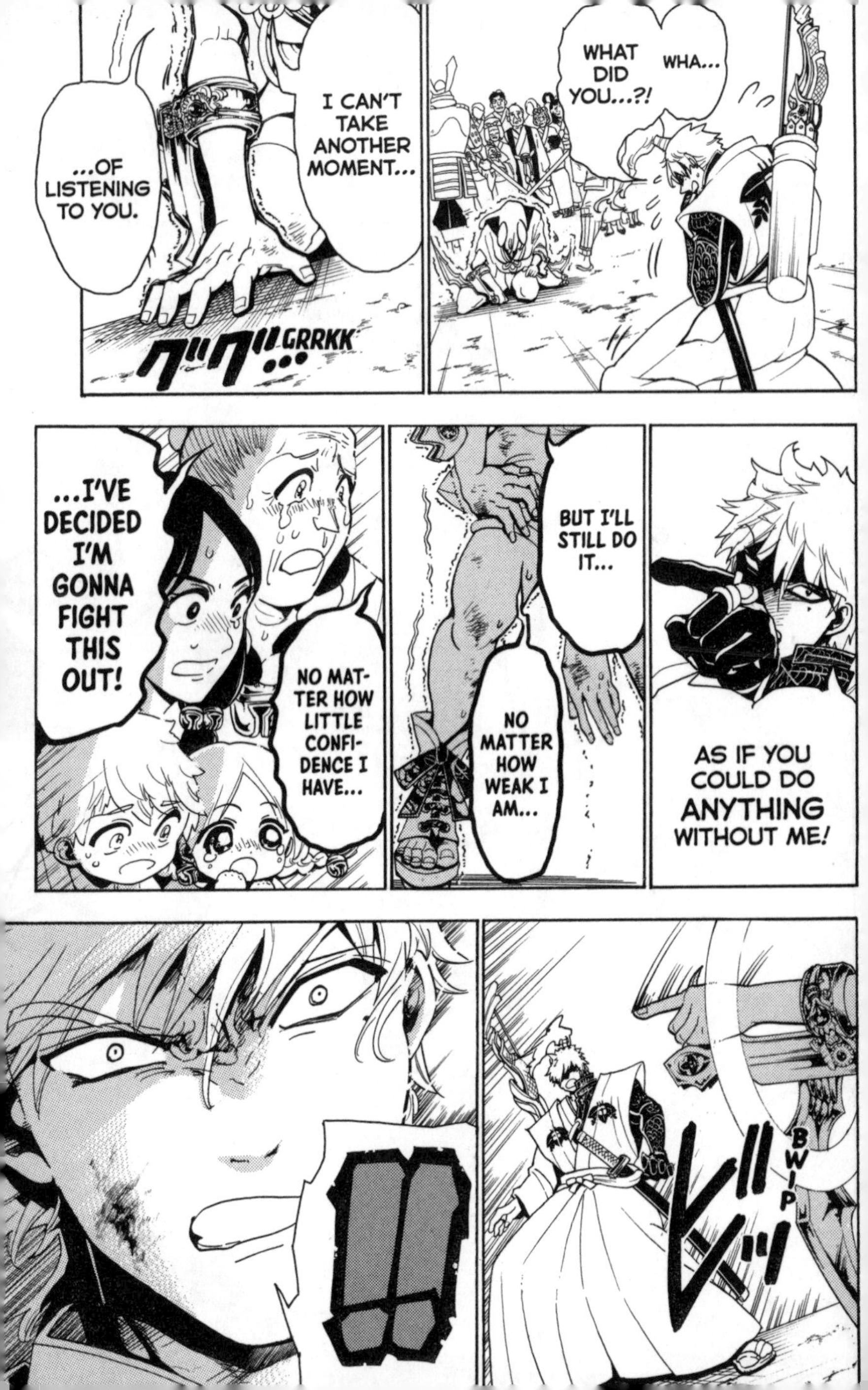
WHA...
WHAT DID YOU...?!
I CAN'T TAKE ANOTHER MOMENT...
...OF LISTENING TO YOU.
GRRKK
AS IF YOU COULD DO ANYTHING WITHOUT ME!
BUT I'LL STILL DO IT...
NO MATTER HOW WEAK I AM...
NO MAT-TER HOW LITTLE CONFI-DENCE I HAVE...
...I'VE DECIDED I'M GONNA FIGHT THIS OUT!
BWIP

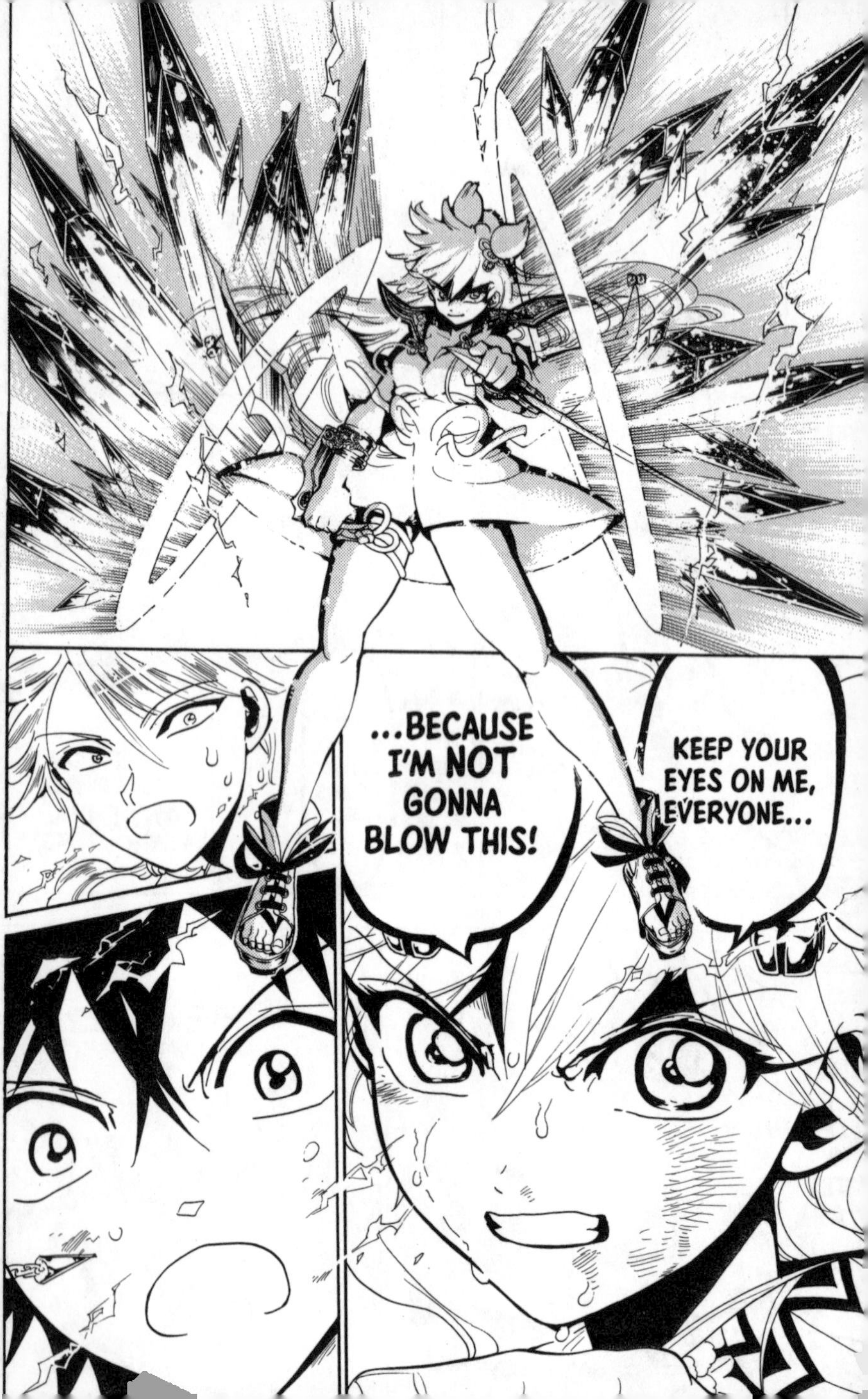
KEEP YOUR EYES ON ME, EVERYONE...
...BECAUSE I'M NOT GONNA BLOW THIS!

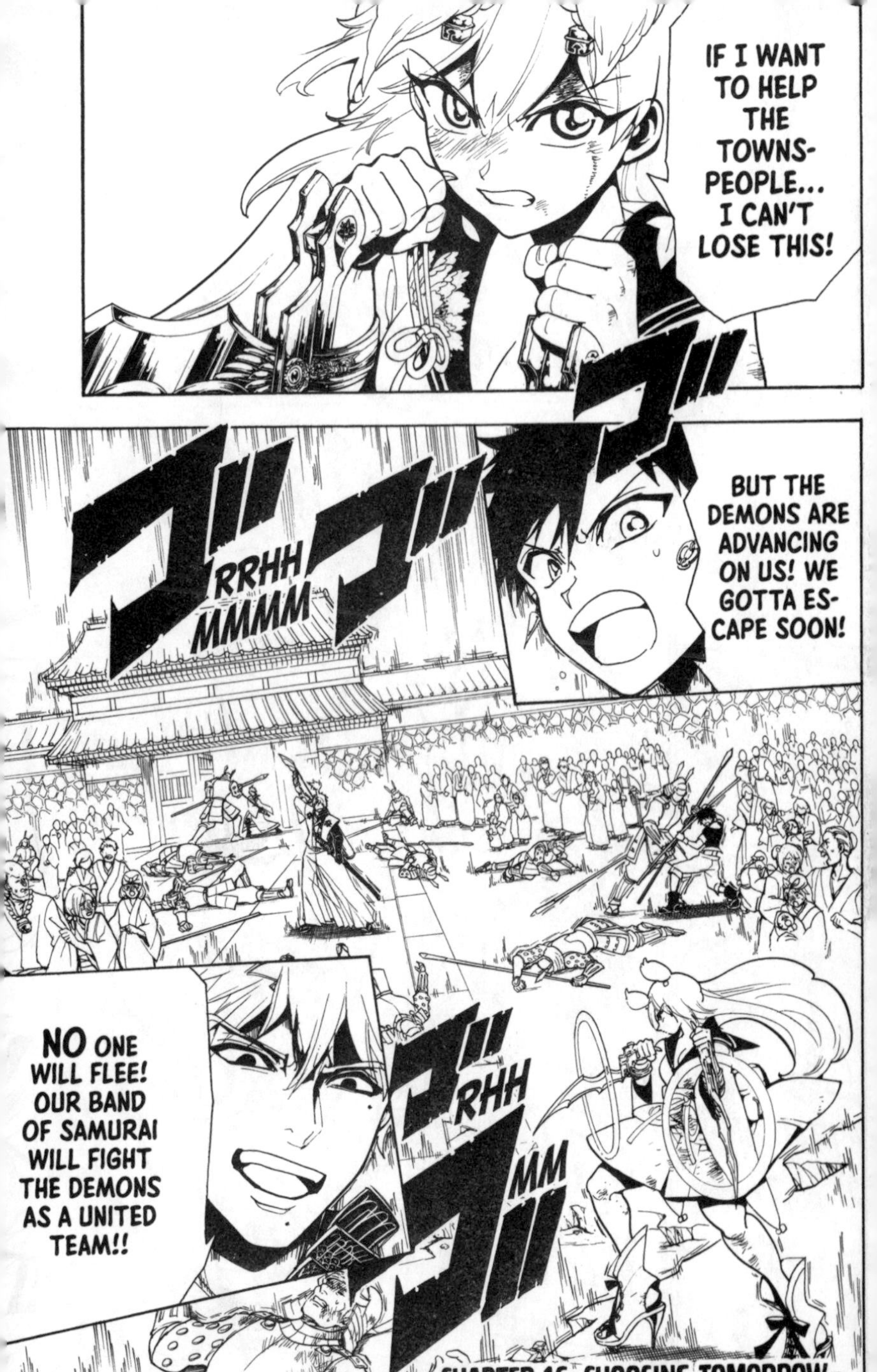
IF I WANT TO HELP THE TOWNS-PEOPLE... I CAN'T LOSE THIS!
BUT THE DEMONS ARE ADVANCING ON US! WE GOTTA ESCAPE SOON!
RRHH MMMM
RHH MM
NO ONE WILL FLEE! OUR BAND OF SAMURAI WILL FIGHT THE DEMONS AS A UNITED TEAM!!

CHAPTER 16: CHOOSING TOMORROW

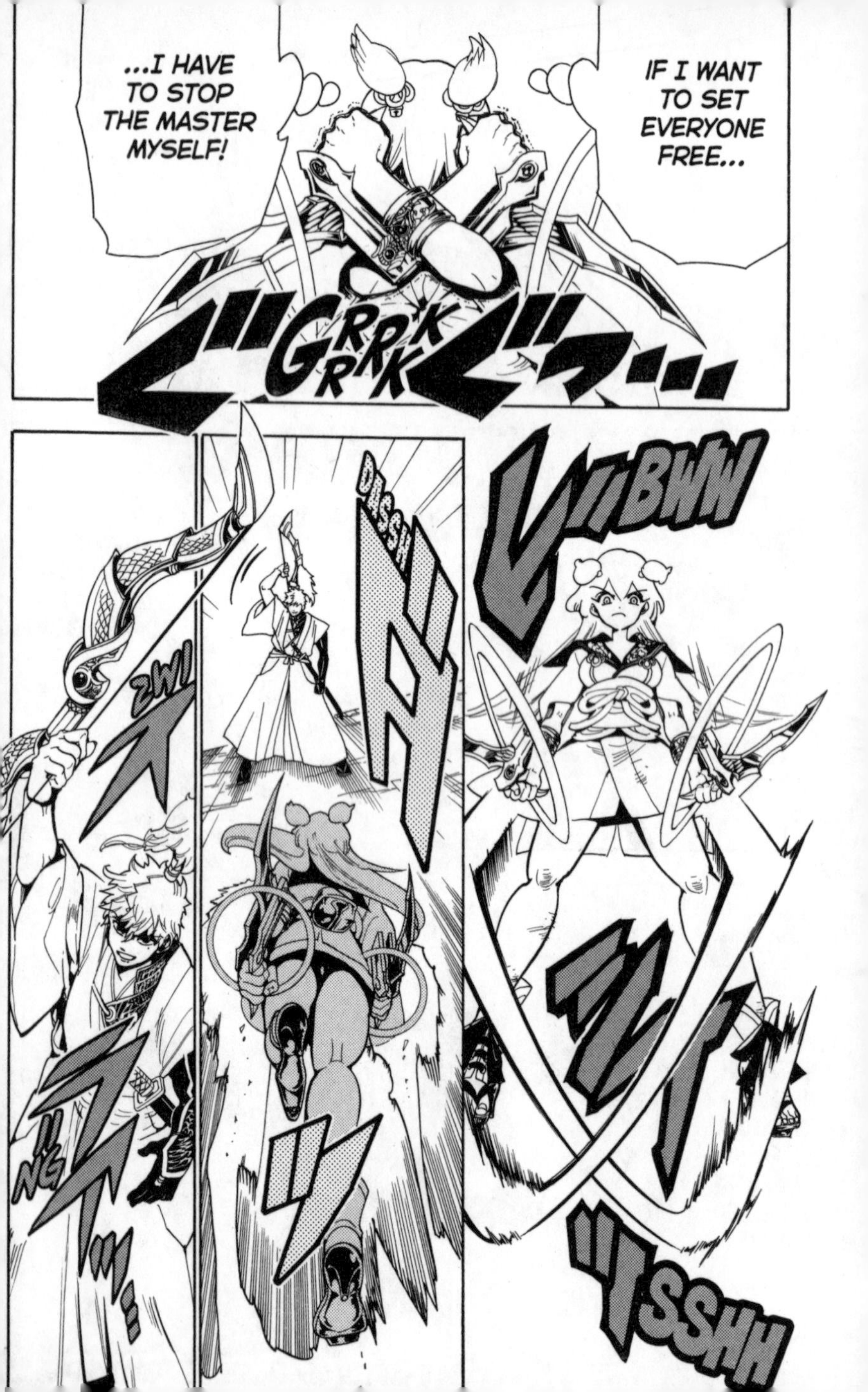
IF I WANT TO SET EVERYONE FREE...
...I HAVE TO STOP THE MASTER MYSELF!
GRRK RRK
BWW
SSHH
DASSH
ZWI
NG

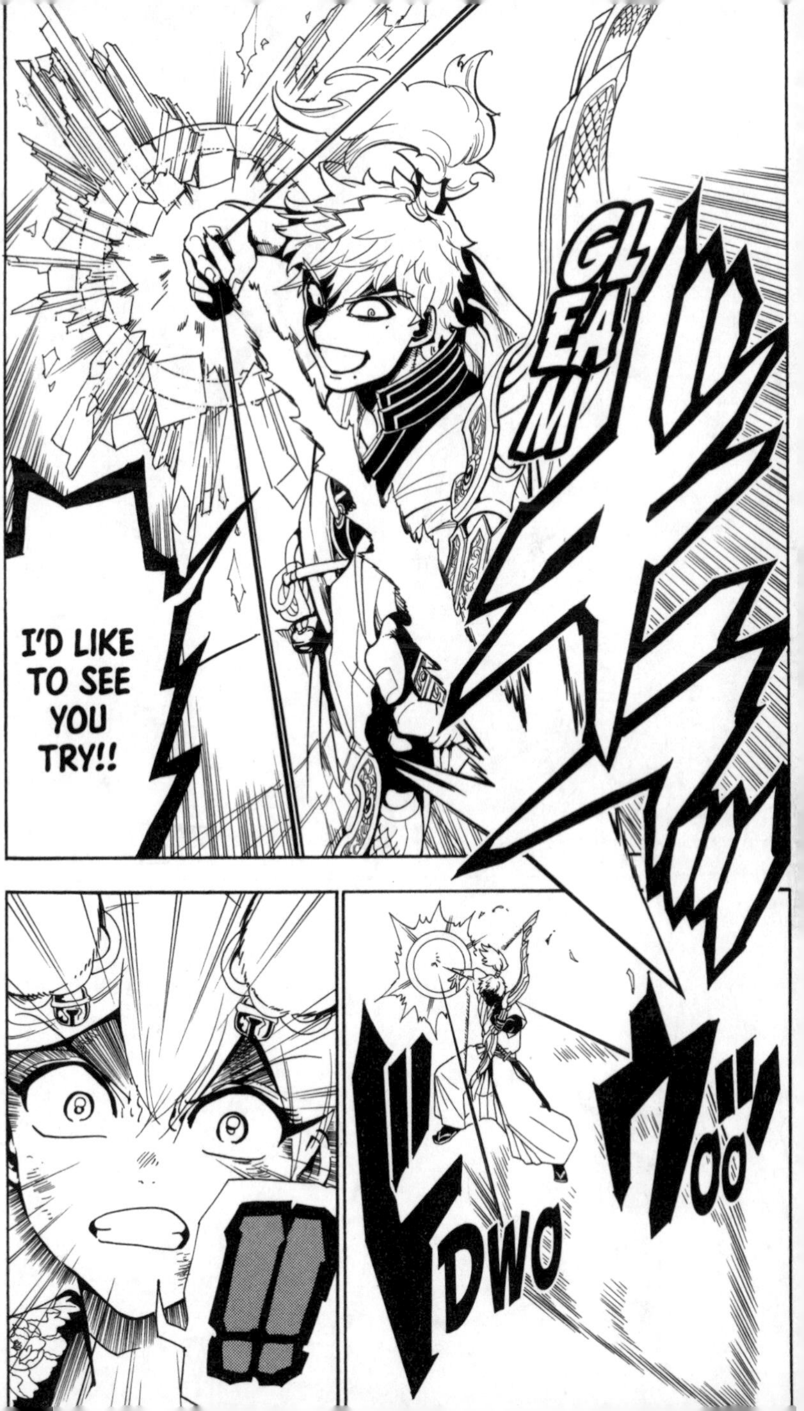
GLEAM
I'D LIKE TO SEE YOU TRY!!
DWOOO

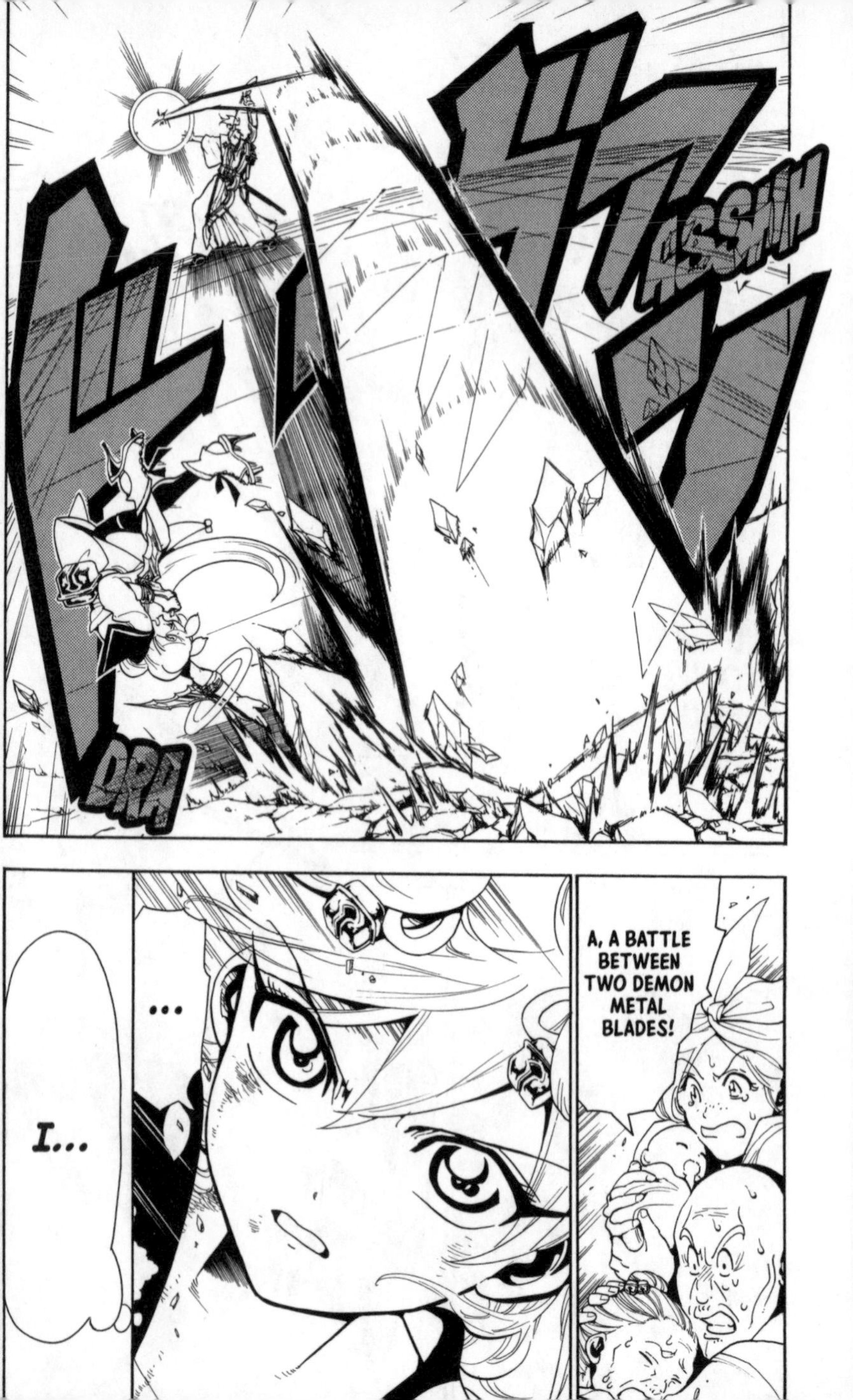
GASHIN
DRA
A, A BATTLE BETWEEN TWO DEMON METAL BLADES!
...
I...

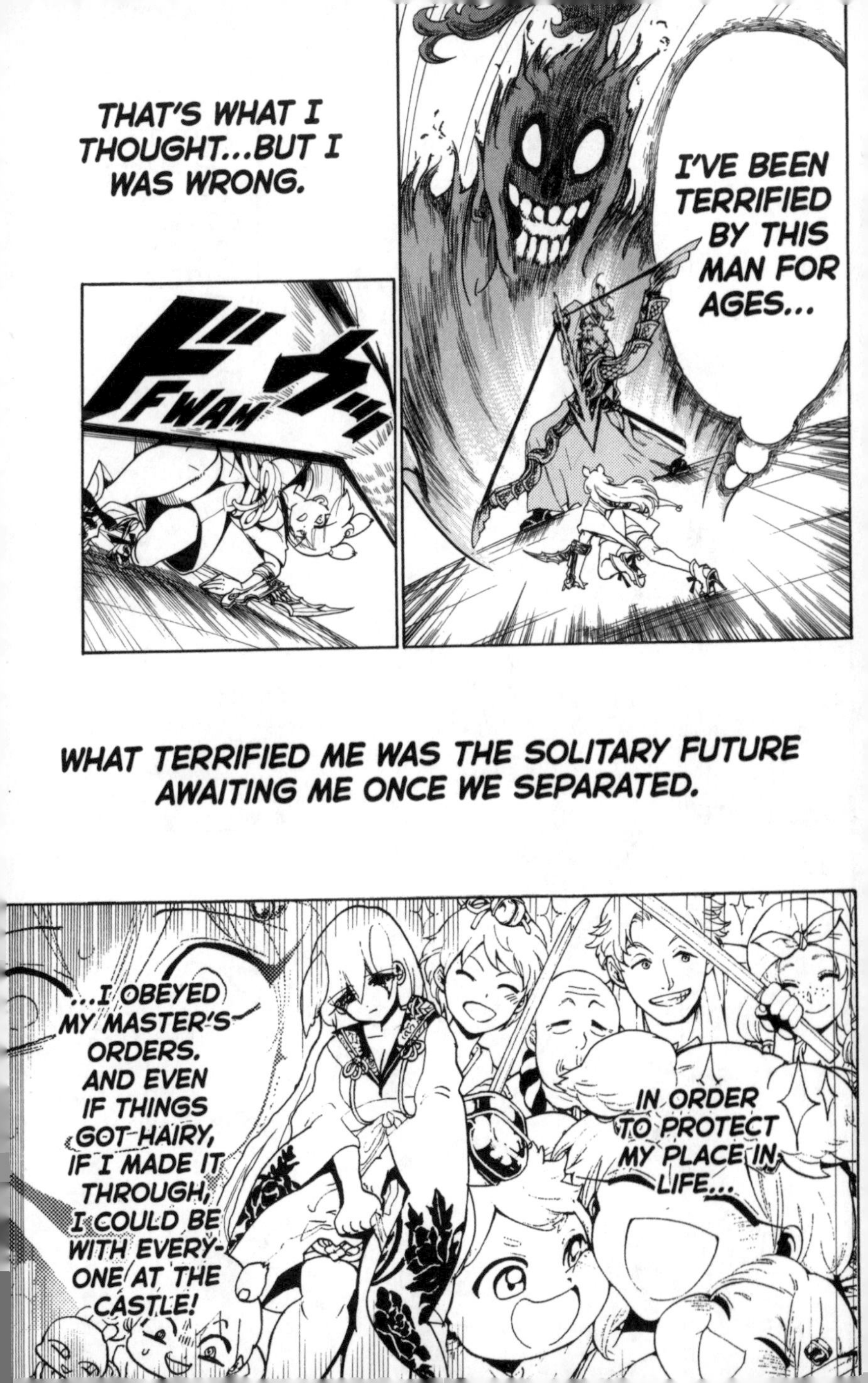
I'VE BEEN TERRIFIED BY THIS MAN FOR AGES...
THAT'S WHAT I THOUGHT...BUT I WAS WRONG.
FWAM
WHAT TERRIFIED ME WAS THE SOLITARY FUTURE AWAITING ME ONCE WE SEPARATED.
IN ORDER TO PROTECT MY PLACE IN LIFE...
...I OBEYED MY MASTER'S ORDERS. AND EVEN IF THINGS GOT HAIRY, IF I MADE IT THROUGH, I COULD BE WITH EVERY-ONE AT THE CASTLE!

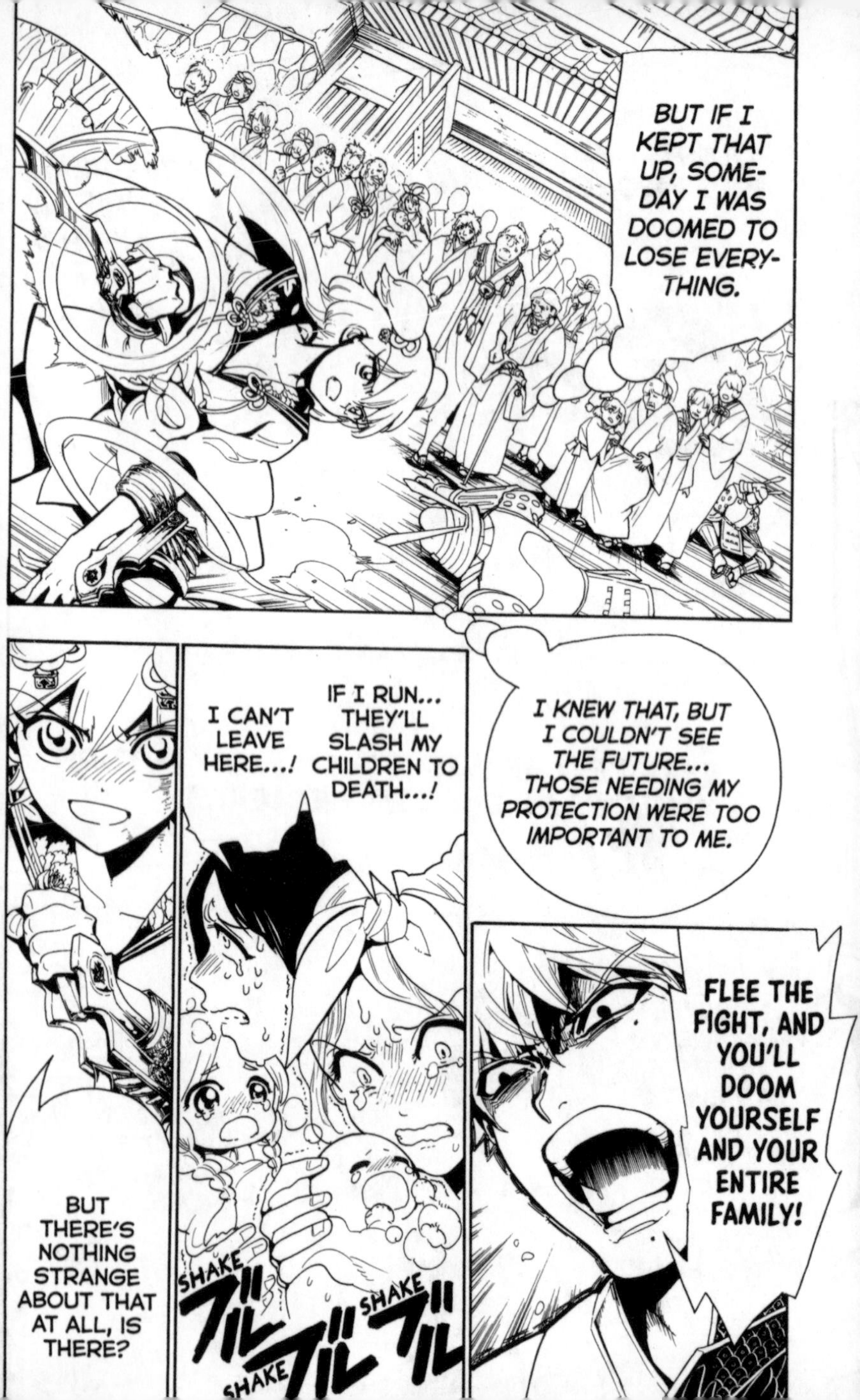
BUT IF I KEPT THAT UP, SOME-DAY I WAS DOOMED TO LOSE EVERY-THING.
I KNEW THAT, BUT I COULDN'T SEE THE FUTURE... THOSE NEEDING MY PROTECTION WERE TOO IMPORTANT TO ME.
FLEE THE FIGHT, AND YOU'LL DOOM YOURSELF AND YOUR ENTIRE FAMILY!
IF I RUN... THEY'LL SLASH MY CHILDREN TO DEATH...!
I CAN'T LEAVE HERE...!
SHAKE
SHAKE
SHAKE
SHAKE
BUT THERE'S NOTHING STRANGE ABOUT THAT AT ALL, IS THERE?

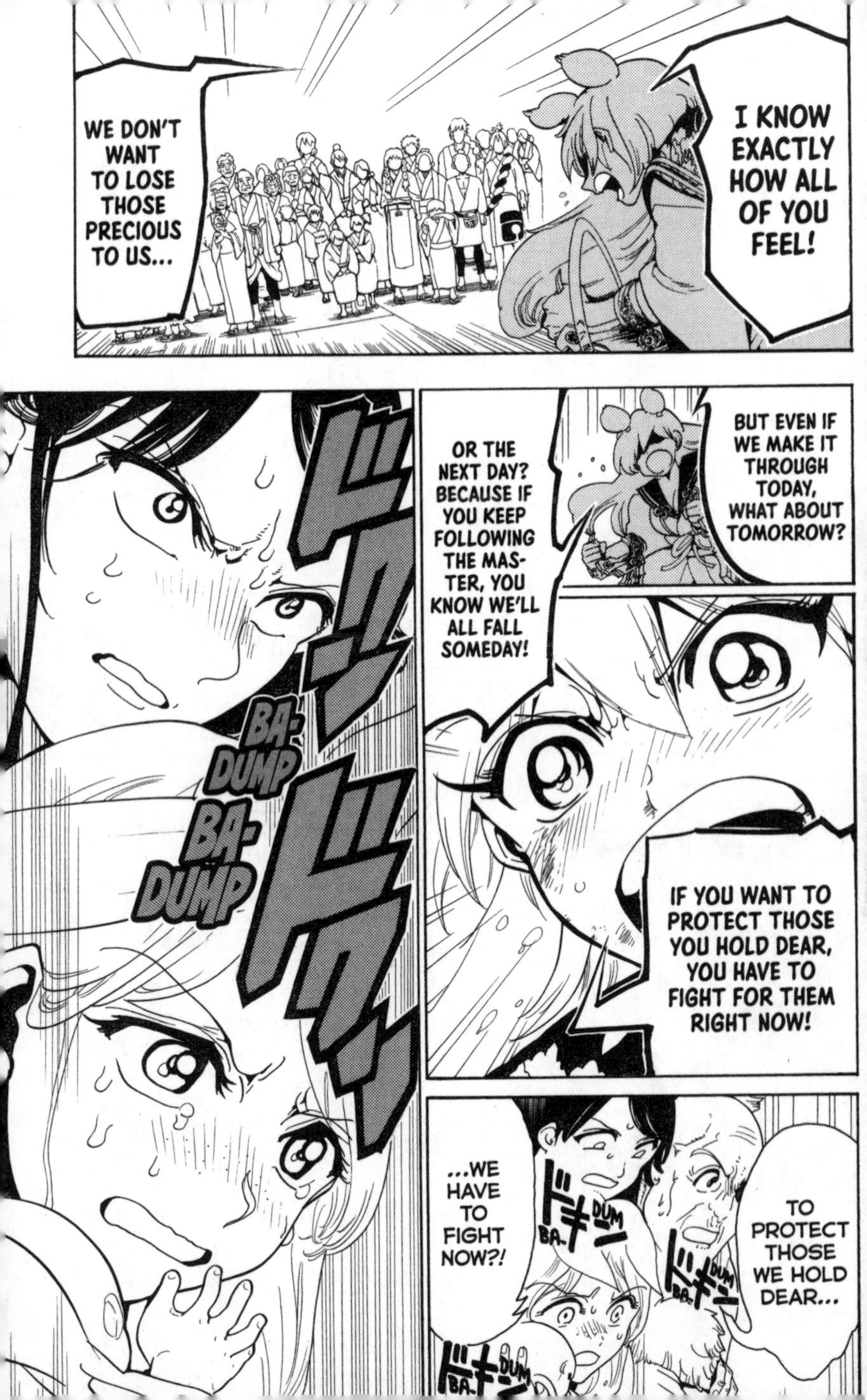
I KNOW EXACTLY HOW ALL OF YOU FEEL!
WE DON'T WANT TO LOSE THOSE PRECIOUS TO US...
BUT EVEN IF WE MAKE IT THROUGH TODAY, WHAT ABOUT TOMORROW?
OR THE NEXT DAY? BECAUSE IF YOU KEEP FOLLOWING THE MASTER, YOU KNOW WE'LL ALL FALL SOMEDAY!
IF YOU WANT TO PROTECT THOSE YOU HOLD DEAR, YOU HAVE TO FIGHT FOR THEM RIGHT NOW!
TO PROTECT THOSE WE HOLD DEAR...
BA-DUM
BA-DUM
...WE HAVE TO FIGHT NOW?!
BA-DUM
BA-DUMP
BA-DUMP

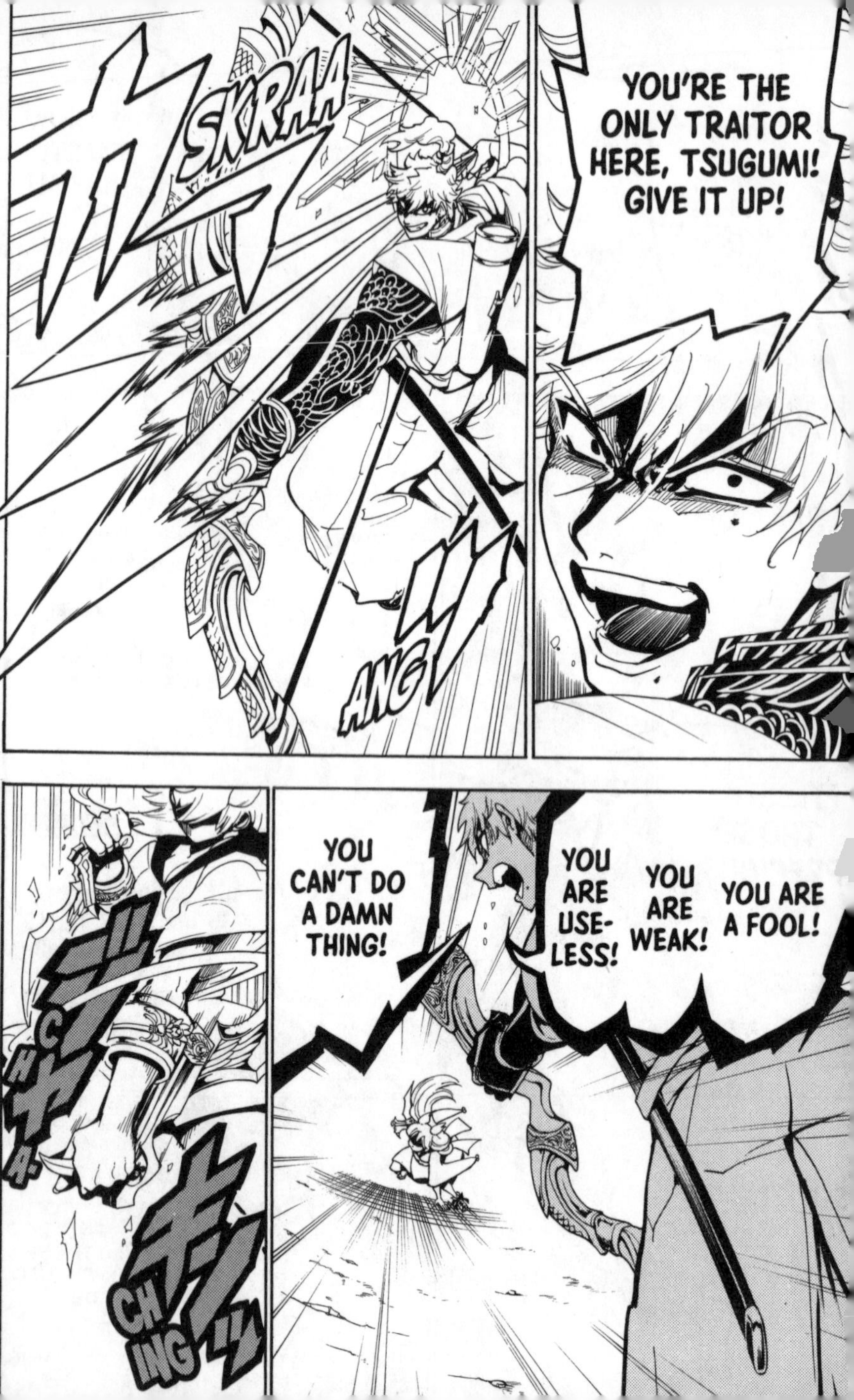
YOU'RE THE ONLY TRAITOR HERE, TSUGUMI! GIVE IT UP!
SKRAA
ANG
YOU ARE A FOOL!
YOU ARE WEAK!
YOU ARE USE-LESS!
YOU CAN'T DO A DAMN THING!
CHA-
CHING

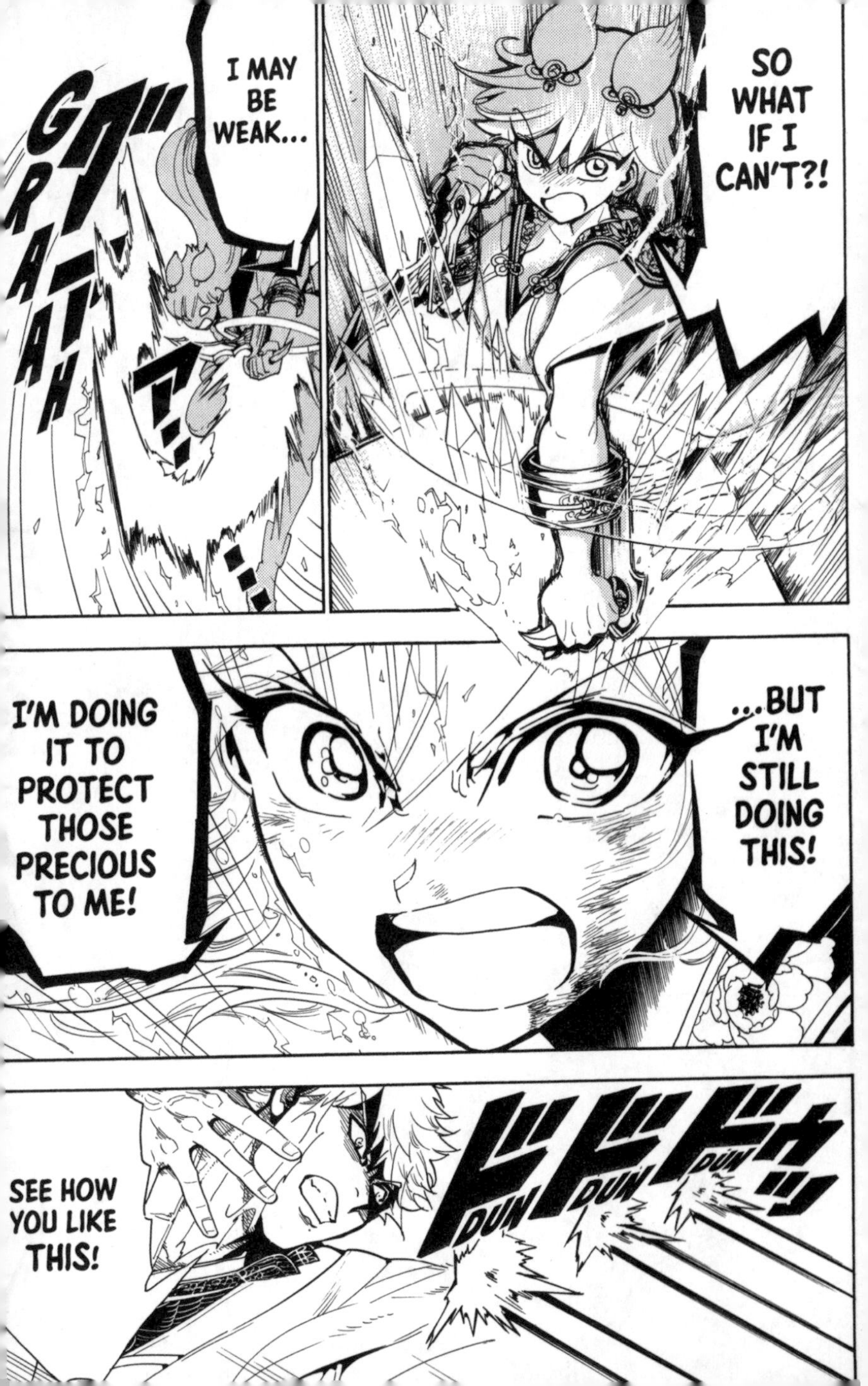
SO WHAT IF I CAN'T?!
I MAY BE WEAK...
GRAAAH
?!
...
...BUT I'M STILL DOING THIS!
I'M DOING IT TO PROTECT THOSE PRECIOUS TO ME!
DUN DUN DUN
SEE HOW YOU LIKE THIS!

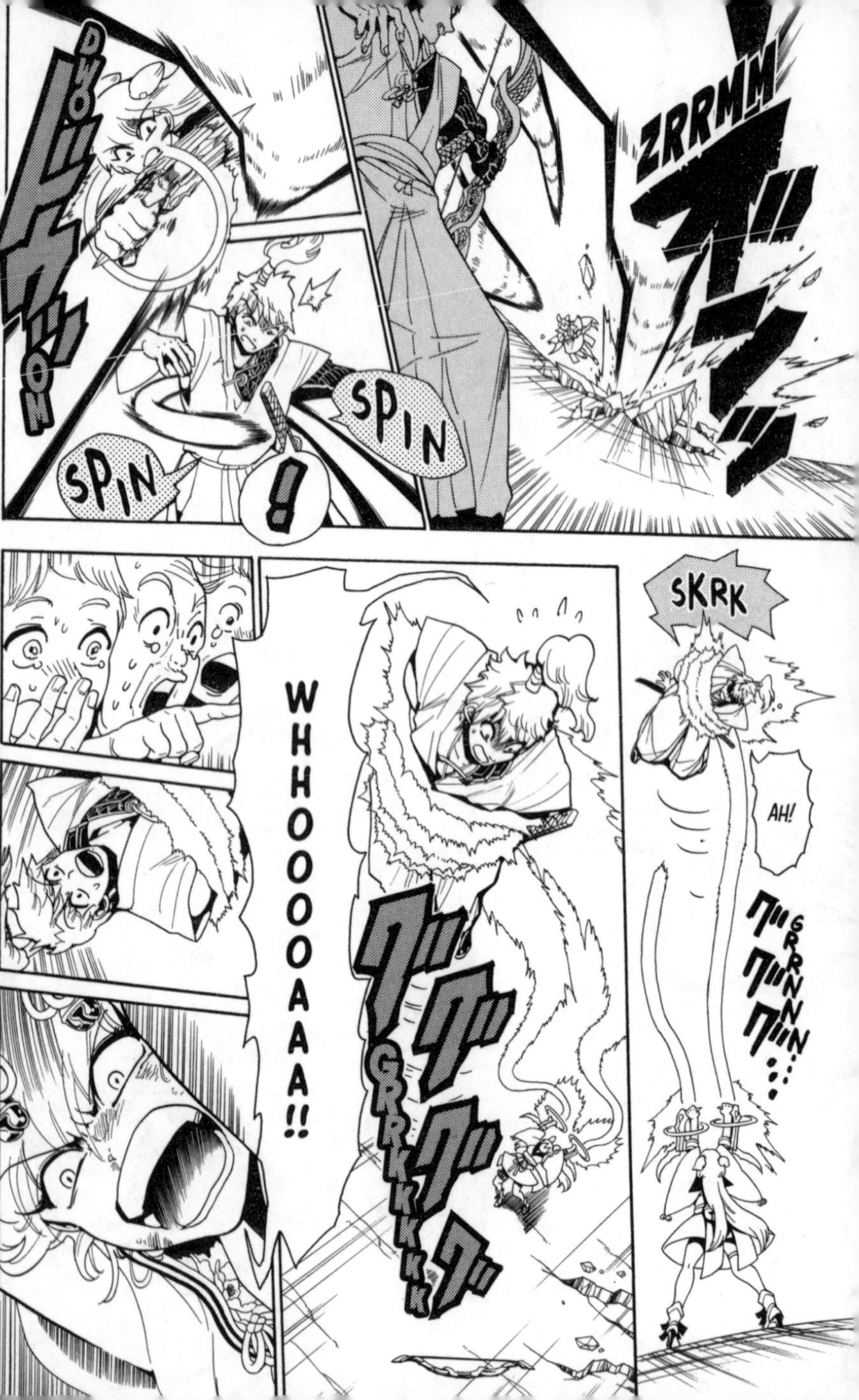
ZRRMM
SPIN
SPIN
!
DWOOM
SKRK
AH!
GRRNNN...
WHHOOOOOAAA!!
GRRKKKKK

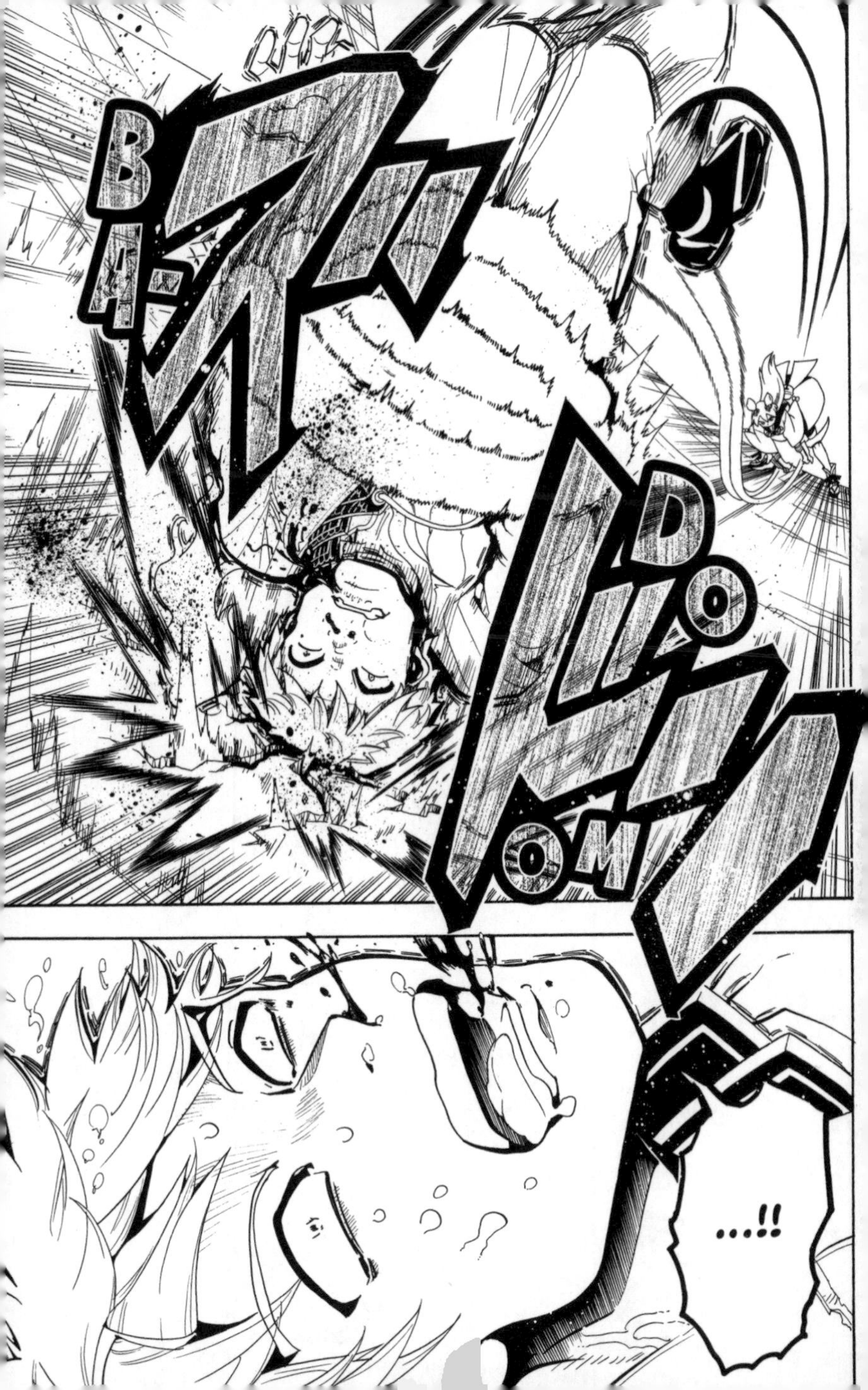
DOOM
BA-
...!!

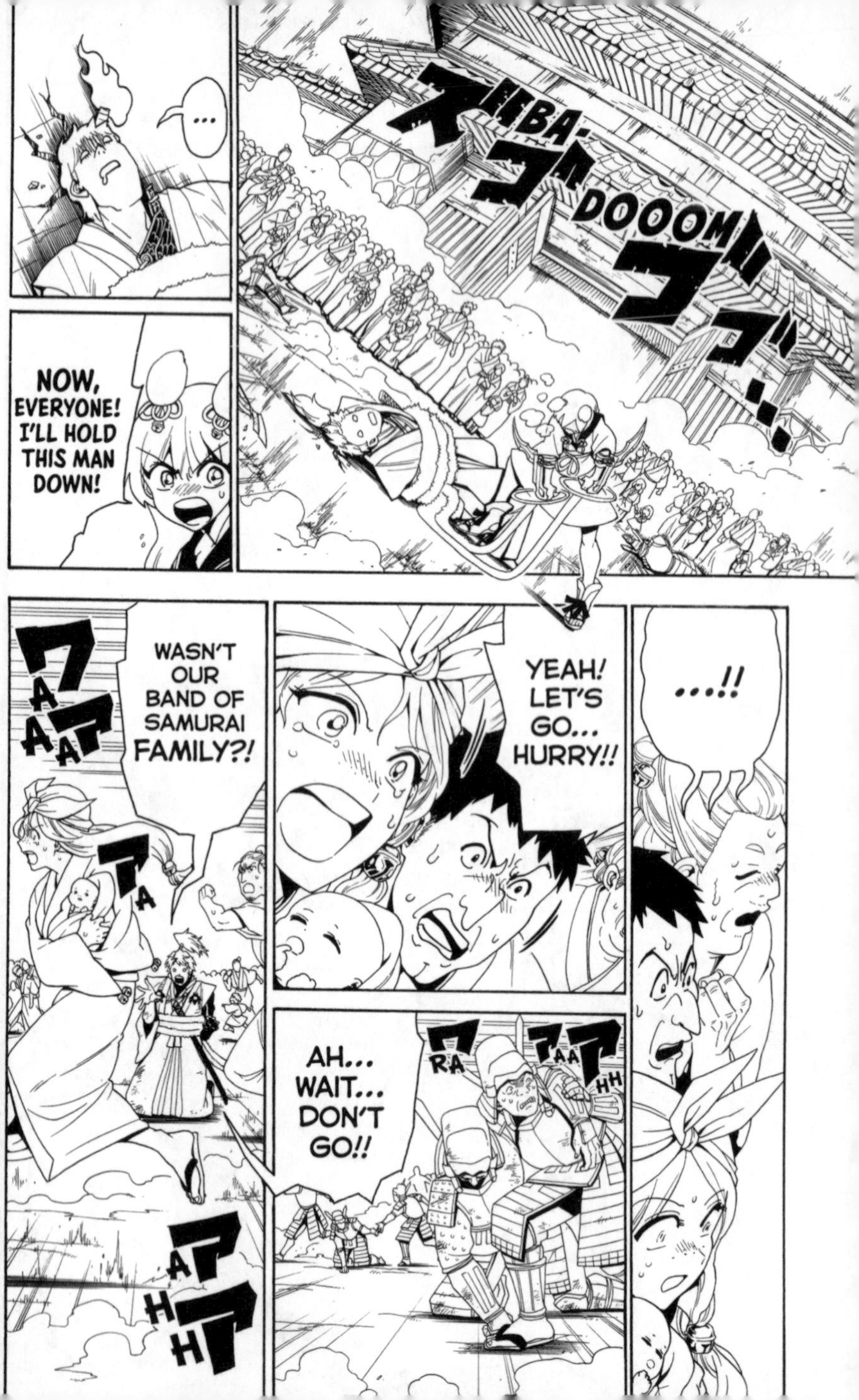
BA-DOOOM!!
...
NOW, EVERYONE! I'LL HOLD THIS MAN DOWN!
...!!
YEAH! LET'S GO... HURRY!!
RA
AAHH
AH... WAIT... DON'T GO!!
WASN'T OUR BAND OF SAMURAI FAMILY?!

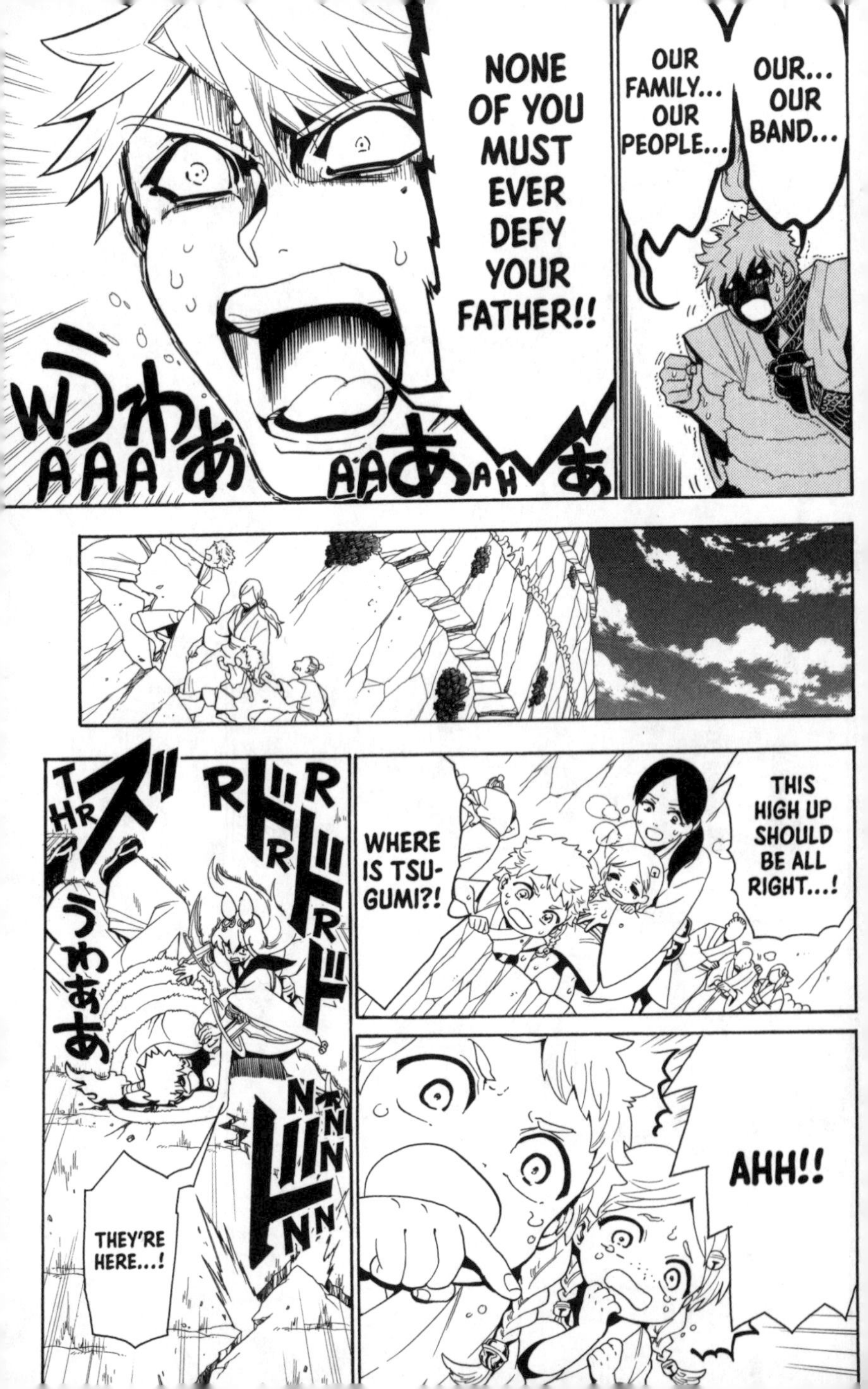
OUR... OUR BAND...
OUR FAMILY... OUR PEOPLE...
NONE OF YOU MUST EVER DEFY YOUR FATHER!!
うわああああ
WAAAAAAH
THIS HIGH UP SHOULD BE ALL RIGHT...!
WHERE IS TSU-GUMI?!
AHH!!
ズ
THR
ドドド
RRRRR
うわああ
ドン
NNNNNN
THEY'RE HERE...!

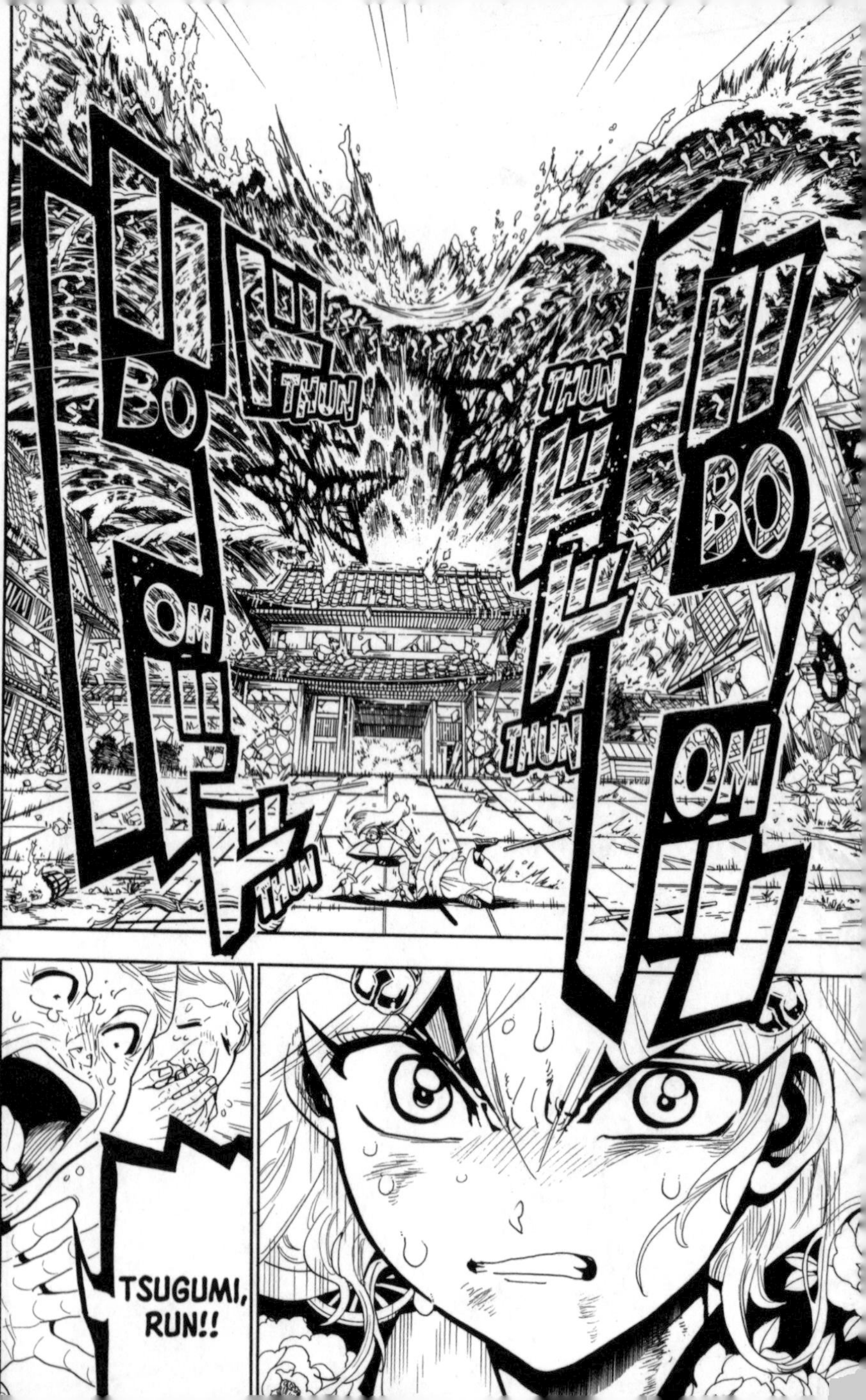
THUN
BOOM!!
THUN
BOOM!!
THUN
THUN
TSUGUMI, RUN!!

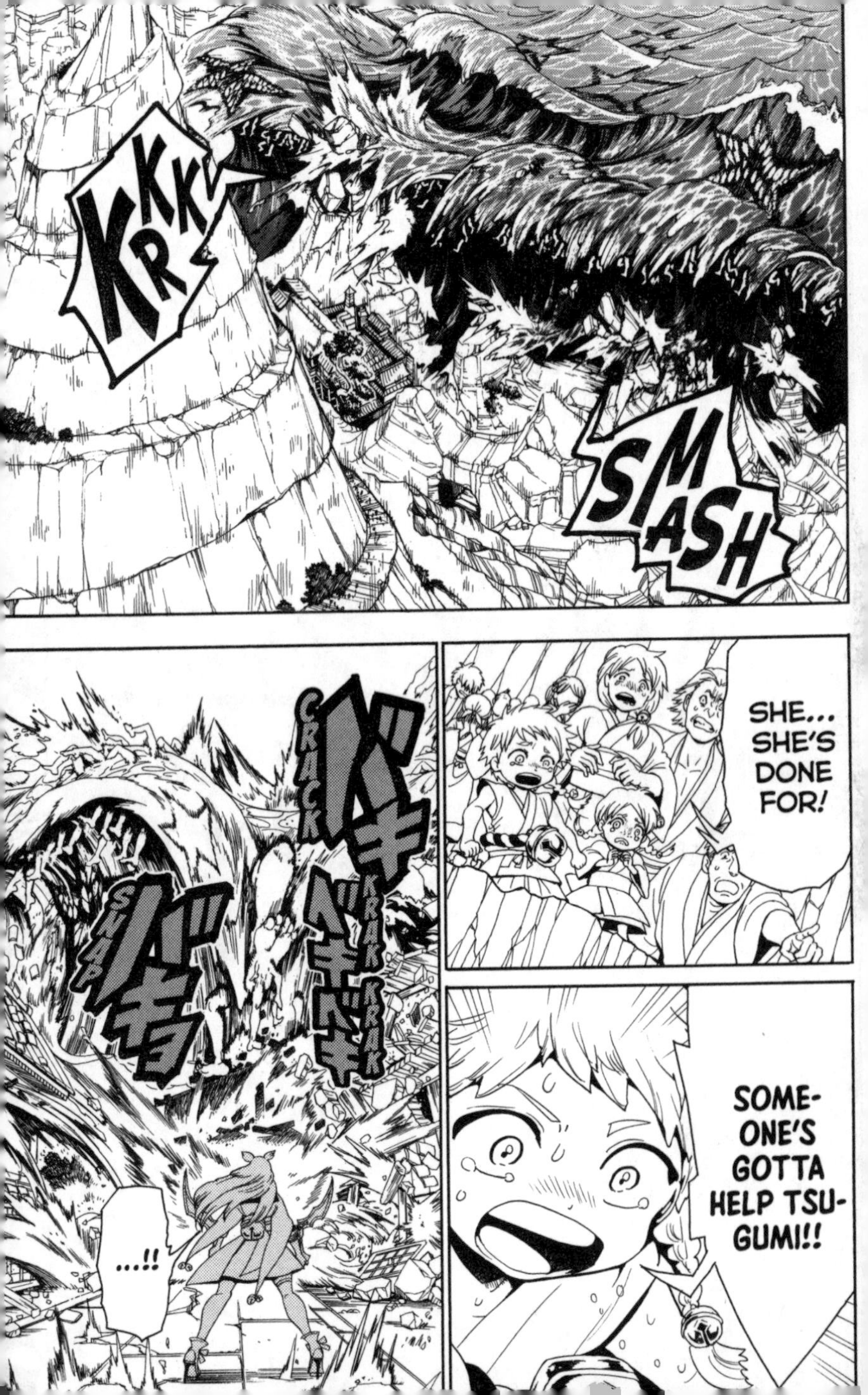
KRKK
SMASH
SHE... SHE'S DONE FOR!
SOME-ONE'S GOTTA HELP TSU-GUMI!!
CRACK
バキ
KRAK KRAK
ベキベキ
SNAP
バキョ
...!!

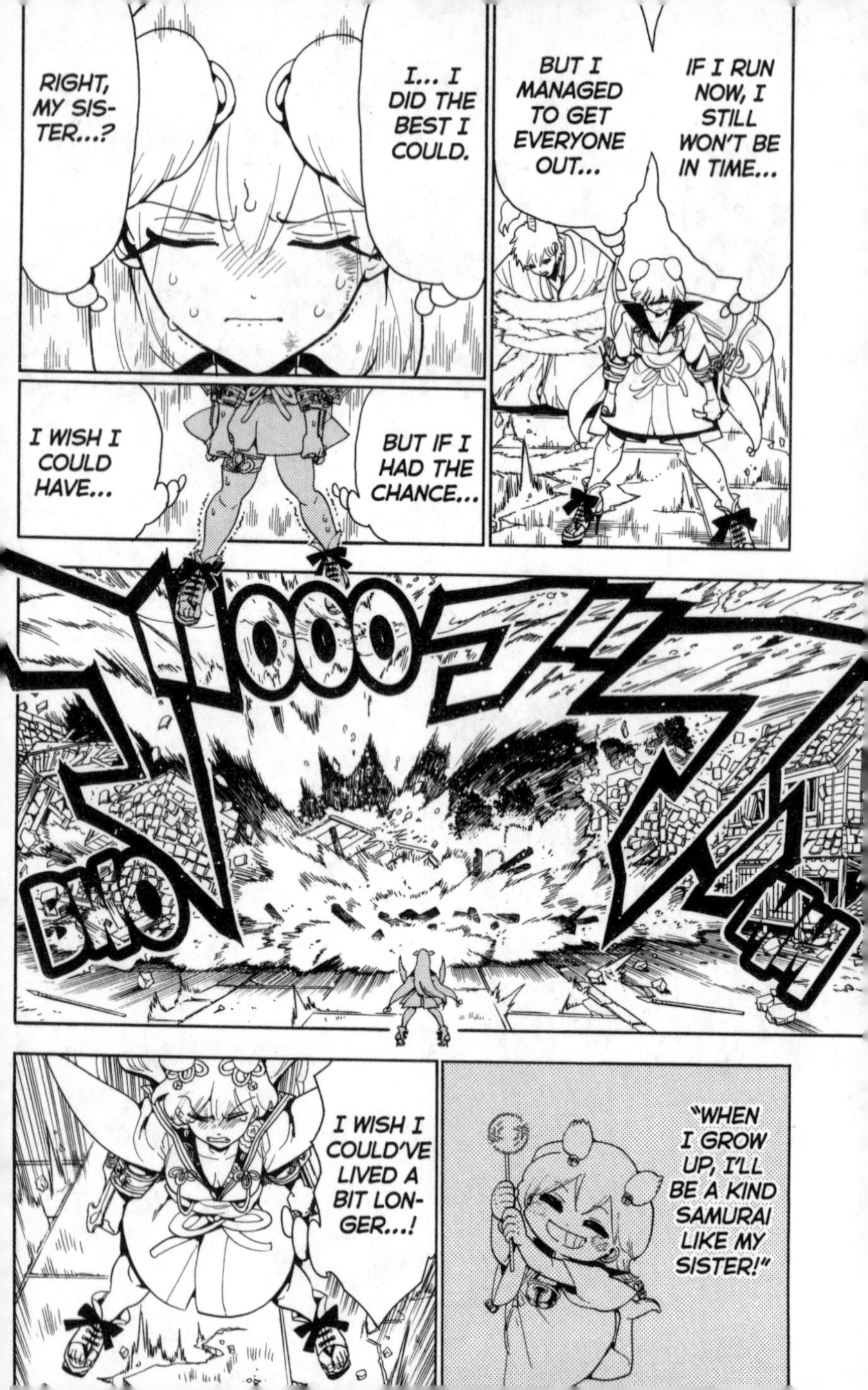
IF I RUN NOW, I STILL WON'T BE IN TIME...
BUT I MANAGED TO GET EVERYONE OUT...
I... I DID THE BEST I COULD.
RIGHT, MY SIS-TER...?
BUT IF I HAD THE CHANCE...
I WISH I COULD HAVE...
"WHEN I GROW UP, I'LL BE A KIND SAMURAI LIKE MY SISTER!"
I WISH I COULD'VE LIVED A BIT LON-GER...!

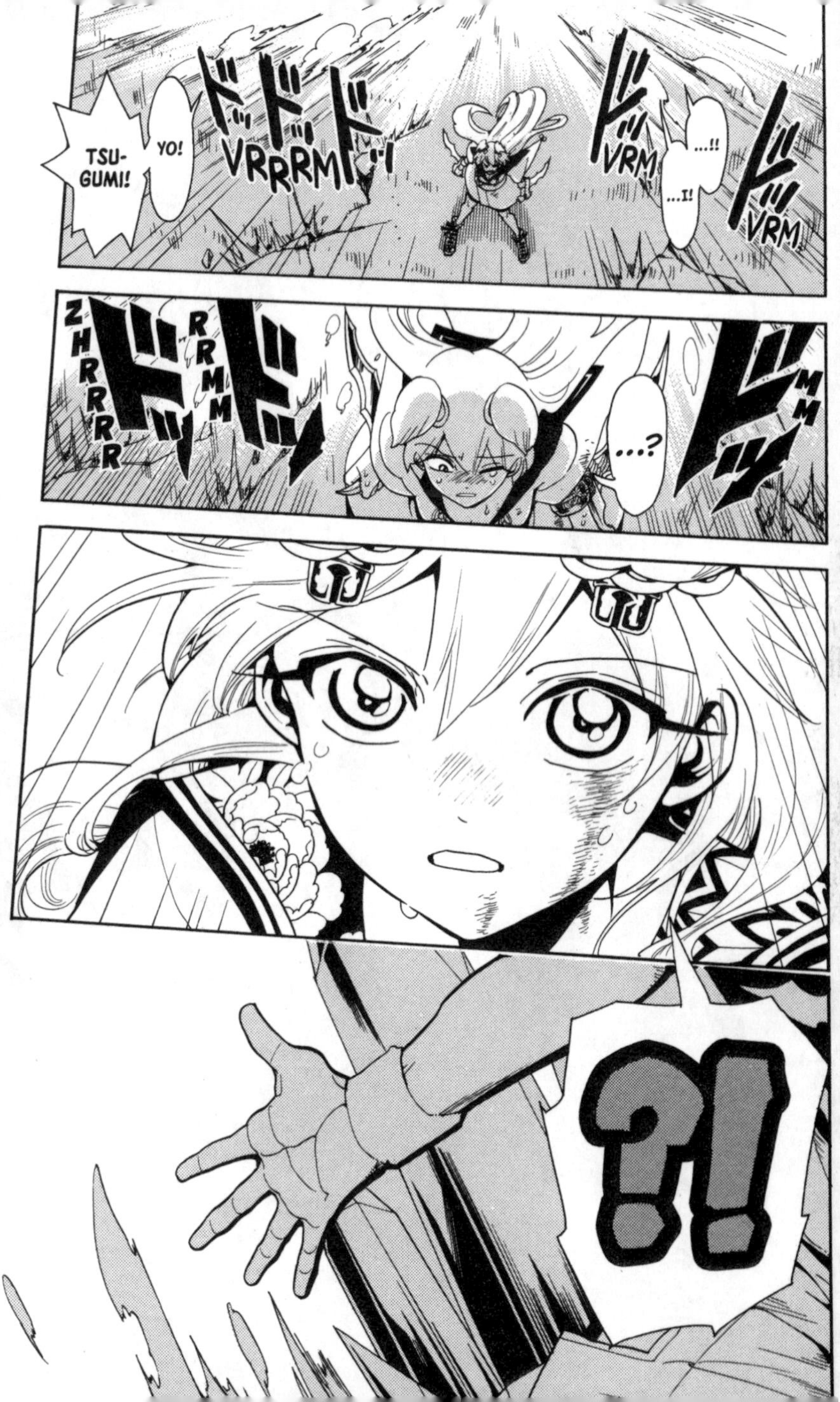
VRM
...!!
...I!
VRM
VRRRM
YO!
TSU-GUMI!
MM
...?
RRRMM
ZHRRRRR
?!

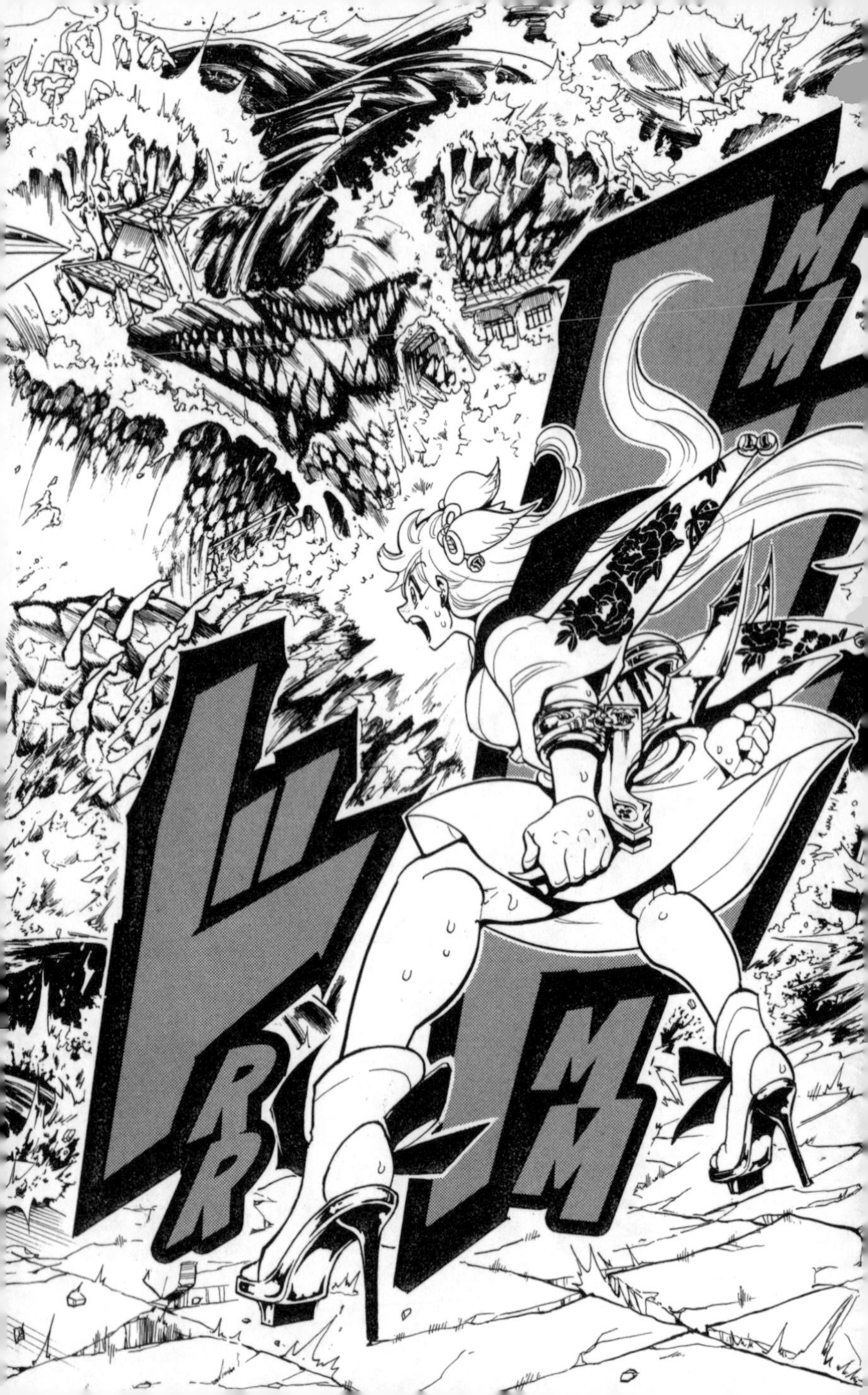
RRMMMM

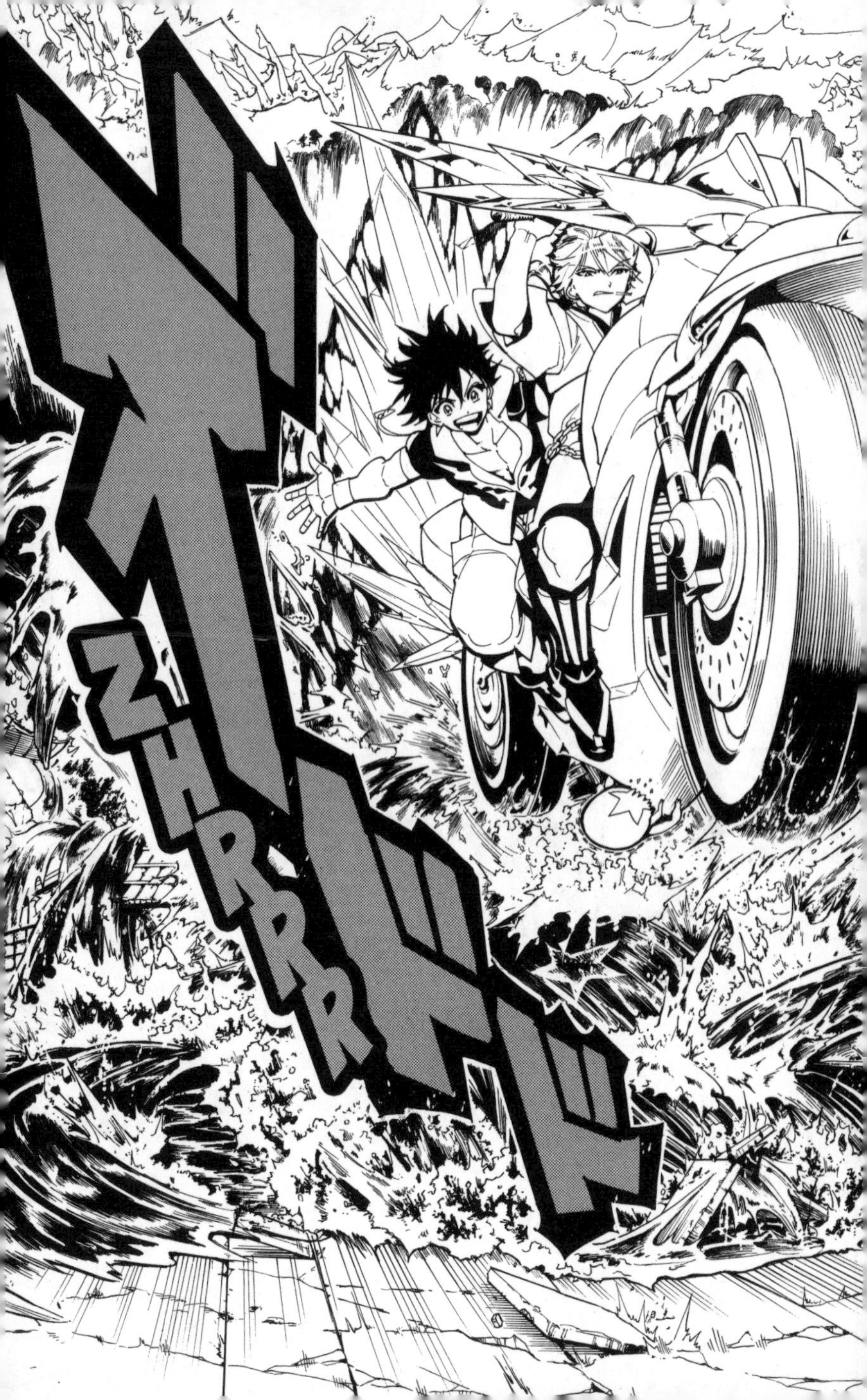
ZHRRR

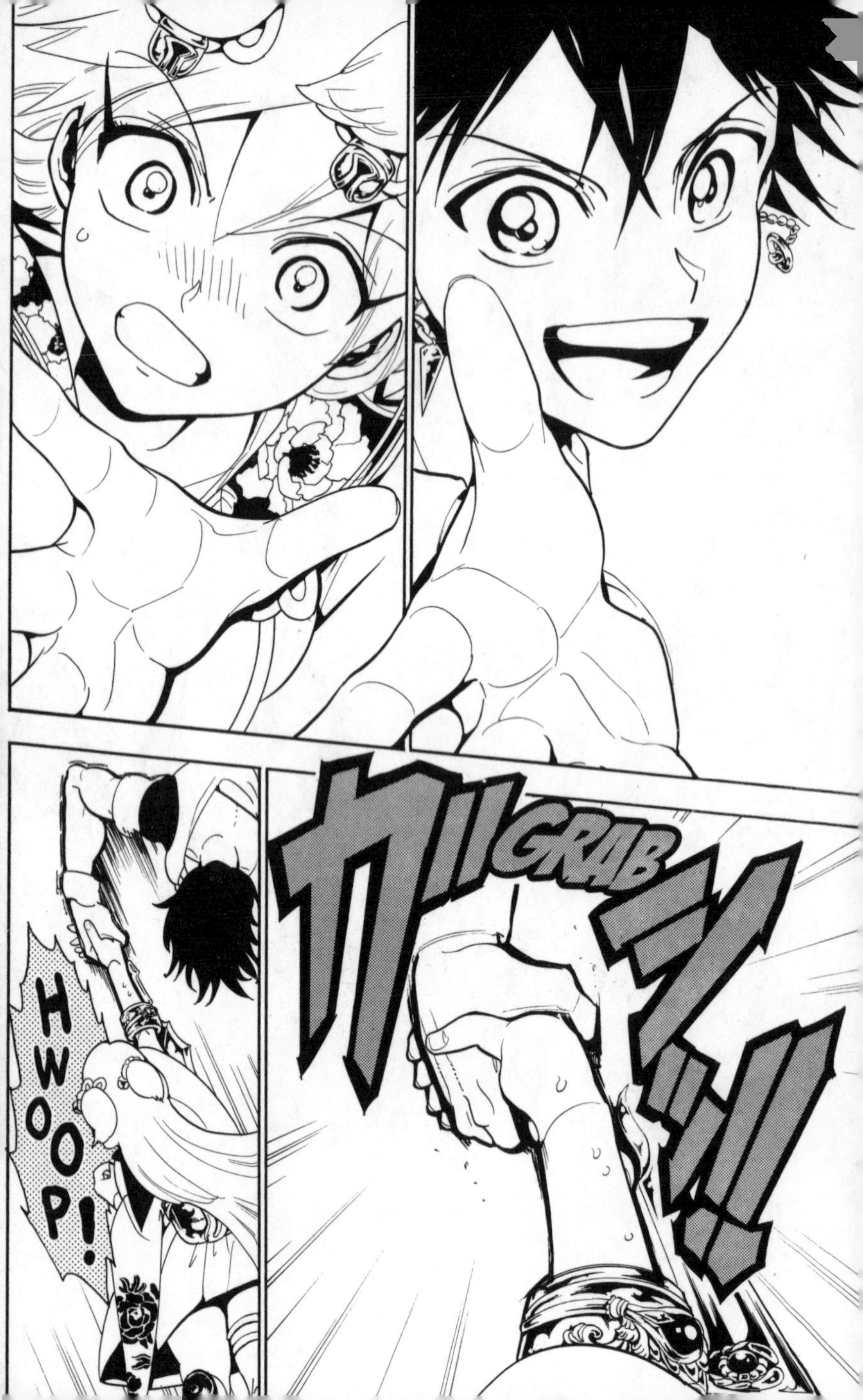
カッ GRAB ーッ!!
HWOOP!

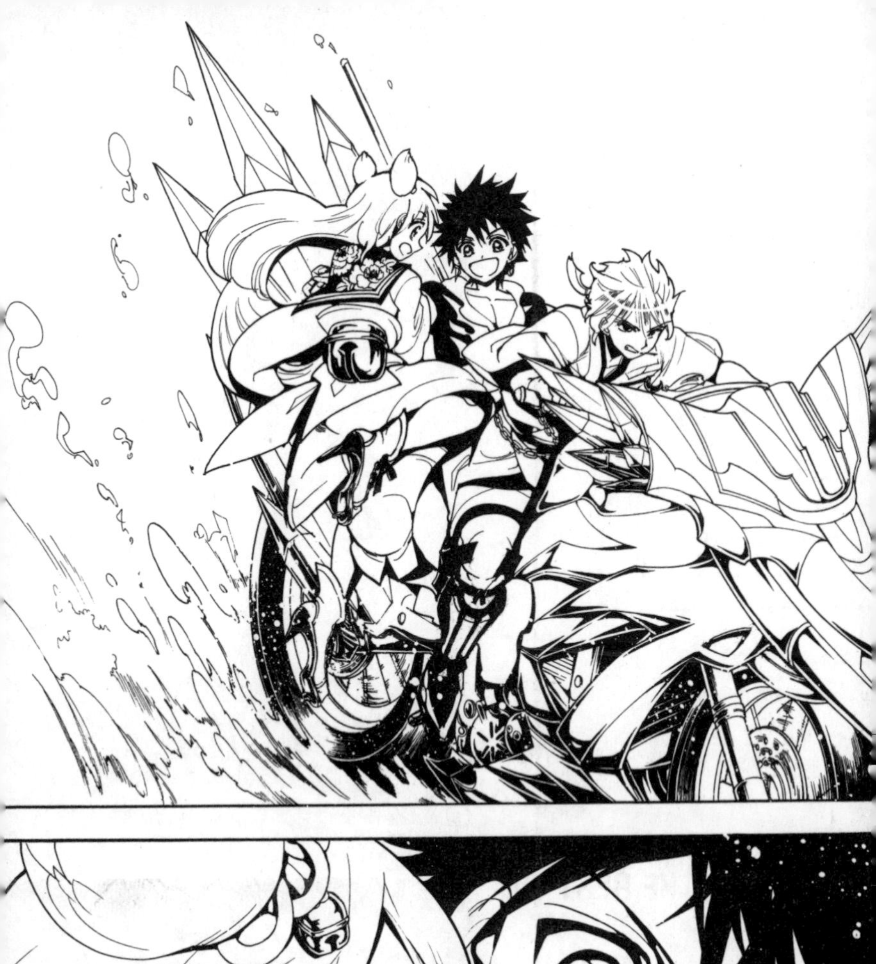

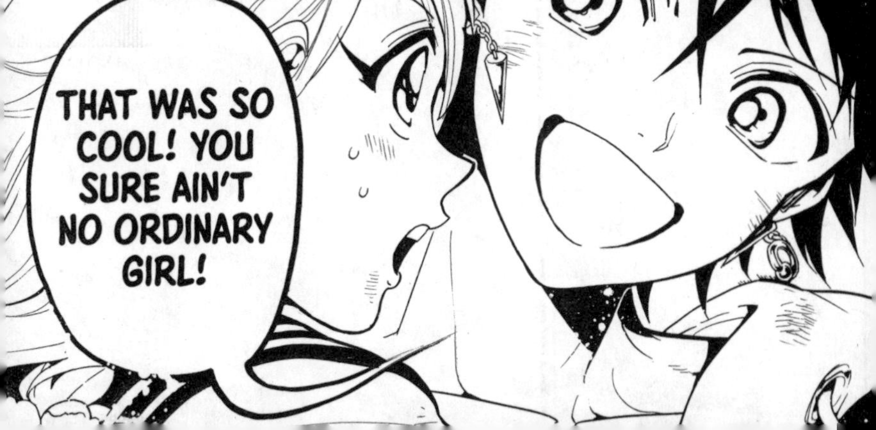
THAT WAS SO COOL! YOU SURE AIN'T NO ORDINARY GIRL!

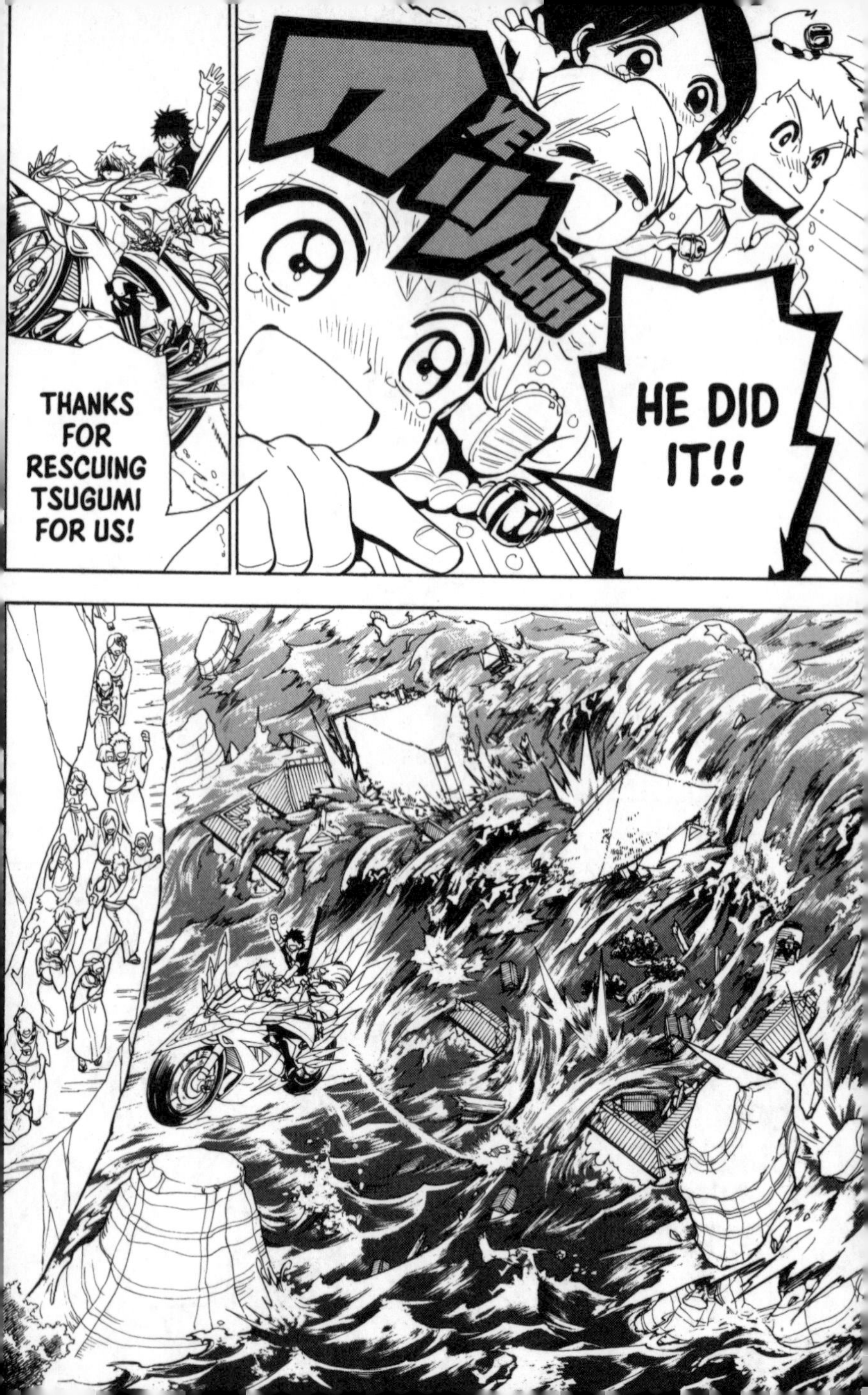
YEAHH
HE DID IT!!
THANKS FOR RESCUING TSUGUMI FOR US!

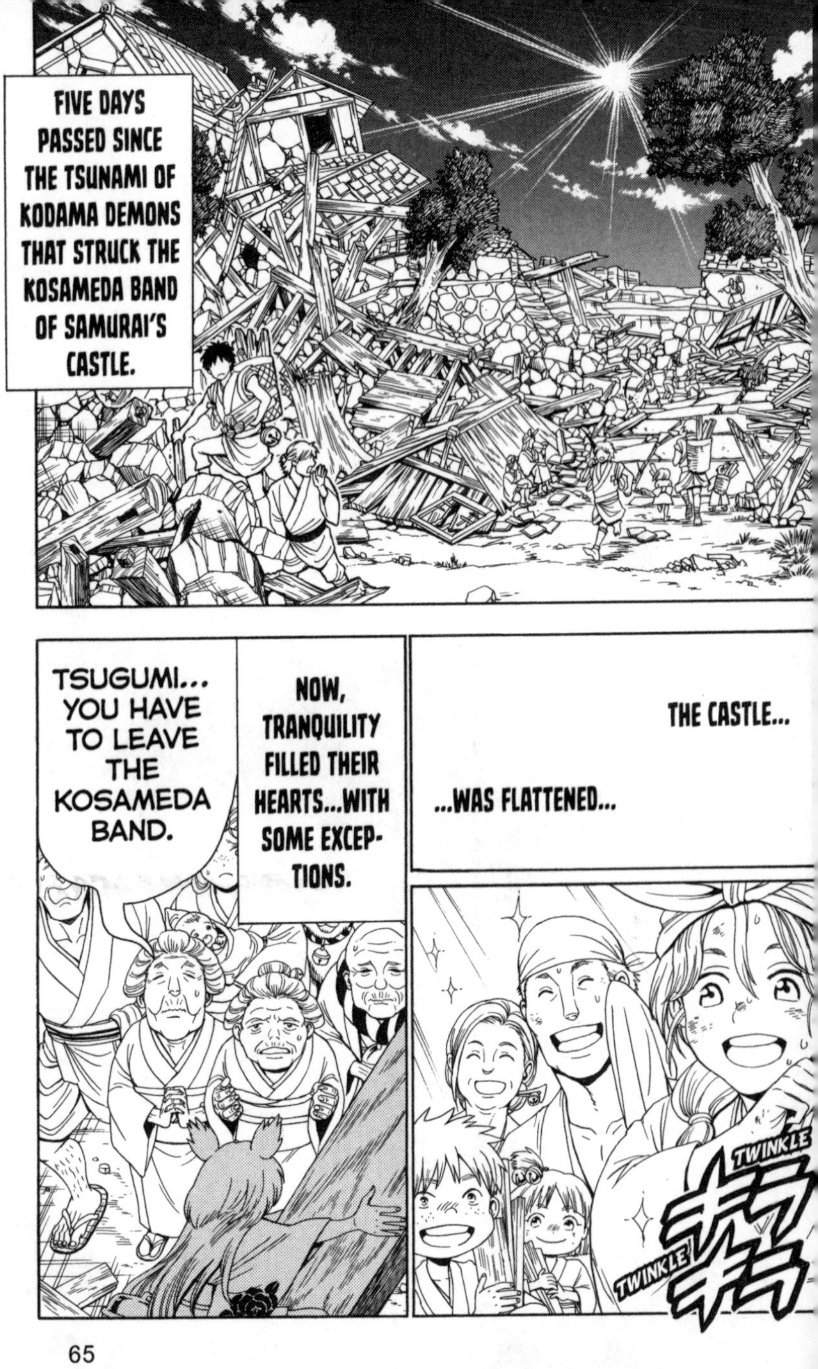
FIVE DAYS PASSED SINCE THE TSUNAMI OF KODAMA DEMONS THAT STRUCK THE KOSAMEDA BAND OF SAMURAI'S CASTLE.
THE CASTLE...
...WAS FLATTENED...
TWINKLE キラ
TWINKLE キラ
NOW, TRANQUILITY FILLED THEIR HEARTS...WITH SOME EXCEP-TIONS.
TSUGUMI... YOU HAVE TO LEAVE THE KOSAMEDA BAND.

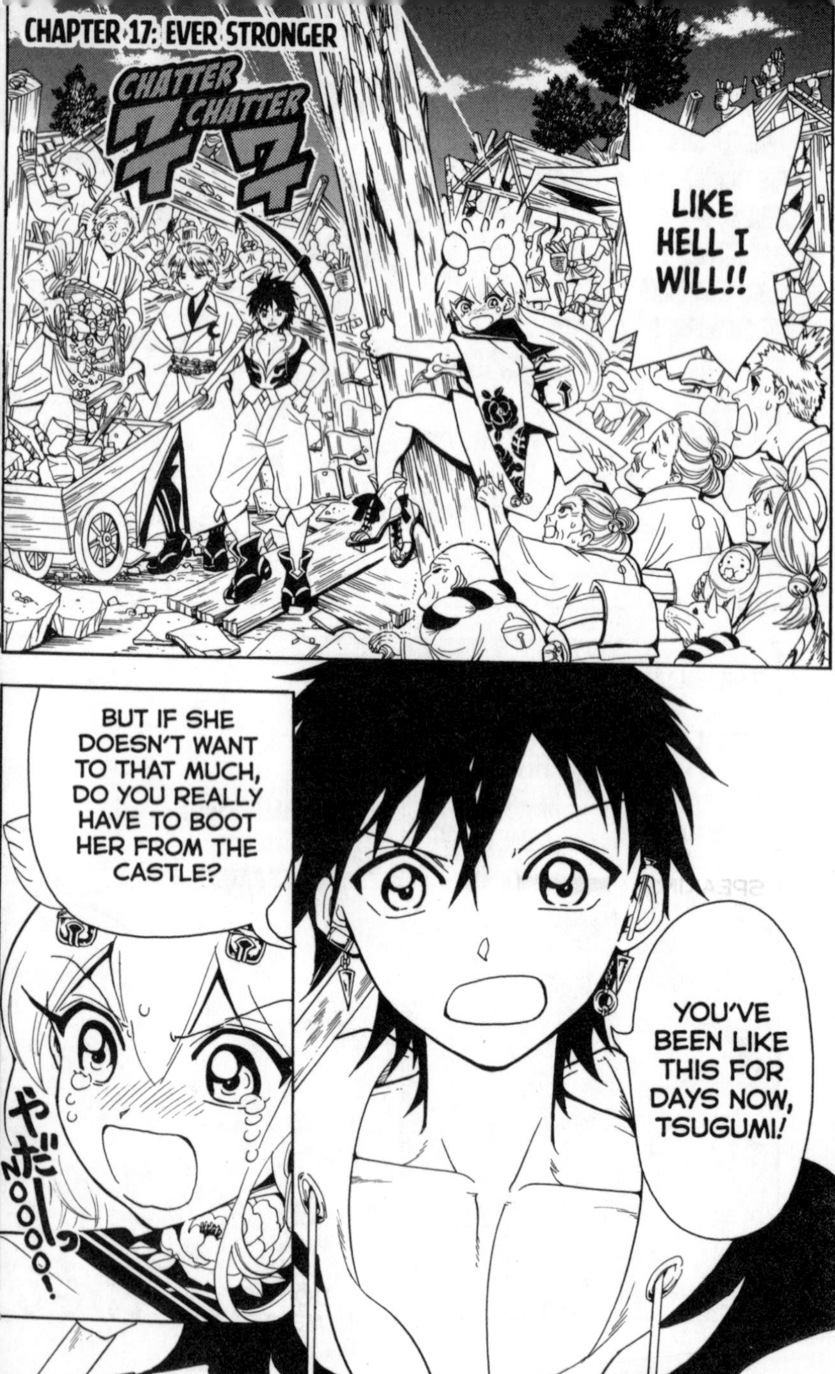
CHAPTER 17: EVER STRONGER
CHATTER CHATTER
ワイワイ
LIKE HELL I WILL!!
YOU'VE BEEN LIKE THIS FOR DAYS NOW, TSUGUMI!
BUT IF SHE DOESN'T WANT TO THAT MUCH, DO YOU REALLY HAVE TO BOOT HER FROM THE CASTLE?
やだー NOOOOO!

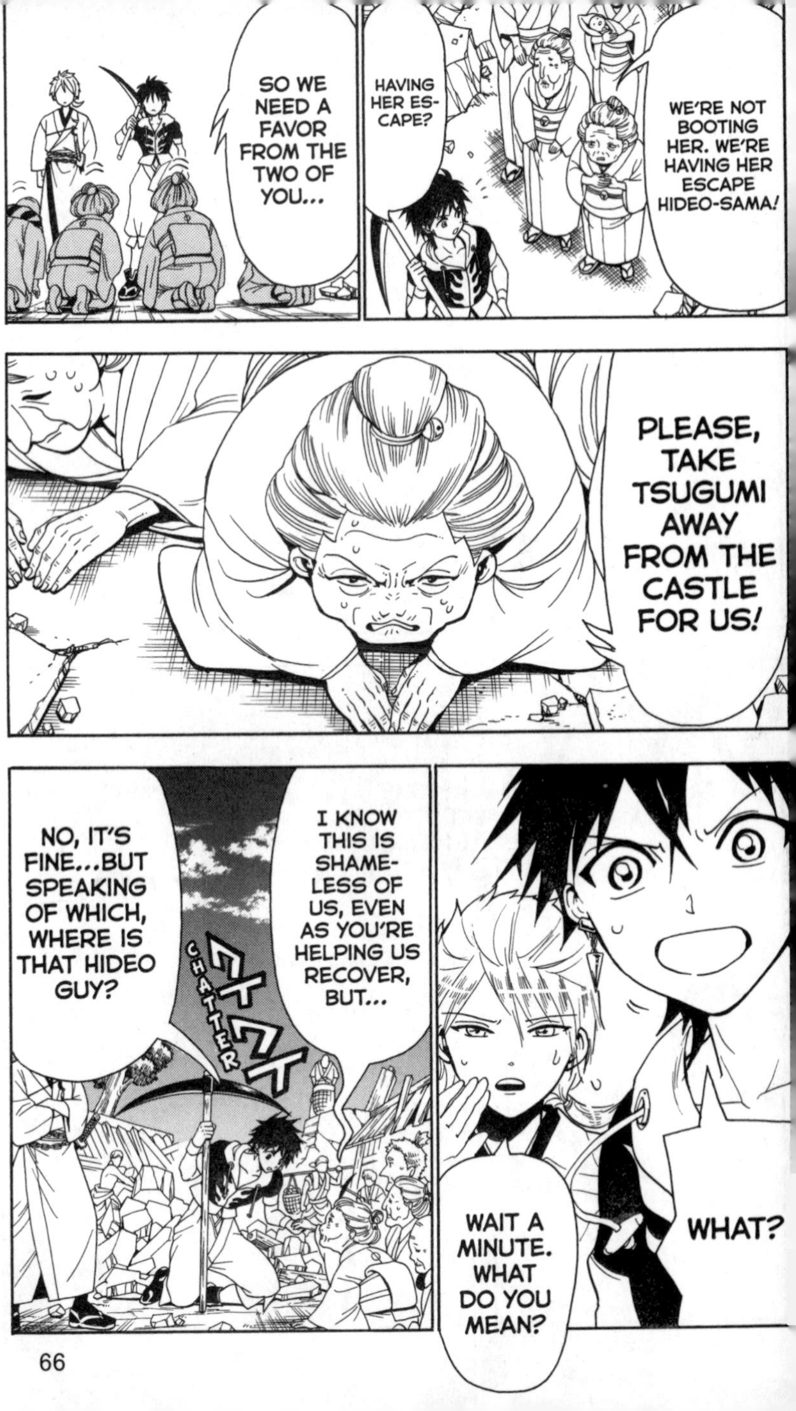
WE'RE NOT BOOTING HER. WE'RE HAVING HER ESCAPE HIDEO-SAMA!
HAVING HER ES-CAPE?
SO WE NEED A FAVOR FROM THE TWO OF YOU...
PLEASE, TAKE TSUGUMI AWAY FROM THE CASTLE FOR US!
WHAT?
WAIT A MINUTE. WHAT DO YOU MEAN?
I KNOW THIS IS SHAME-LESS OF US, EVEN AS YOU'RE HELPING US RECOVER, BUT...
CHATTER
NO, IT'S FINE...BUT SPEAKING OF WHICH, WHERE IS THAT HIDEO GUY?

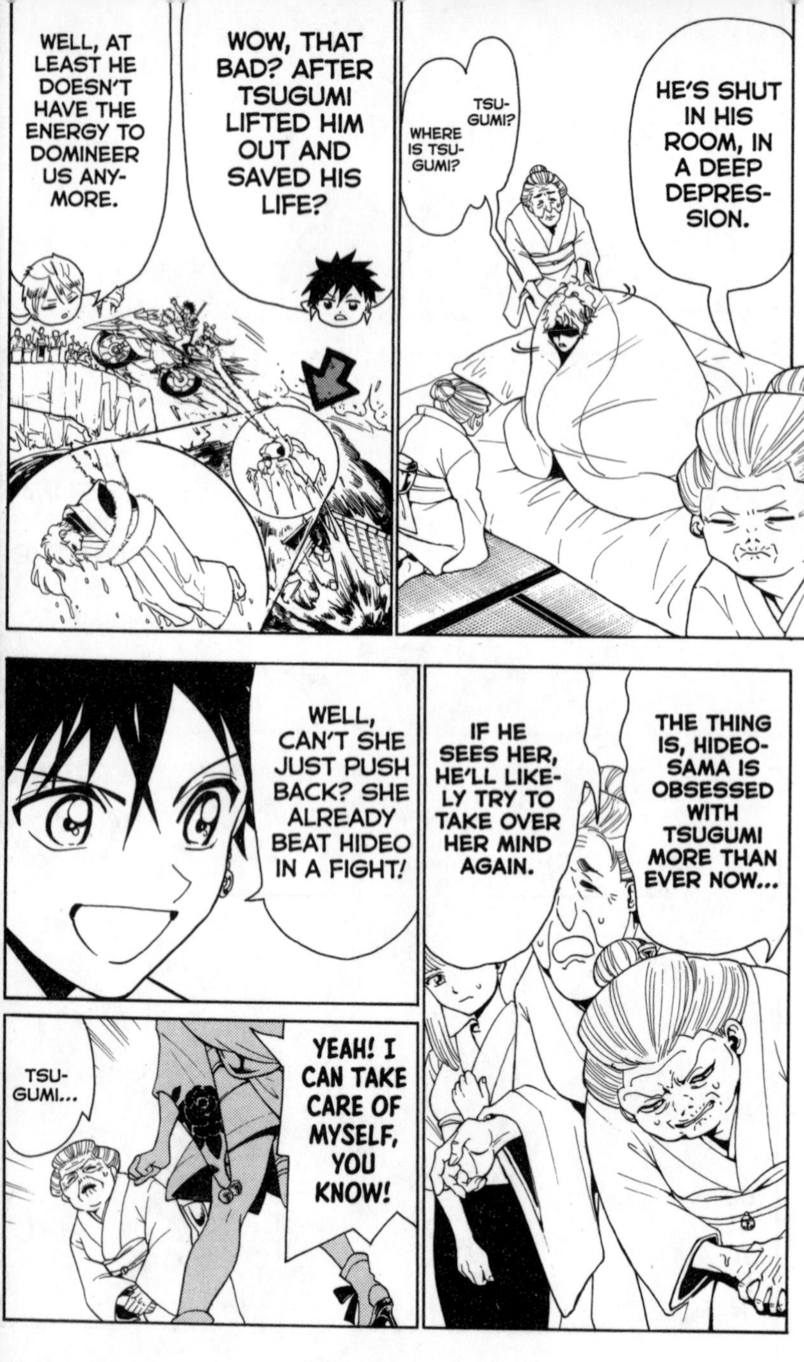
HE'S SHUT IN HIS ROOM, IN A DEEP DEPRESSION.
TSU-GUMI?
WHERE IS TSU-GUMI?
WOW, THAT BAD? AFTER TSUGUMI LIFTED HIM OUT AND SAVED HIS LIFE?
WELL, AT LEAST HE DOESN'T HAVE THE ENERGY TO DOMINEER US ANYMORE.
THE THING IS, HIDEO-SAMA IS OBSESSED WITH TSUGUMI MORE THAN EVER NOW...
IF HE SEES HER, HE'LL LIKELY TRY TO TAKE OVER HER MIND AGAIN.
WELL, CAN'T SHE JUST PUSH BACK? SHE ALREADY BEAT HIDEO IN A FIGHT!
YEAH! I CAN TAKE CARE OF MYSELF, YOU KNOW!
TSU-GUMI...

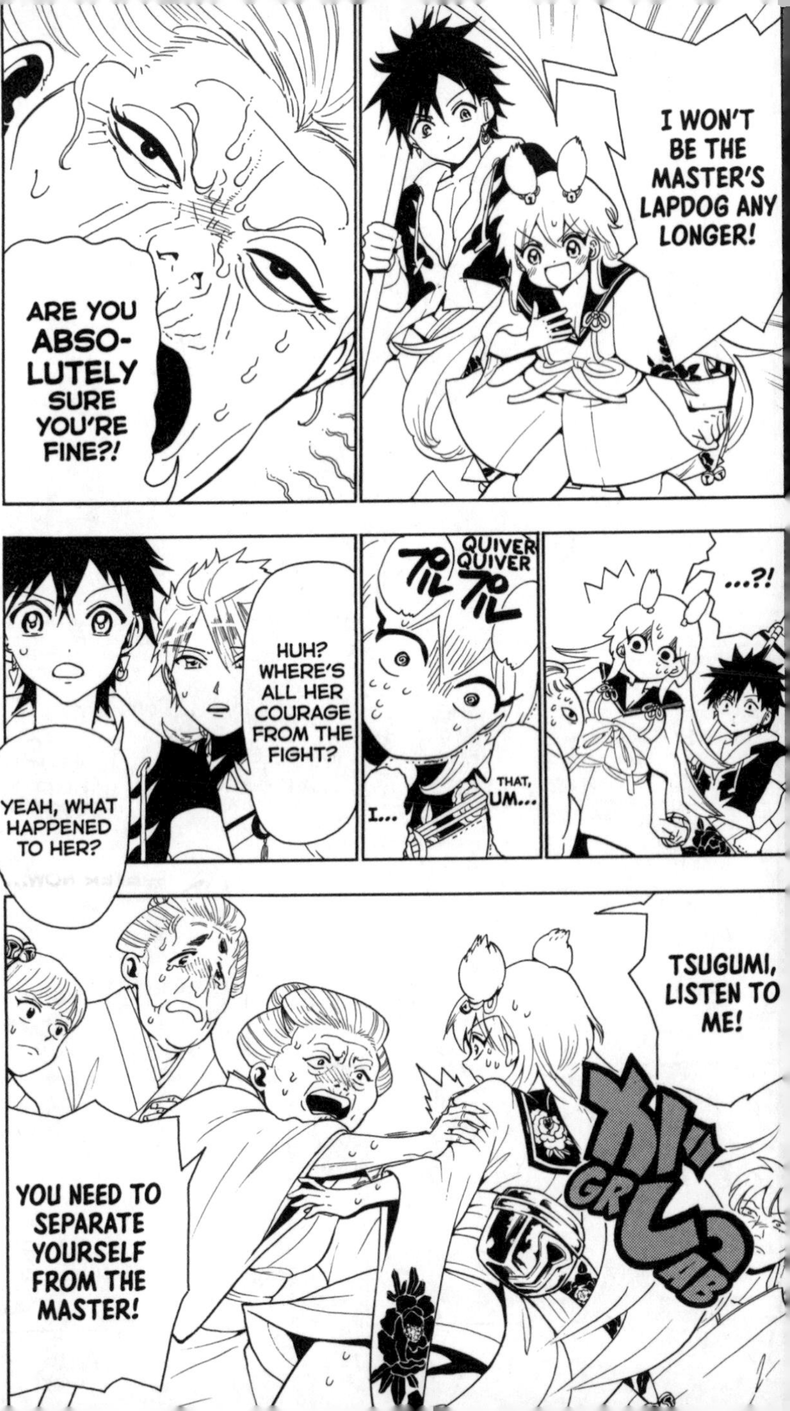
I WON'T BE THE MASTER'S LAPDOG ANY LONGER!
ARE YOU ABSO-LUTELY SURE YOU'RE FINE?!
...?!
プルプル
QUIVER QUIVER
THAT, UM...
I...
HUH? WHERE'S ALL HER COURAGE FROM THE FIGHT?
YEAH, WHAT HAPPENED TO HER?
TSUGUMI, LISTEN TO ME!
GRAB
YOU NEED TO SEPARATE YOURSELF FROM THE MASTER!

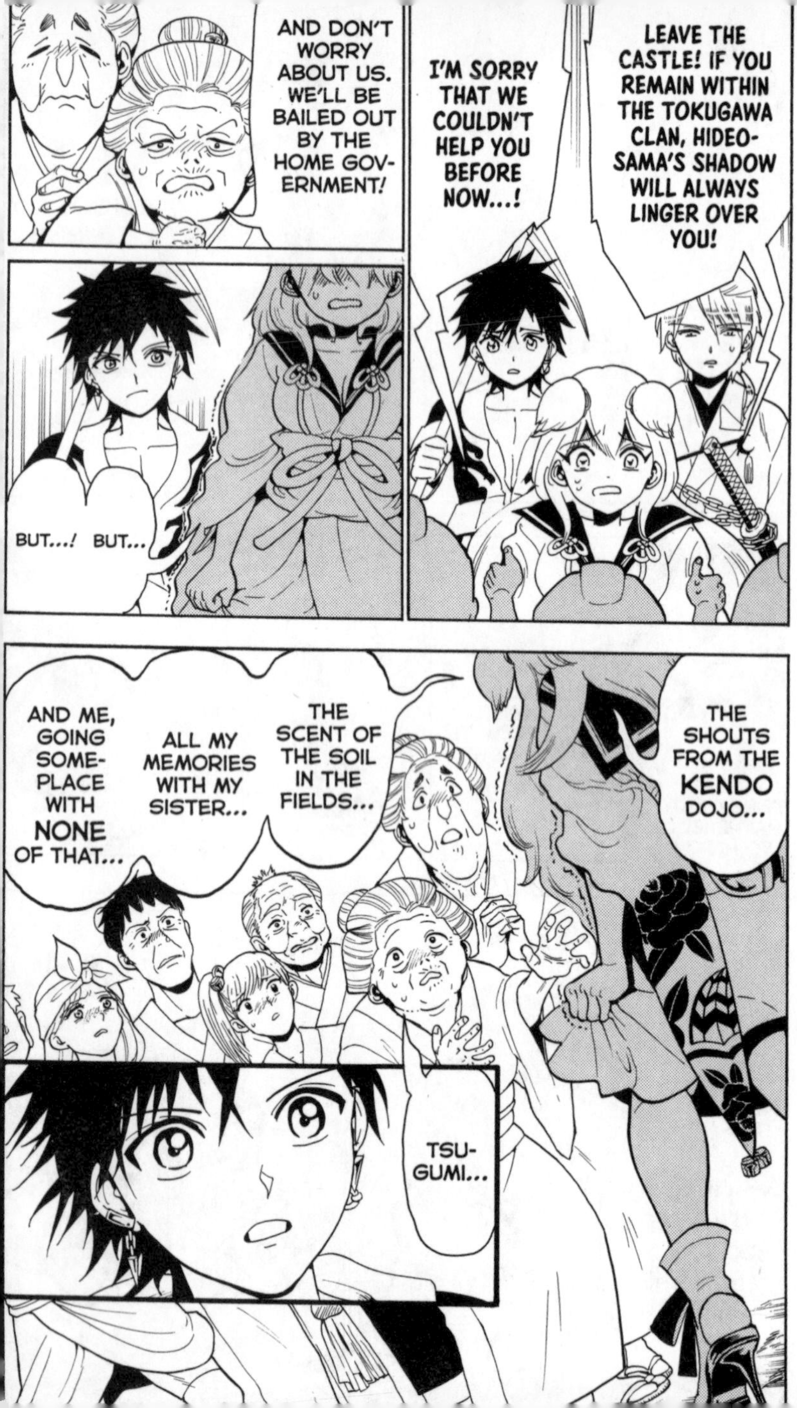
LEAVE THE CASTLE! IF YOU REMAIN WITHIN THE TOKUGAWA CLAN, HIDEO-SAMA'S SHADOW WILL ALWAYS LINGER OVER YOU!
I'M SORRY THAT WE COULDN'T HELP YOU BEFORE NOW...!
AND DON'T WORRY ABOUT US. WE'LL BE BAILED OUT BY THE HOME GOVERNMENT!
BUT...! BUT...
THE SHOUTS FROM THE KENDO DOJO...
THE SCENT OF THE SOIL IN THE FIELDS...
ALL MY MEMORIES WITH MY SISTER...
AND ME, GOING SOMEPLACE WITH NONE OF THAT...
TSUGUMI...

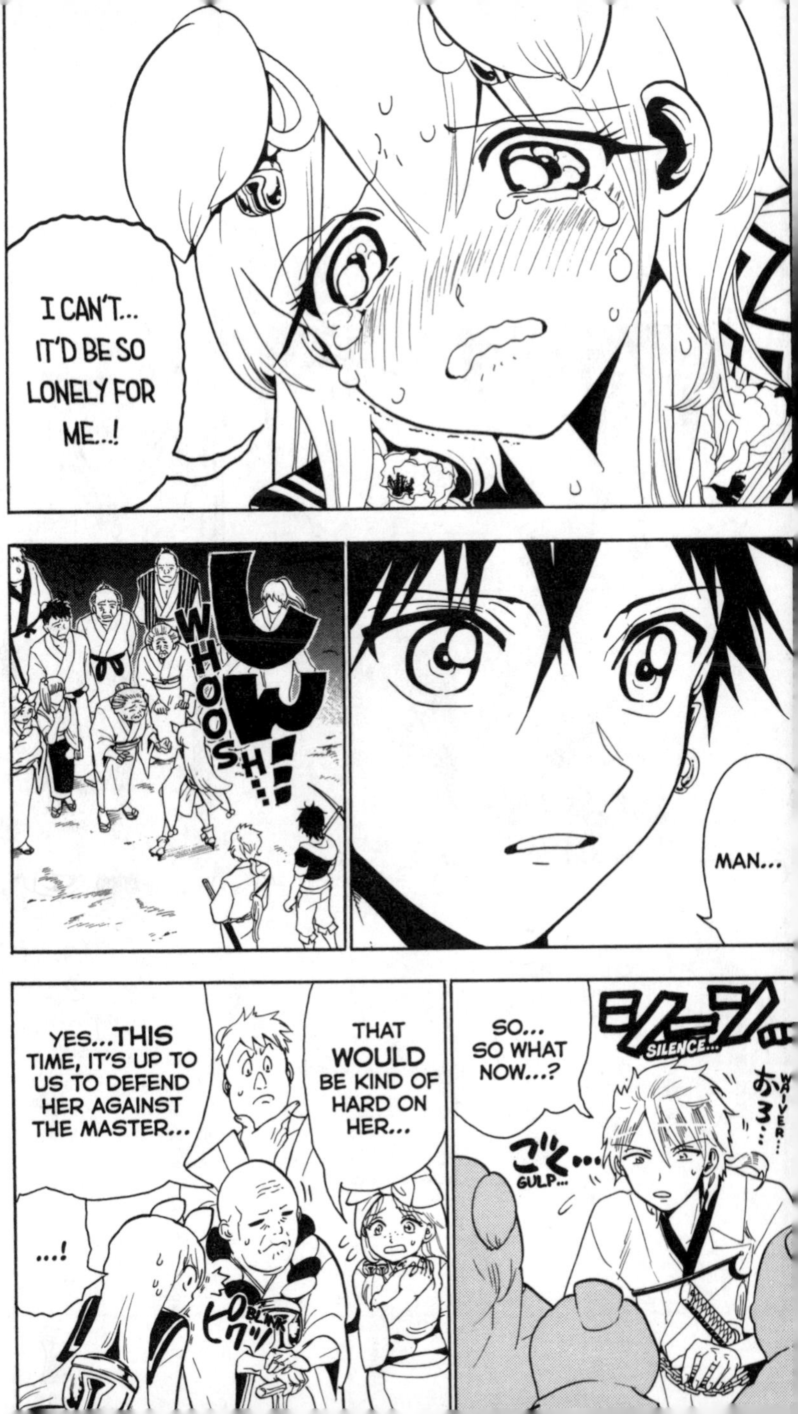
I CAN'T... IT'D BE SO LONELY FOR ME...!
MAN...
WHOOSH!!
シーン...
SILENCE...
SO... SO WHAT NOW...?
おろ...
WAVER...
ごく...
GULP...
THAT WOULD BE KIND OF HARD ON HER...
YES...THIS TIME, IT'S UP TO US TO DEFEND HER AGAINST THE MASTER...
ピクッ
BLINK
...!

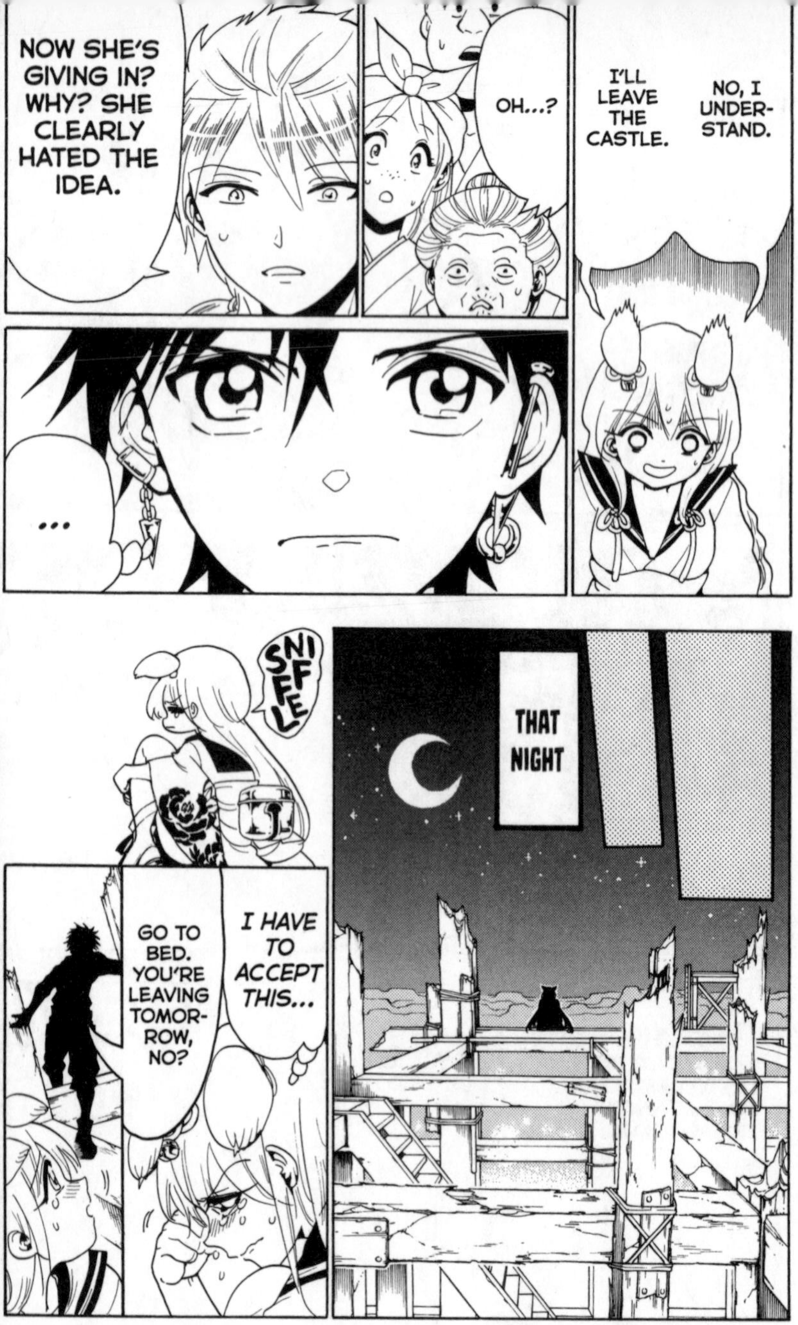
NO, I UNDER-STAND.
I'LL LEAVE THE CASTLE.
OH...?
NOW SHE'S GIVING IN? WHY? SHE CLEARLY HATED THE IDEA.
...
THAT NIGHT
SNIFFLE
I HAVE TO ACCEPT THIS...
GO TO BED. YOU'RE LEAVING TOMOR-ROW, NO?

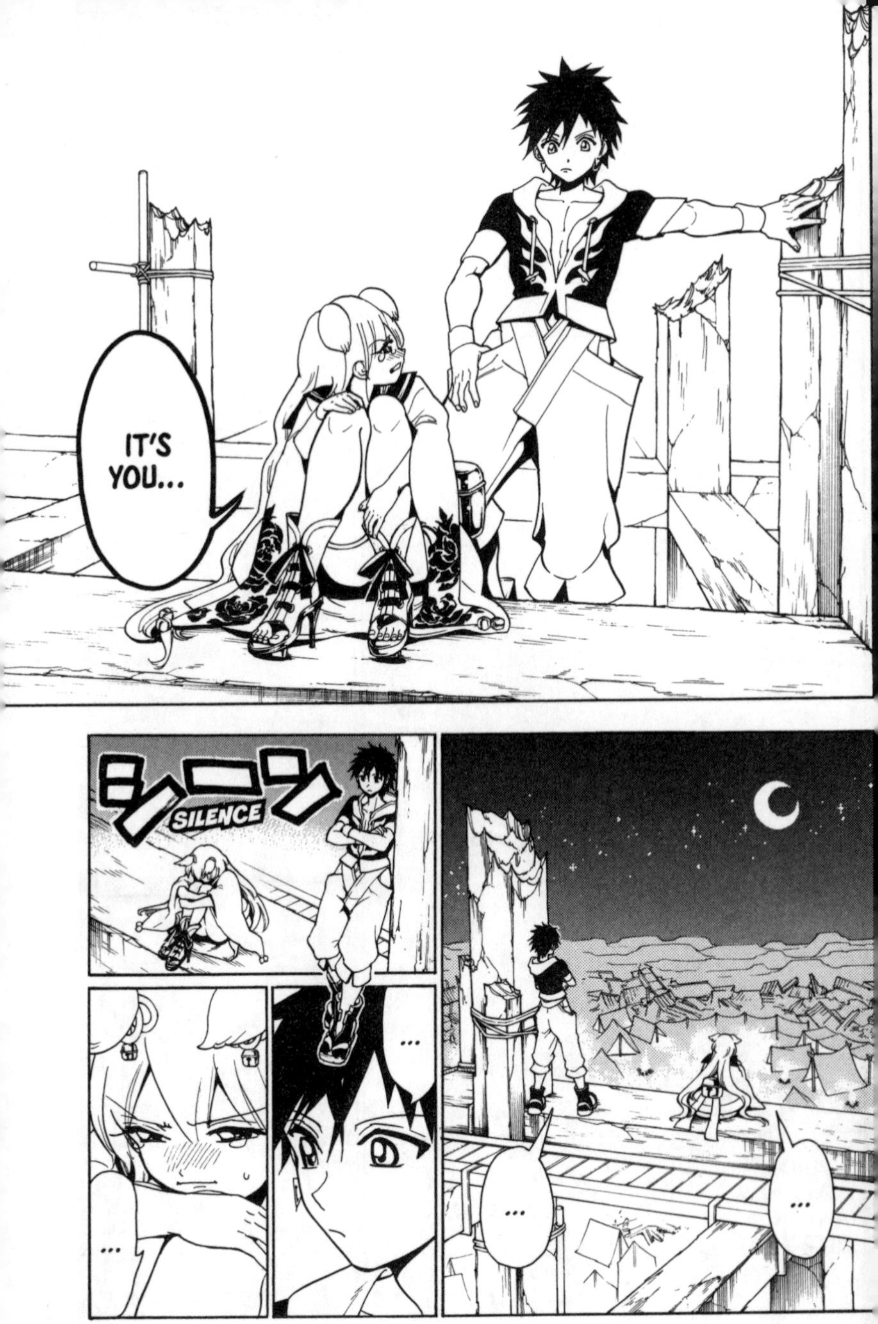
IT'S YOU...
...
...
シーン
SILENCE
...
...

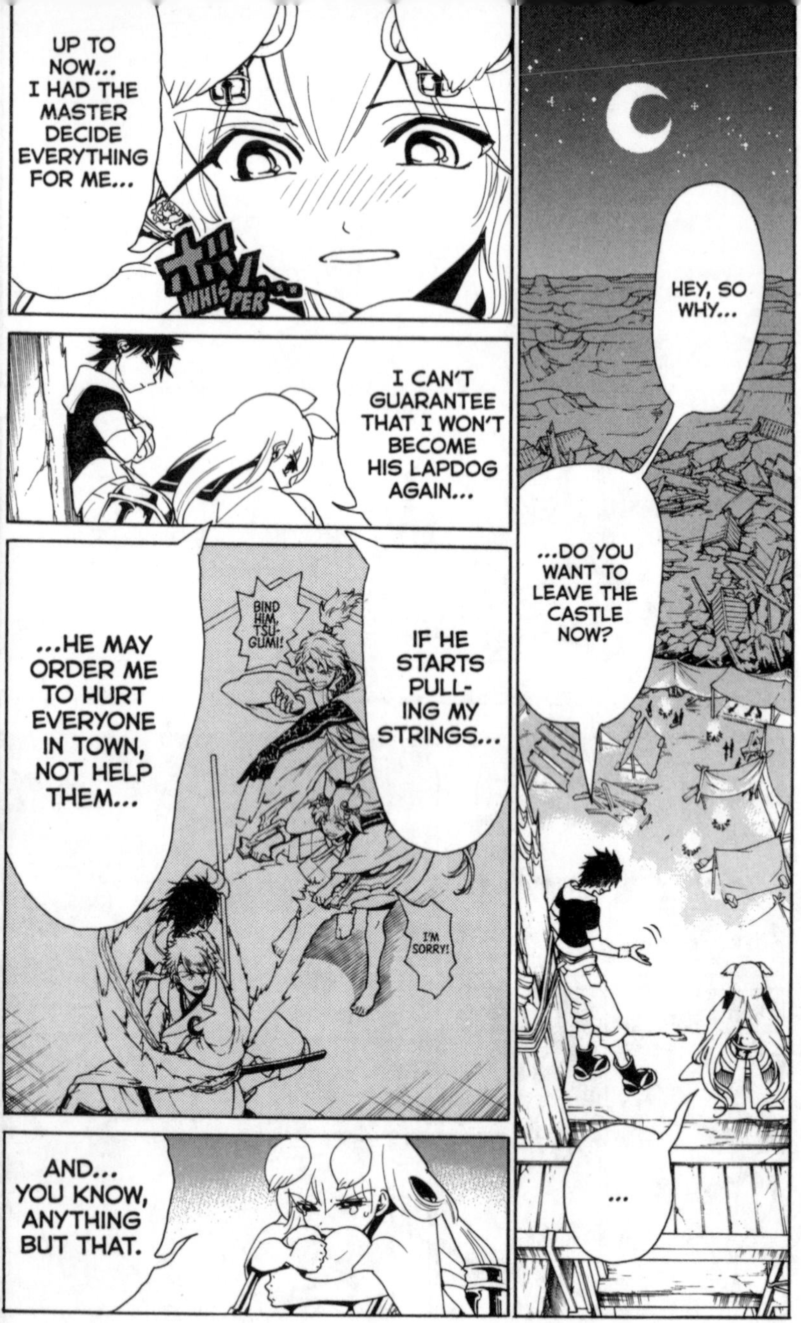
HEY, SO WHY...
...DO YOU WANT TO LEAVE THE CASTLE NOW?
...
UP TO NOW... I HAD THE MASTER DECIDE EVERYTHING FOR ME...
WHISPER
I CAN'T GUARANTEE THAT I WON'T BECOME HIS LAPDOG AGAIN...
IF HE STARTS PULL-ING MY STRINGS...
BIND HIM, TSU-GUMI!
...HE MAY ORDER ME TO HURT EVERYONE IN TOWN, NOT HELP THEM...
I'M SORRY!
AND... YOU KNOW, ANYTHING BUT THAT.

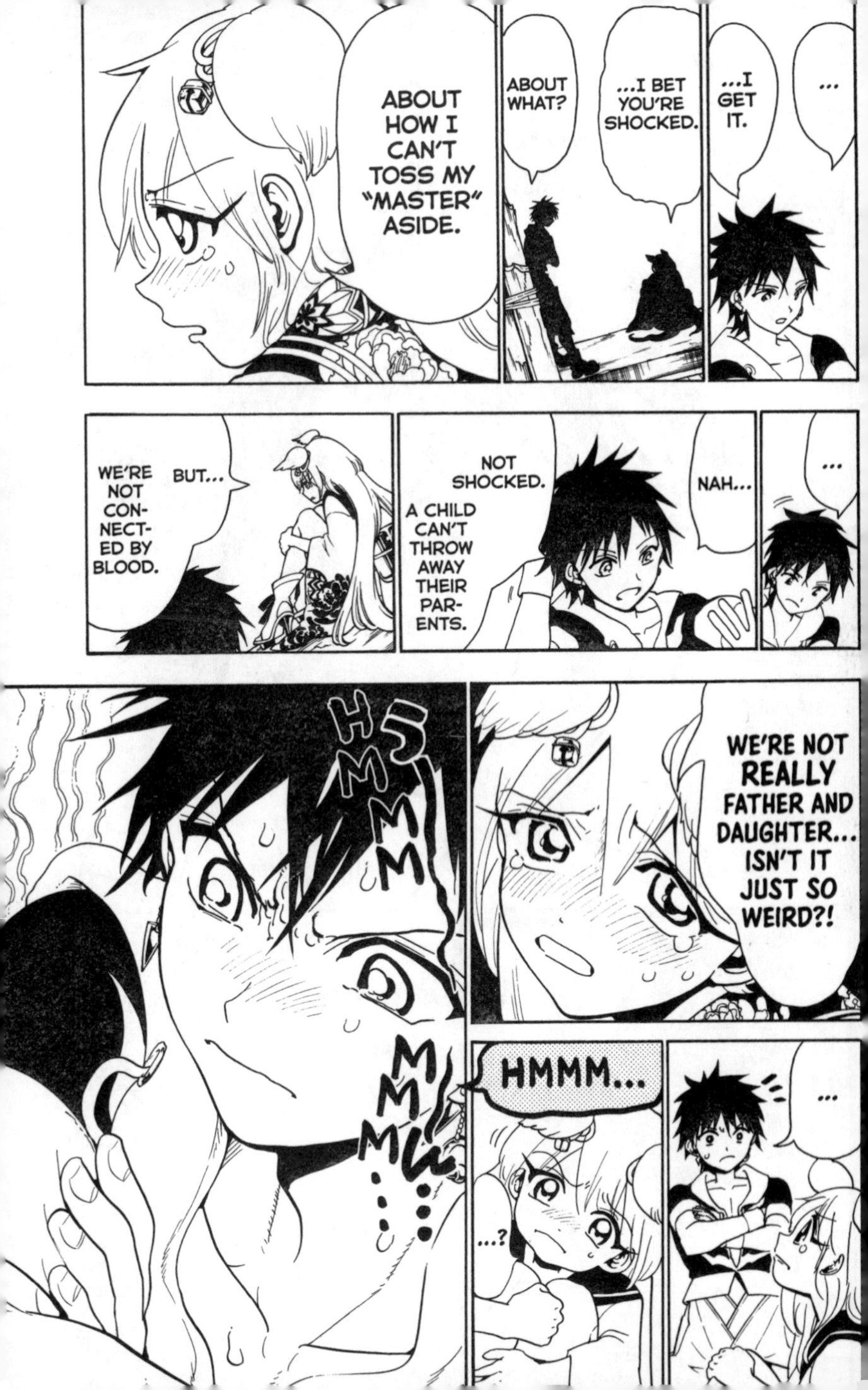
...
...I GET IT.
...I BET YOU'RE SHOCKED.
ABOUT WHAT?
ABOUT HOW I CAN'T TOSS MY "MASTER" ASIDE.
...
NAH...
NOT SHOCKED.
A CHILD CAN'T THROW AWAY THEIR PARENTS.
BUT...
WE'RE NOT CONNECTED BY BLOOD.
WE'RE NOT REALLY FATHER AND DAUGHTER... ISN'T IT JUST SO WEIRD?!
...
HMMM...
...?
HMMMM
MMMMU...

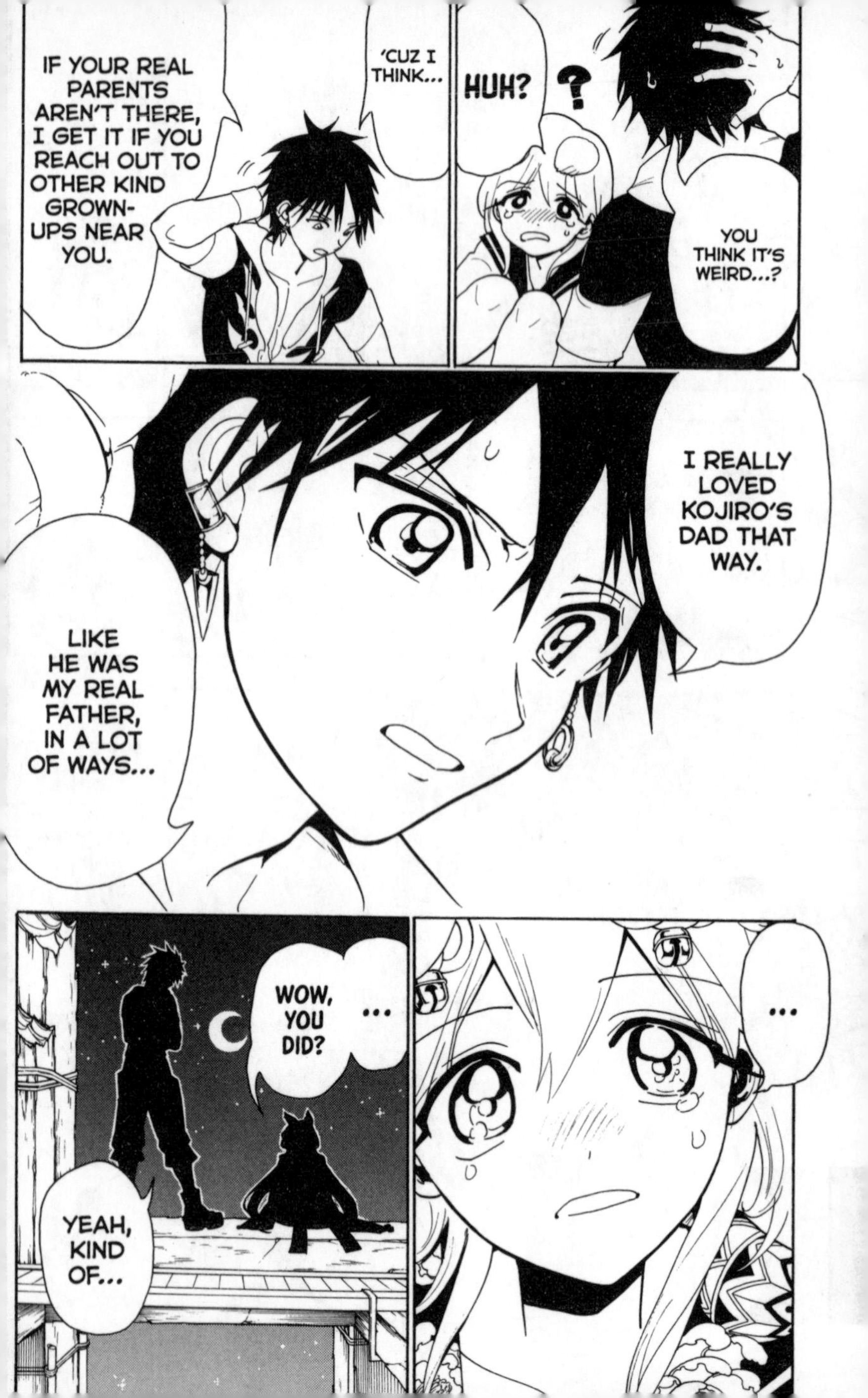
YOU THINK IT'S WEIRD...?
HUH?
?
'CUZ I THINK...
IF YOUR REAL PARENTS AREN'T THERE, I GET IT IF YOU REACH OUT TO OTHER KIND GROWN-UPS NEAR YOU.
I REALLY LOVED KOJIRO'S DAD THAT WAY.
LIKE HE WAS MY REAL FATHER, IN A LOT OF WAYS...
...
...
WOW, YOU DID?
YEAH, KIND OF...

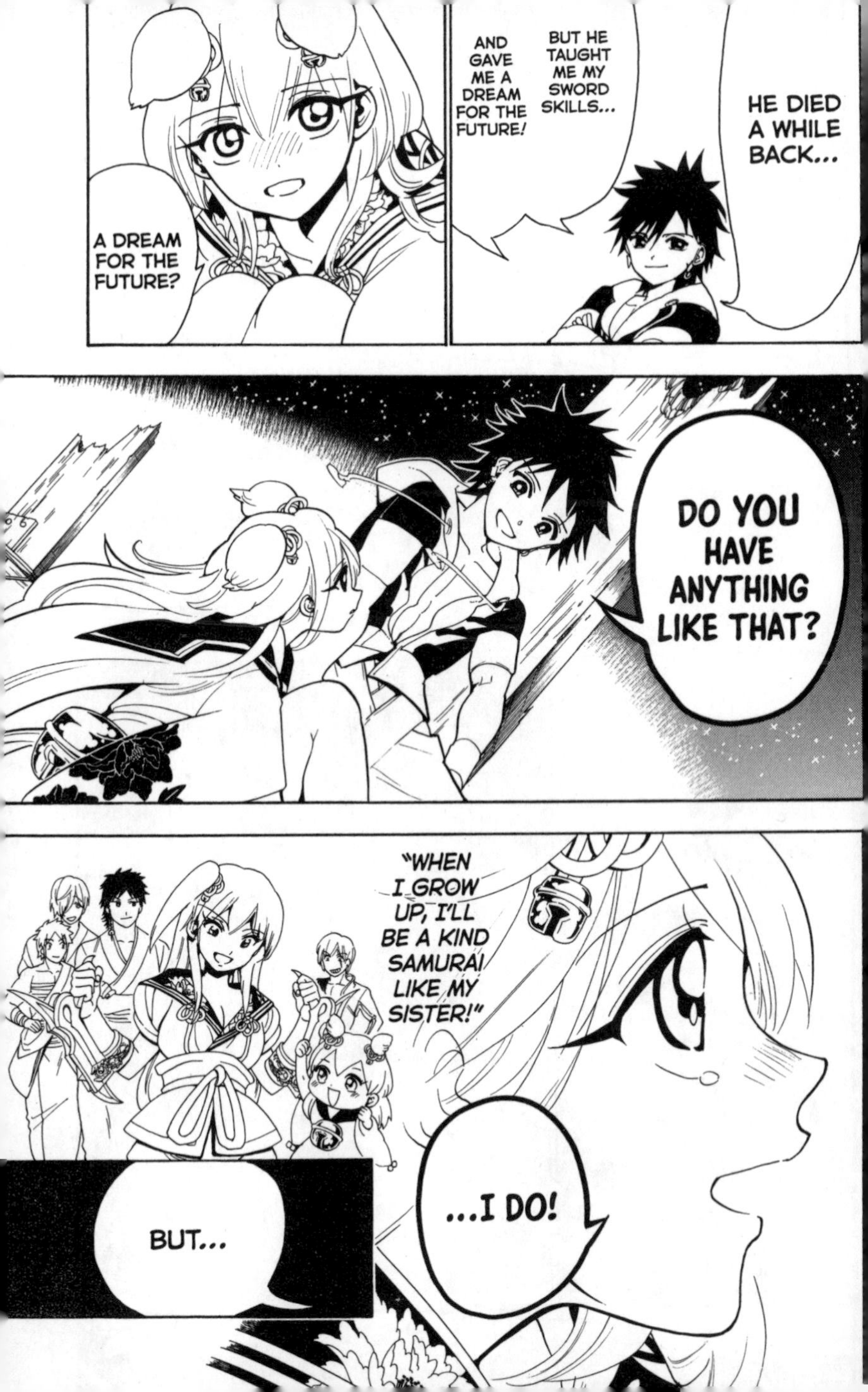
HE DIED A WHILE BACK...
BUT HE TAUGHT ME MY SWORD SKILLS...
AND GAVE ME A DREAM FOR THE FUTURE!
A DREAM FOR THE FUTURE?
DO YOU HAVE ANYTHING LIKE THAT?
"WHEN I GROW UP, I'LL BE A KIND SAMURAI LIKE MY SISTER!"
...I DO!
BUT...

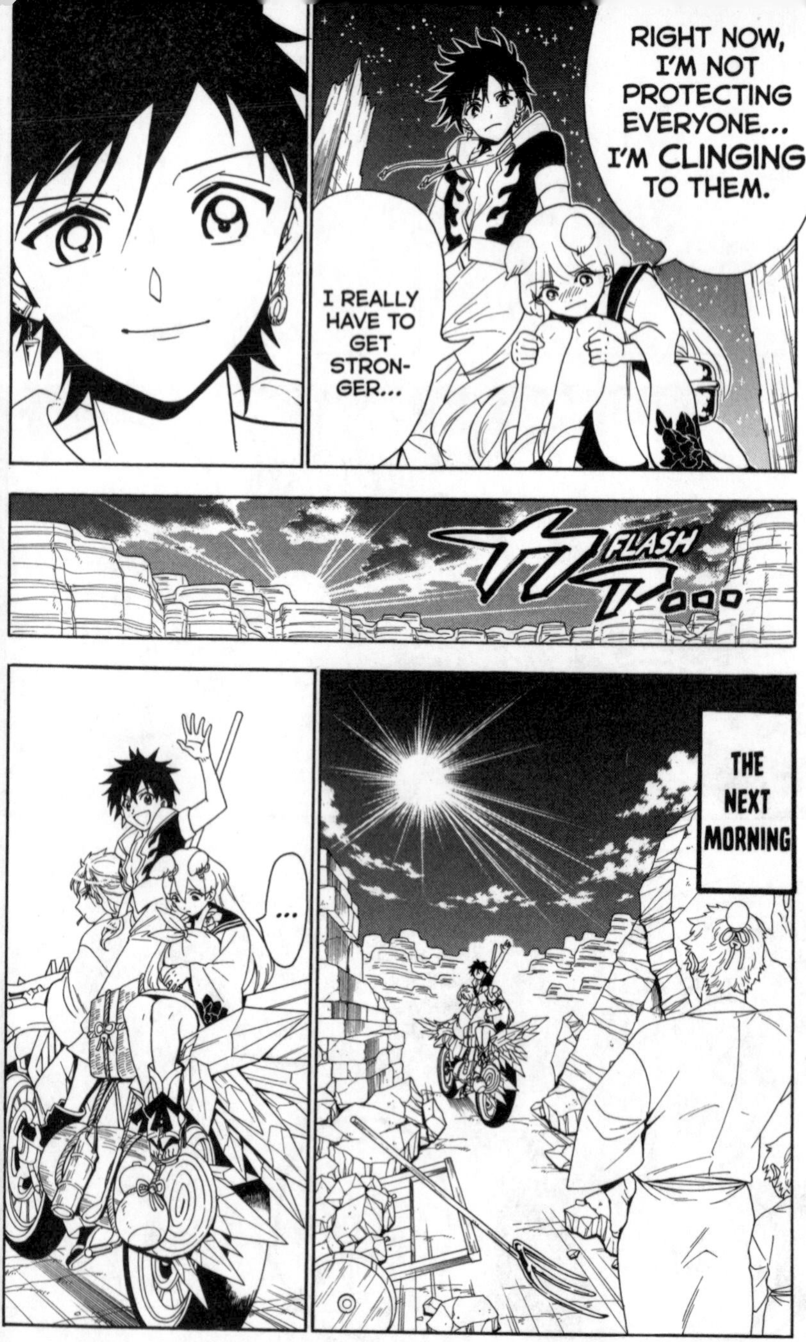
RIGHT NOW, I'M NOT PROTECTING EVERYONE... I'M CLINGING TO THEM.
I REALLY HAVE TO GET STRONGER...
FLASH
THE NEXT MORNING
...

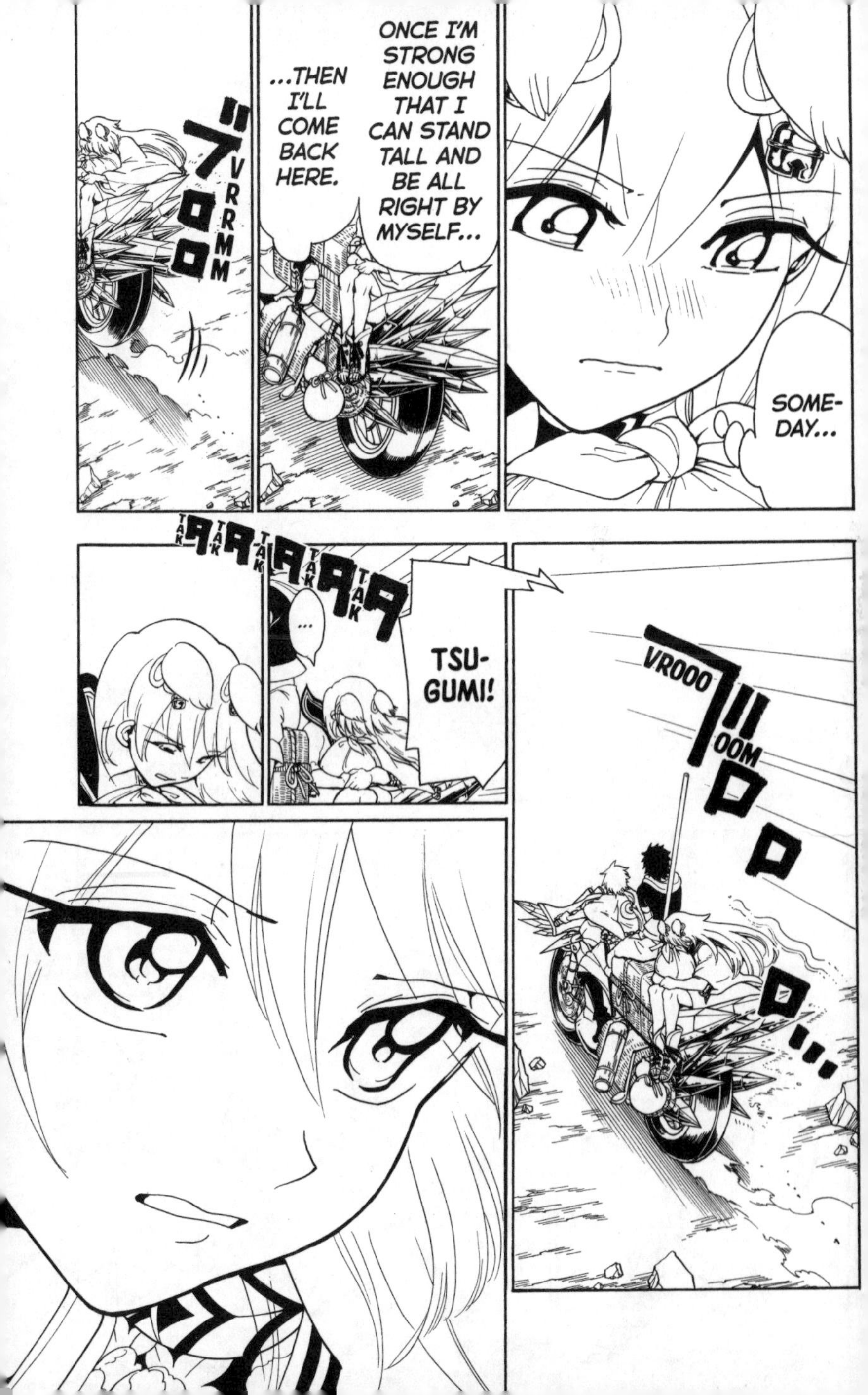
SOME-DAY...
ONCE I'M STRONG ENOUGH THAT I CAN STAND TALL AND BE ALL RIGHT BY MYSELF...
...THEN I'LL COME BACK HERE.
VRRMM
VROOOOOM
TSU-GUMI!
...
TAK TAK TAK TAK TAK

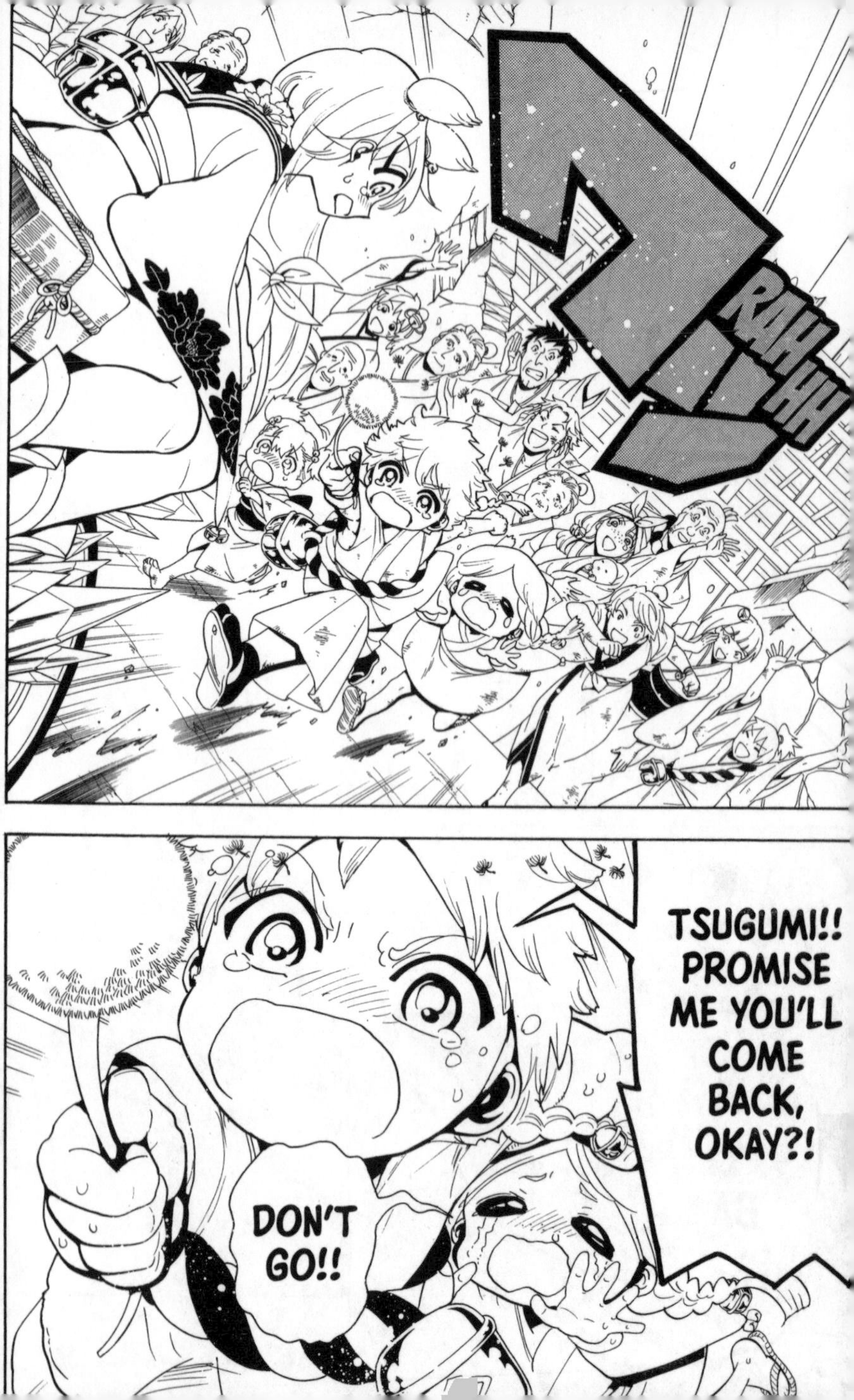
RAHHHH
TSUGUMI!! PROMISE ME YOU'LL COME BACK, OKAY?!
DON'T GO!!

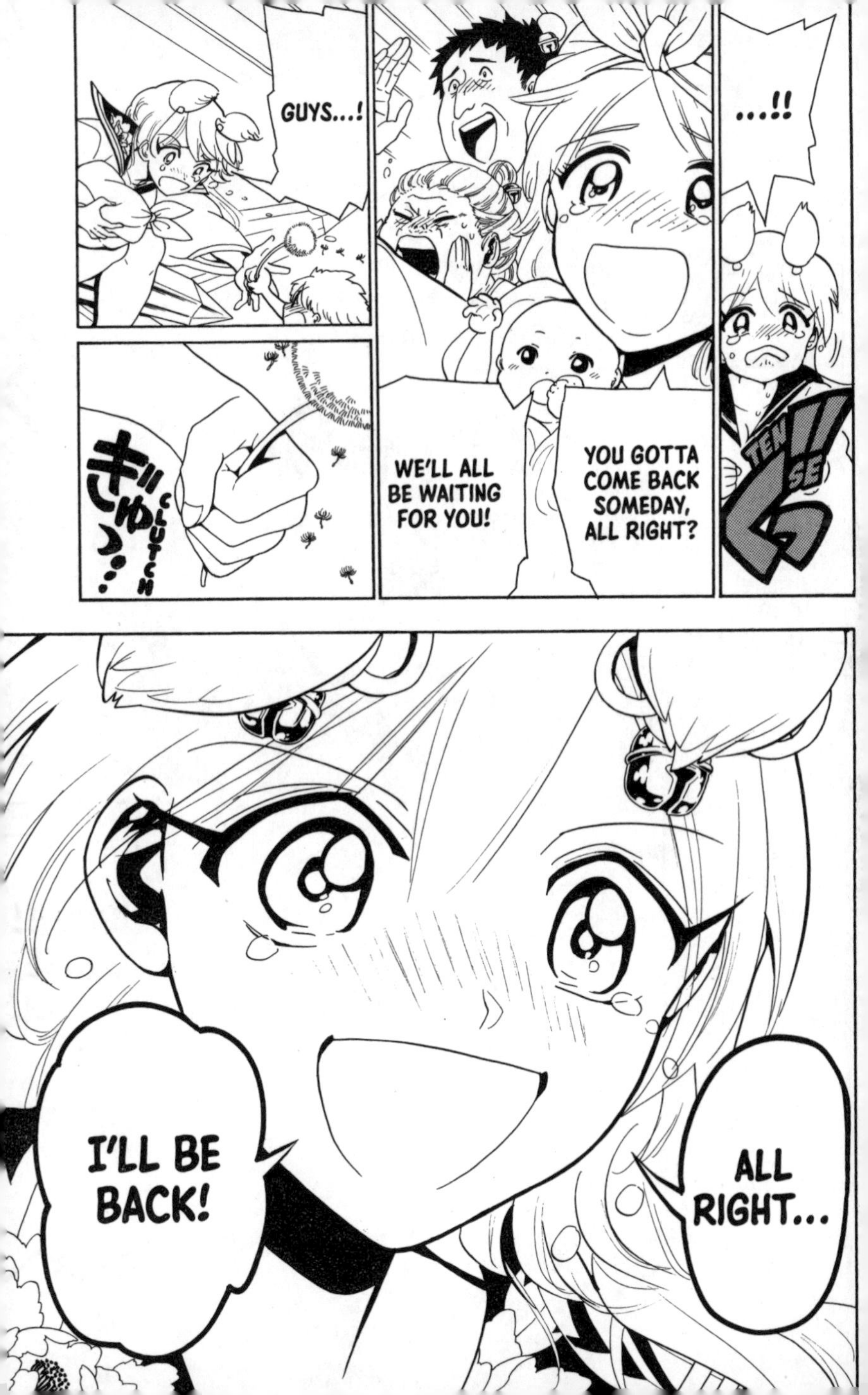
...!!
TENSE
YOU GOTTA COME BACK SOMEDAY, ALL RIGHT?
WE'LL ALL BE WAITING FOR YOU!
GUYS...!
きゅっ…
CLUTCH
ALL RIGHT...
I'LL BE BACK!

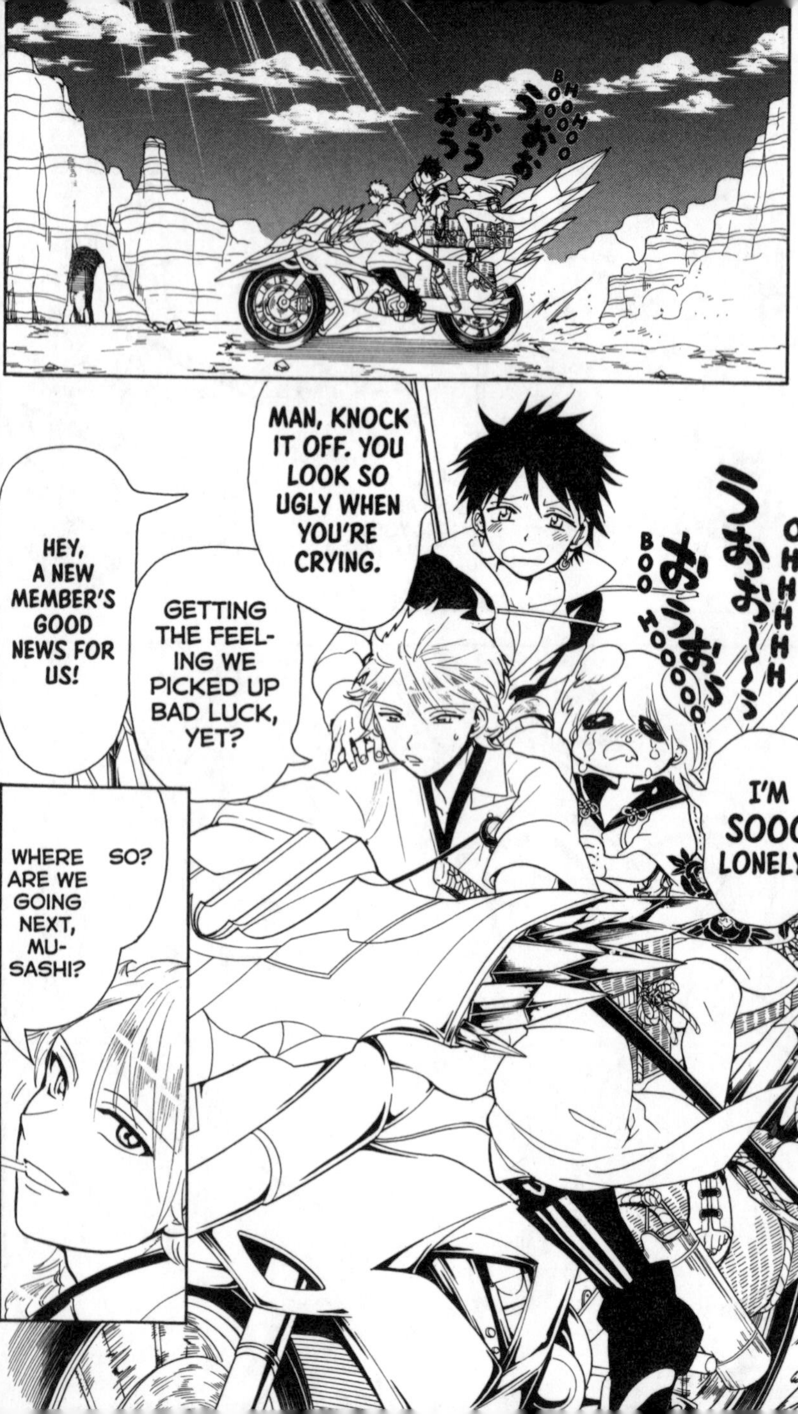
BOOHOOHOOO
うおおおおうう
OHHHHHH
うおお～～
BOO HOOOOOOO
おうおう
I'M SOOO LONELY!
MAN, KNOCK IT OFF. YOU LOOK SO UGLY WHEN YOU'RE CRYING.
GETTING THE FEEL-ING WE PICKED UP BAD LUCK, YET?
HEY, A NEW MEMBER'S GOOD NEWS FOR US!
SO? WHERE ARE WE GOING NEXT, MU-SASHI?

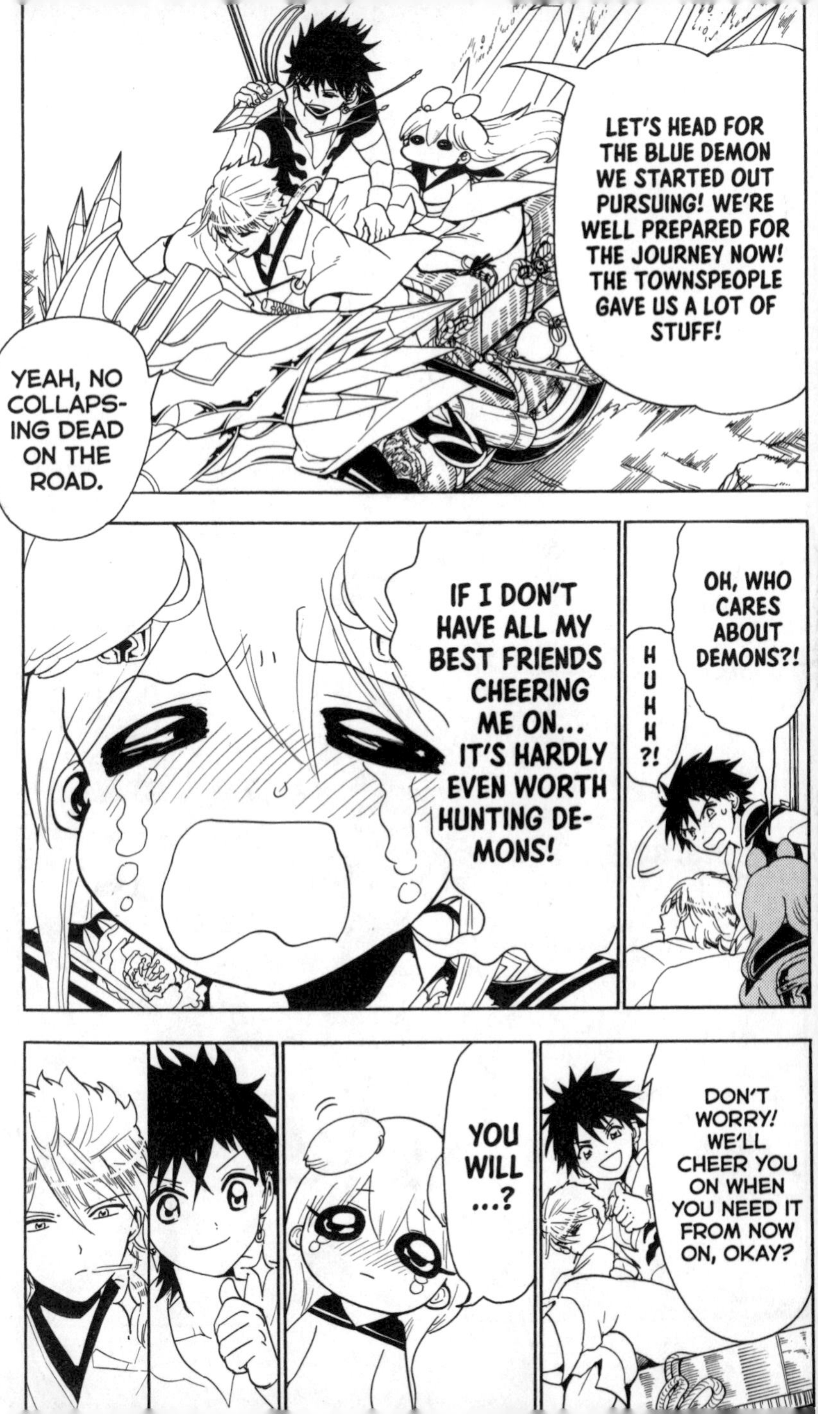
LET'S HEAD FOR THE BLUE DEMON WE STARTED OUT PURSUING! WE'RE WELL PREPARED FOR THE JOURNEY NOW! THE TOWNSPEOPLE GAVE US A LOT OF STUFF!
YEAH, NO COLLAPSING DEAD ON THE ROAD.
OH, WHO CARES ABOUT DEMONS?!
HUHHH?!
IF I DON'T HAVE ALL MY BEST FRIENDS CHEERING ME ON... IT'S HARDLY EVEN WORTH HUNTING DEMONS!
DON'T WORRY! WE'LL CHEER YOU ON WHEN YOU NEED IT FROM NOW ON, OKAY?
YOU WILL ...?

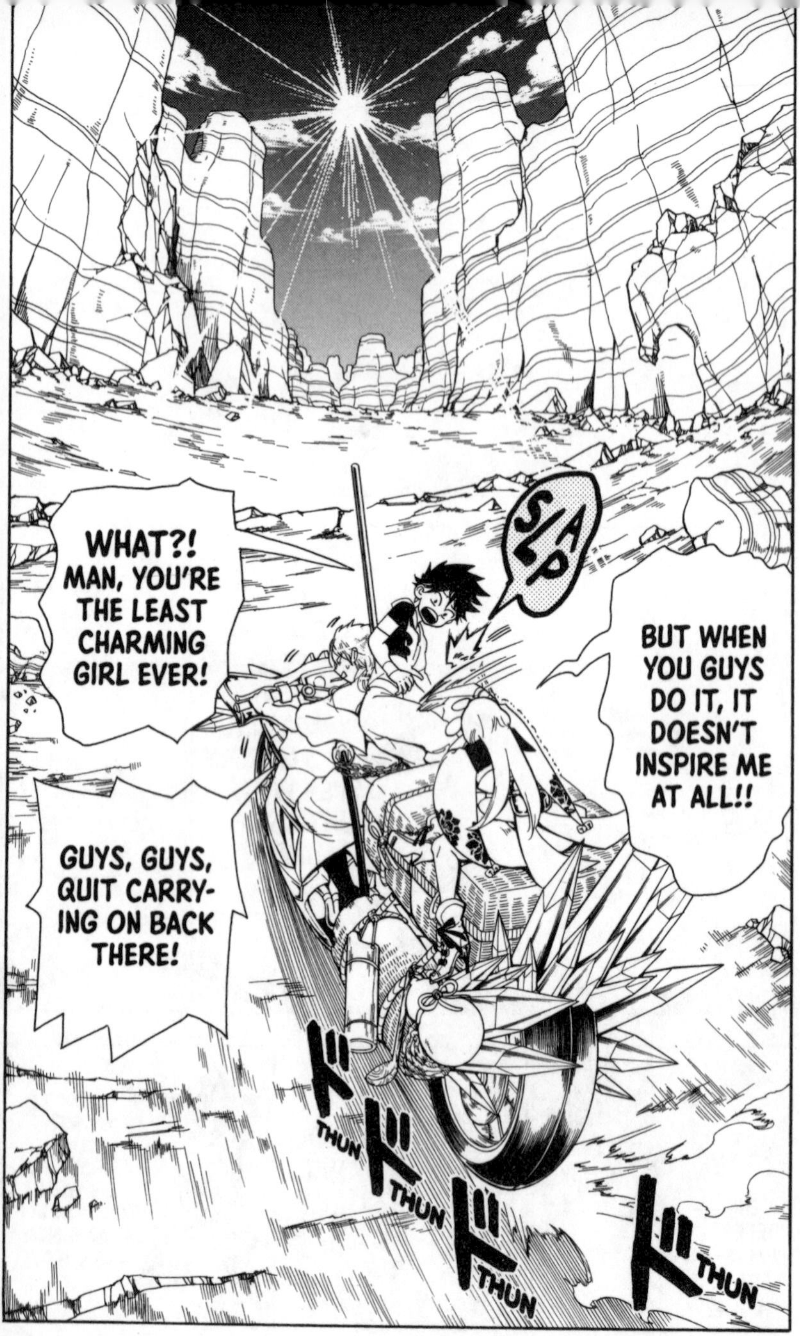
SLAP
BUT WHEN YOU GUYS DO IT, IT DOESN'T INSPIRE ME AT ALL!!
WHAT?! MAN, YOU'RE THE LEAST CHARMING GIRL EVER!
GUYS, GUYS, QUIT CARRYING ON BACK THERE!
THUN THUN THUN THUN

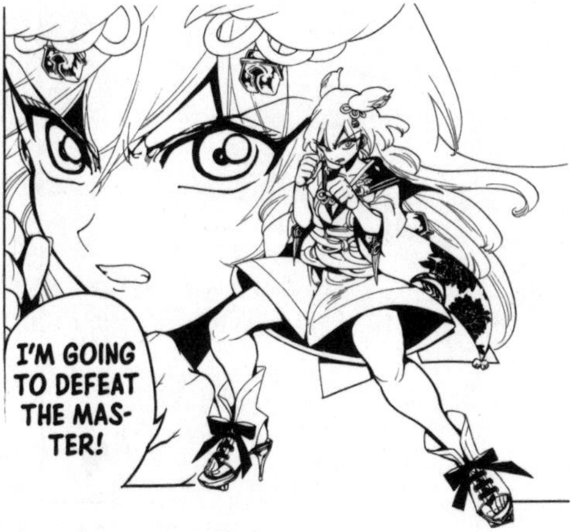
I'M GOING TO DEFEAT THE MAS-TER!

ORIENT

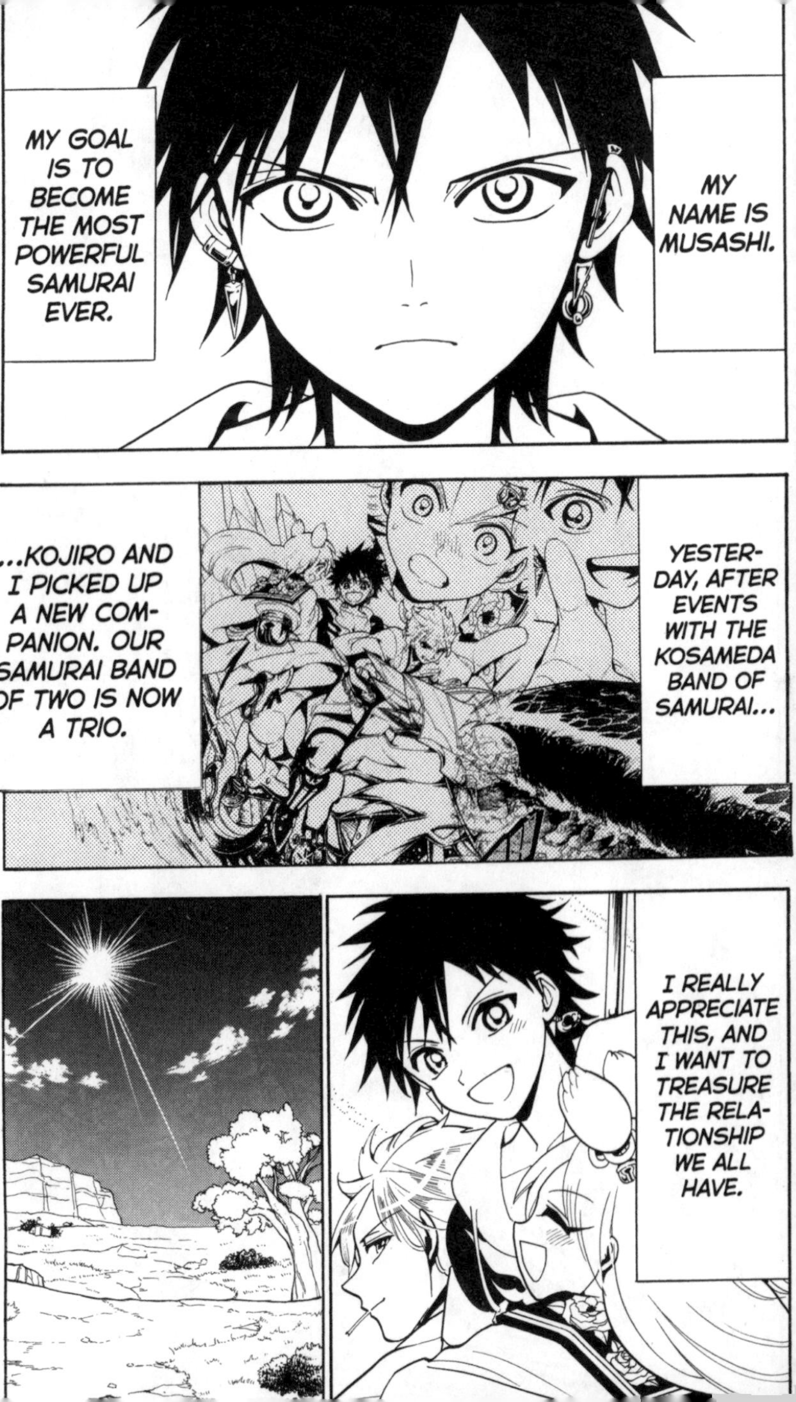
MY NAME IS MUSASHI.
MY GOAL IS TO BECOME THE MOST POWERFUL SAMURAI EVER.
YESTER-DAY, AFTER EVENTS WITH THE KOSAMEDA BAND OF SAMURAI...
...KOJIRO AND I PICKED UP A NEW COM-PANION. OUR SAMURAI BAND OF TWO IS NOW A TRIO.
I REALLY APPRECIATE THIS, AND I WANT TO TREASURE THE RELA-TIONSHIP WE ALL HAVE.

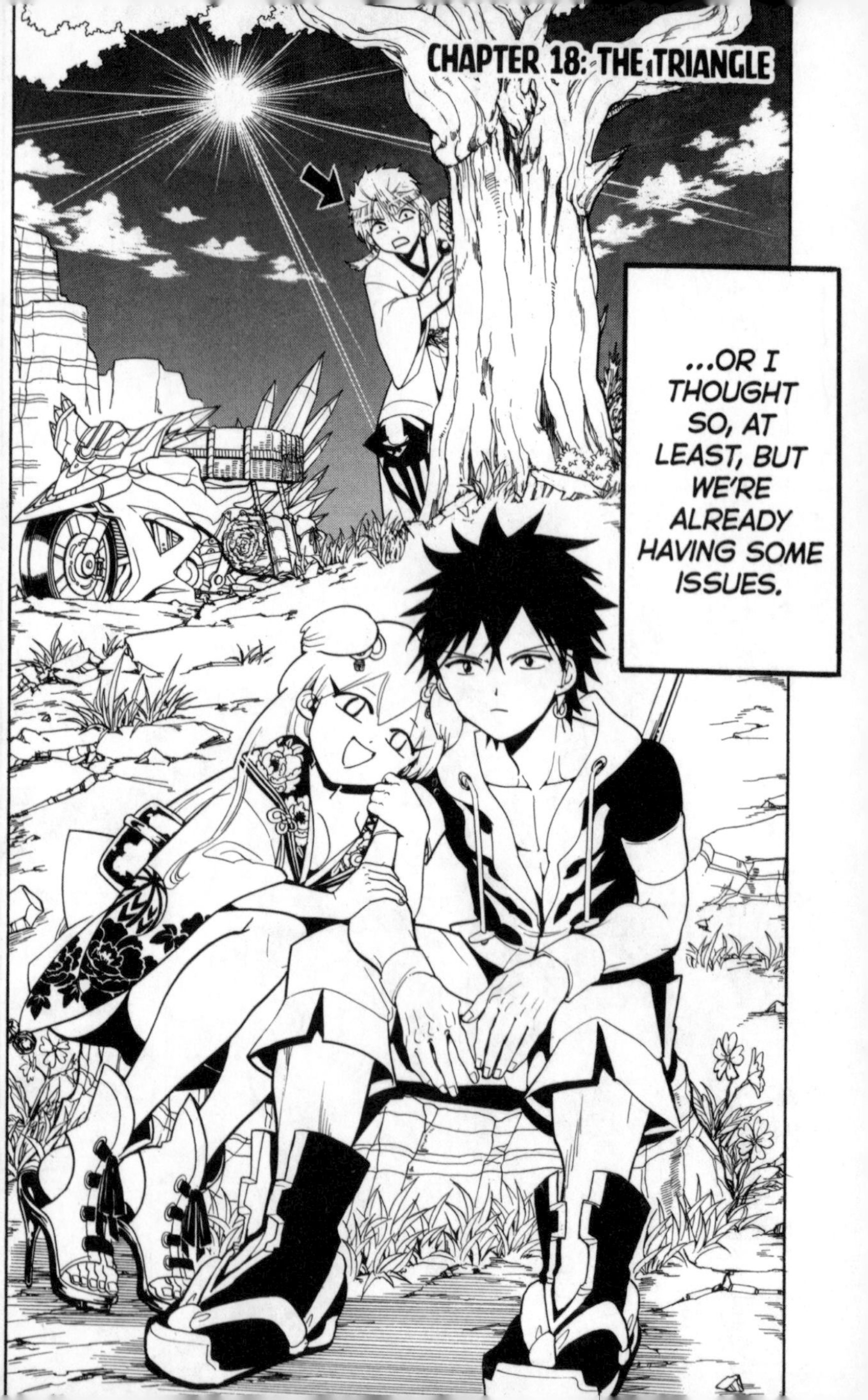
CHAPTER 18: THE TRIANGLE
...OR I THOUGHT SO, AT LEAST, BUT WE'RE ALREADY HAVING SOME ISSUES.

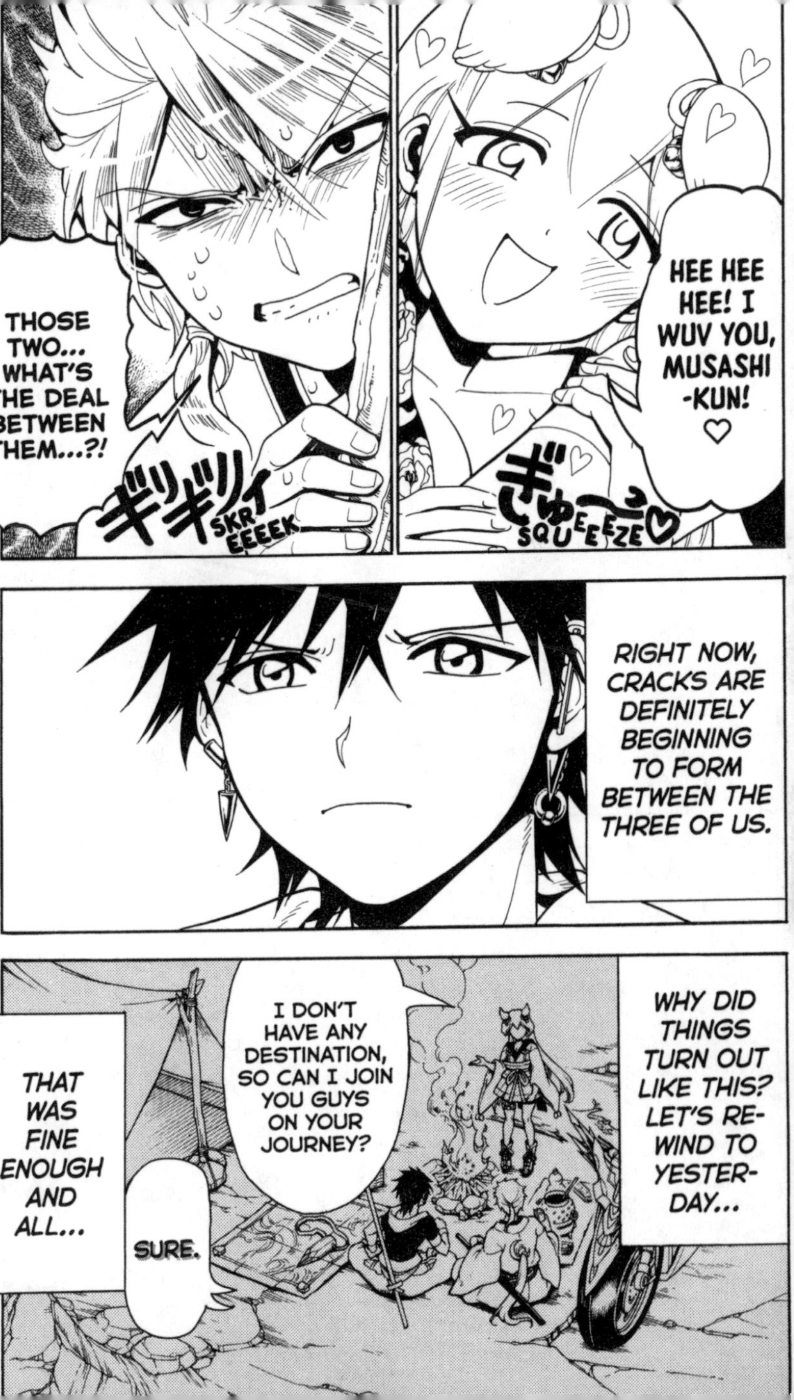

HEE HEE HEE! I WUV YOU, MUSASHI-KUN! ♡
ぎゅーっ SQUEEEZE♡
THOSE TWO... WHAT'S THE DEAL BETWEEN THEM...?!
ギリギリィ SKREEEEK
RIGHT NOW, CRACKS ARE DEFINITELY BEGINNING TO FORM BETWEEN THE THREE OF US.
WHY DID THINGS TURN OUT LIKE THIS? LET'S RE-WIND TO YESTER-DAY...
I DON'T HAVE ANY DESTINATION, SO CAN I JOIN YOU GUYS ON YOUR JOURNEY?
SURE.
THAT WAS FINE ENOUGH AND ALL...

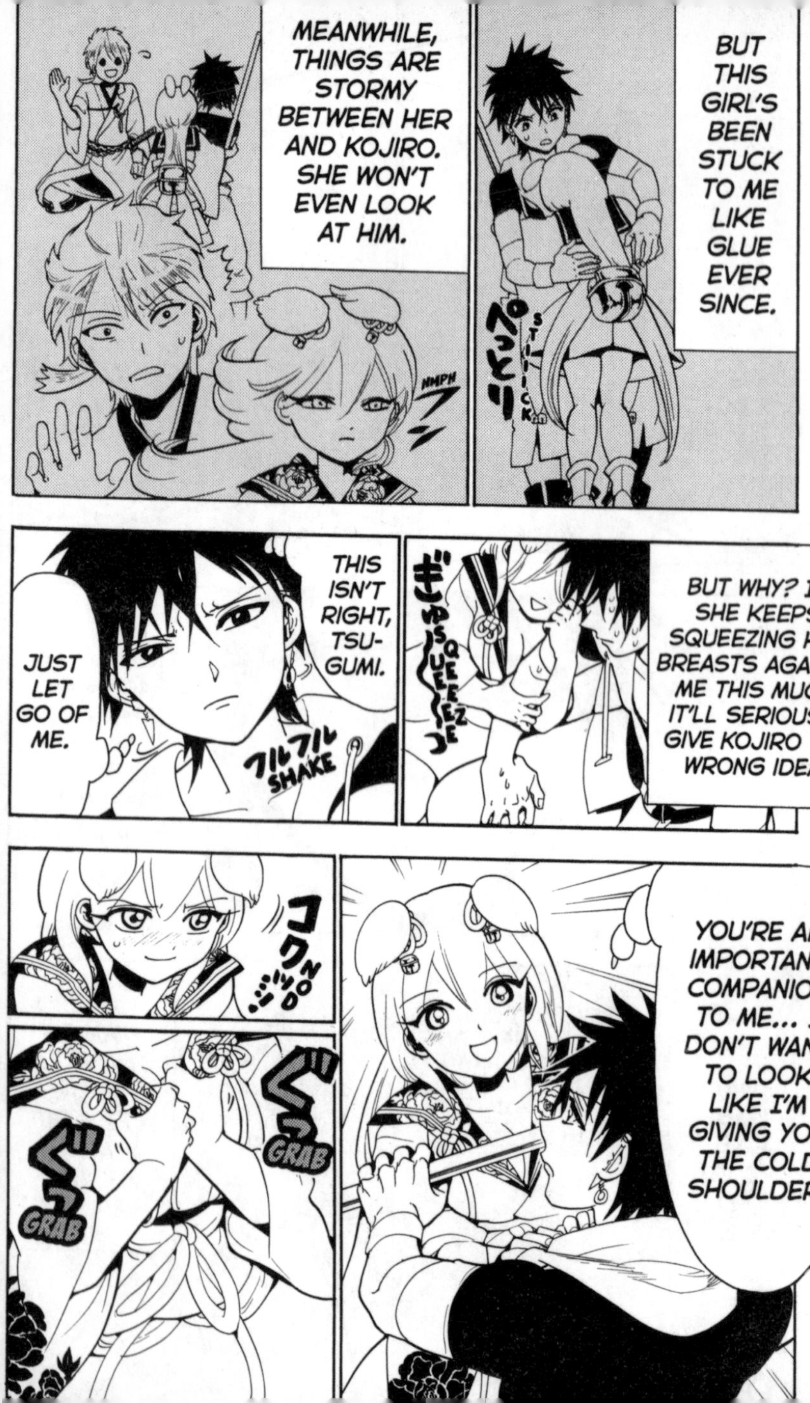
BUT THIS GIRL'S BEEN STUCK TO ME LIKE GLUE EVER SINCE.
ぺっとり
STICK
MEANWHILE, THINGS ARE STORMY BETWEEN HER AND KOJIRO. SHE WON'T EVEN LOOK AT HIM.
HMPH
BUT WHY? IF SHE KEEPS SQUEEZING HER BREASTS AGAINST ME THIS MUCH, IT'LL SERIOUSLY GIVE KOJIRO THE WRONG IDEA!
ぎゅ
SQUEEZE
THIS ISN'T RIGHT, TSU-GUMI.
JUST LET GO OF ME.
フルフル
SHAKE
YOU'RE AN IMPORTANT COMPANION TO ME... I DON'T WANT TO LOOK LIKE I'M GIVING YOU THE COLD SHOULDER!
コク
NOD
ぐっ
GRAB
ぐっ
GRAB

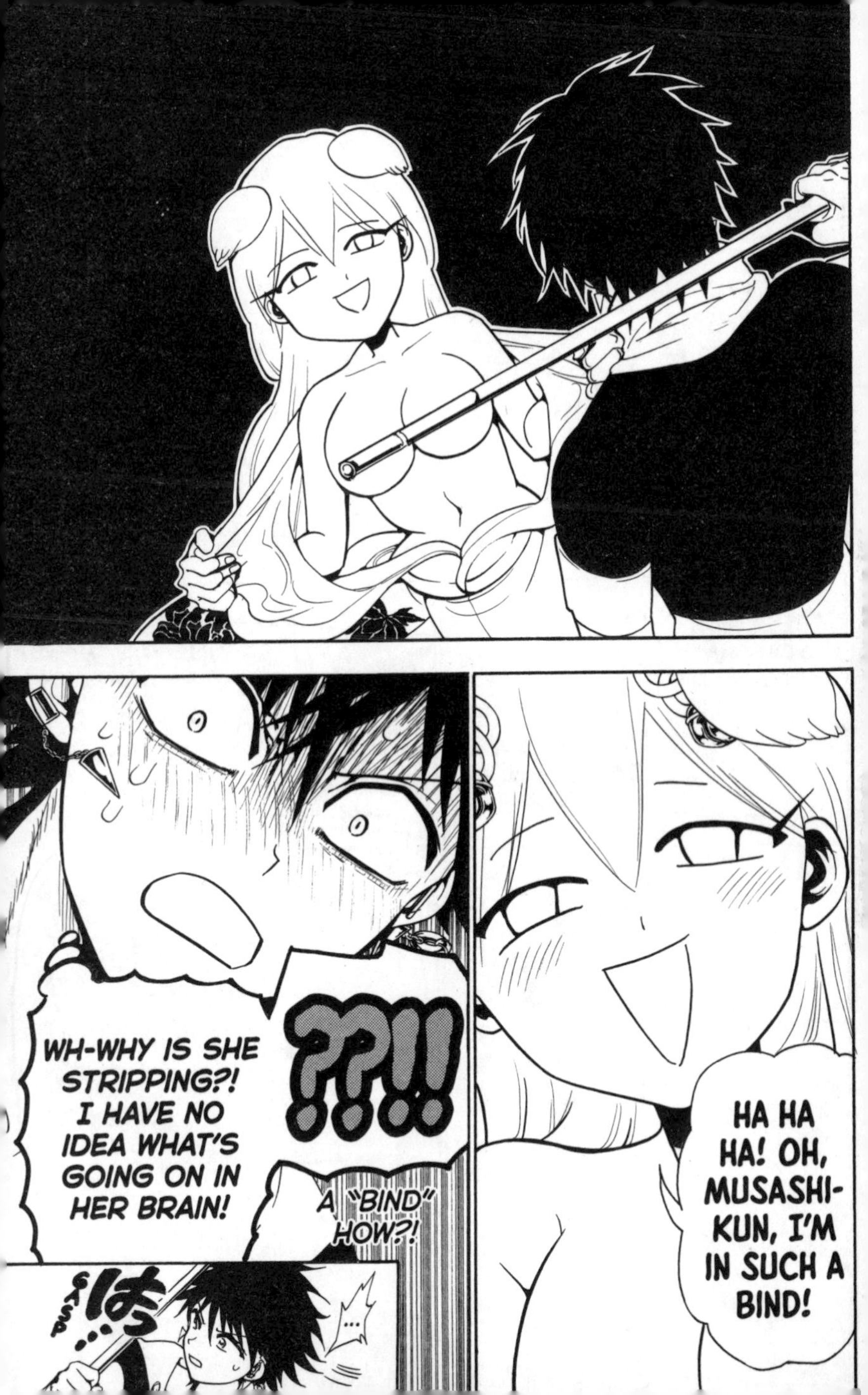
HA HA HA! OH, MUSASHI-KUN, I'M IN SUCH A BIND!
??!!
WH-WHY IS SHE STRIPPING?! I HAVE NO IDEA WHAT'S GOING ON IN HER BRAIN!
A "BIND" HOW?!
...
はっ
GASP

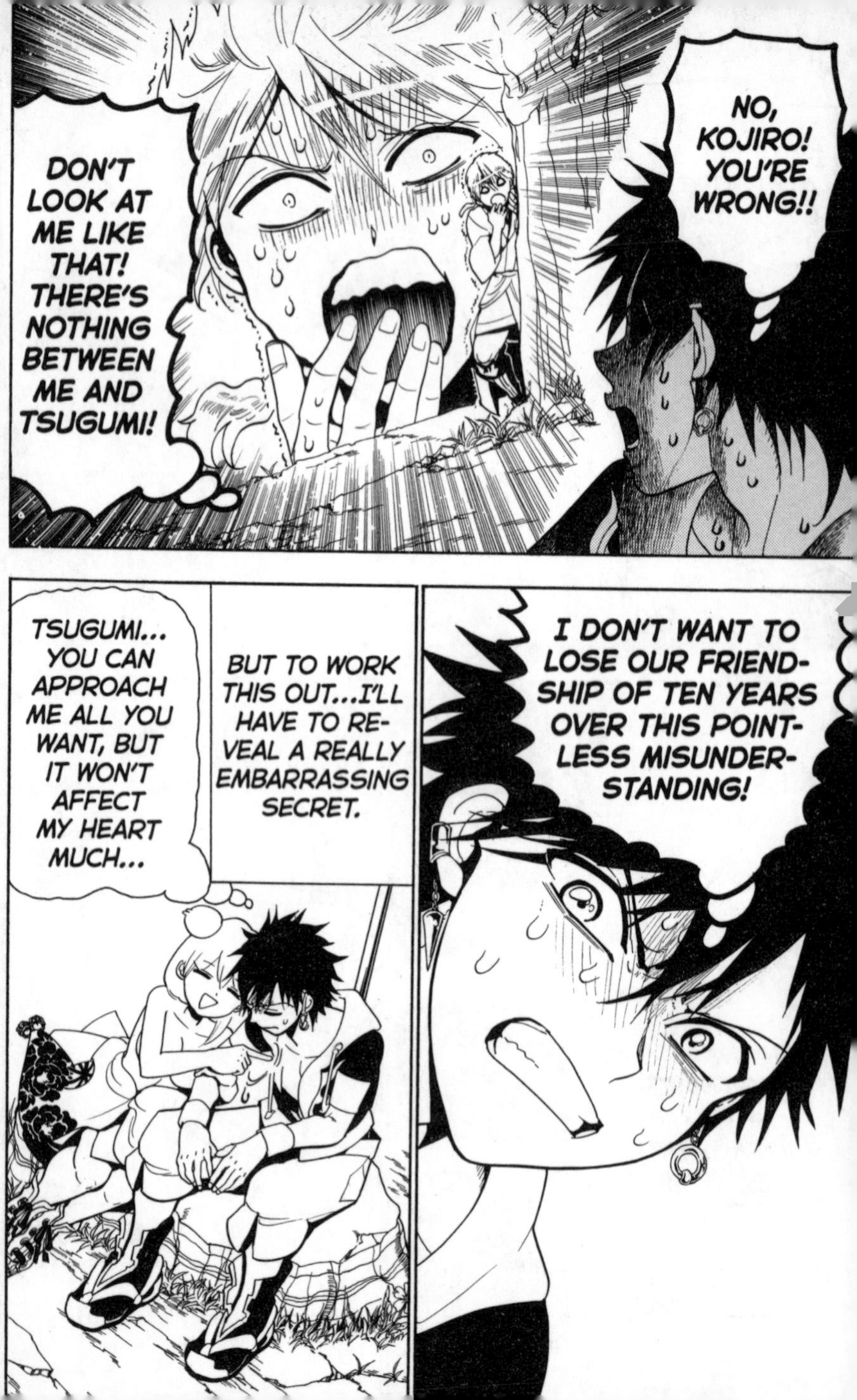
NO, KOJIRO! YOU'RE WRONG!!
DON'T LOOK AT ME LIKE THAT! THERE'S NOTHING BETWEEN ME AND TSUGUMI!
I DON'T WANT TO LOSE OUR FRIEND-SHIP OF TEN YEARS OVER THIS POINT-LESS MISUNDER-STANDING!
BUT TO WORK THIS OUT...I'LL HAVE TO RE-VEAL A REALLY EMBARRASSING SECRET.
TSUGUMI... YOU CAN APPROACH ME ALL YOU WANT, BUT IT WON'T AFFECT MY HEART MUCH...

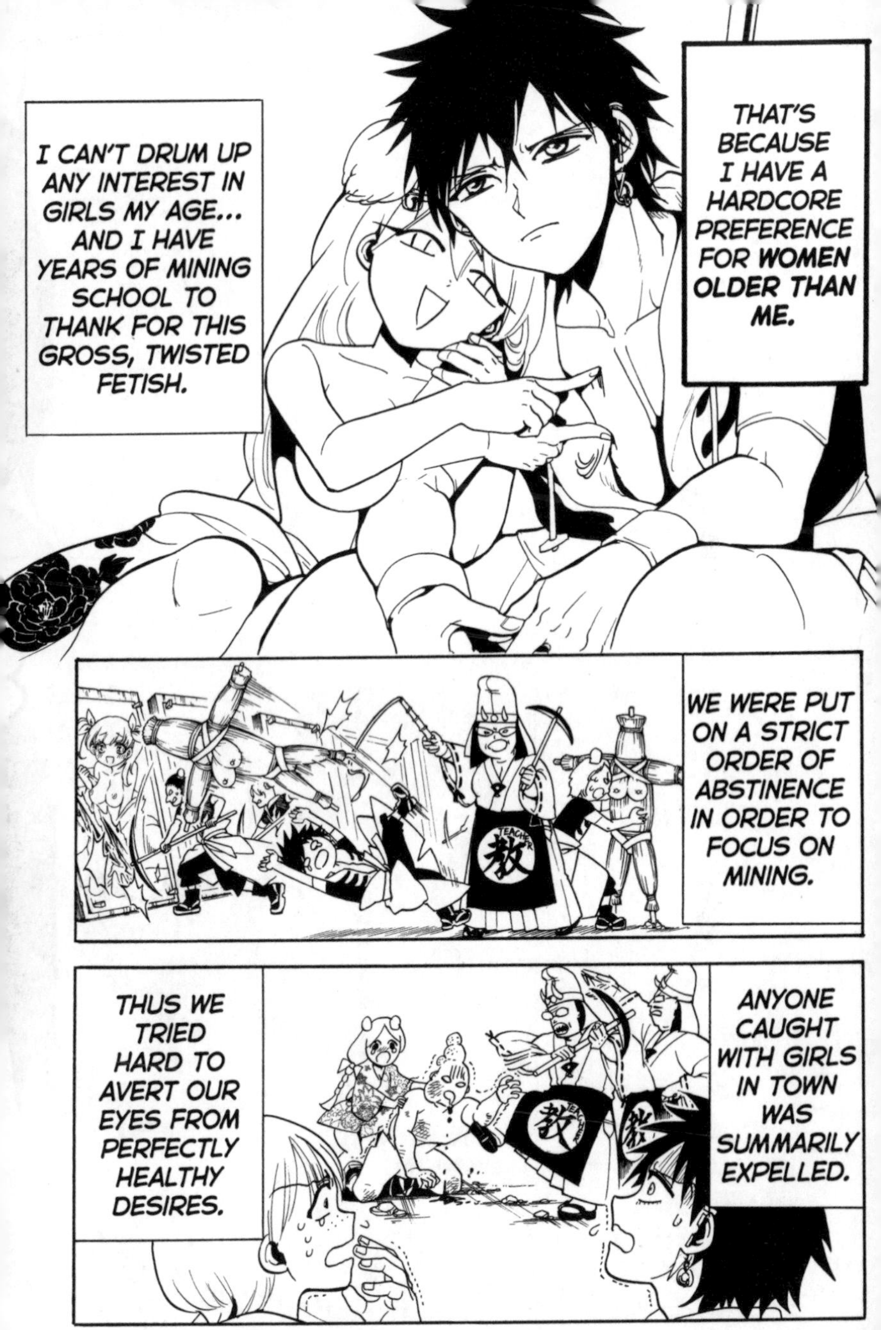
THAT'S BECAUSE I HAVE A HARDCORE PREFERENCE FOR WOMEN OLDER THAN ME.
I CAN'T DRUM UP ANY INTEREST IN GIRLS MY AGE... AND I HAVE YEARS OF MINING SCHOOL TO THANK FOR THIS GROSS, TWISTED FETISH.
WE WERE PUT ON A STRICT ORDER OF ABSTINENCE IN ORDER TO FOCUS ON MINING.
ANYONE CAUGHT WITH GIRLS IN TOWN WAS SUMMARILY EXPELLED.
THUS WE TRIED HARD TO AVERT OUR EYES FROM PERFECTLY HEALTHY DESIRES.

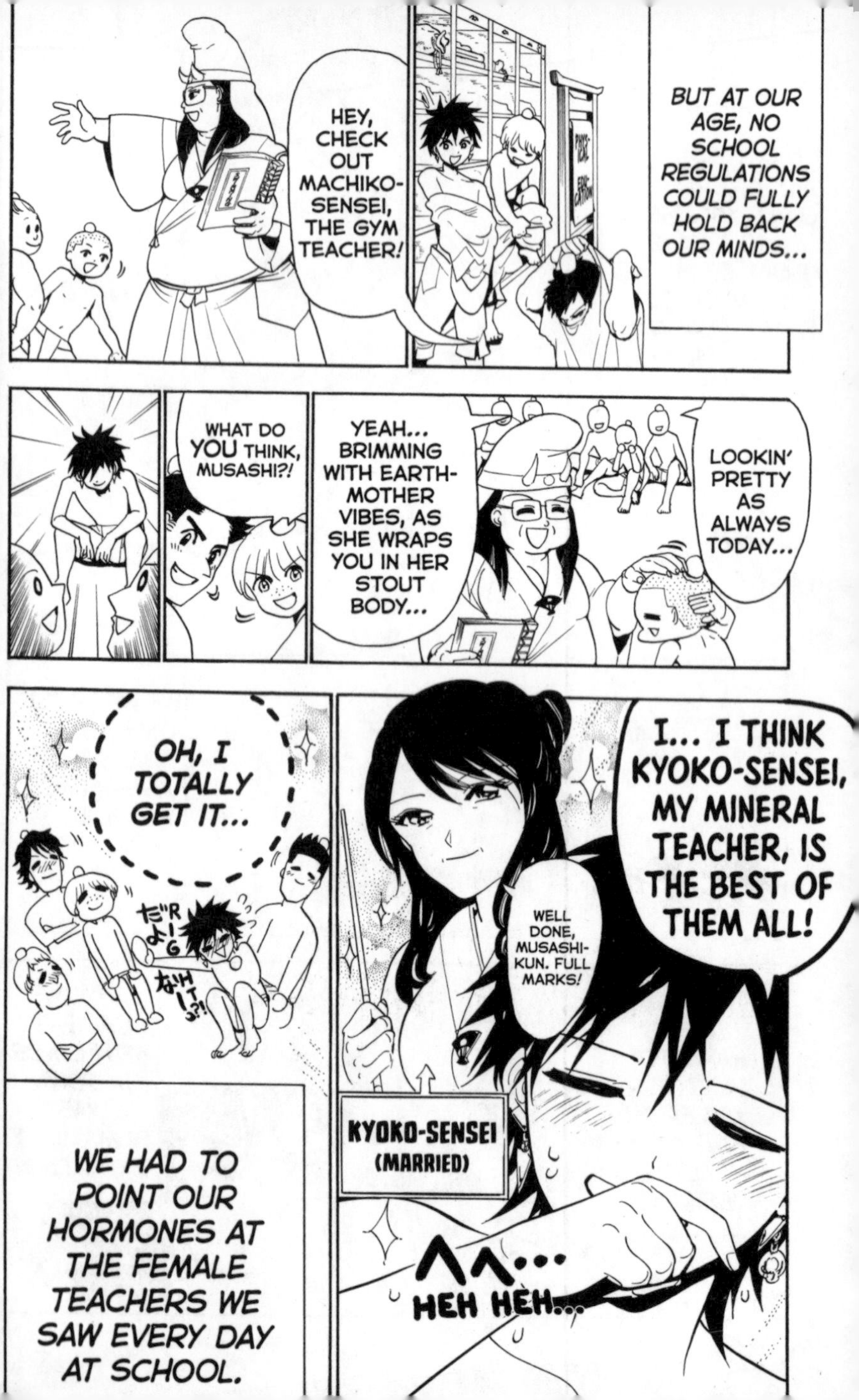
BUT AT OUR AGE, NO SCHOOL REGULATIONS COULD FULLY HOLD BACK OUR MINDS...
HEY, CHECK OUT MACHIKO-SENSEI, THE GYM TEACHER!
LOOKIN' PRETTY AS ALWAYS TODAY...
YEAH... BRIMMING WITH EARTH-MOTHER VIBES, AS SHE WRAPS YOU IN HER STOUT BODY...
WHAT DO YOU THINK, MUSASHI?!
I... I THINK KYOKO-SENSEI, MY MINERAL TEACHER, IS THE BEST OF THEM ALL!
WELL DONE, MUSASHI-KUN. FULL MARKS!
KYOKO-SENSEI
(MARRIED)
ヘヘ...
HEH HEH...
OH, I TOTALLY GET IT...
だよな
RIGHT?!
WE HAD TO POINT OUR HORMONES AT THE FEMALE TEACHERS WE SAW EVERY DAY AT SCHOOL.

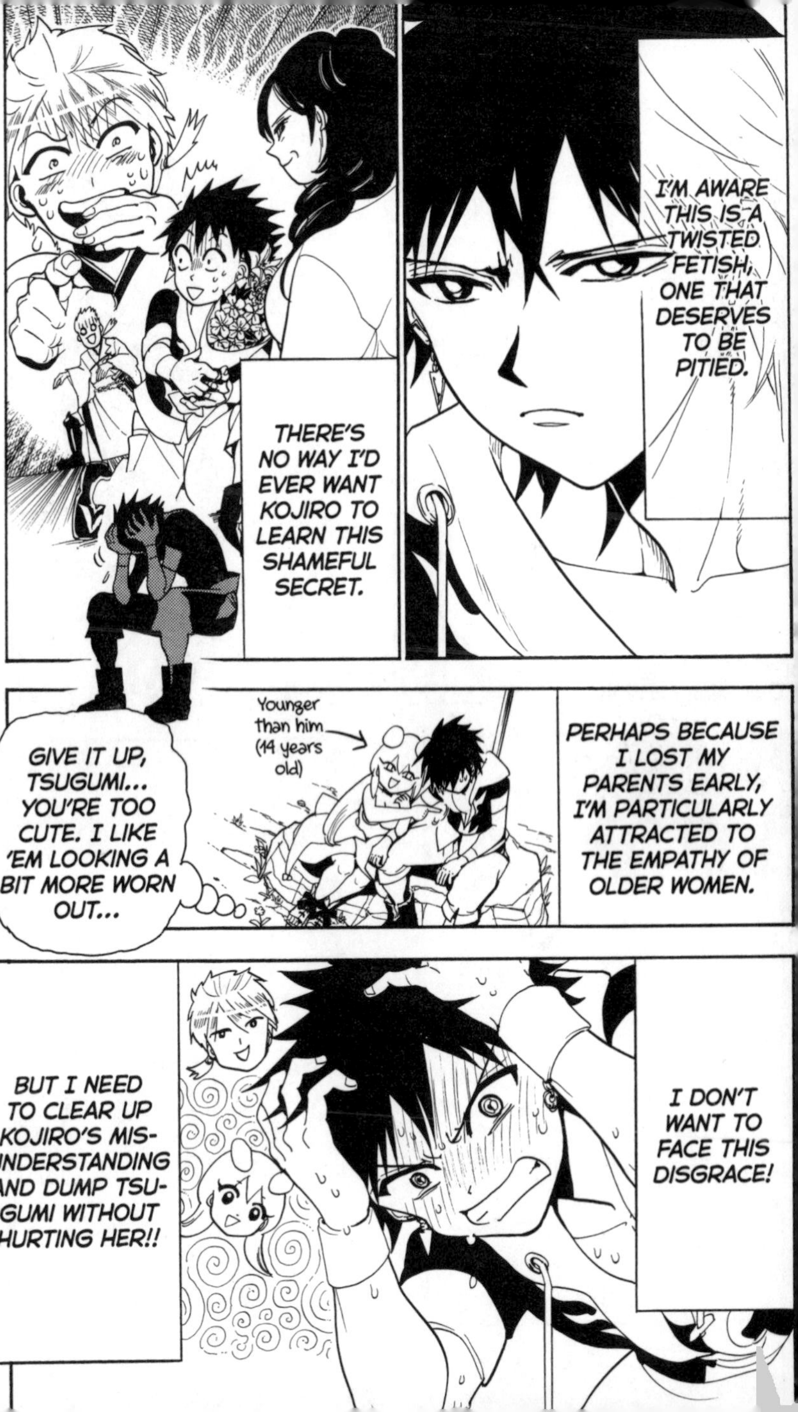
I'M AWARE THIS IS A TWISTED FETISH, ONE THAT DESERVES TO BE PITIED.
THERE'S NO WAY I'D EVER WANT KOJIRO TO LEARN THIS SHAMEFUL SECRET.
PERHAPS BECAUSE I LOST MY PARENTS EARLY, I'M PARTICULARLY ATTRACTED TO THE EMPATHY OF OLDER WOMEN.
Younger than him (14 years old)
GIVE IT UP, TSUGUMI... YOU'RE TOO CUTE. I LIKE 'EM LOOKING A BIT MORE WORN OUT...
I DON'T WANT TO FACE THIS DISGRACE!
BUT I NEED TO CLEAR UP KOJIRO'S MIS-UNDERSTANDING AND DUMP TSU-GUMI WITHOUT HURTING HER!!

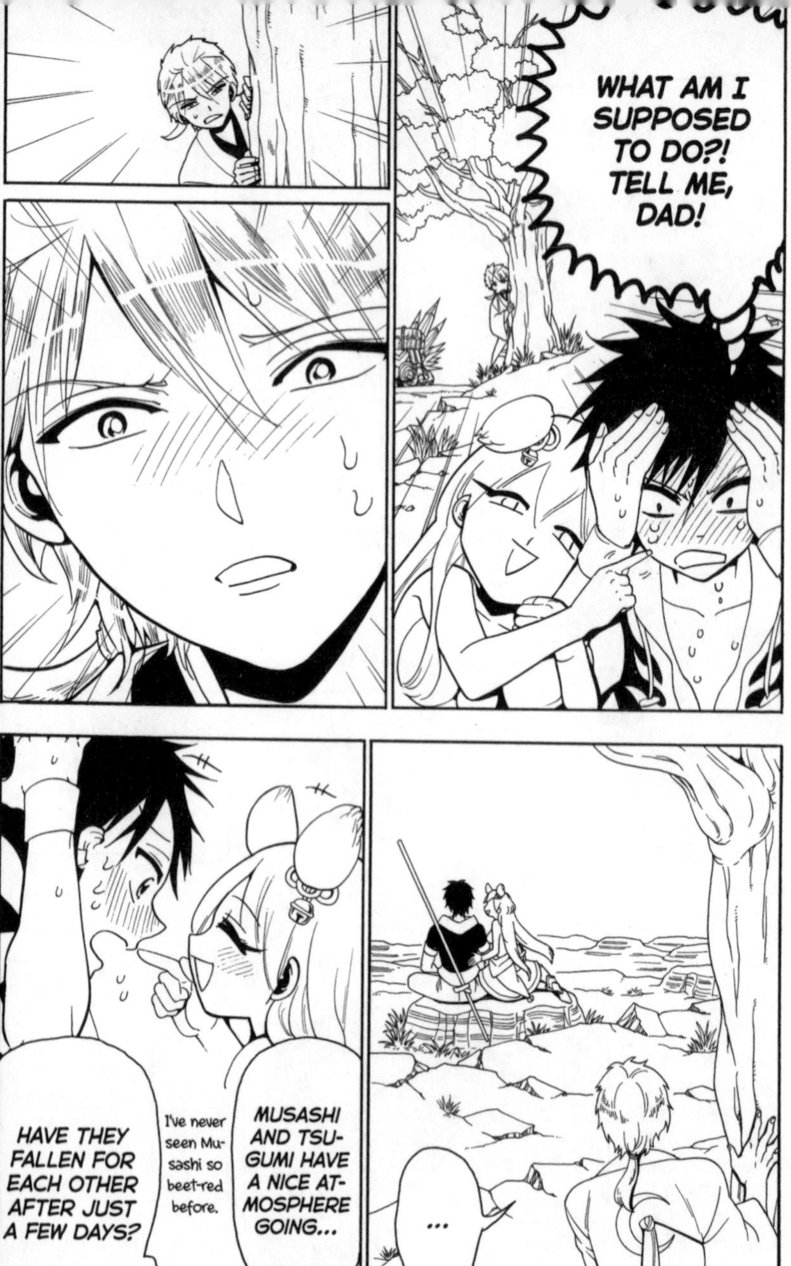
WHAT AM I SUPPOSED TO DO?! TELL ME, DAD!
...
MUSASHI AND TSU-GUMI HAVE A NICE AT-MOSPHERE GOING...
I've never seen Mu-sashi so beet-red before.
HAVE THEY FALLEN FOR EACH OTHER AFTER JUST A FEW DAYS?

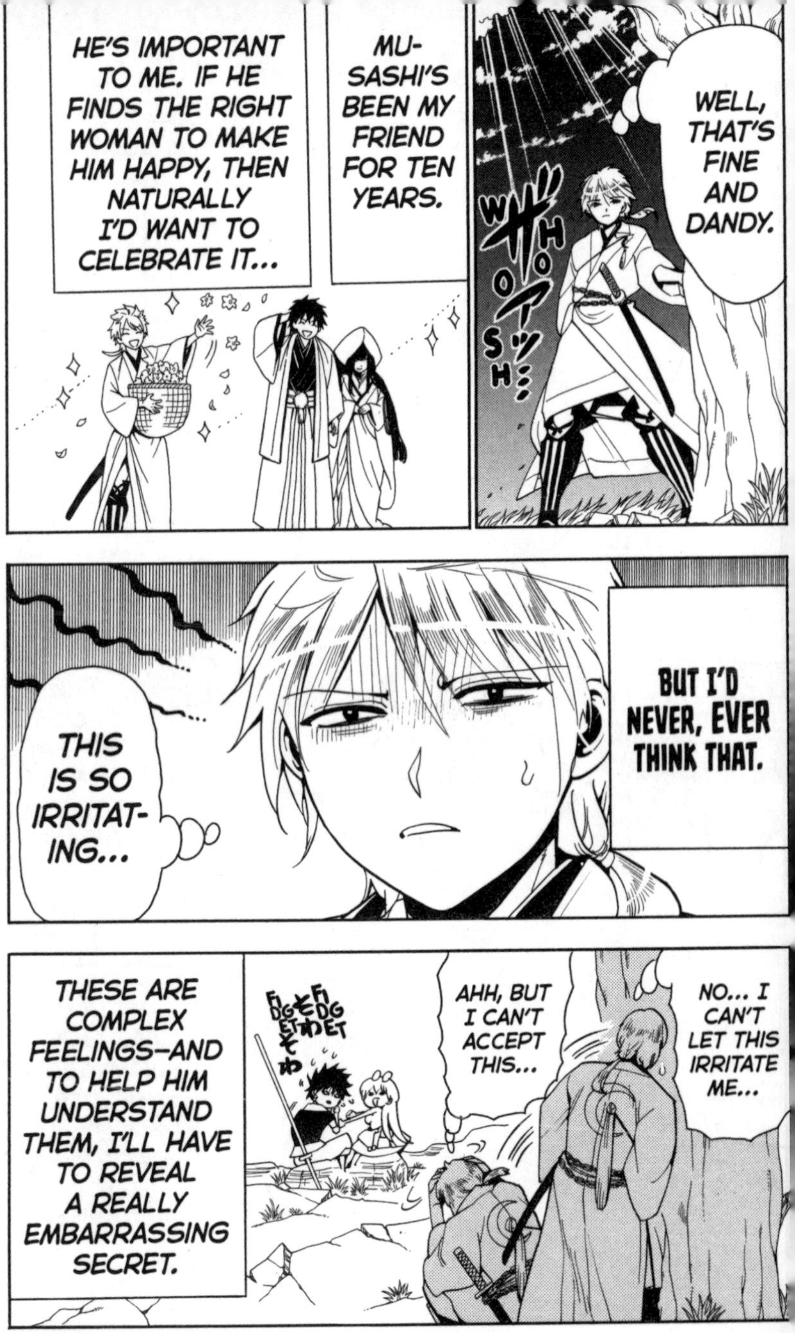
WELL, THAT'S FINE AND DANDY.
WHOOSH
MU-SASHI'S BEEN MY FRIEND FOR TEN YEARS.
HE'S IMPORTANT TO ME. IF HE FINDS THE RIGHT WOMAN TO MAKE HIM HAPPY, THEN NATURALLY I'D WANT TO CELEBRATE IT...
BUT I'D NEVER, EVER THINK THAT.
THIS IS SO IRRITAT-ING...
NO... I CAN'T LET THIS IRRITATE ME...
AHH, BUT I CAN'T ACCEPT THIS...
FIDGET FIDGET
THESE ARE COMPLEX FEELINGS—AND TO HELP HIM UNDERSTAND THEM, I'LL HAVE TO REVEAL A REALLY EMBARRASSING SECRET.

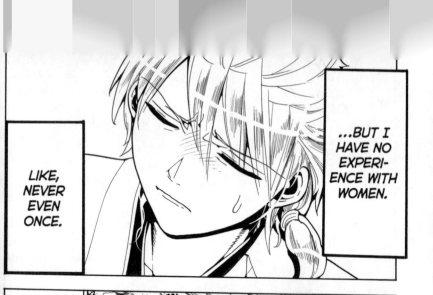

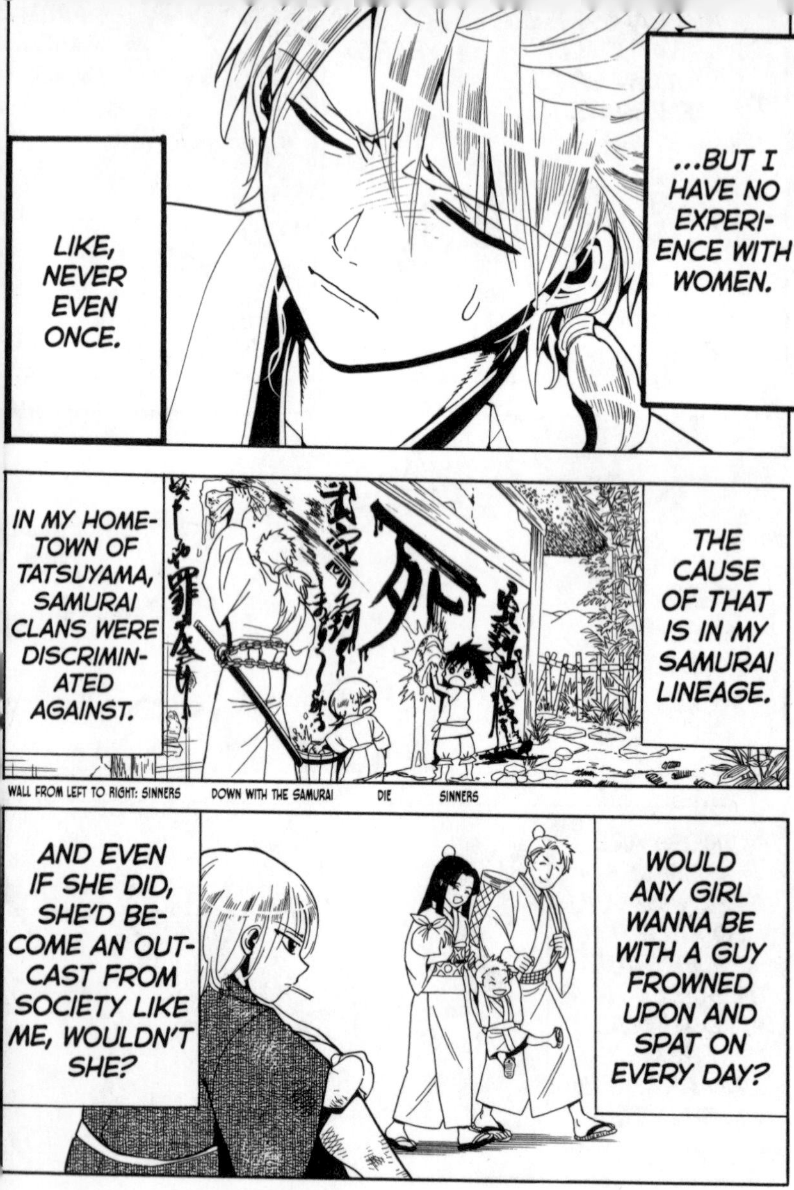
...BUT I HAVE NO EXPERIENCE WITH WOMEN.
LIKE, NEVER EVEN ONCE.
THE CAUSE OF THAT IS IN MY SAMURAI LINEAGE.
IN MY HOMETOWN OF TATSUYAMA, SAMURAI CLANS WERE DISCRIMINATED AGAINST.
WALL FROM LEFT TO RIGHT: SINNERS DOWN WITH THE SAMURAI DIE SINNERS
WOULD ANY GIRL WANNA BE WITH A GUY FROWNED UPON AND SPAT ON EVERY DAY?
AND EVEN IF SHE DID, SHE'D BECOME AN OUTCAST FROM SOCIETY LIKE ME, WOULDN'T SHE?

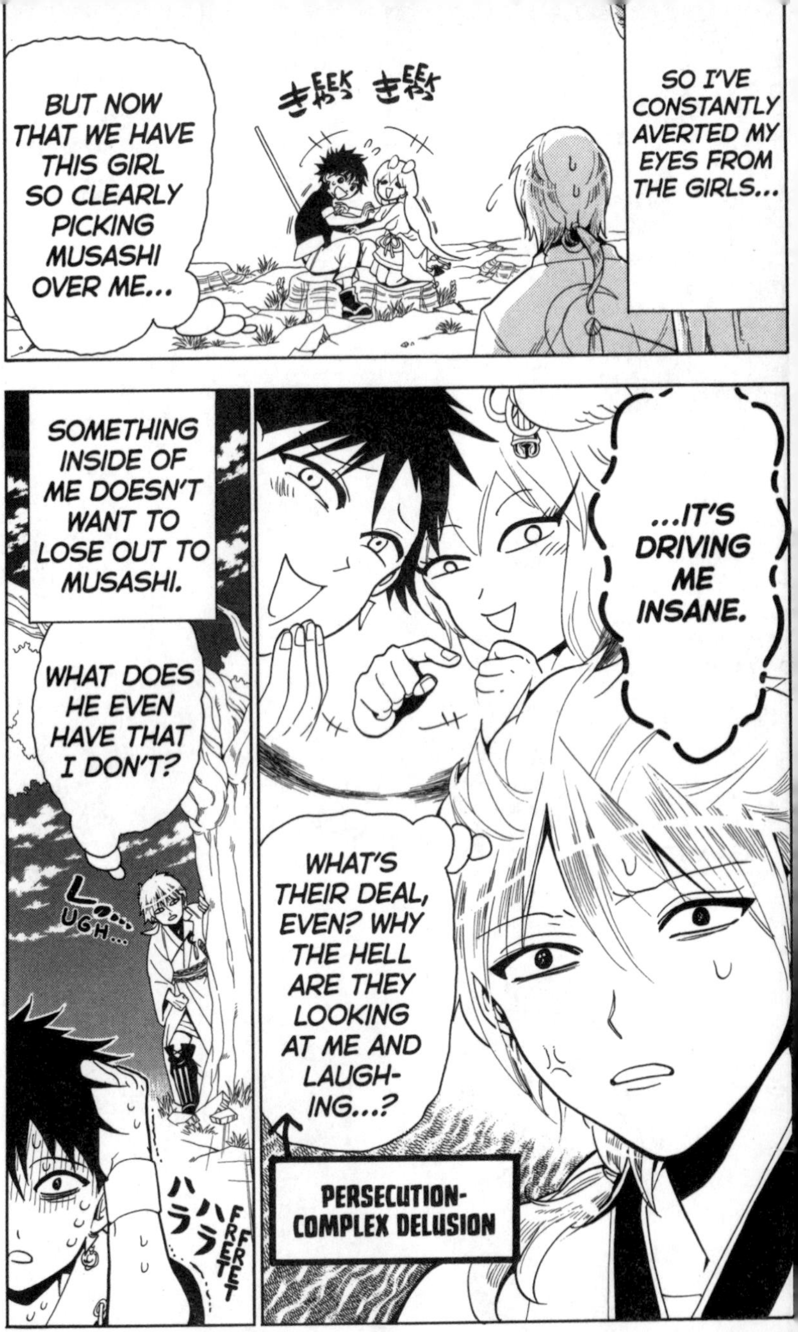
SO I'VE CONSTANTLY AVERTED MY EYES FROM THE GIRLS...
BUT NOW THAT WE HAVE THIS GIRL SO CLEARLY PICKING MUSASHI OVER ME...
...IT'S DRIVING ME INSANE.
WHAT'S THEIR DEAL, EVEN? WHY THE HELL ARE THEY LOOKING AT ME AND LAUGH-ING...?
PERSECUTION-COMPLEX DELUSION
SOMETHING INSIDE OF ME DOESN'T WANT TO LOSE OUT TO MUSASHI.
WHAT DOES HE EVEN HAVE THAT I DON'T?
UGH...
FRET FRET

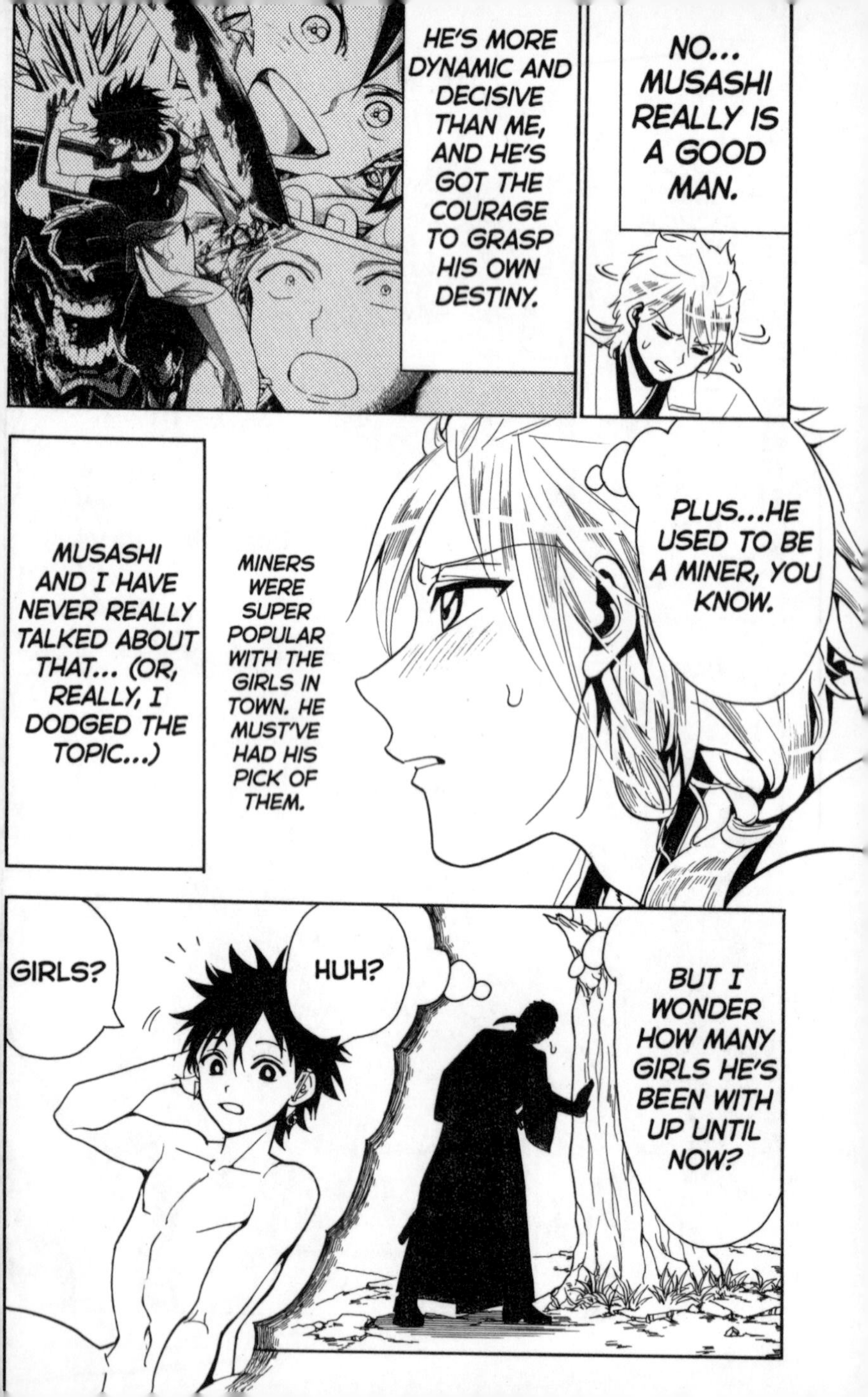

NO... MUSASHI REALLY IS A GOOD MAN.
HE'S MORE DYNAMIC AND DECISIVE THAN ME, AND HE'S GOT THE COURAGE TO GRASP HIS OWN DESTINY.
PLUS...HE USED TO BE A MINER, YOU KNOW.
MINERS WERE SUPER POPULAR WITH THE GIRLS IN TOWN. HE MUST'VE HAD HIS PICK OF THEM.
MUSASHI AND I HAVE NEVER REALLY TALKED ABOUT THAT... (OR, REALLY, I DODGED THE TOPIC...)
BUT I WONDER HOW MANY GIRLS HE'S BEEN WITH UP UNTIL NOW?
HUH?
GIRLS?

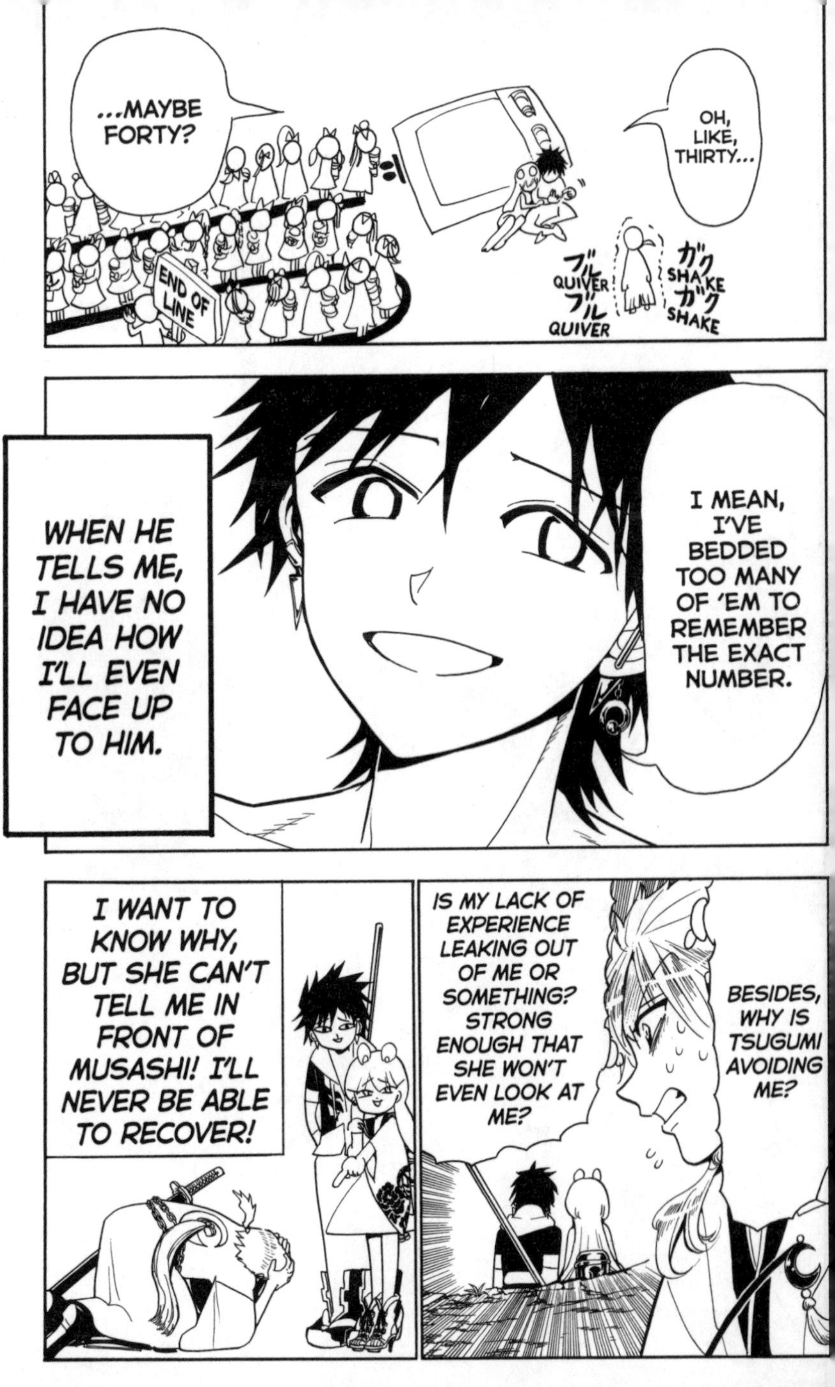
OH, LIKE, THIRTY...
ガク SHAKE ガク SHAKE
ブル QUIVER ブル QUIVER
...MAYBE FORTY?
END OF LINE
I MEAN, I'VE BEDDED TOO MANY OF 'EM TO REMEMBER THE EXACT NUMBER.
WHEN HE TELLS ME, I HAVE NO IDEA HOW I'LL EVEN FACE UP TO HIM.
BESIDES, WHY IS TSUGUMI AVOIDING ME?
IS MY LACK OF EXPERIENCE LEAKING OUT OF ME OR SOMETHING? STRONG ENOUGH THAT SHE WON'T EVEN LOOK AT ME?
I WANT TO KNOW WHY, BUT SHE CAN'T TELL ME IN FRONT OF MUSASHI! I'LL NEVER BE ABLE TO RECOVER!

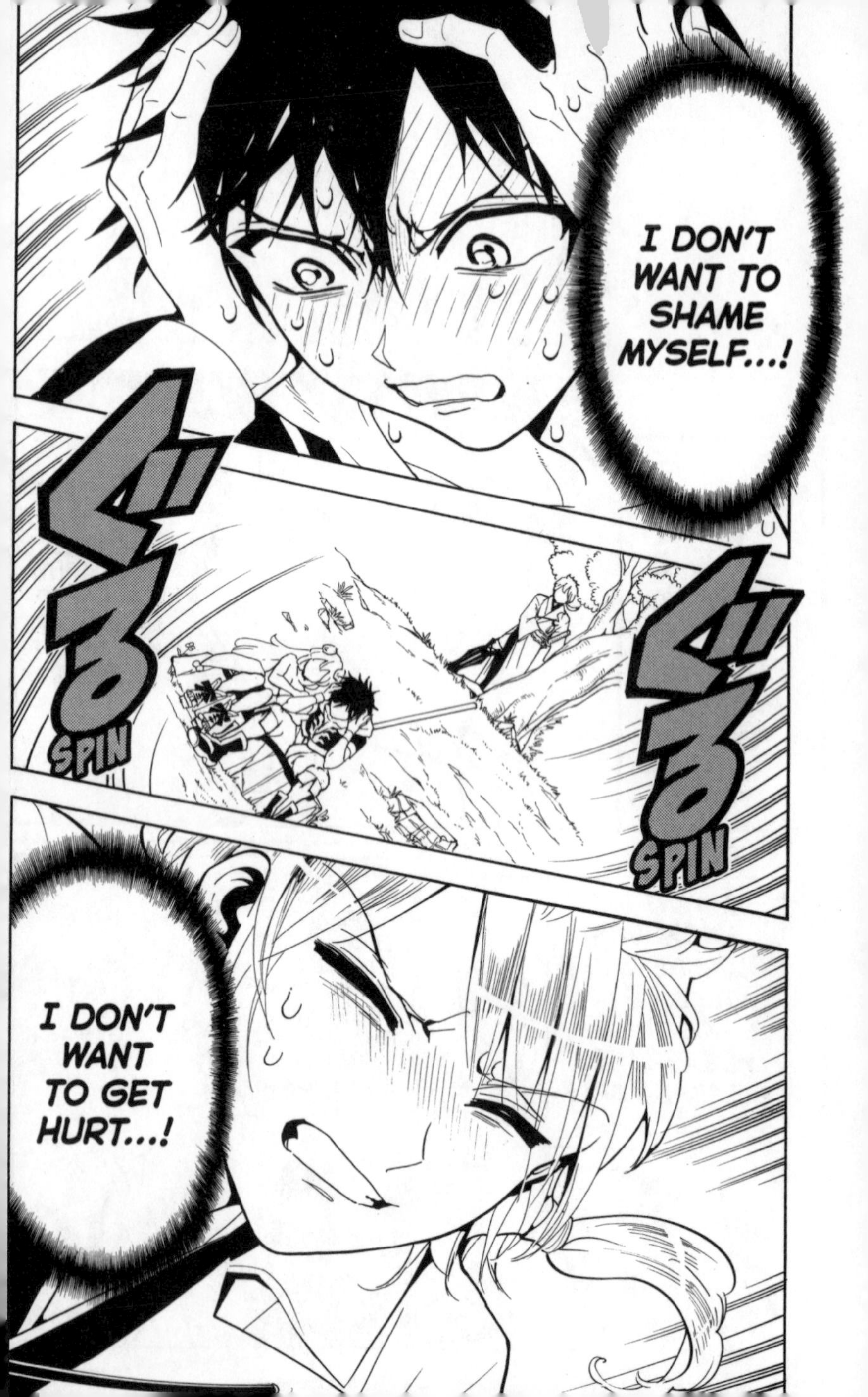
I DON'T WANT TO SHAME MYSELF...!
ぐる
SPIN
ぐる
SPIN
I DON'T WANT TO GET HURT...!

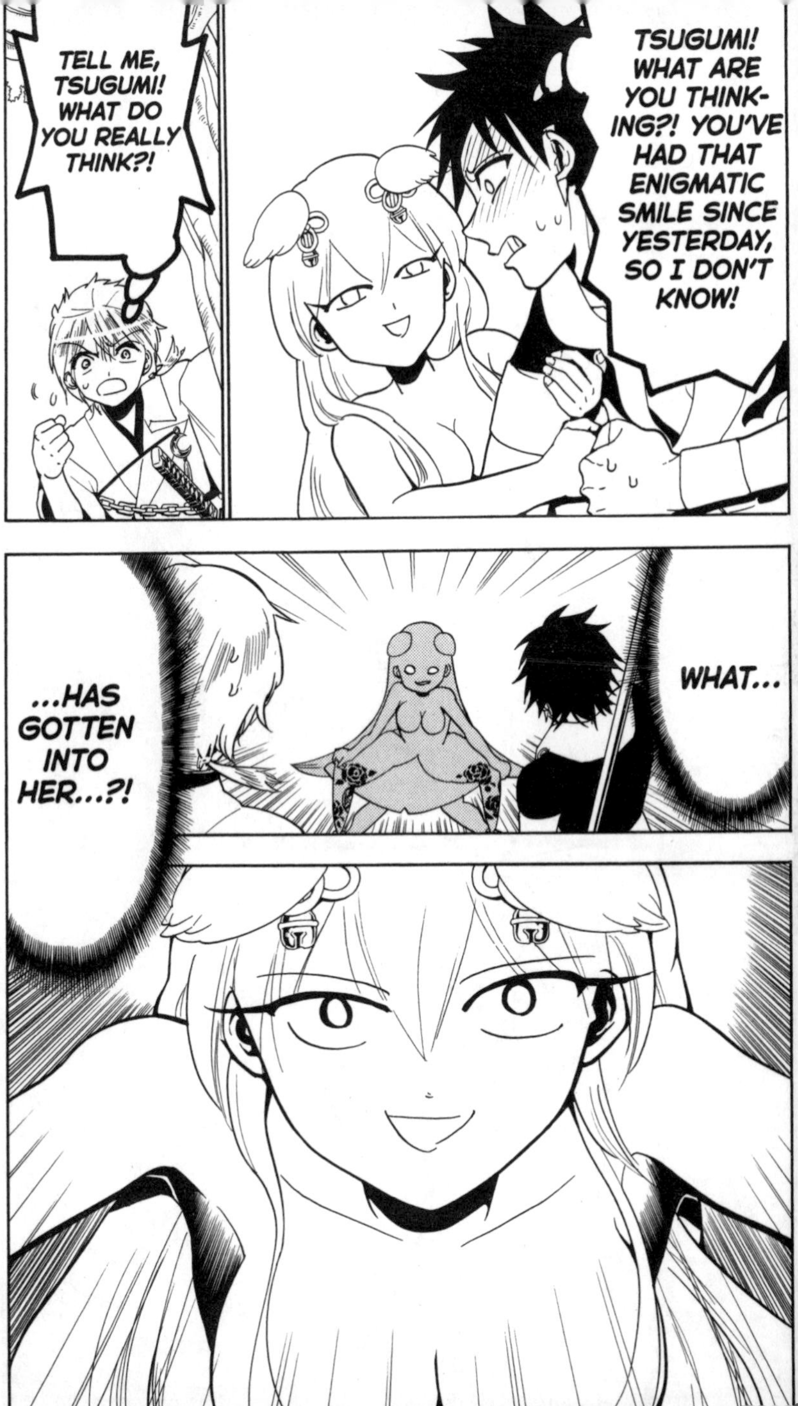
TSUGUMI! WHAT ARE YOU THINKING?! YOU'VE HAD THAT ENIGMATIC SMILE SINCE YESTERDAY, SO I DON'T KNOW!
TELL ME, TSUGUMI! WHAT DO YOU REALLY THINK?!
WHAT...
...HAS GOTTEN INTO HER...?!

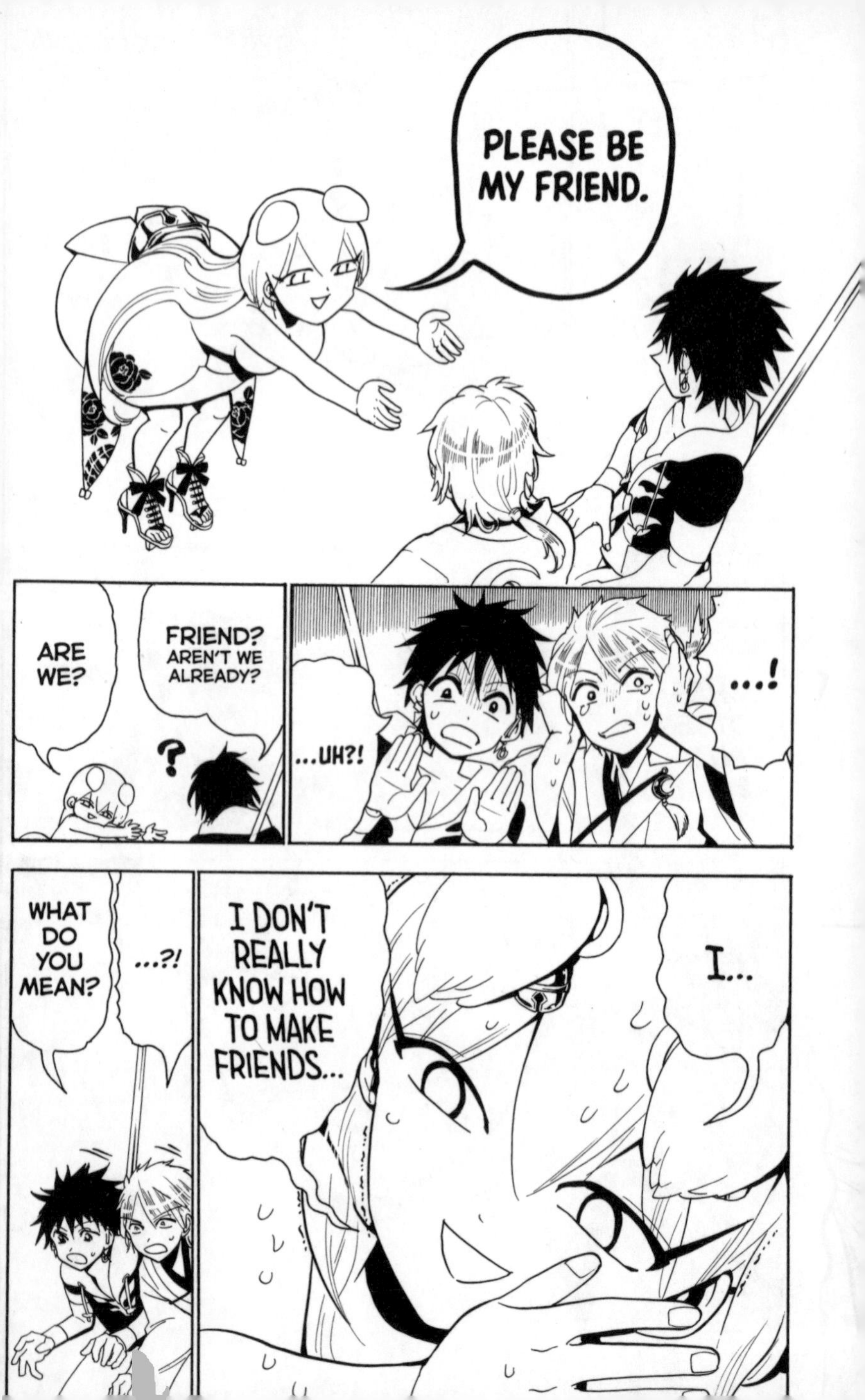
PLEASE BE MY FRIEND.
...!
...UH?!
FRIEND? AREN'T WE ALREADY?
ARE WE?
?
I...
I DON'T REALLY KNOW HOW TO MAKE FRIENDS...
...?!
WHAT DO YOU MEAN?

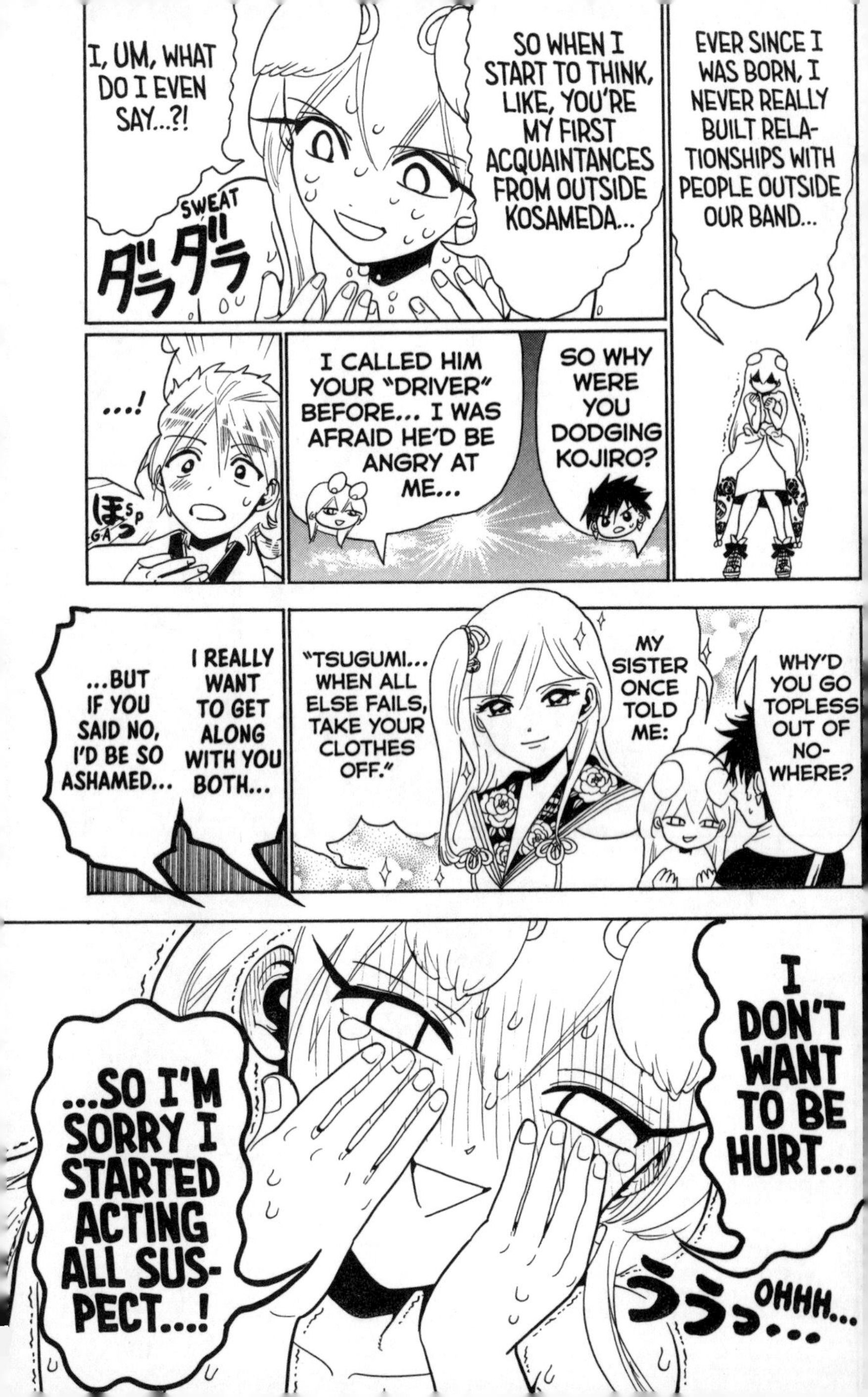
EVER SINCE I WAS BORN, I NEVER REALLY BUILT RELA-TIONSHIPS WITH PEOPLE OUTSIDE OUR BAND...
SO WHEN I START TO THINK, LIKE, YOU'RE MY FIRST ACQUAINTANCES FROM OUTSIDE KOSAMEDA...
I, UM, WHAT DO I EVEN SAY...?!
ダラダラ
SWEAT
SO WHY WERE YOU DODGING KOJIRO?
I CALLED HIM YOUR "DRIVER" BEFORE... I WAS AFRAID HE'D BE ANGRY AT ME...
...!
ぼっ
GASP
WHY'D YOU GO TOPLESS OUT OF NO-WHERE?
MY SISTER ONCE TOLD ME:
"TSUGUMI... WHEN ALL ELSE FAILS, TAKE YOUR CLOTHES OFF."
I REALLY WANT TO GET ALONG WITH YOU BOTH...
...BUT IF YOU SAID NO, I'D BE SO ASHAMED...
I DON'T WANT TO BE HURT...
...SO I'M SORRY I STARTED ACTING ALL SUS-PECT...!
うぅっ...
OHHH...

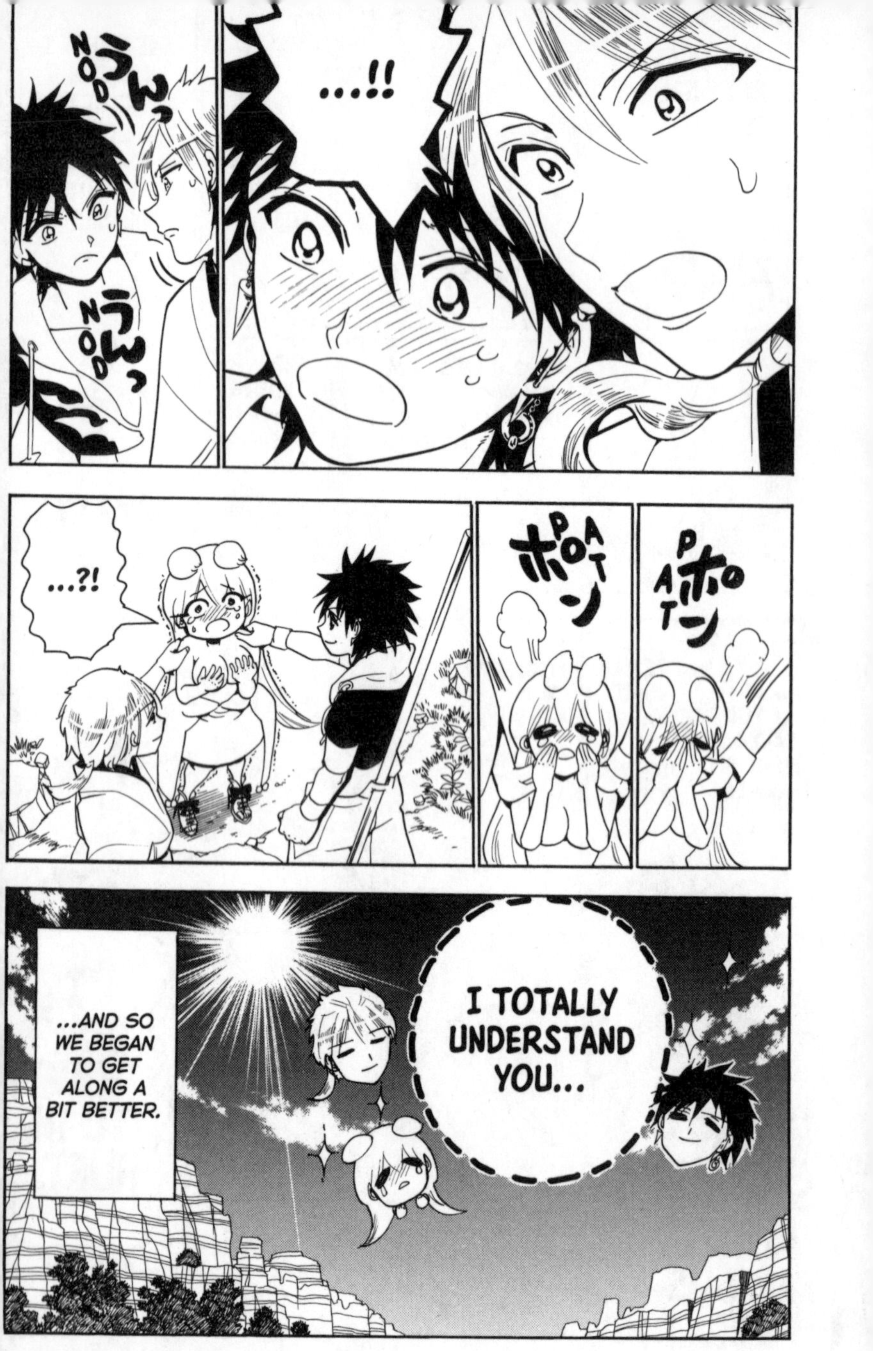
...!!
うんっ NOD
うんっ NOD
ポン PAT
ポン PAT
...?!
I TOTALLY UNDERSTAND YOU...
...AND SO WE BEGAN TO GET ALONG A BIT BETTER.

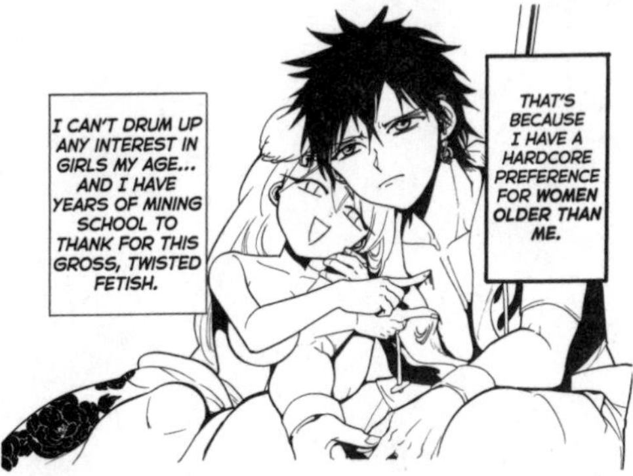
THAT'S BECAUSE I HAVE A HARDCORE PREFERENCE FOR WOMEN OLDER THAN ME.
I CAN'T DRUM UP ANY INTEREST IN GIRLS MY AGE... AND I HAVE YEARS OF MINING SCHOOL TO THANK FOR THIS GROSS, TWISTED FETISH.

ORIENT

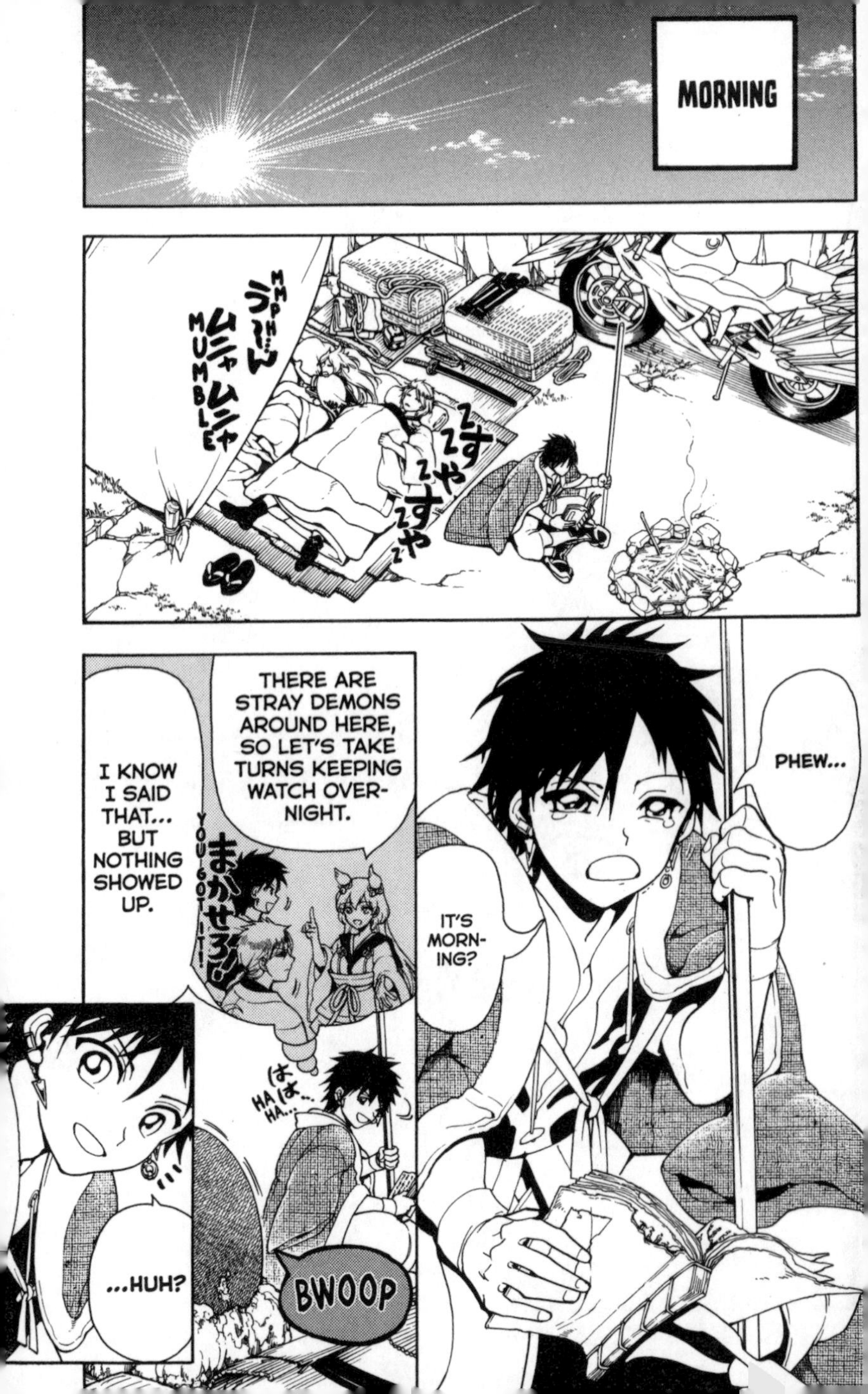
MORNING
うーん
MMPH...
ムニャムニャ
MUMBLE
すやすや
ZZZ
PHEW...
IT'S MORNING?
THERE ARE STRAY DEMONS AROUND HERE, SO LET'S TAKE TURNS KEEPING WATCH OVERNIGHT.
まかせろ!!
YOU GOT IT!
I KNOW I SAID THAT... BUT NOTHING SHOWED UP.
はは...
HA HA...
BWOOP
...HUH?

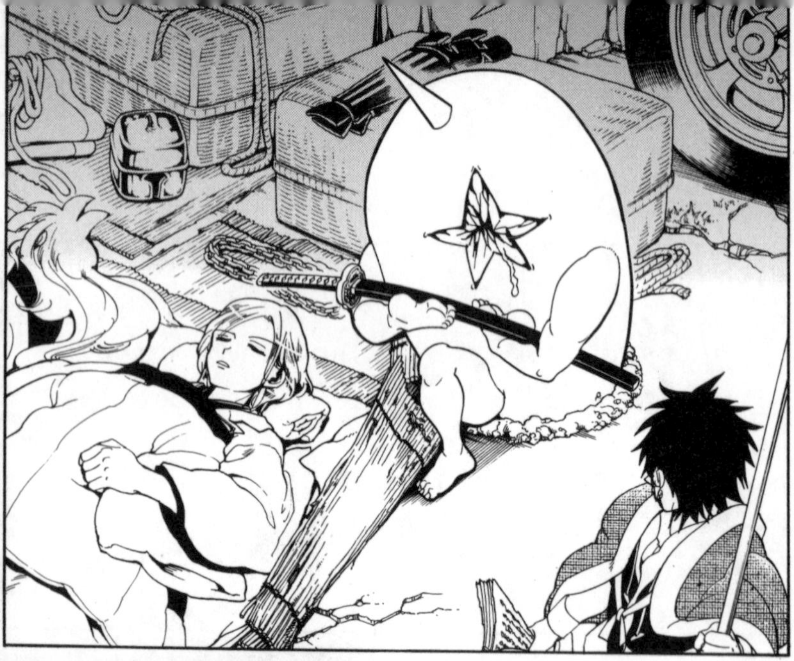

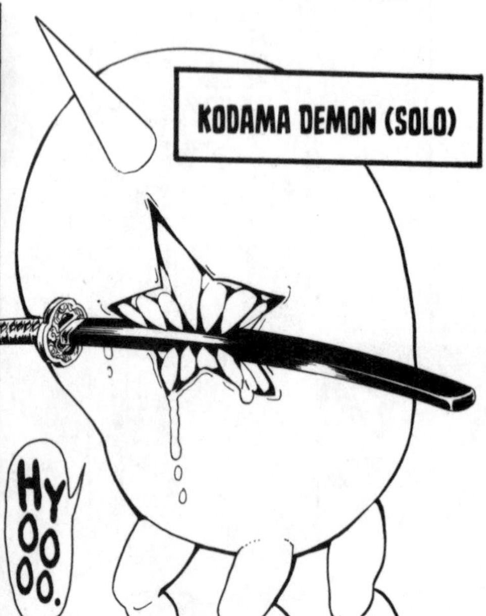
KODAMA DEMON (SOLO)
HYOOOO.

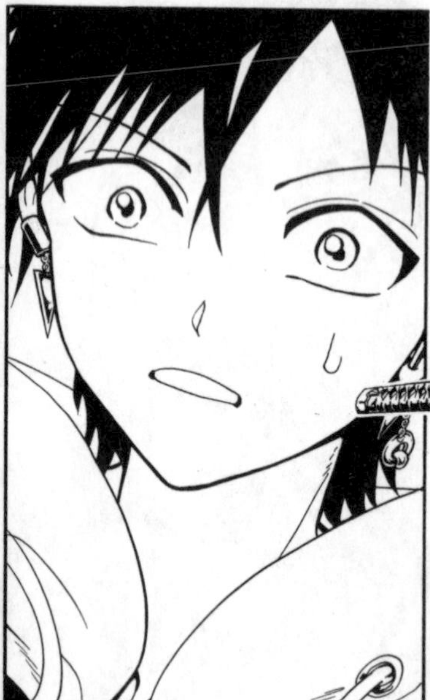

CHAPTER 19: THE KATANA

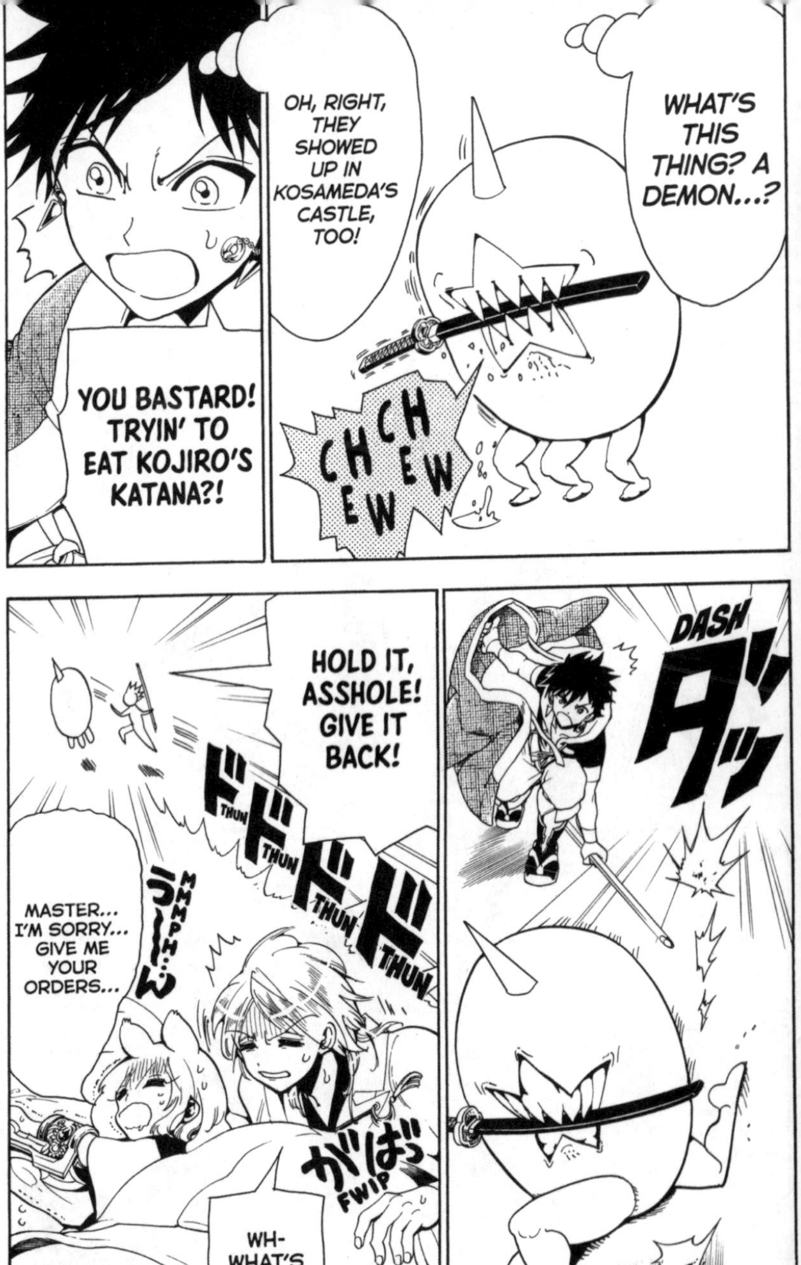
WHAT'S THIS THING? A DEMON...?
OH, RIGHT, THEY SHOWED UP IN KOSAMEDA'S CASTLE, TOO!
CHEW CHEW
YOU BASTARD! TRYIN' TO EAT KOJIRO'S KATANA?!
DASH
ダッ
HOLD IT, ASSHOLE! GIVE IT BACK!
ドドドド
THUN THUN THUN THUN
うーん
MMMPH...
MASTER... I'M SORRY... GIVE ME YOUR ORDERS...
がばっ
FWIP
WH- WHAT'S UP?!

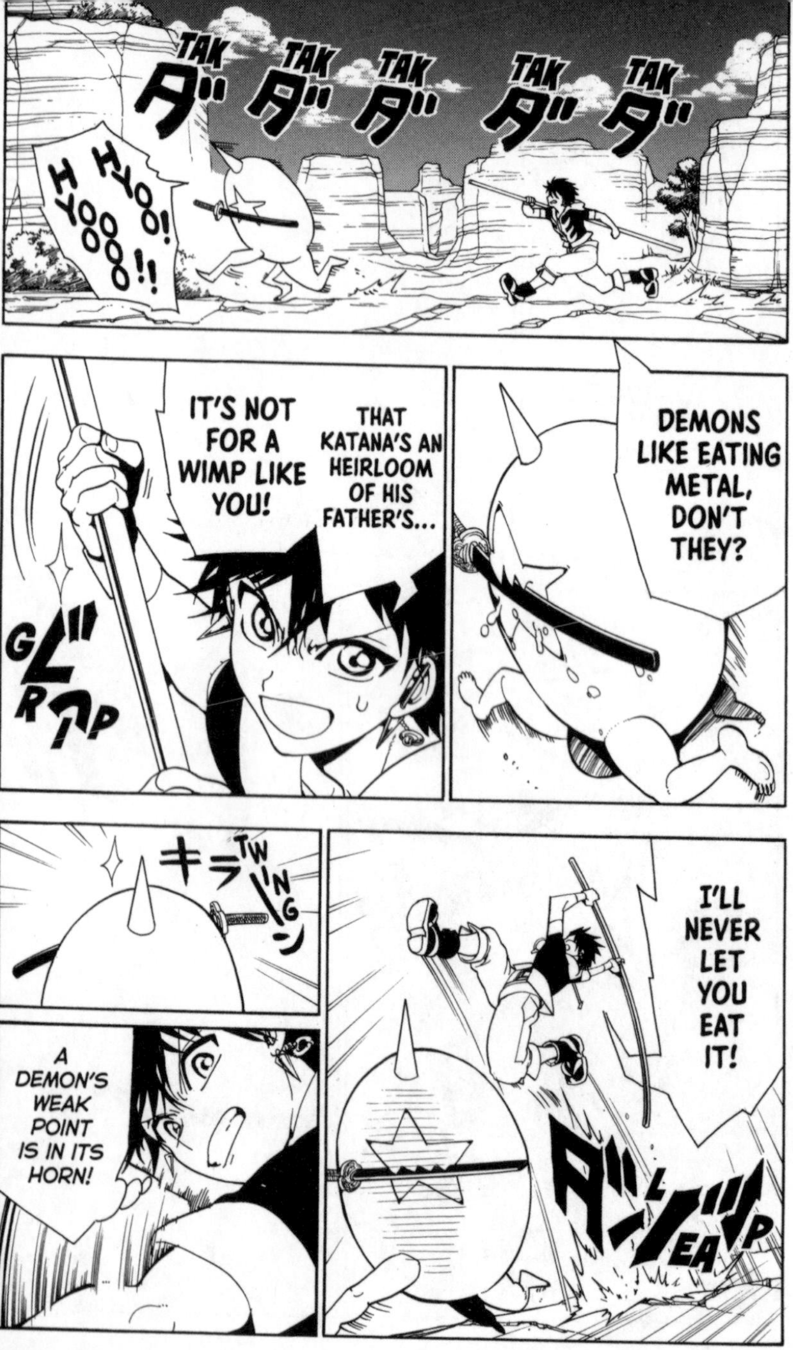
TAK
TAK
TAK
TAK
TAK
HYOOO! HYOOOOO!!
DEMONS LIKE EATING METAL, DON'T THEY?
THAT KATANA'S AN HEIRLOOM OF HIS FATHER'S...
IT'S NOT FOR A WIMP LIKE YOU!
GRIP
I'LL NEVER LET YOU EAT IT!
LEAP
TWING
A DEMON'S WEAK POINT IS IN ITS HORN!

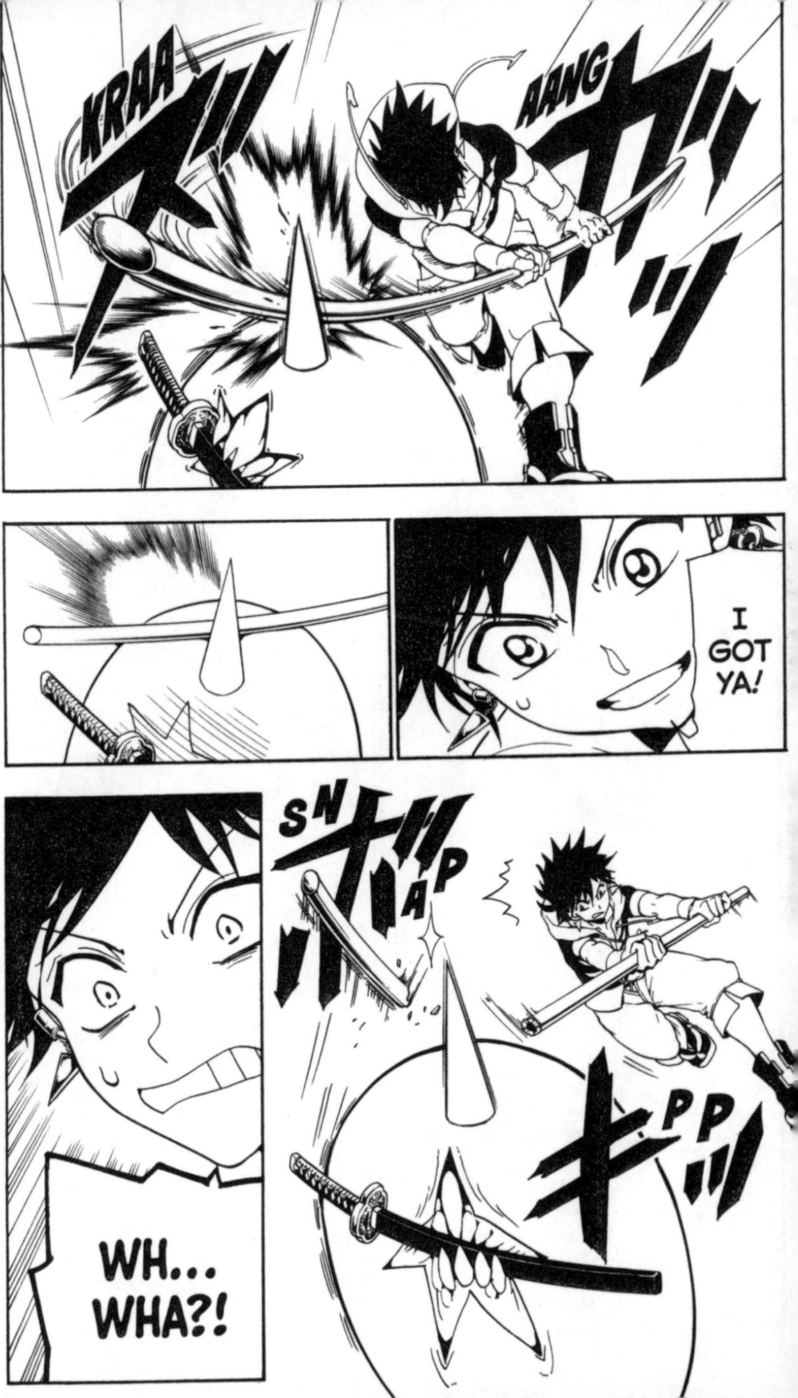
AANG
KRAA
I GOT YA!
SNAP
PP
WH... WHA?!

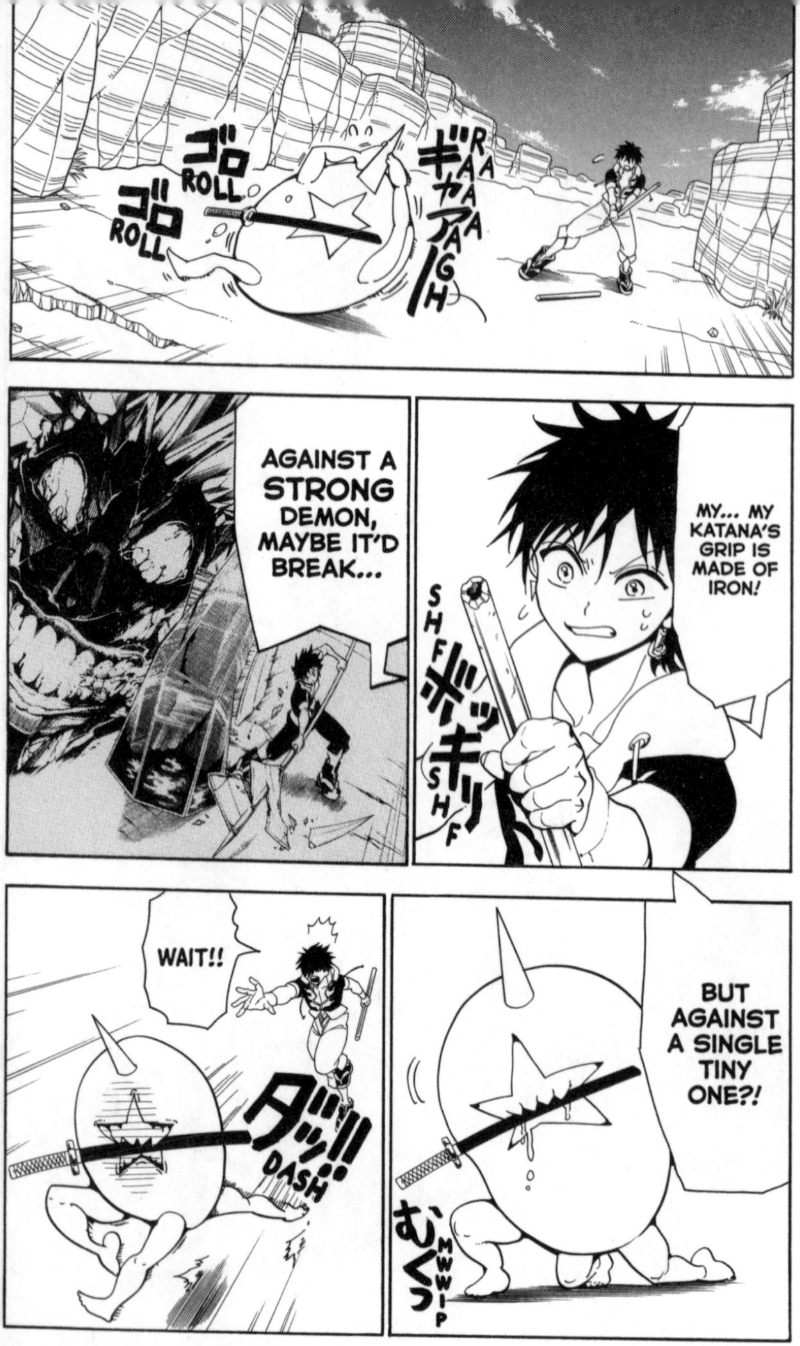
ギャアア
RAAAAGH
ゴロ
ROLL
ゴロ
ROLL
MY... MY KATANA'S GRIP IS MADE OF IRON!
ボッキリ
SHF SHF
AGAINST A STRONG DEMON, MAYBE IT'D BREAK...
BUT AGAINST A SINGLE TINY ONE?!
むくっ
MWWIP
WAIT!!
ダッ!!
DASH

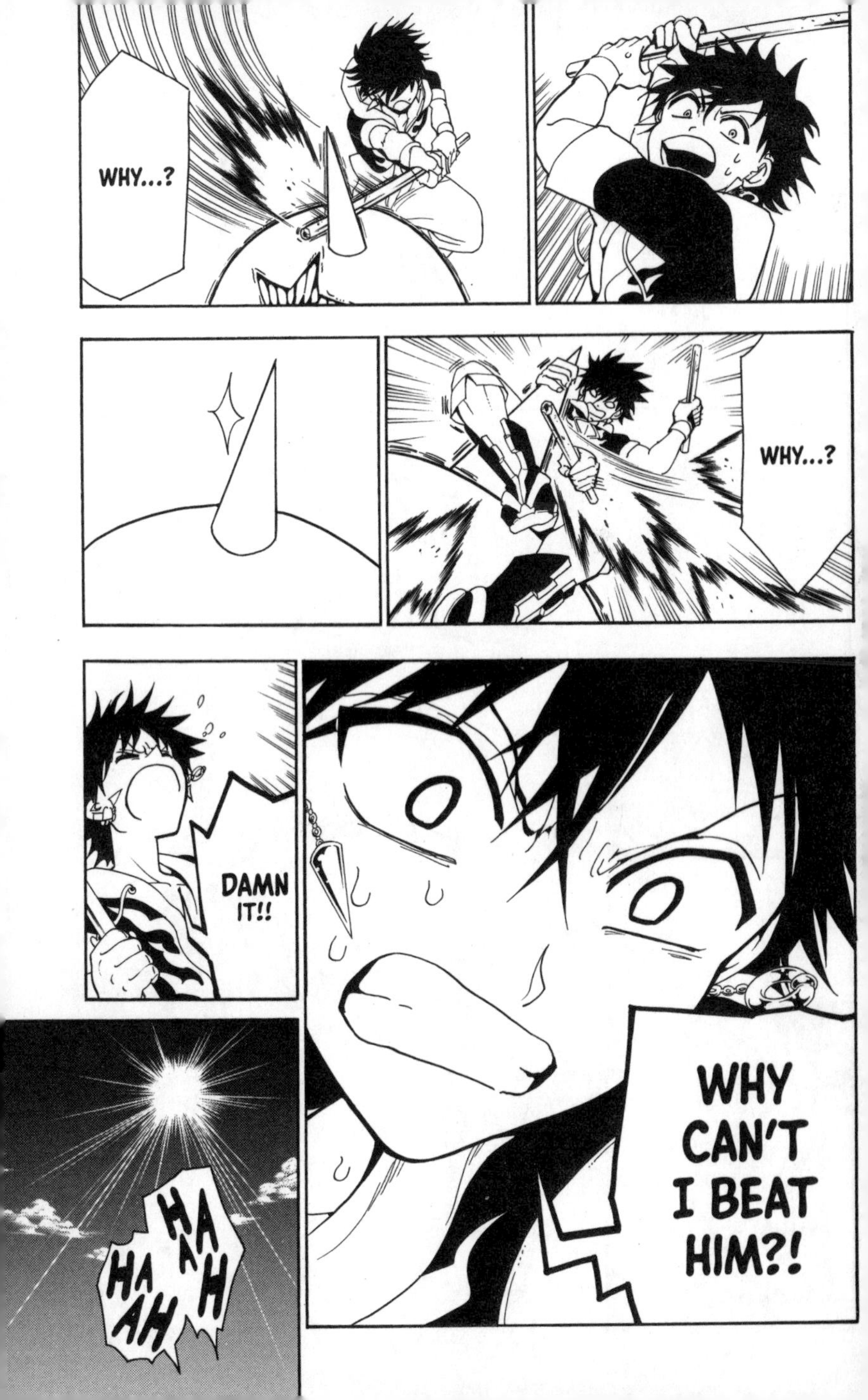
WHY...?
WHY...?
WHY CAN'T I BEAT HIM?!
DAMN IT!!
HAAH
HAAH

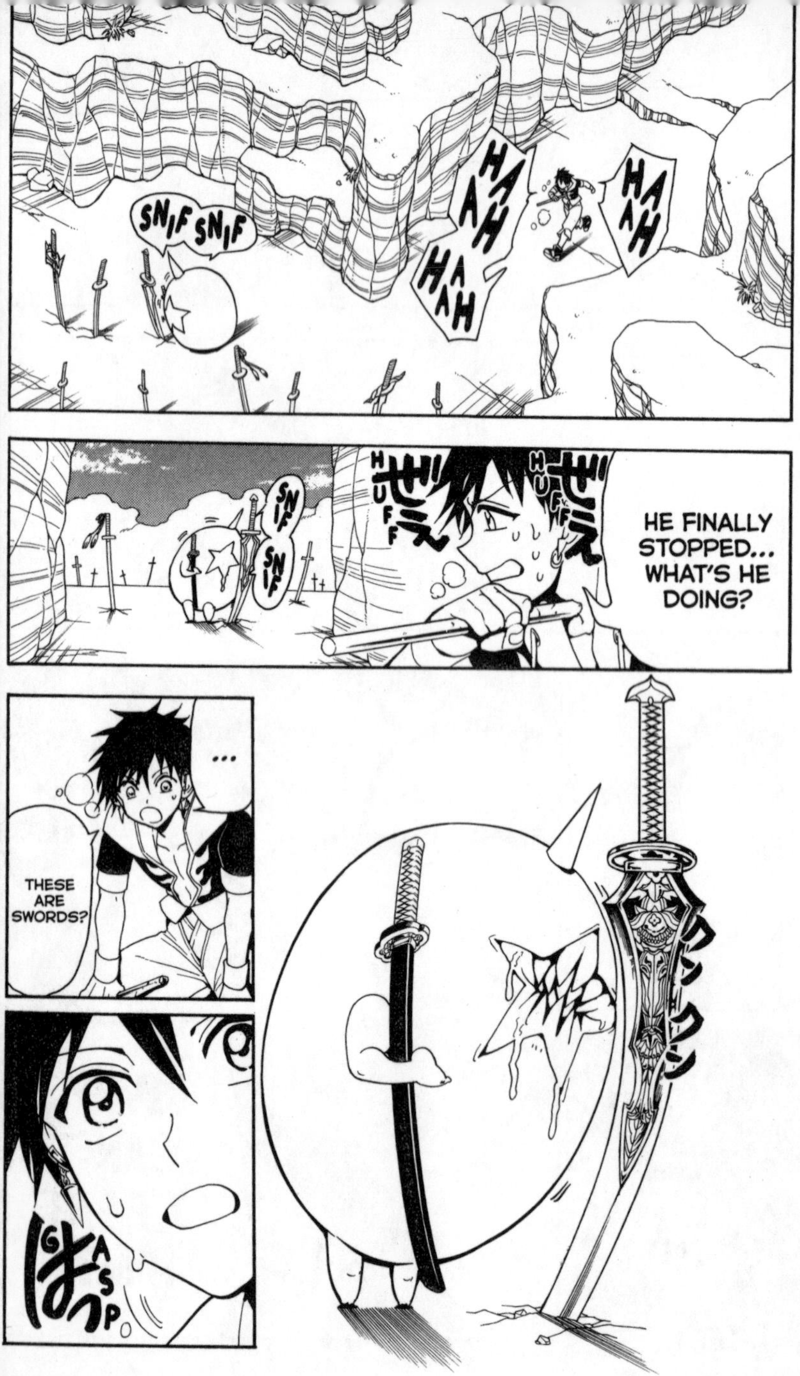
HAAH
HAAH HAAH
SNIF SNIF
HE FINALLY STOPPED... WHAT'S HE DOING?
HUFF
HUFF
SNIF SNIF
...
THESE ARE SWORDS?
GASP

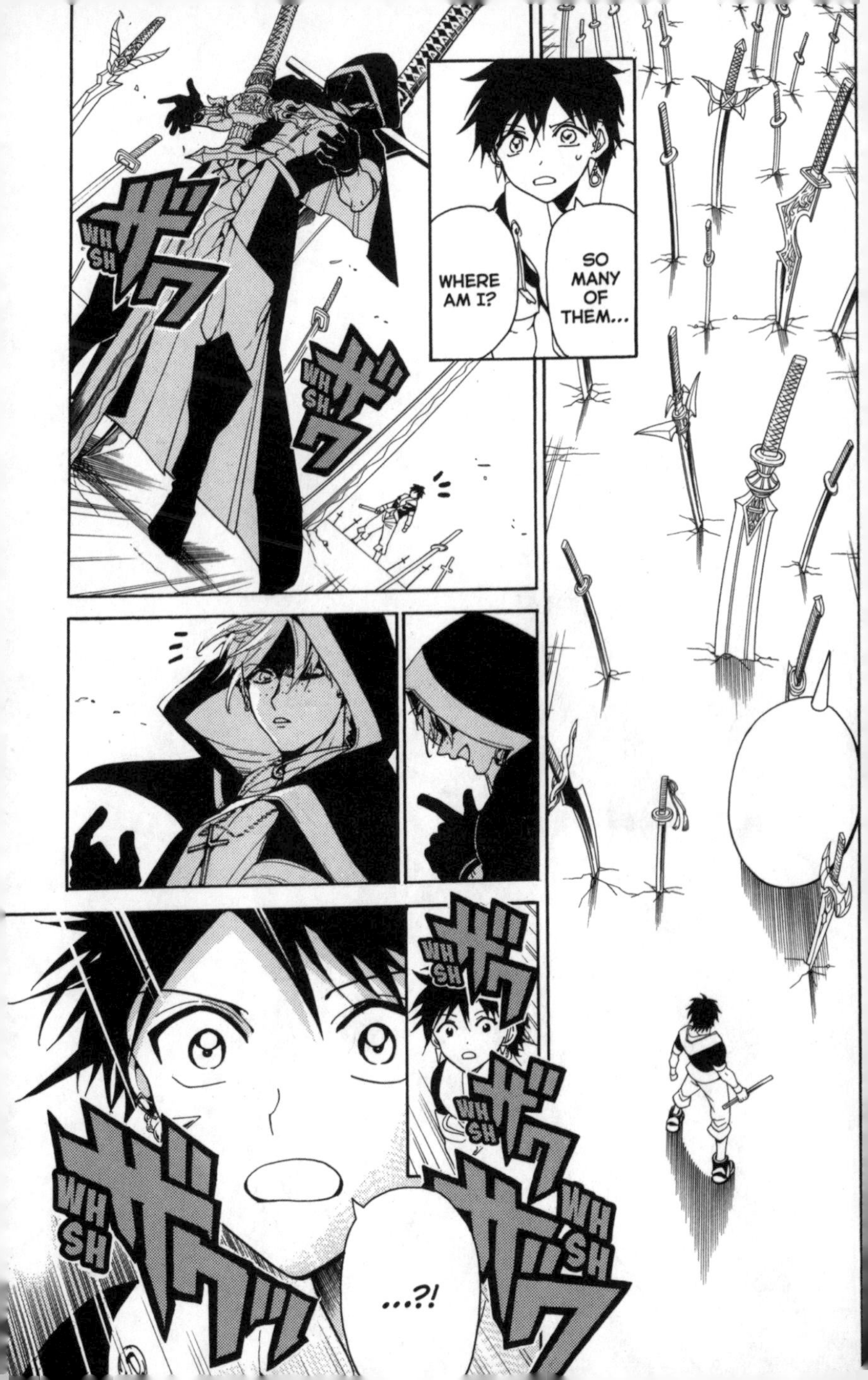

SO MANY OF THEM...
WHERE AM I?
WHSH
WHSH
WHSH
WHSH
WHSH
WHSH
...?!

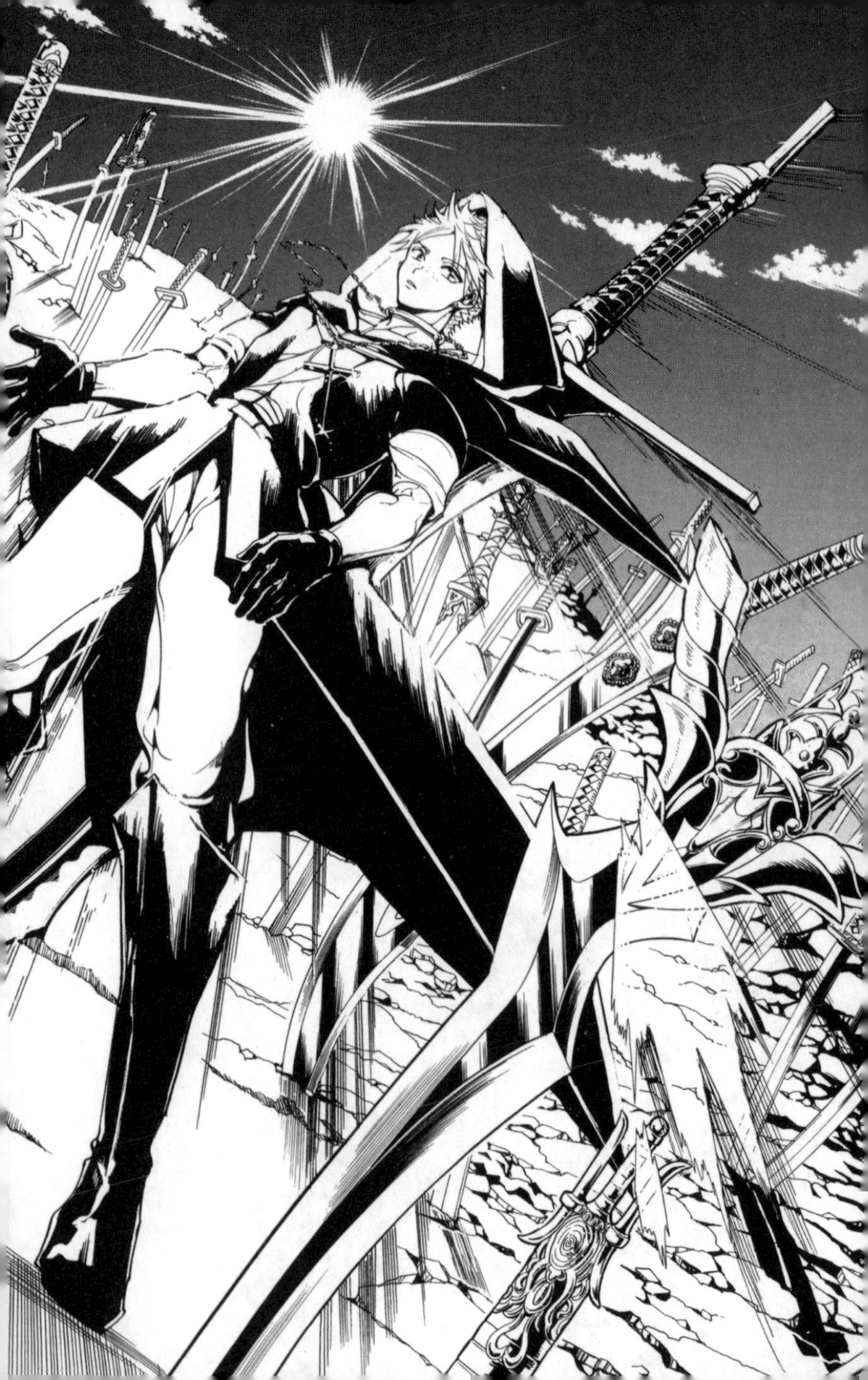

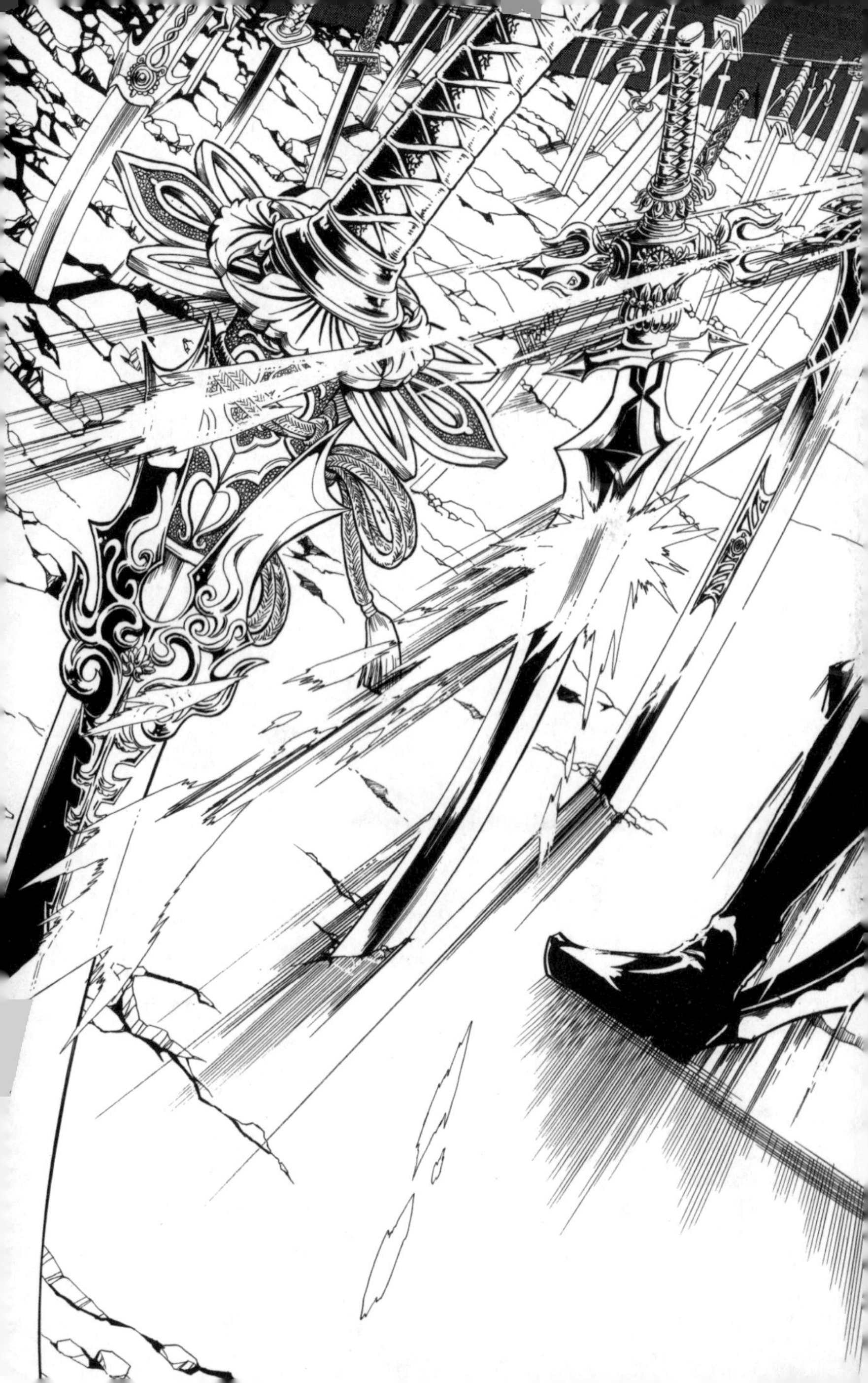

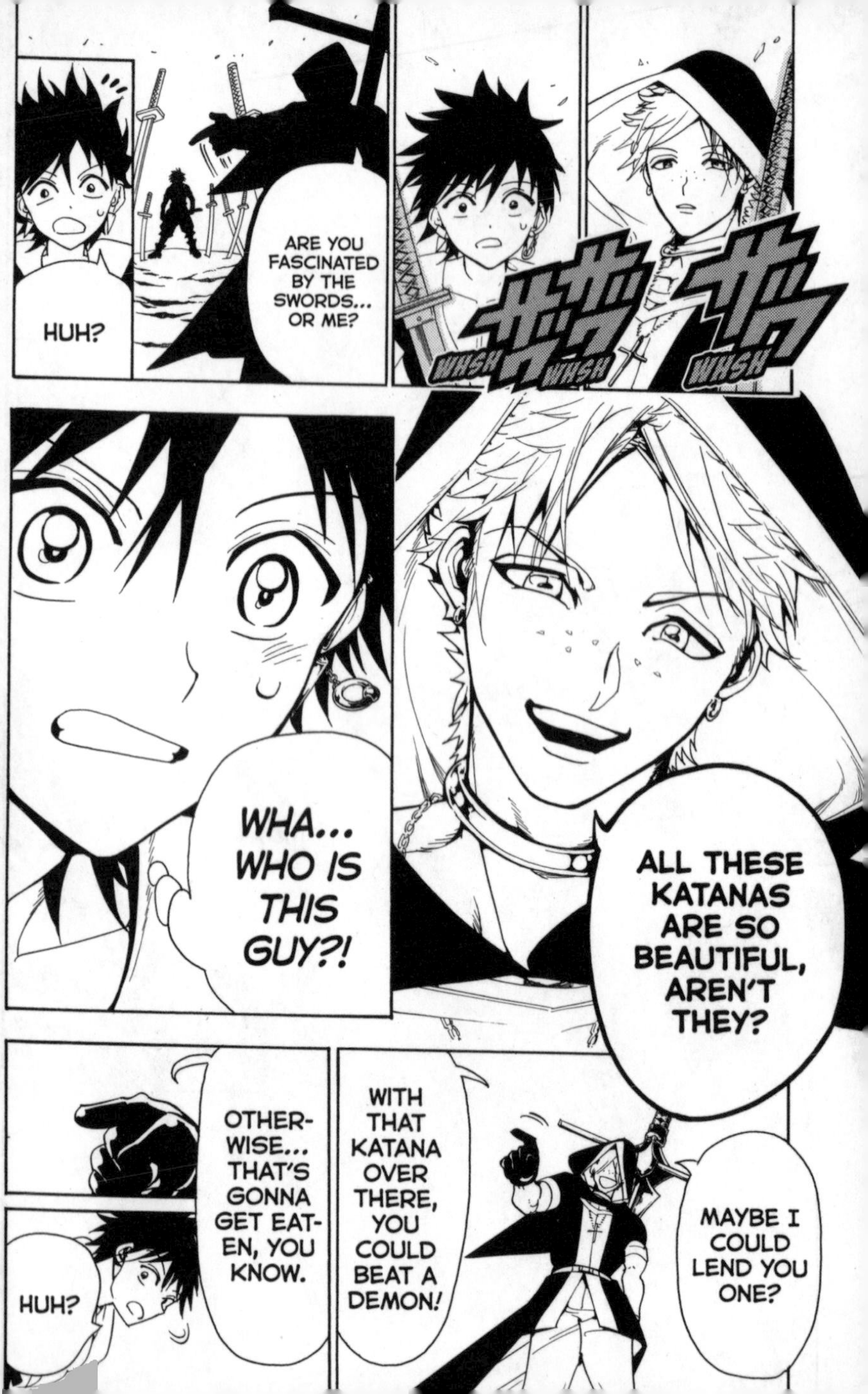
WHSH
WHSH
WHSH
ARE YOU FASCINATED BY THE SWORDS... OR ME?
HUH?
ALL THESE KATANAS ARE SO BEAUTIFUL, AREN'T THEY?
WHA... WHO IS THIS GUY?!
MAYBE I COULD LEND YOU ONE?
WITH THAT KATANA OVER THERE, YOU COULD BEAT A DEMON!
OTHERWISE... THAT'S GONNA GET EATEN, YOU KNOW.
HUH?

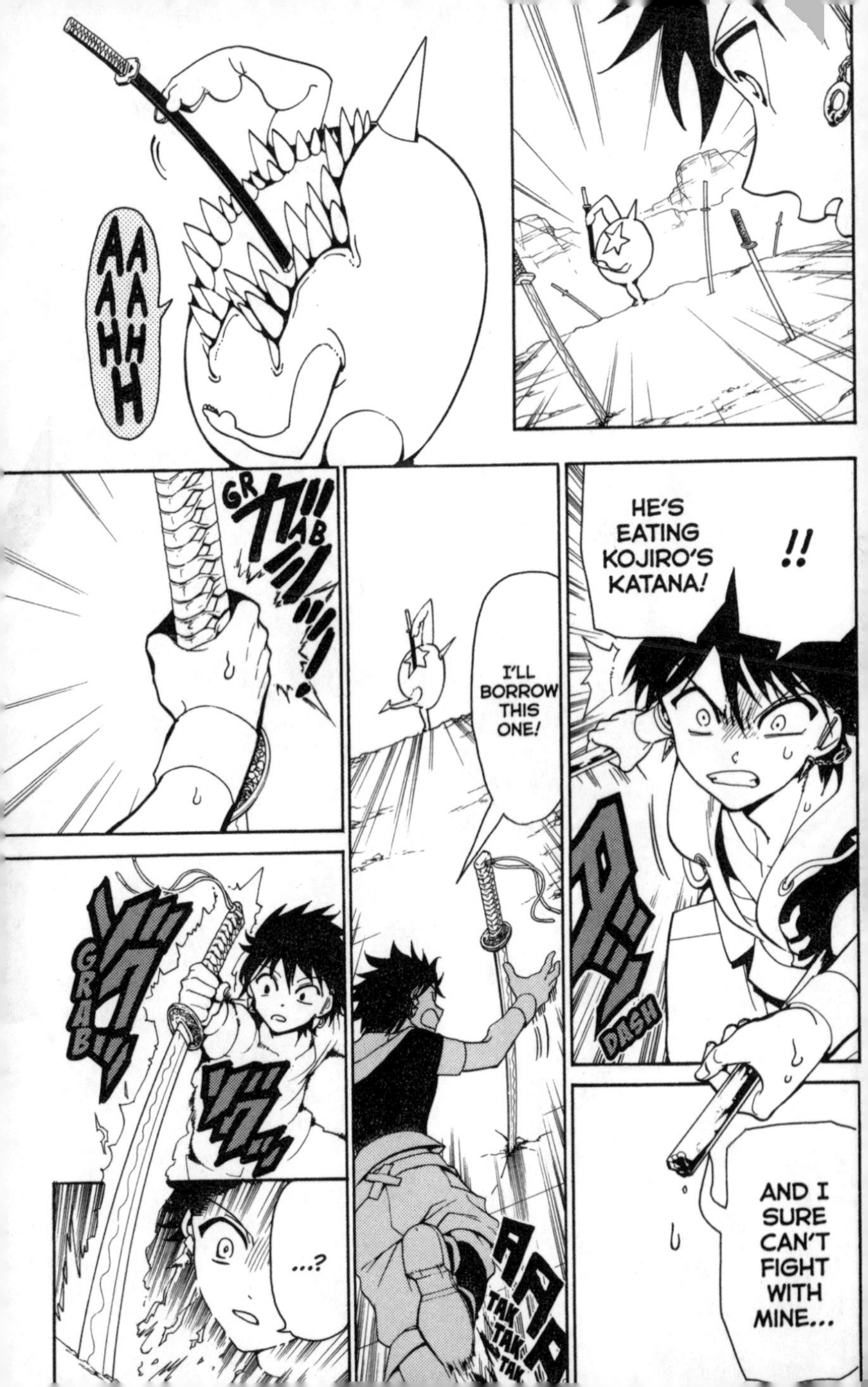
AAAAHHH
HE'S EATING KOJIRO'S KATANA!
!!
DASH
AND I SURE CAN'T FIGHT WITH MINE...
I'LL BORROW THIS ONE!
TAK TAK TAK TAK
GRAB
GRAB!!
...?

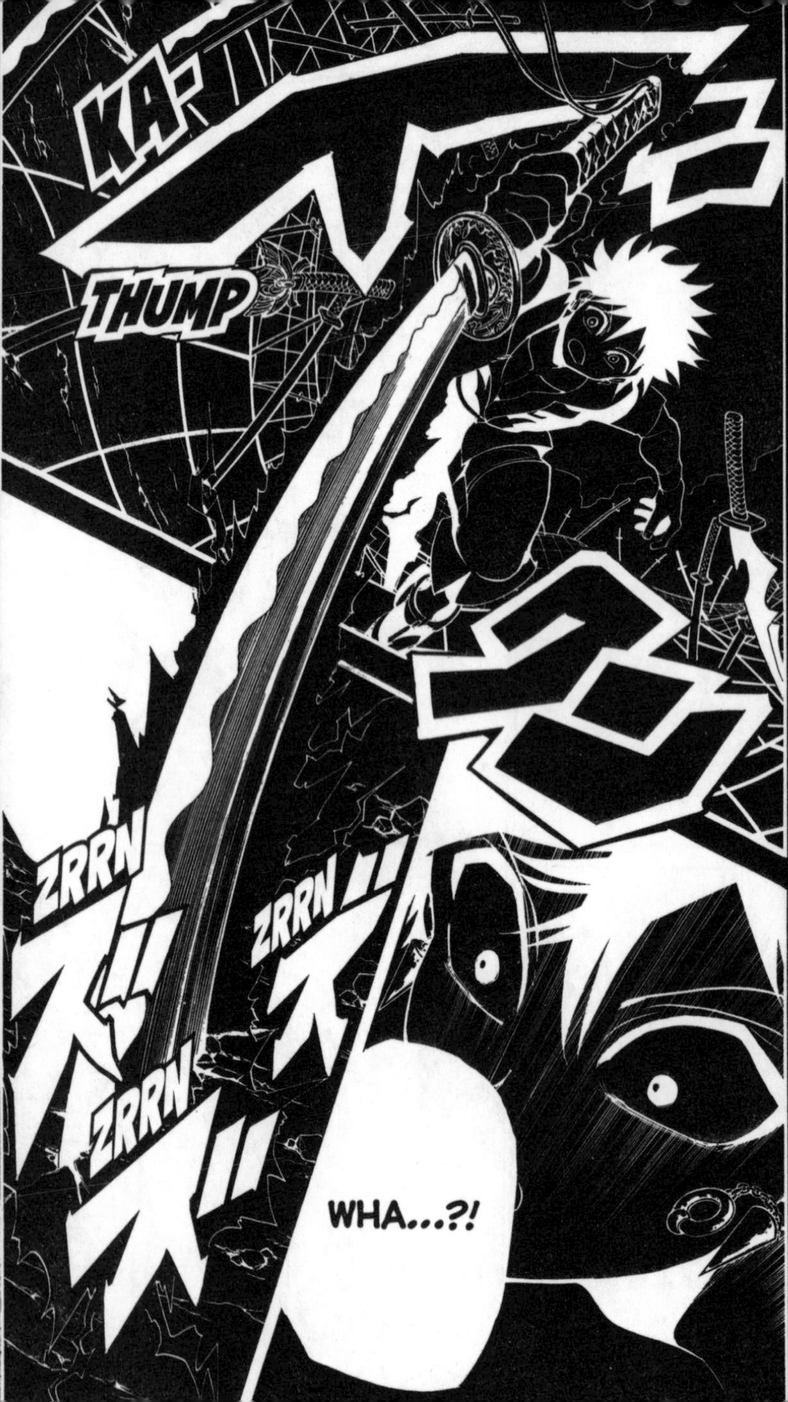
KA-
THUMP
ZRRN
ZRRN
ZRRN
WHA...?!

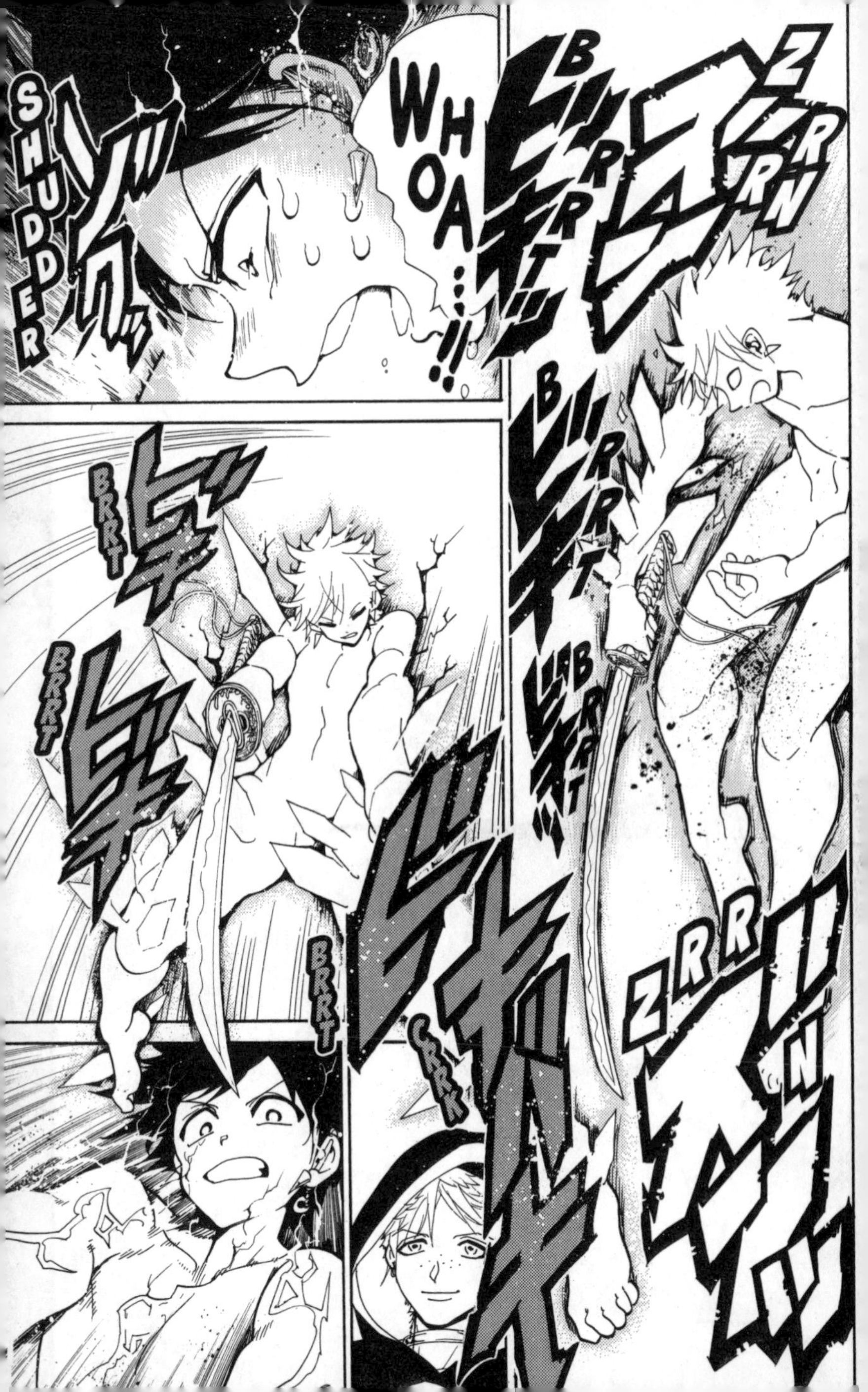
ZRRN
BRRT
BRRRT
BRRT
ZRRRN
WHOA...!!
SHUDDER
BRRT
BRRT
BRRT
CRRRK

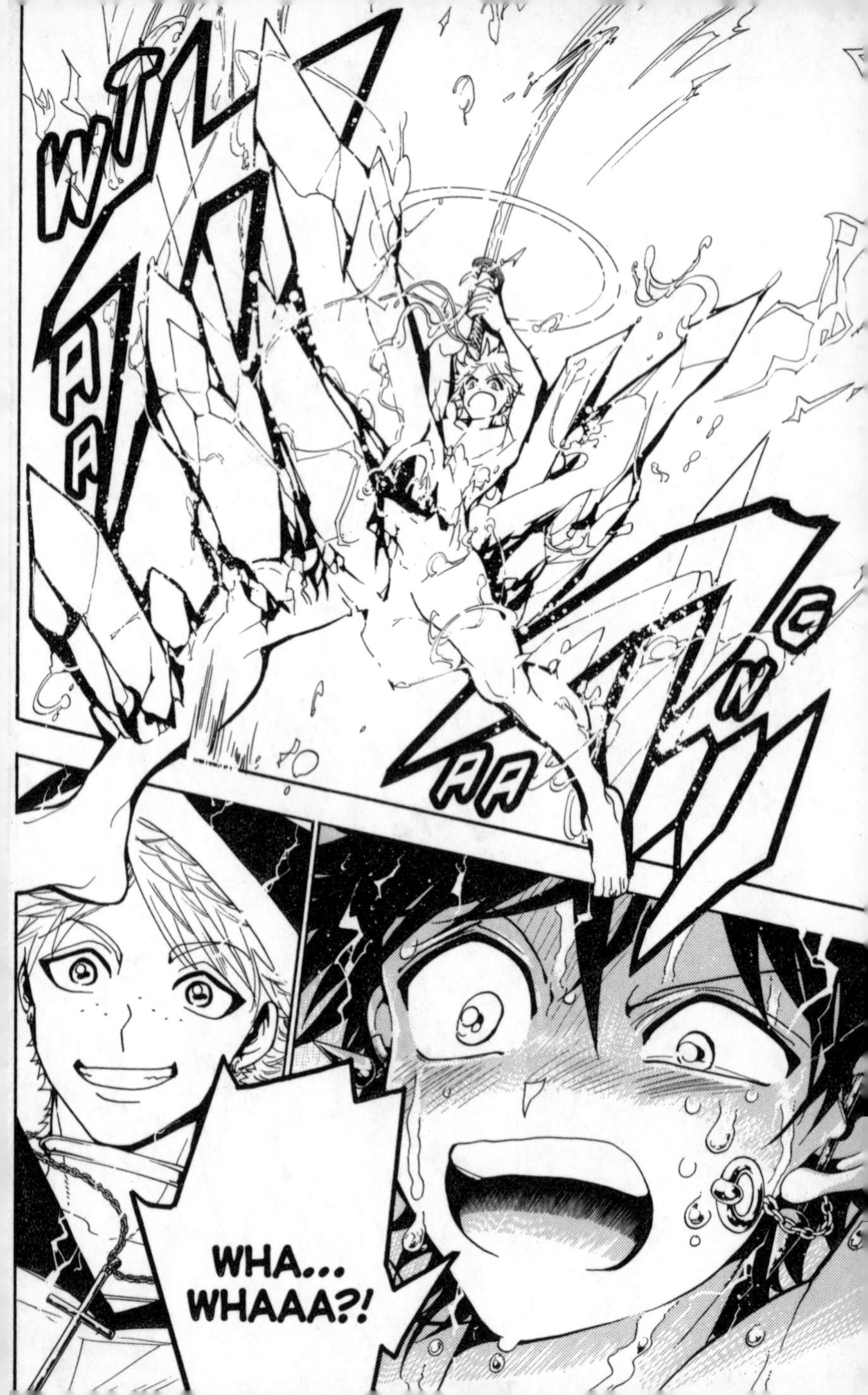
WHA...
WHAAA?!

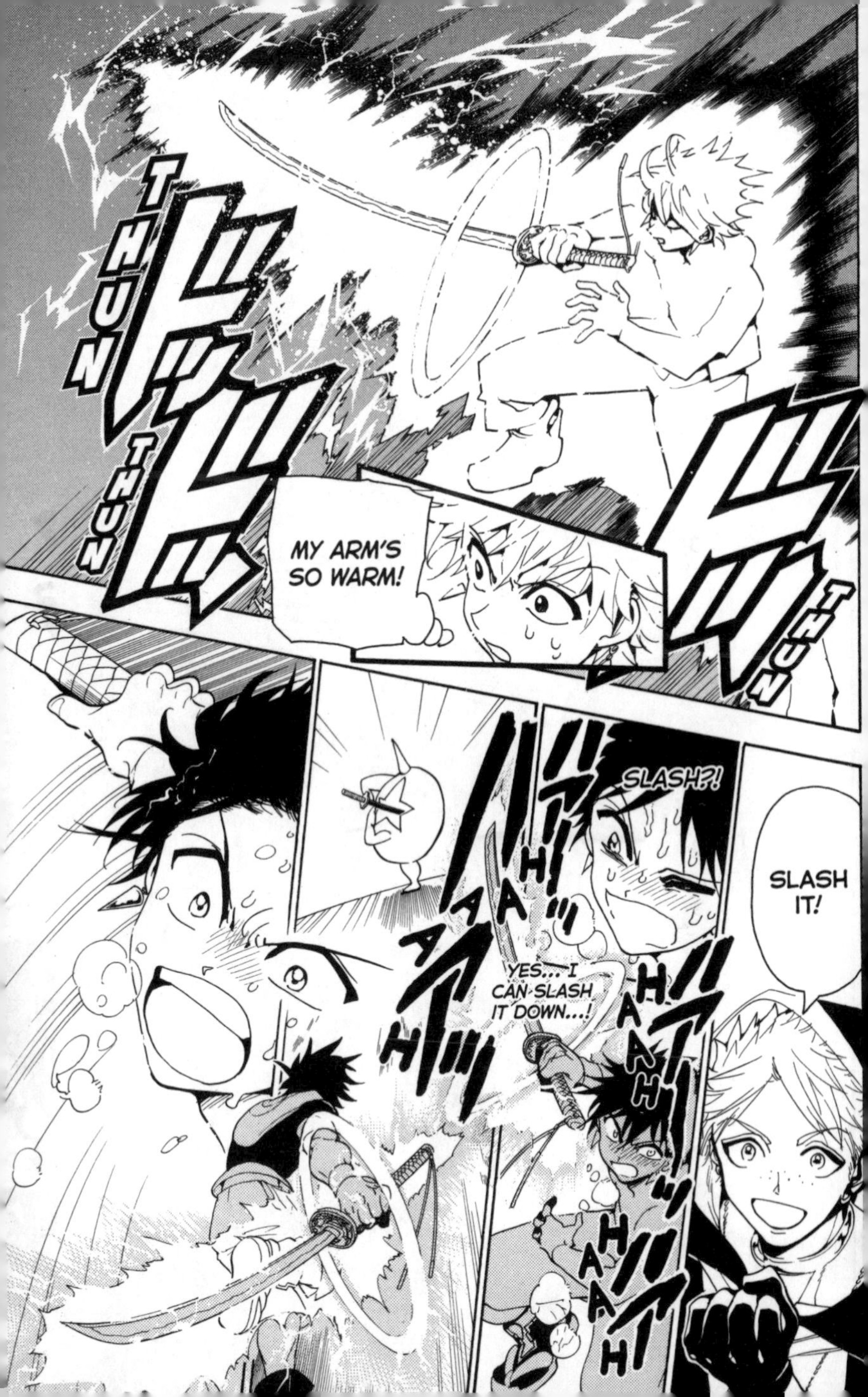
THUN
MY ARM'S SO WARM!
THUN THUN
SLASH IT!
SLASH?!
HAAAH
YES... I CAN SLASH IT DOWN...!
HAAH
HAAAH

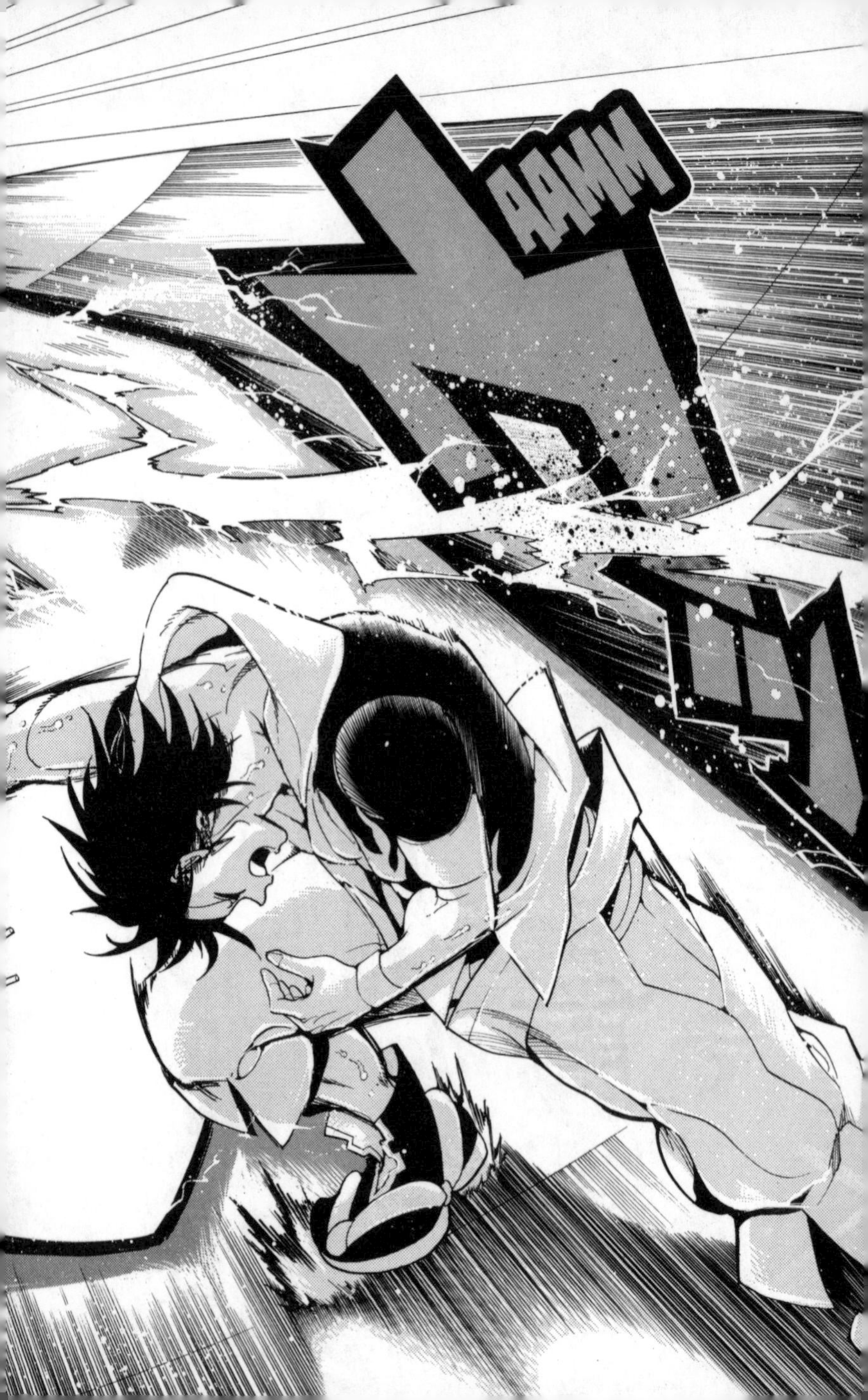
AAMM

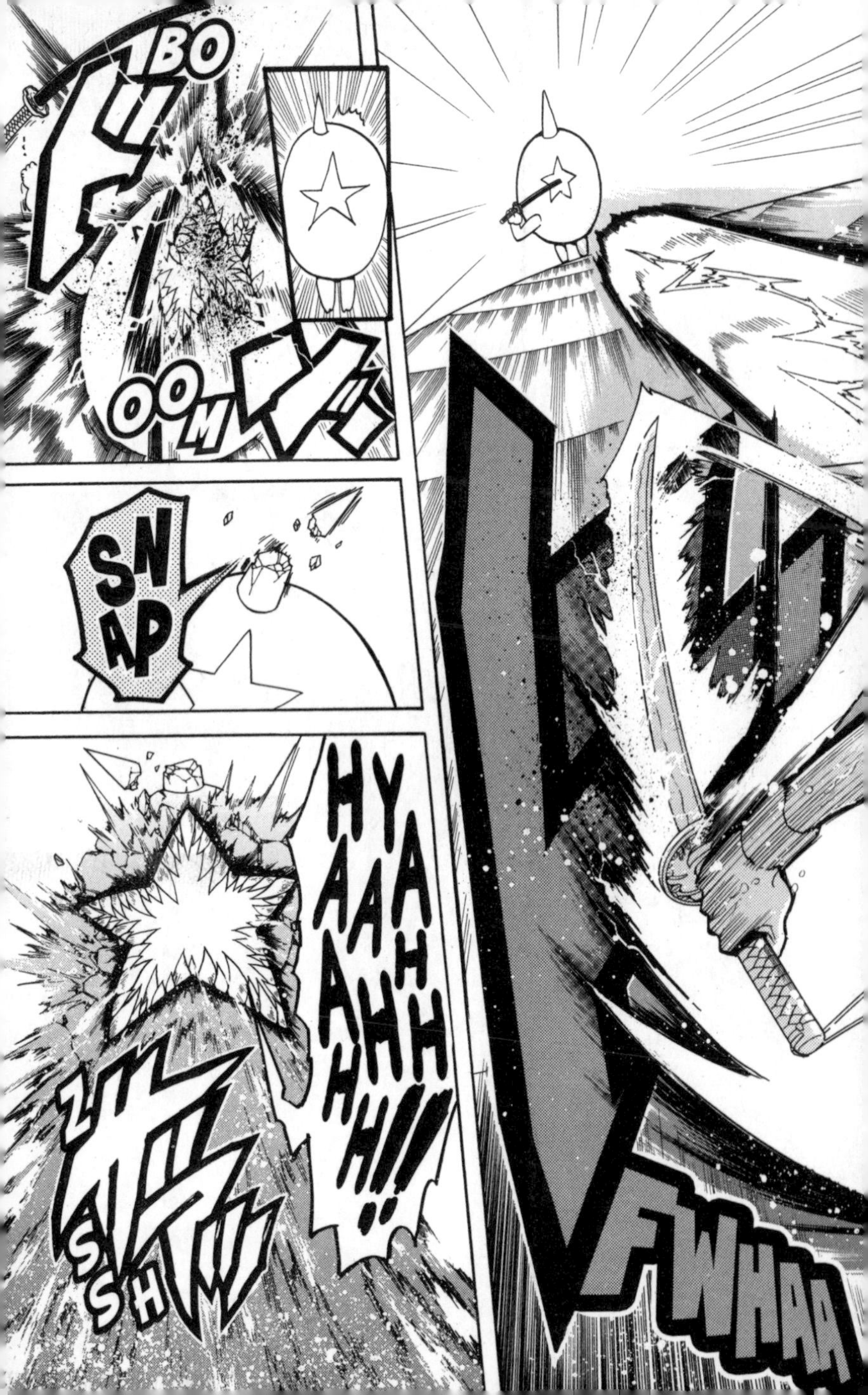
FWHAAA
BOOM
SNAP
HYAAAAHHHHH!!
ZSSH

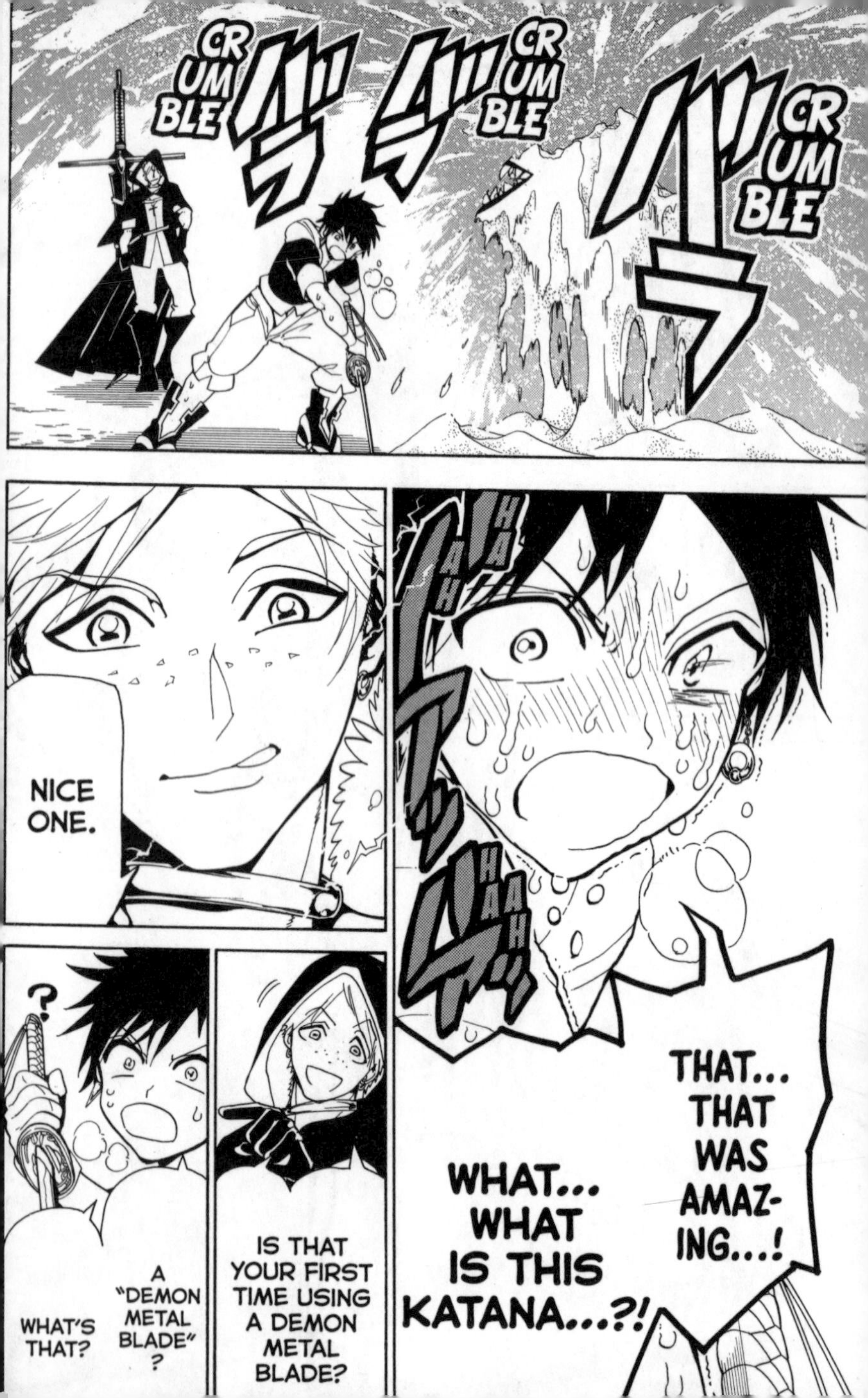
CRUMBLE
CRUMBLE
CRUMBLE
THAT... THAT WAS AMAZING...!
WHAT... WHAT IS THIS KATANA...?!
NICE ONE.
IS THAT YOUR FIRST TIME USING A DEMON METAL BLADE?
A "DEMON METAL BLADE"?
WHAT'S THAT?

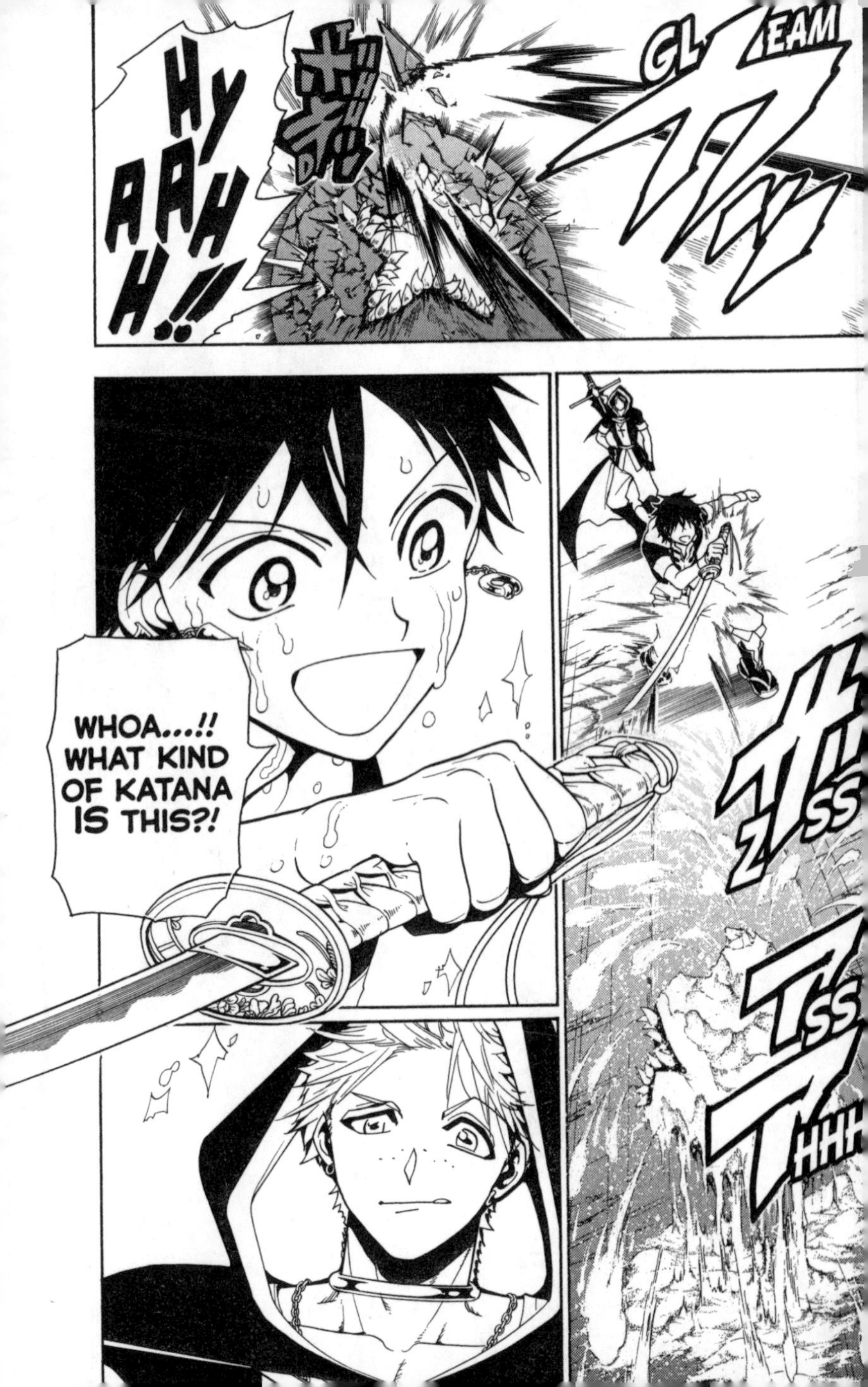
GLEAM
HYAAHHH!!
ZSS
TSS
THHH
WHOA...!! WHAT KIND OF KATANA IS THIS?!

CHAPTER 20: THE NAMELESS DOG

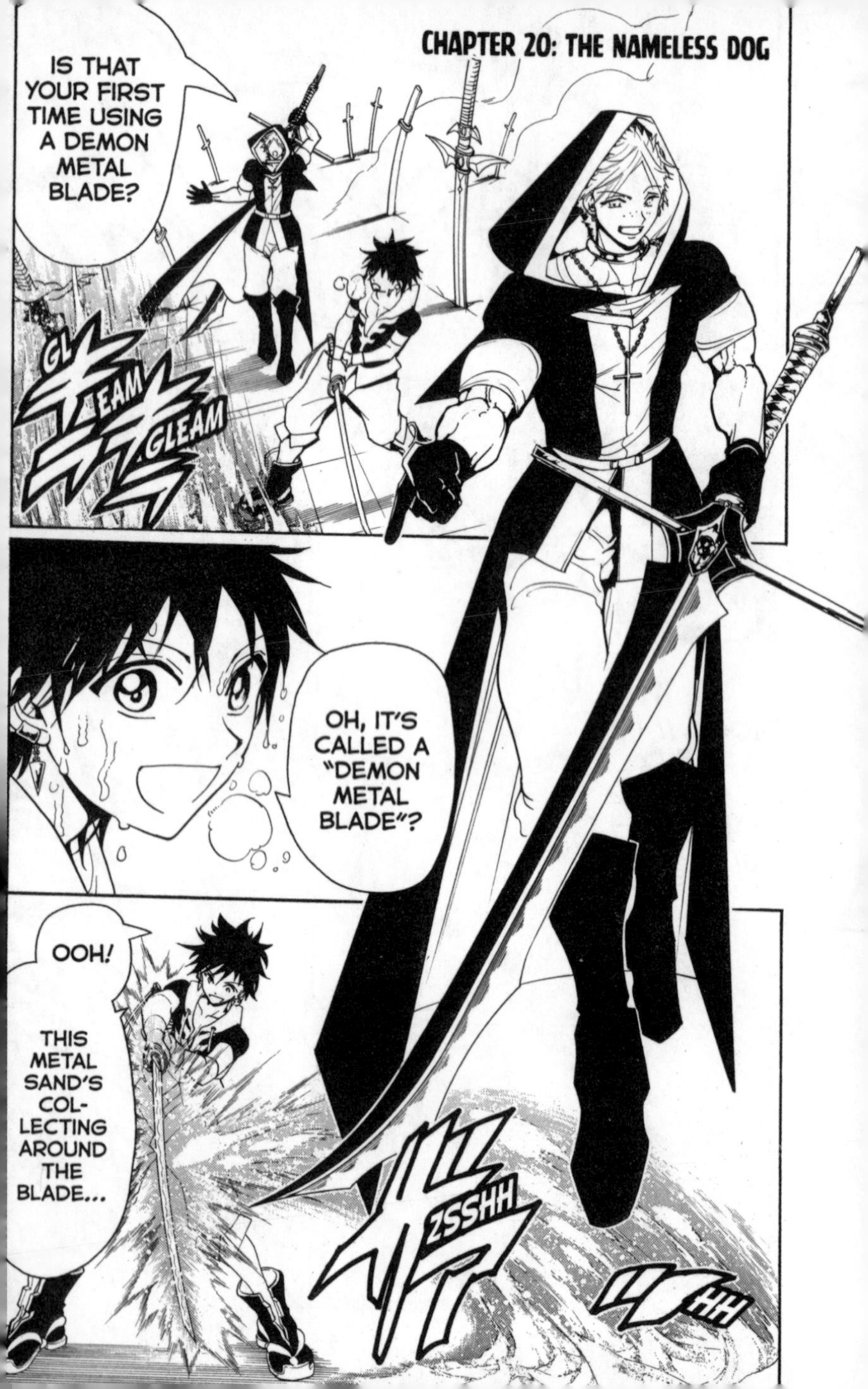
IS THAT YOUR FIRST TIME USING A DEMON METAL BLADE?
GLEAM GLEAM
OH, IT'S CALLED A "DEMON METAL BLADE"?
OOH!
THIS METAL SAND'S COL-LECTING AROUND THE BLADE...
ZSSHH
HH

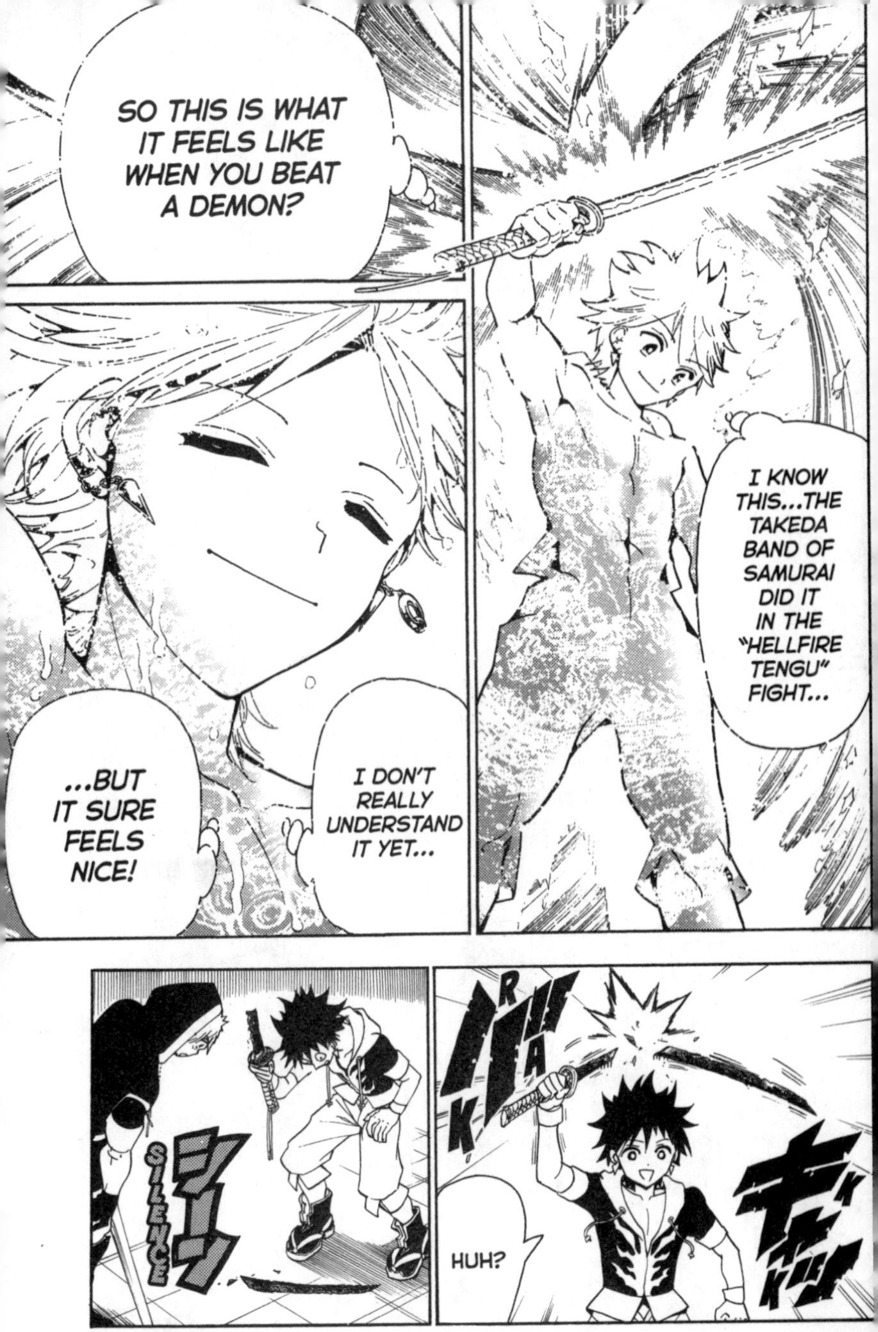
I KNOW THIS...THE TAKEDA BAND OF SAMURAI DID IT IN THE "HELLFIRE TENGU" FIGHT...
SO THIS IS WHAT IT FEELS LIKE WHEN YOU BEAT A DEMON?
I DON'T REALLY UNDERSTAND IT YET...
...BUT IT SURE FEELS NICE!
HUH?
SILENCE

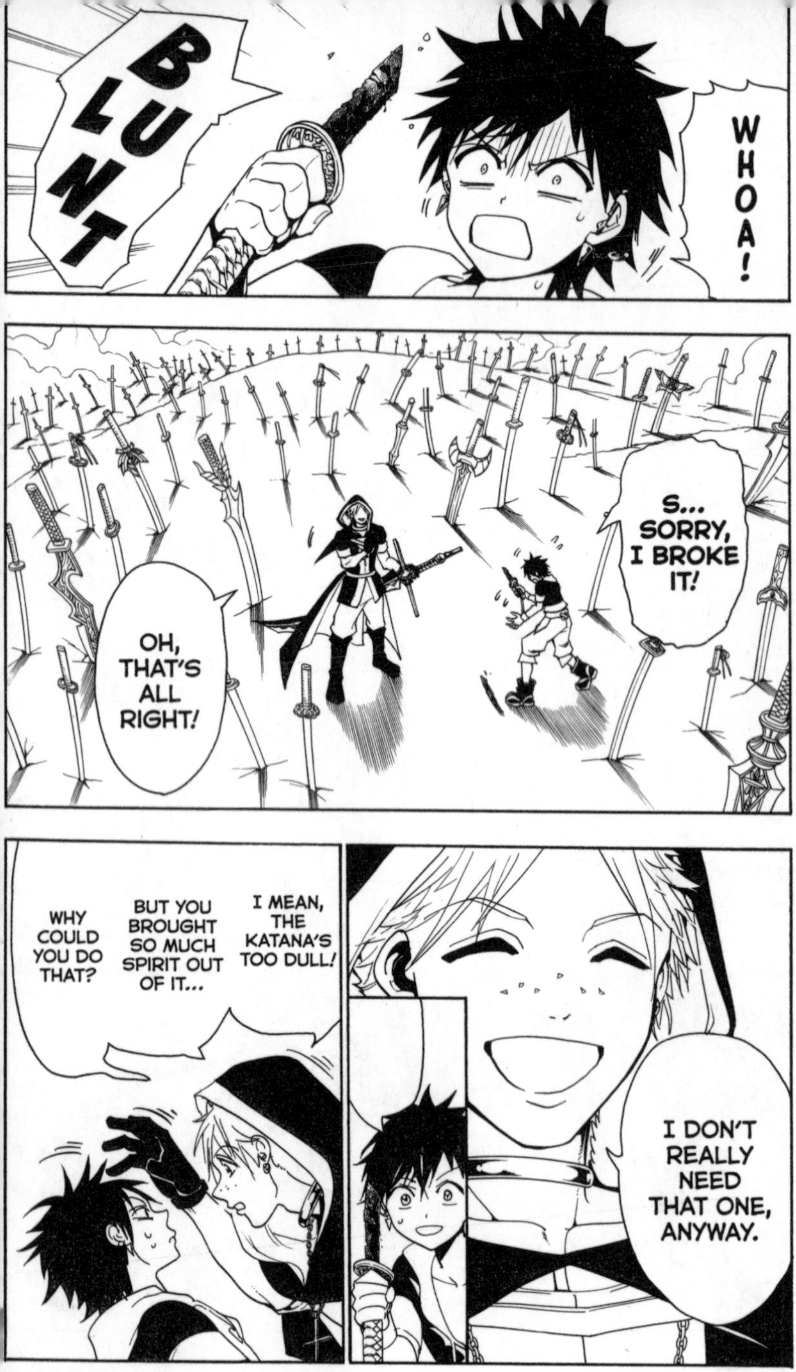
WHOA!
BLUNT
S... SORRY, I BROKE IT!
OH, THAT'S ALL RIGHT!
I DON'T REALLY NEED THAT ONE, ANYWAY.
I MEAN, THE KATANA'S TOO DULL!
BUT YOU BROUGHT SO MUCH SPIRIT OUT OF IT...
WHY COULD YOU DO THAT?

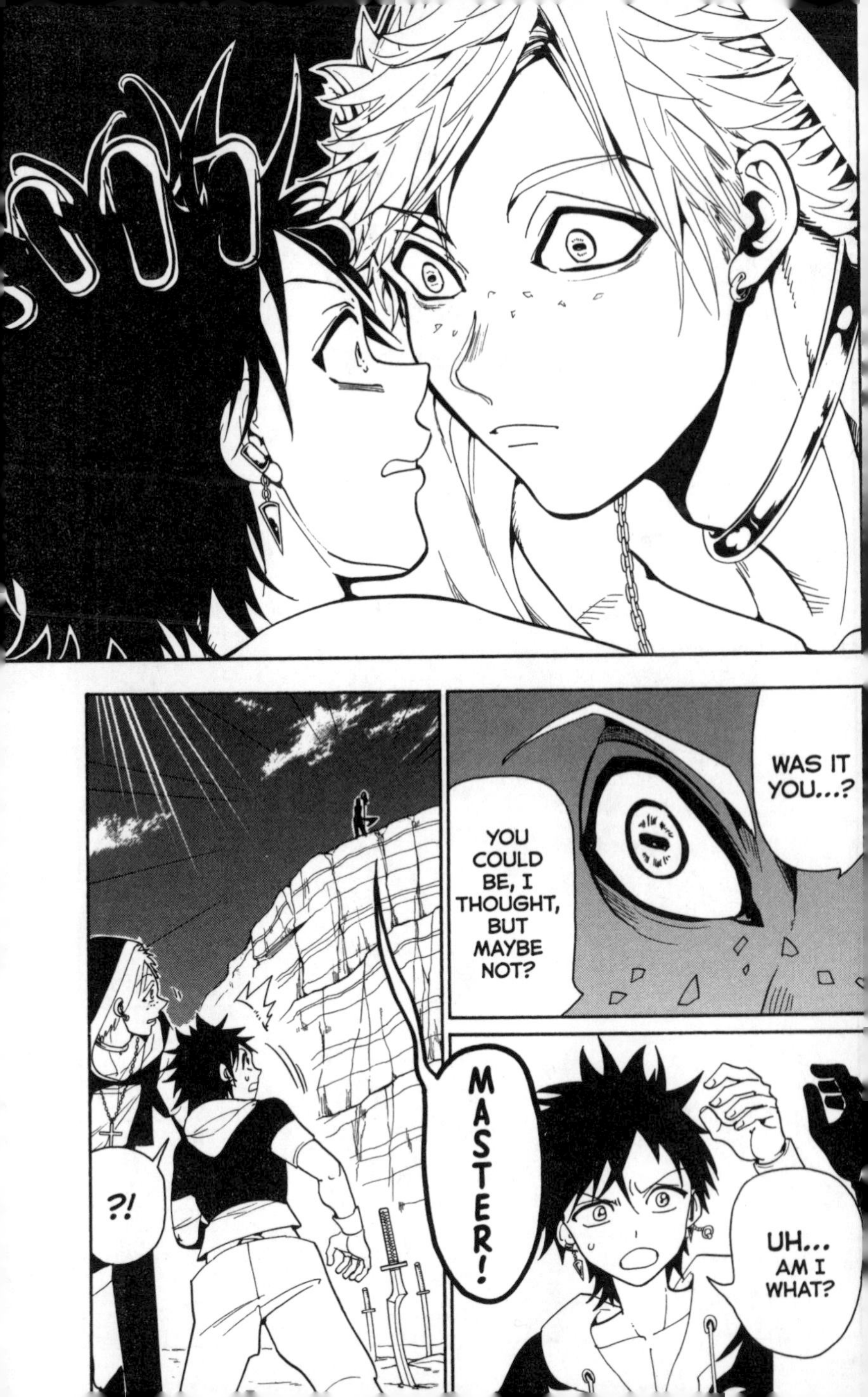
WAS IT YOU...?
YOU COULD BE, I THOUGHT, BUT MAYBE NOT?
UH... AM I WHAT?
MASTER!
?!

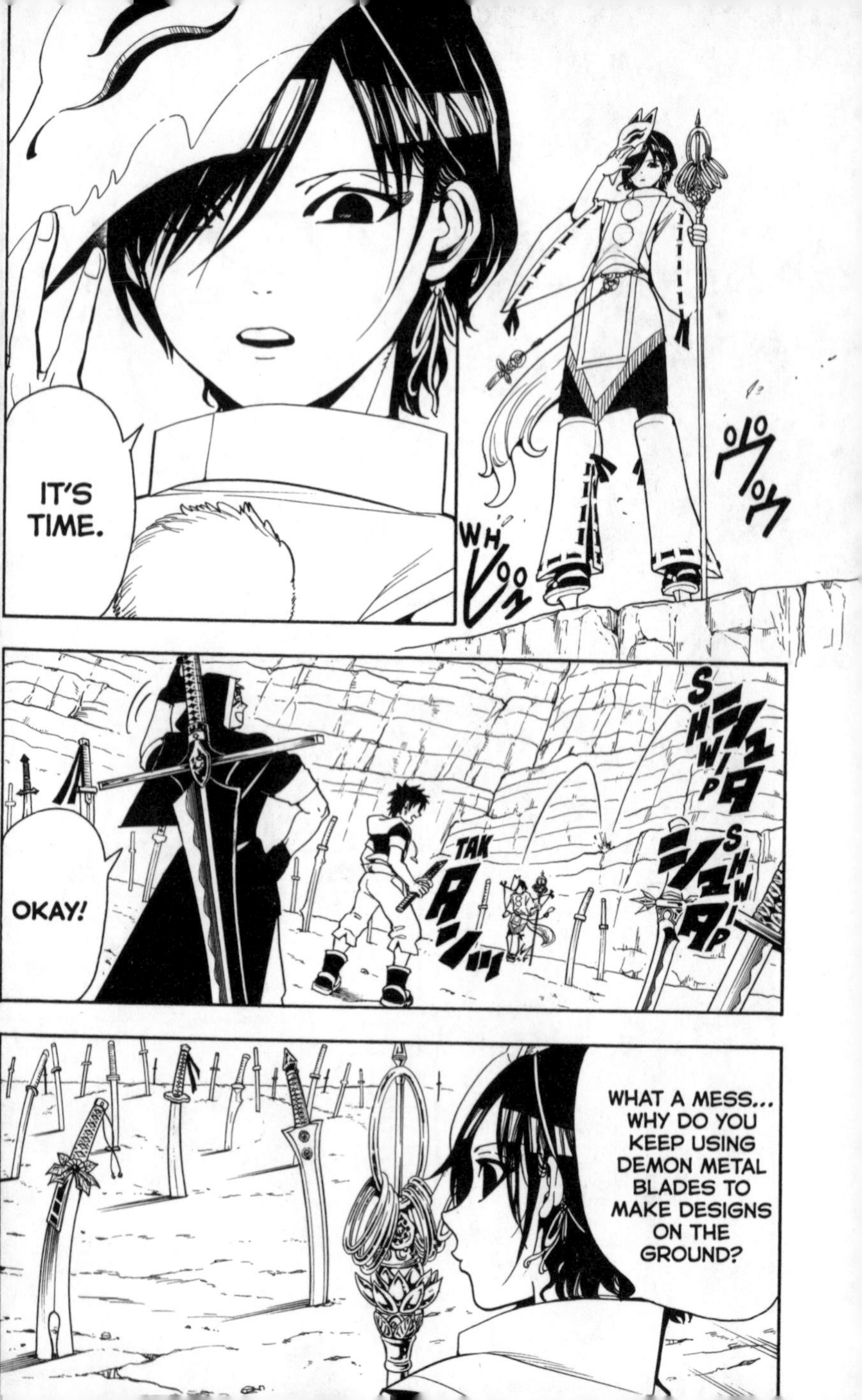
WH
IT'S TIME.
SHWIP
SHWIP
TAK
OKAY!
WHAT A MESS... WHY DO YOU KEEP USING DEMON METAL BLADES TO MAKE DESIGNS ON THE GROUND?

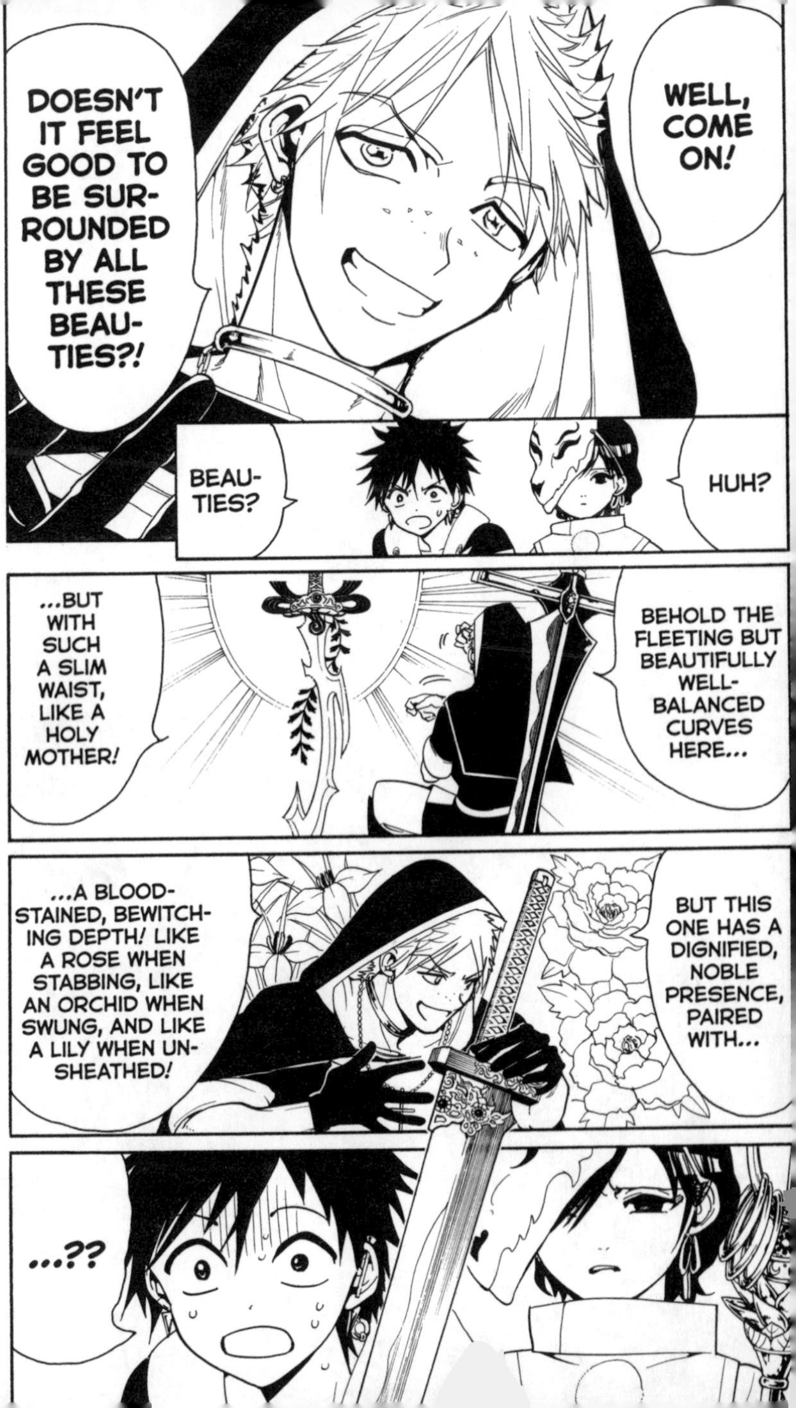
WELL, COME ON!
DOESN'T IT FEEL GOOD TO BE SURROUNDED BY ALL THESE BEAUTIES?!
HUH?
BEAUTIES?
BEHOLD THE FLEETING BUT BEAUTIFULLY WELL-BALANCED CURVES HERE...
...BUT WITH SUCH A SLIM WAIST, LIKE A HOLY MOTHER!
BUT THIS ONE HAS A DIGNIFIED, NOBLE PRESENCE, PAIRED WITH...
...A BLOOD-STAINED, BEWITCHING DEPTH! LIKE A ROSE WHEN STABBING, LIKE AN ORCHID WHEN SWUNG, AND LIKE A LILY WHEN UNSHEATHED!
...??

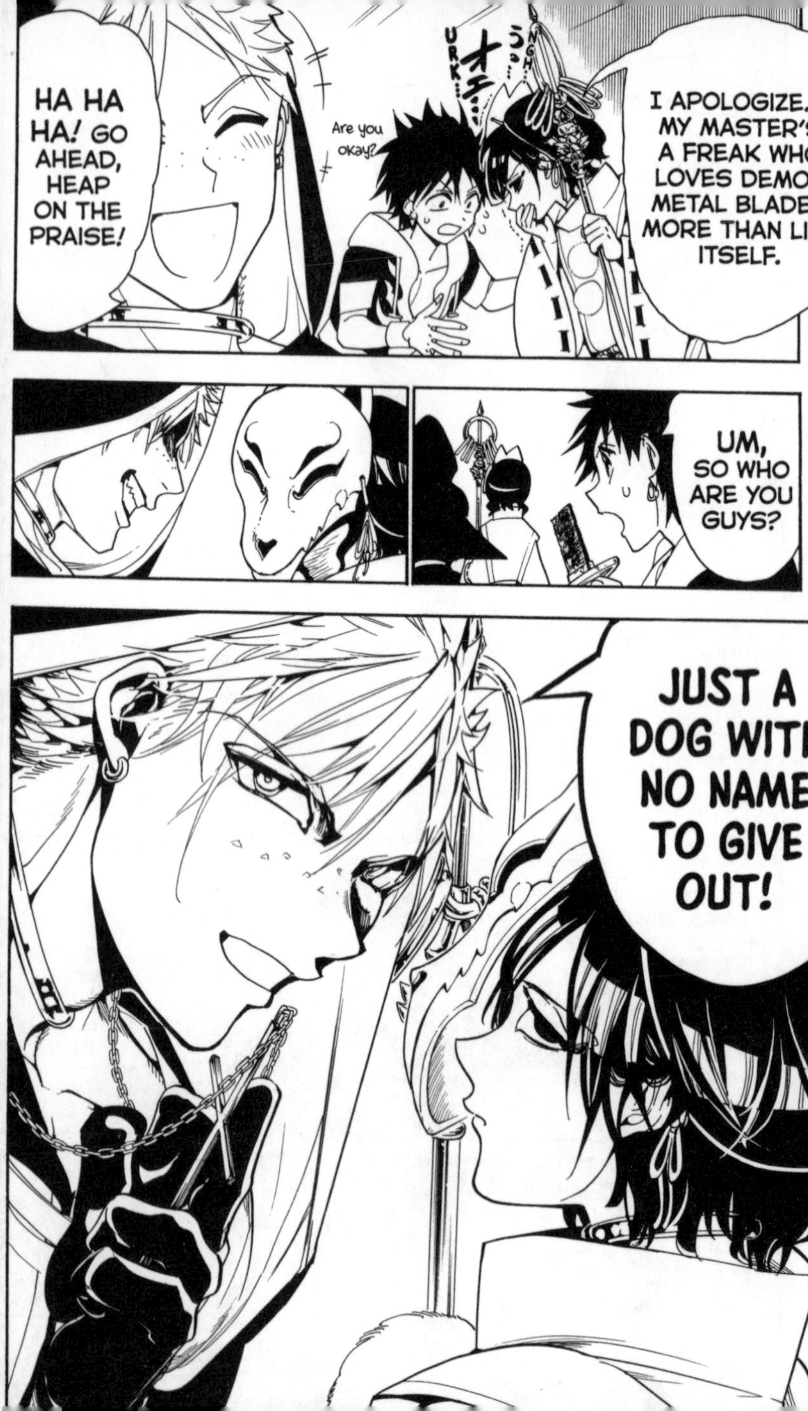
I APOLOGIZE... MY MASTER'S A FREAK WHO LOVES DEMON METAL BLADES MORE THAN LIFE ITSELF.
うっ…
NGH...
オエ…
URK...
Are you okay?
HA HA HA! GO AHEAD, HEAP ON THE PRAISE!
UM, SO WHO ARE YOU GUYS?
JUST A DOG WITH NO NAME TO GIVE OUT!

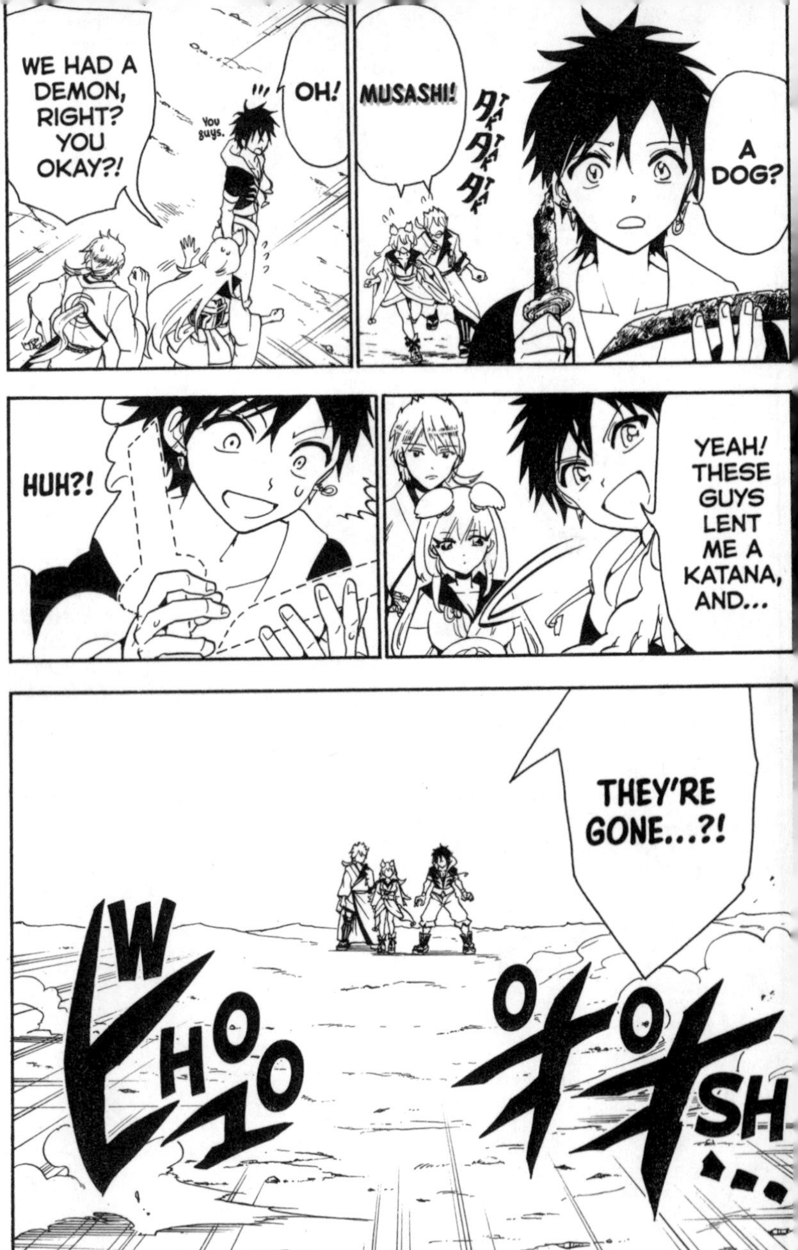

A DOG?
TAK TAK TAK
MUSASHI!
OH!
You guys.
WE HAD A DEMON, RIGHT? YOU OKAY?!
YEAH! THESE GUYS LENT ME A KATANA, AND...
HUH?!
THEY'RE GONE...?!
WHOOOOOSH...

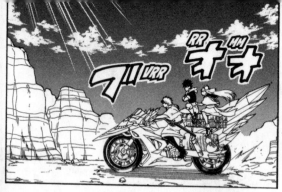

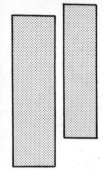

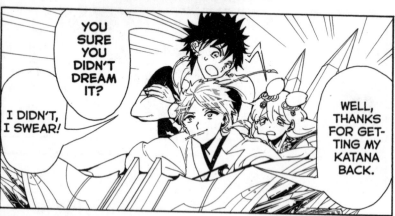

RR MM
VRR
WELL, THANKS FOR GET-TING MY KATANA BACK.
YOU SURE YOU DIDN'T DREAM IT?
I DIDN'T, I SWEAR!
THAT SWORD WAS JUST SO AWE-SOME.
IT WAS LIKE...
KRAK

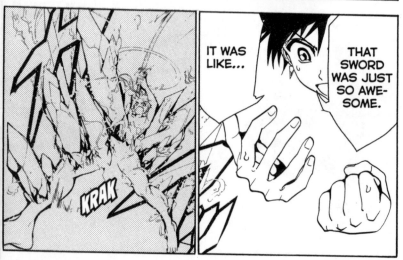

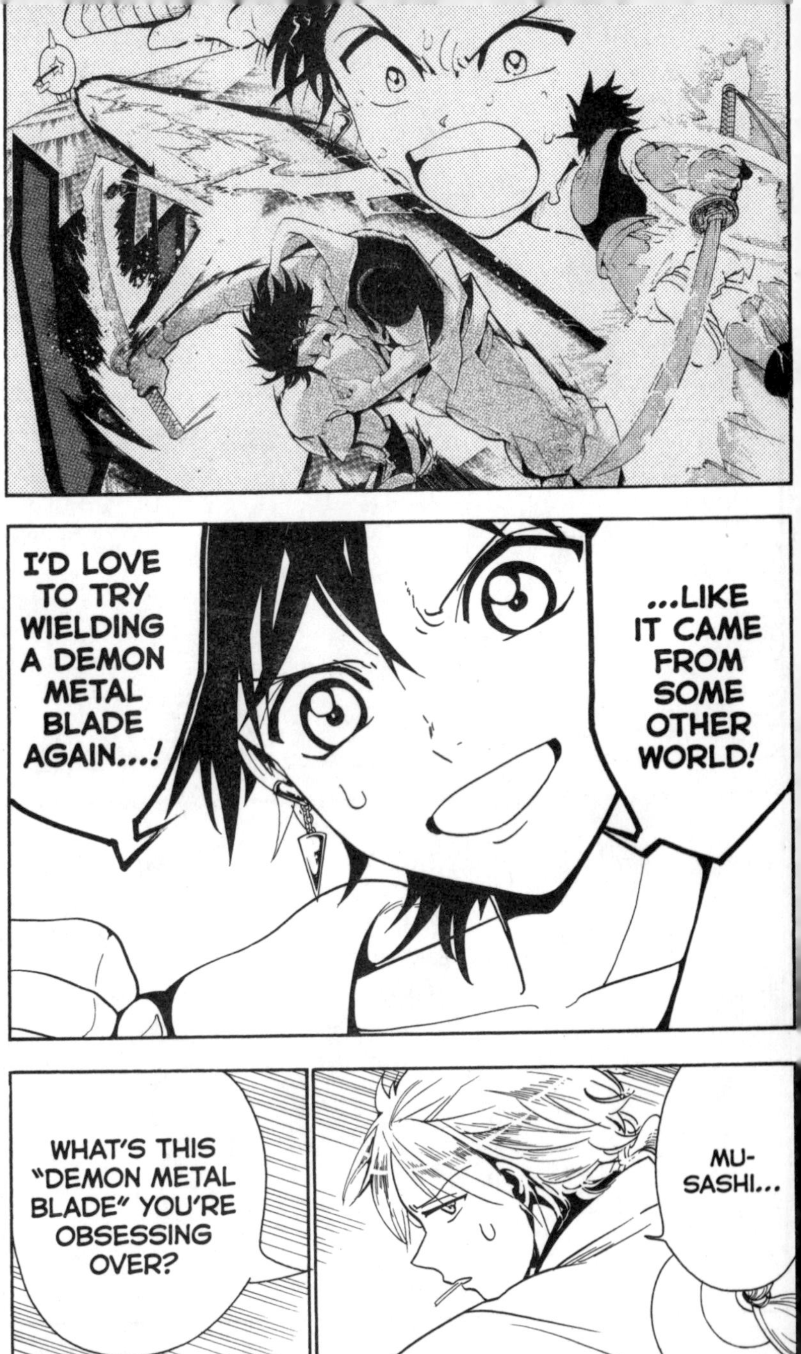
...LIKE IT CAME FROM SOME OTHER WORLD!
I'D LOVE TO TRY WIELDING A DEMON METAL BLADE AGAIN...!
MU-SASHI...
WHAT'S THIS "DEMON METAL BLADE" YOU'RE OBSESSING OVER?

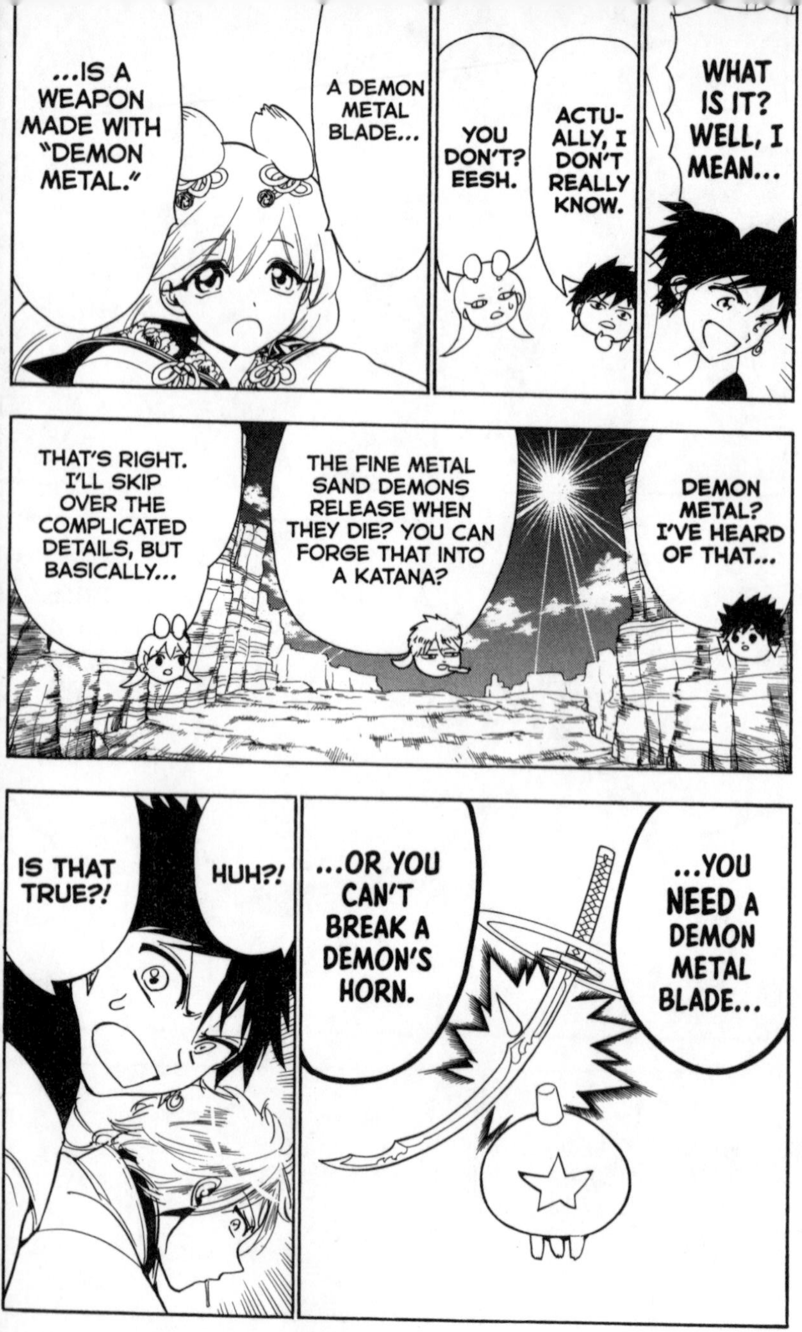
WHAT IS IT? WELL, I MEAN...
ACTU-ALLY, I DON'T REALLY KNOW.
YOU DON'T? EESH.
A DEMON METAL BLADE...
...IS A WEAPON MADE WITH "DEMON METAL."
DEMON METAL? I'VE HEARD OF THAT...
THE FINE METAL SAND DEMONS RELEASE WHEN THEY DIE? YOU CAN FORGE THAT INTO A KATANA?
THAT'S RIGHT. I'LL SKIP OVER THE COMPLICATED DETAILS, BUT BASICALLY...
...YOU NEED A DEMON METAL BLADE...
...OR YOU CAN'T BREAK A DEMON'S HORN.
HUH?!
IS THAT TRUE?!

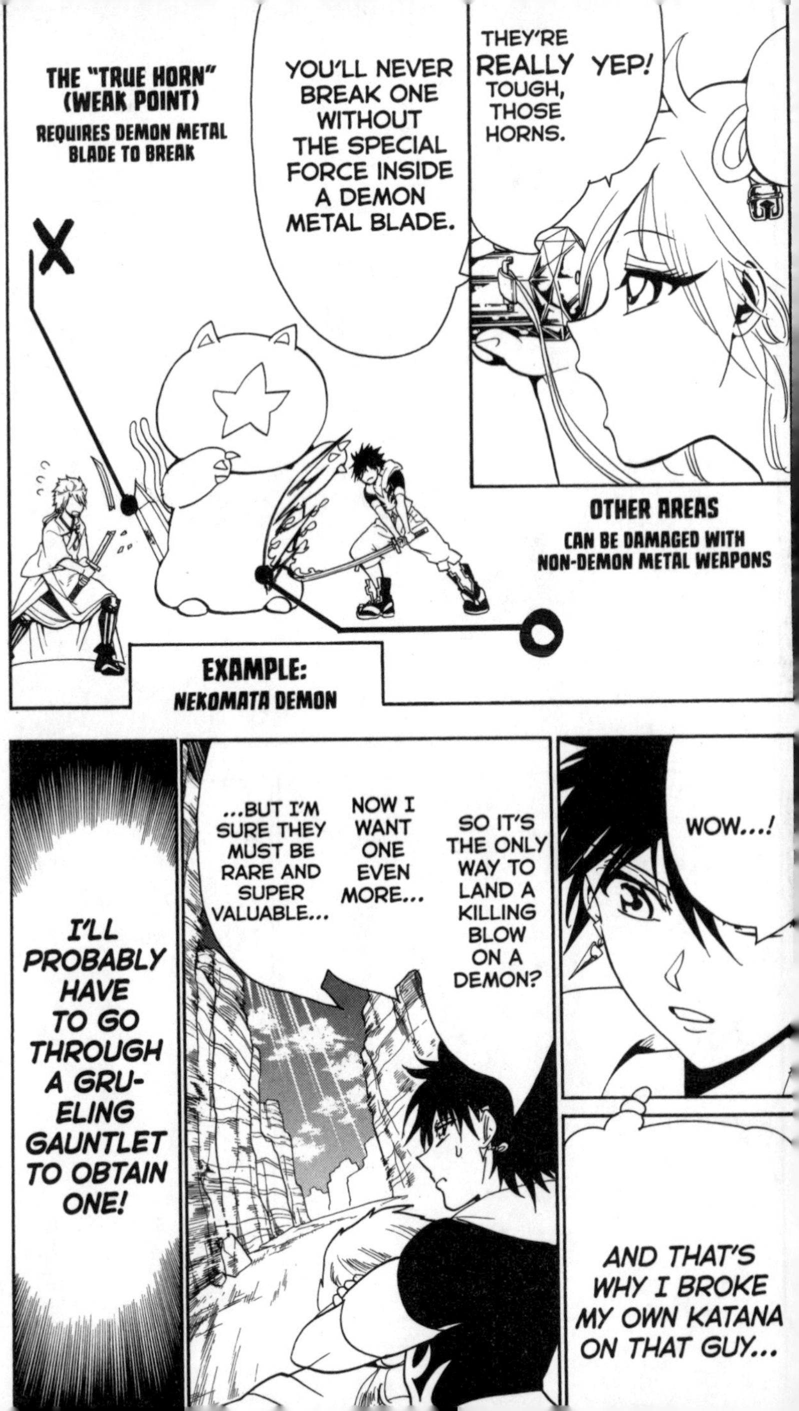

YEP!
THEY'RE REALLY TOUGH, THOSE HORNS.
YOU'LL NEVER BREAK ONE WITHOUT THE SPECIAL FORCE INSIDE A DEMON METAL BLADE.
THE "TRUE HORN" (WEAK POINT)
REQUIRES DEMON METAL BLADE TO BREAK
OTHER AREAS
CAN BE DAMAGED WITH NON-DEMON METAL WEAPONS
EXAMPLE:
NEKOMATA DEMON
WOW...!
AND THAT'S WHY I BROKE MY OWN KATANA ON THAT GUY...
SO IT'S THE ONLY WAY TO LAND A KILLING BLOW ON A DEMON?
NOW I WANT ONE EVEN MORE...
...BUT I'M SURE THEY MUST BE RARE AND SUPER VALUABLE...
I'LL PROBABLY HAVE TO GO THROUGH A GRU-ELING GAUNTLET TO OBTAIN ONE!

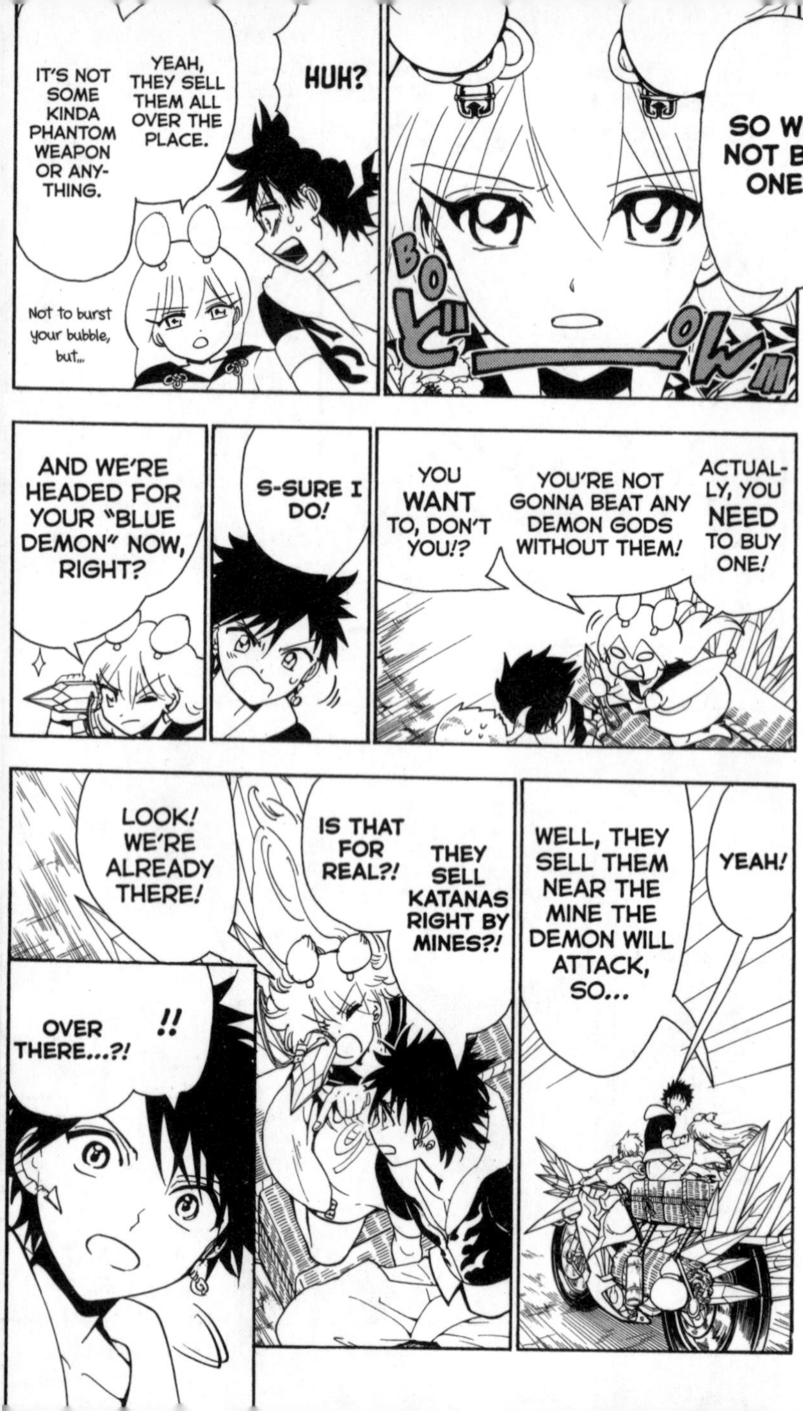
SO WHY NOT BUY ONE?
BOど—OWM
HUH?
YEAH, THEY SELL THEM ALL OVER THE PLACE.
IT'S NOT SOME KINDA PHANTOM WEAPON OR ANY-THING.
Not to burst your bubble, but...
ACTUAL-LY, YOU NEED TO BUY ONE!
YOU'RE NOT GONNA BEAT ANY DEMON GODS WITHOUT THEM!
YOU WANT TO, DON'T YOU!?
S-SURE I DO!
AND WE'RE HEADED FOR YOUR "BLUE DEMON" NOW, RIGHT?
YEAH!
WELL, THEY SELL THEM NEAR THE MINE THE DEMON WILL ATTACK, SO...
THEY SELL KATANAS RIGHT BY MINES?!
IS THAT FOR REAL?!
LOOK! WE'RE ALREADY THERE!
!!
OVER THERE...?!

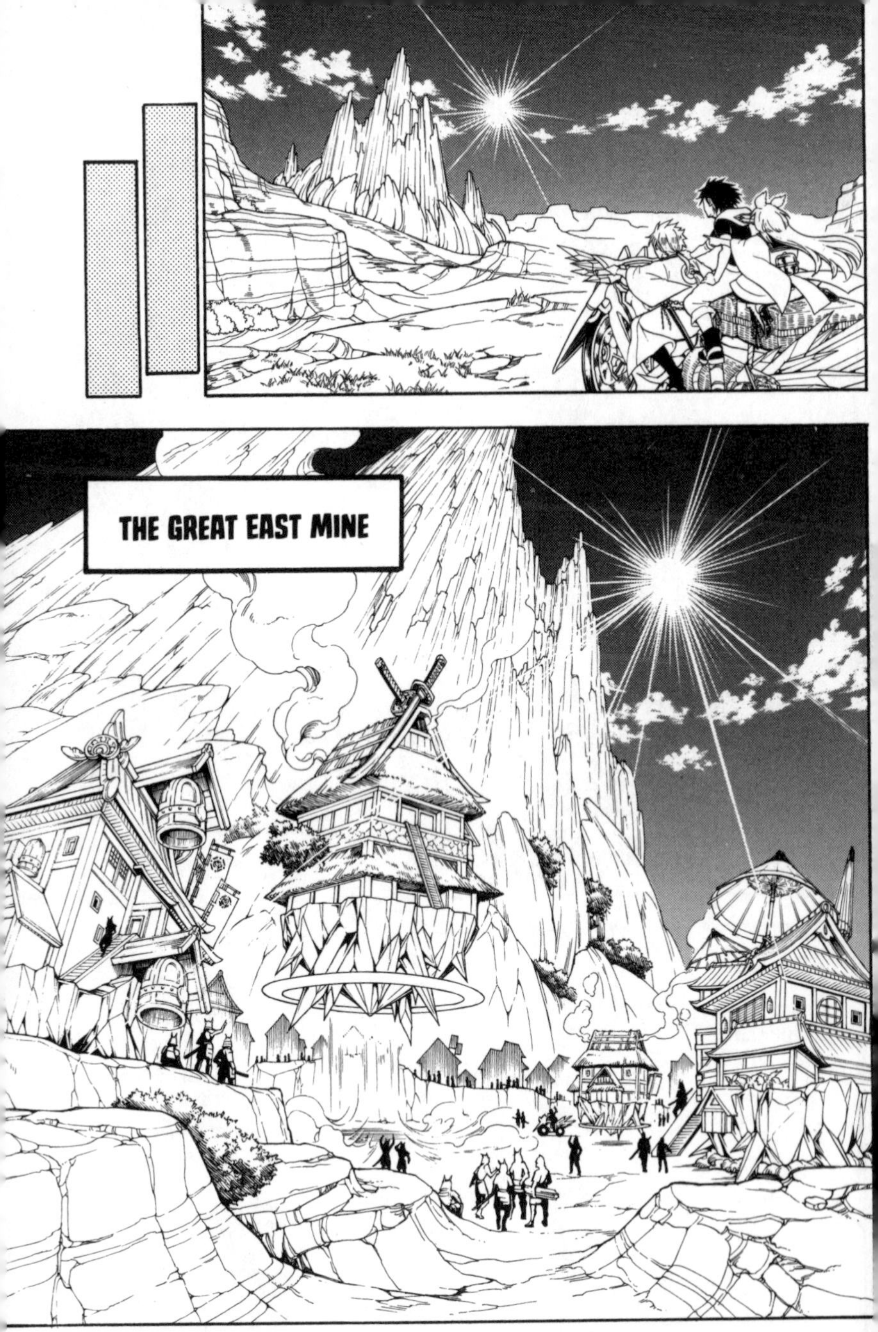
THE GREAT EAST MINE

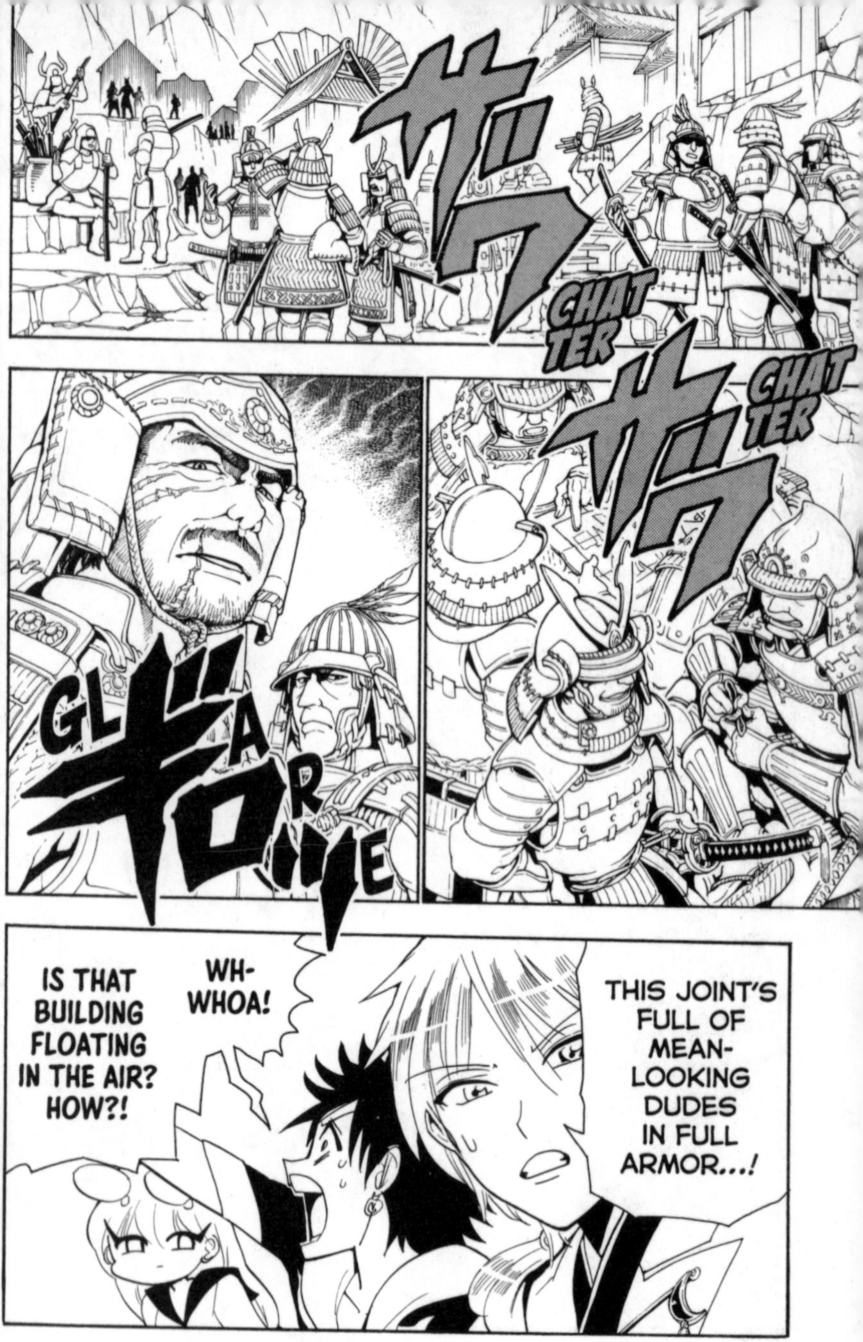
CHATTER
CHATTER
GLARE
THIS JOINT'S FULL OF MEAN-LOOKING DUDES IN FULL ARMOR...!
WH-WHOA!
IS THAT BUILDING FLOATING IN THE AIR? HOW?!

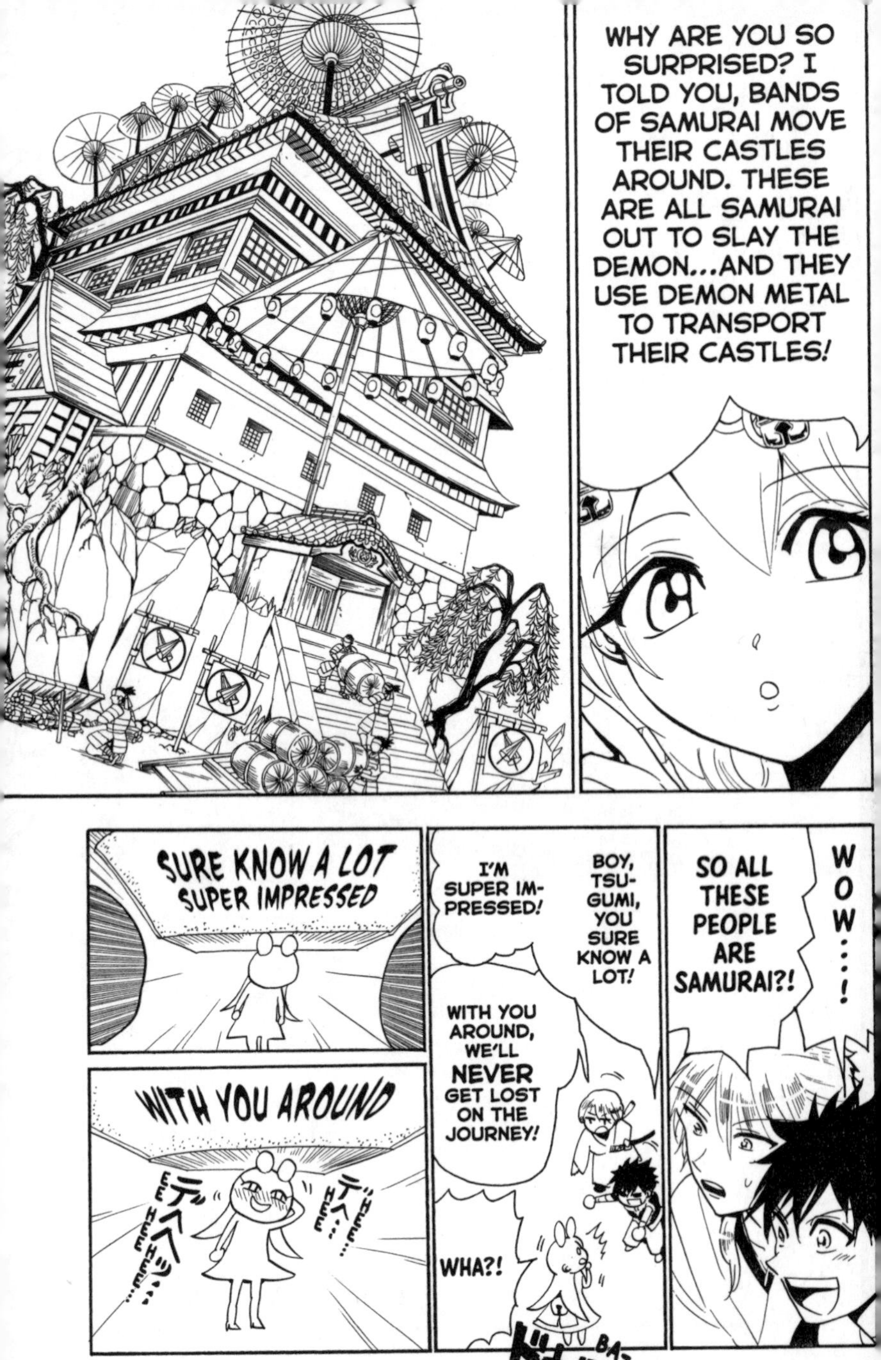
WHY ARE YOU SO SURPRISED? I TOLD YOU, BANDS OF SAMURAI MOVE THEIR CASTLES AROUND. THESE ARE ALL SAMURAI OUT TO SLAY THE DEMON...AND THEY USE DEMON METAL TO TRANSPORT THEIR CASTLES!
WOW...!
SO ALL THESE PEOPLE ARE SAMURAI?!
BOY, TSU-GUMI, YOU SURE KNOW A LOT!
I'M SUPER IM-PRESSED!
WITH YOU AROUND, WE'LL NEVER GET LOST ON THE JOURNEY!
WHA?!
BA-DUM
SURE KNOW A LOT
SUPER IMPRESSED
WITH YOU AROUND
HEE... HEE...
HEE HEE HEE...

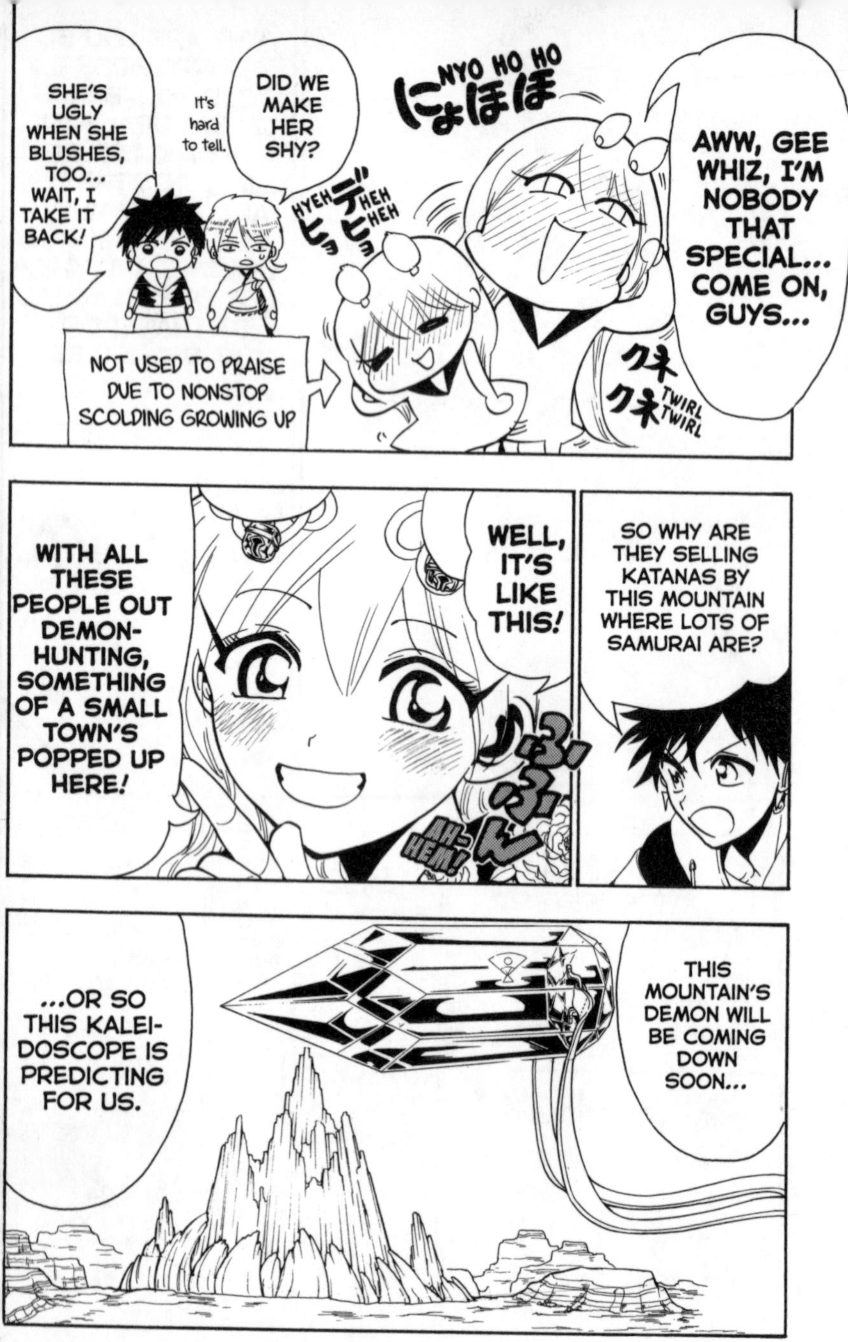
AWW, GEE WHIZ, I'M NOBODY THAT SPECIAL... COME ON, GUYS...
にょほほ NYO HO HO
DID WE MAKE HER SHY?
It's hard to tell.
SHE'S UGLY WHEN SHE BLUSHES, TOO... WAIT, I TAKE IT BACK!
HYEH HEH HEH
NOT USED TO PRAISE DUE TO NONSTOP SCOLDING GROWING UP
クネクネ TWIRL TWIRL
SO WHY ARE THEY SELLING KATANAS BY THIS MOUNTAIN WHERE LOTS OF SAMURAI ARE?
WELL, IT'S LIKE THIS!
WITH ALL THESE PEOPLE OUT DEMON-HUNTING, SOMETHING OF A SMALL TOWN'S POPPED UP HERE!
ふふん AH-HEM!
THIS MOUNTAIN'S DEMON WILL BE COMING DOWN SOON...
...OR SO THIS KALEIDOSCOPE IS PREDICTING FOR US.

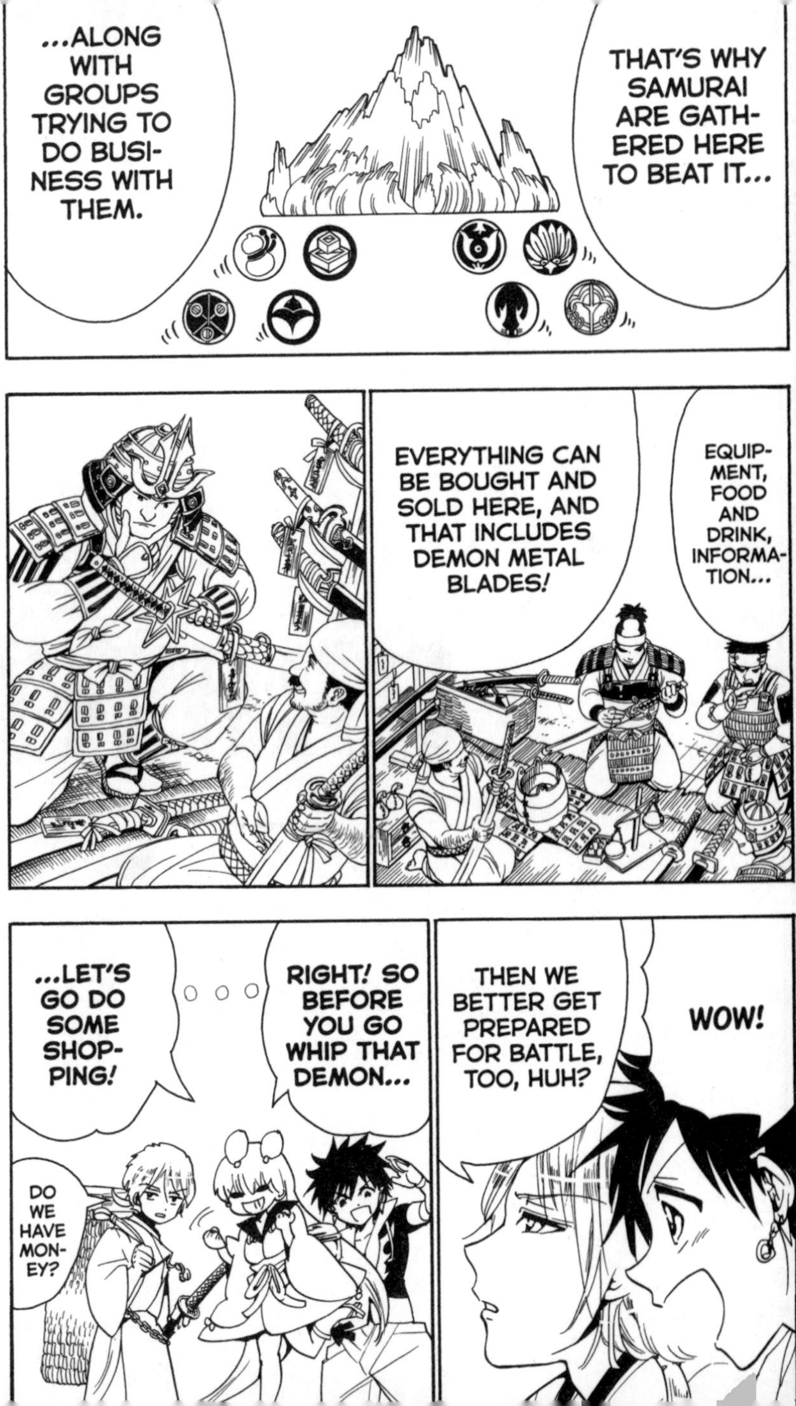
THAT'S WHY SAMURAI ARE GATHERED HERE TO BEAT IT...
...ALONG WITH GROUPS TRYING TO DO BUSINESS WITH THEM.
EQUIPMENT, FOOD AND DRINK, INFORMATION...
EVERYTHING CAN BE BOUGHT AND SOLD HERE, AND THAT INCLUDES DEMON METAL BLADES!
WOW!
THEN WE BETTER GET PREPARED FOR BATTLE, TOO, HUH?
RIGHT! SO BEFORE YOU GO WHIP THAT DEMON...
...LET'S GO DO SOME SHOPPING!
DO WE HAVE MONEY?

ORIENT

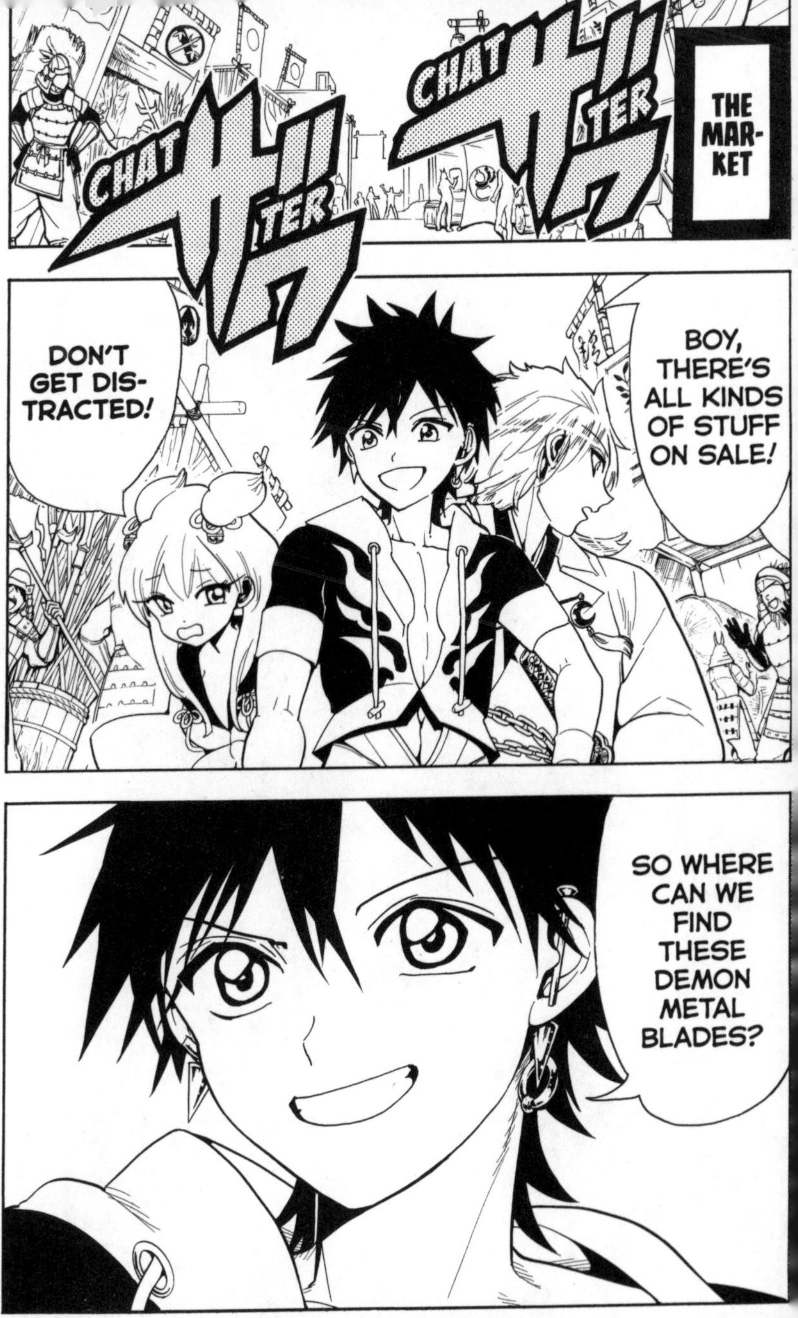
THE MARKET
CHAT ザワ TER
CHAT ザワ TER
BOY, THERE'S ALL KINDS OF STUFF ON SALE!
DON'T GET DISTRACTED!
SO WHERE CAN WE FIND THESE DEMON METAL BLADES?

CHAPTER 21: THE KANEMAKI BAND OF SAMURAI

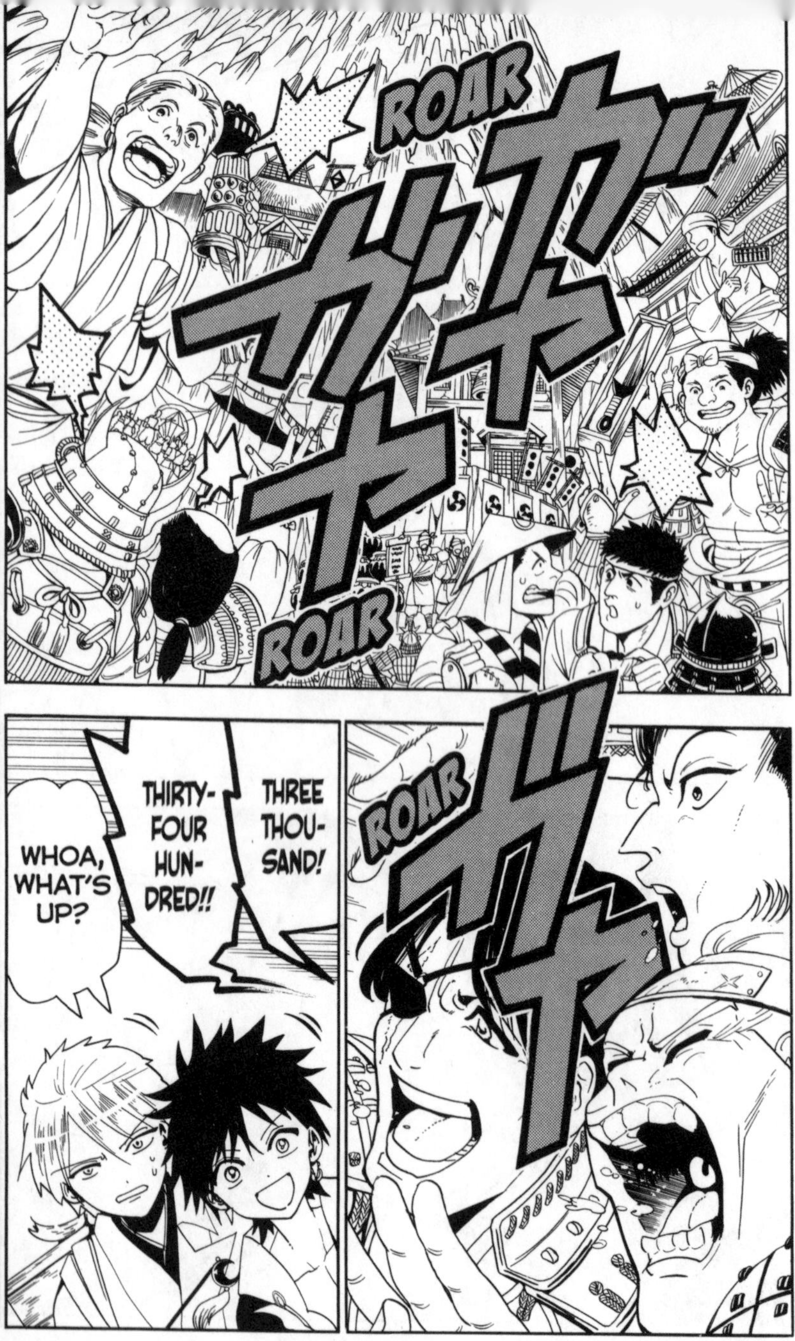
ROAR
ガヤガヤ
ROAR
ROAR
ガヤ
THREE THOU-SAND!
THIRTY-FOUR HUN-DRED!!
WHOA, WHAT'S UP?

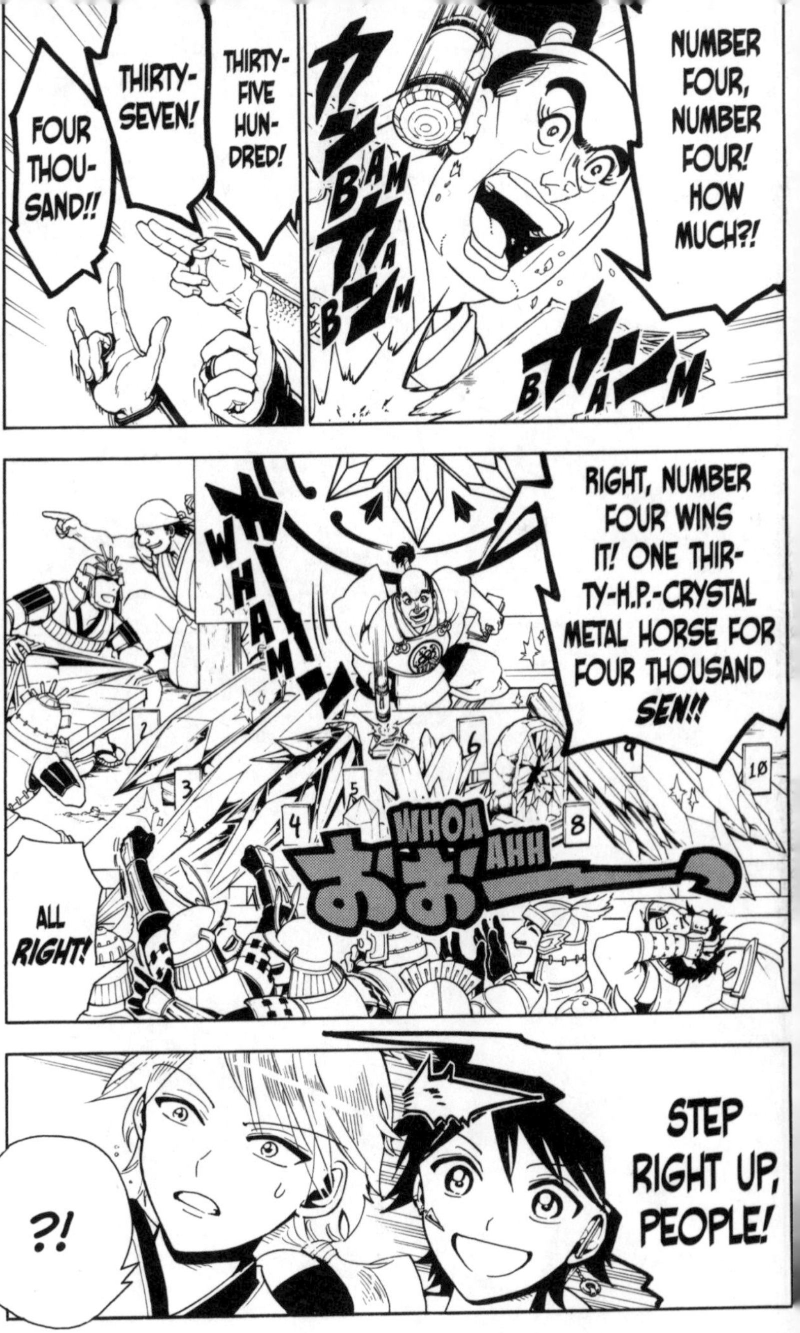
NUMBER FOUR, NUMBER FOUR! HOW MUCH?!
BAM
BAM
BAM
THIRTY-FIVE HUNDRED!
THIRTY-SEVEN!
FOUR THOUSAND!!
RIGHT, NUMBER FOUR WINS IT! ONE THIRTY-H.P.-CRYSTAL METAL HORSE FOR FOUR THOUSAND *SEN*!!
WHAM
WHOA AHH
ALL *RIGHT*!
STEP RIGHT UP, PEOPLE!
?!

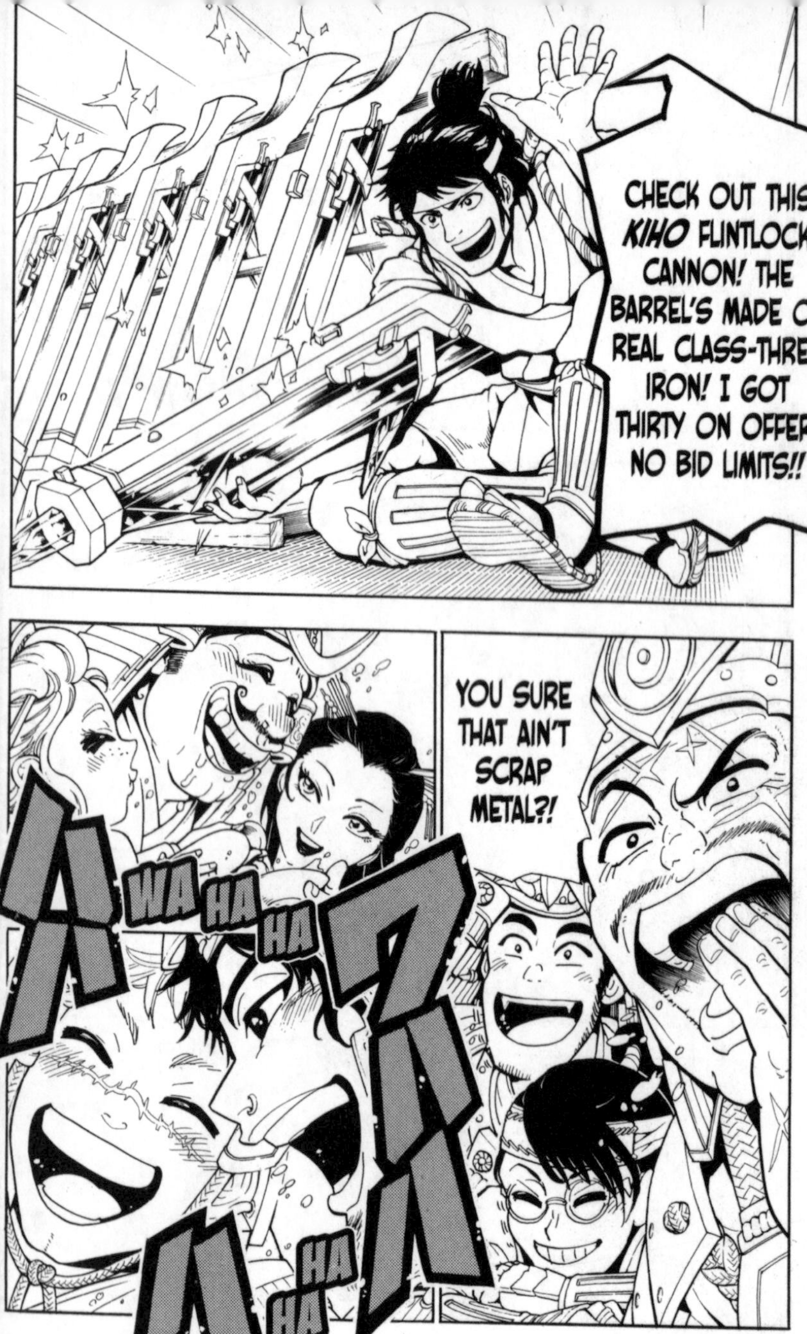
CHECK OUT THIS *KIHO* FLINTLOCK CANNON! THE BARREL'S MADE OF REAL CLASS-THREE IRON! I GOT THIRTY ON OFFER, NO BID LIMITS!!
YOU SURE THAT AIN'T SCRAP METAL?!
WA HA HA
HA HA

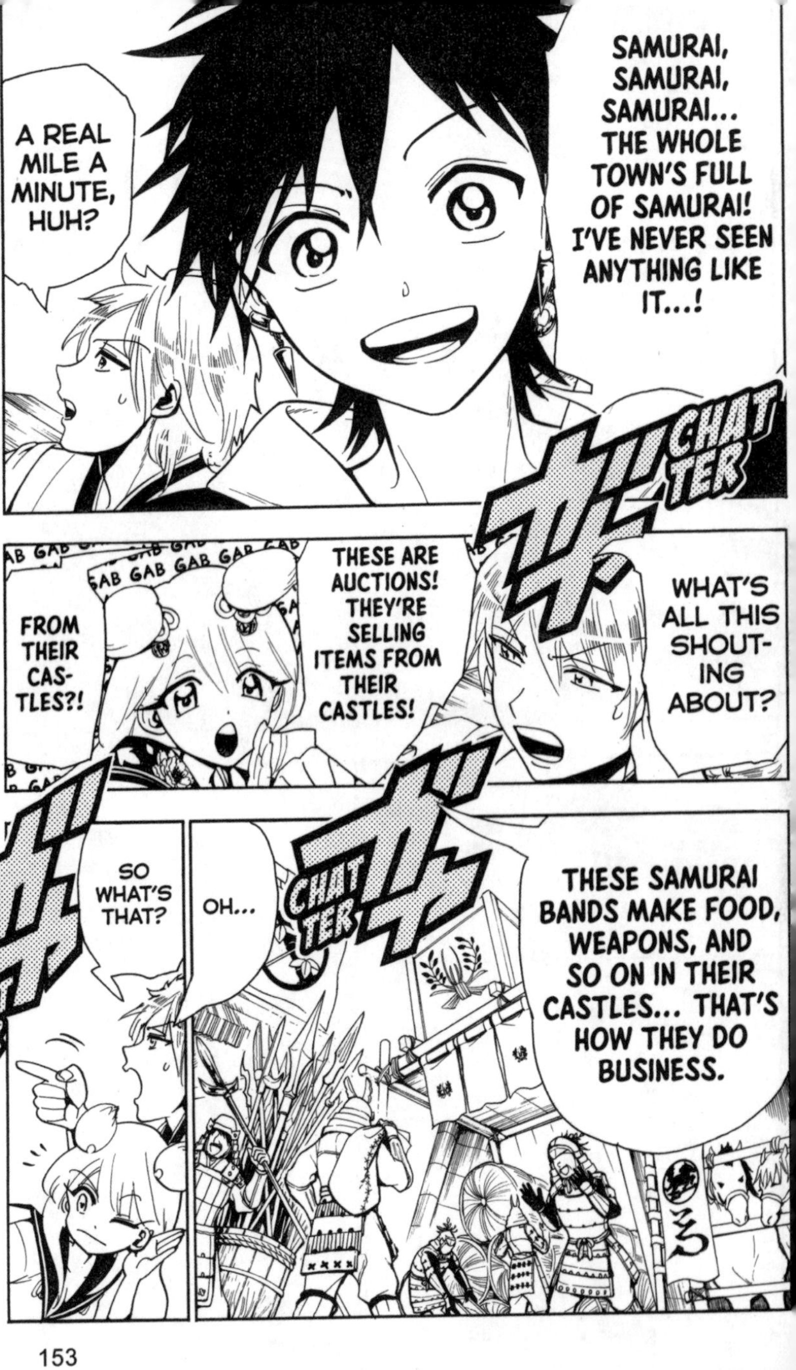
SAMURAI, SAMURAI, SAMURAI... THE WHOLE TOWN'S FULL OF SAMURAI! I'VE NEVER SEEN ANYTHING LIKE IT...!
A REAL MILE A MINUTE, HUH?
CHATTER
WHAT'S ALL THIS SHOUTING ABOUT?
THESE ARE AUCTIONS! THEY'RE SELLING ITEMS FROM THEIR CASTLES!
FROM THEIR CASTLES?!
CHATTER
THESE SAMURAI BANDS MAKE FOOD, WEAPONS, AND SO ON IN THEIR CASTLES... THAT'S HOW THEY DO BUSINESS.
OH...
SO WHAT'S THAT?
CHATTER

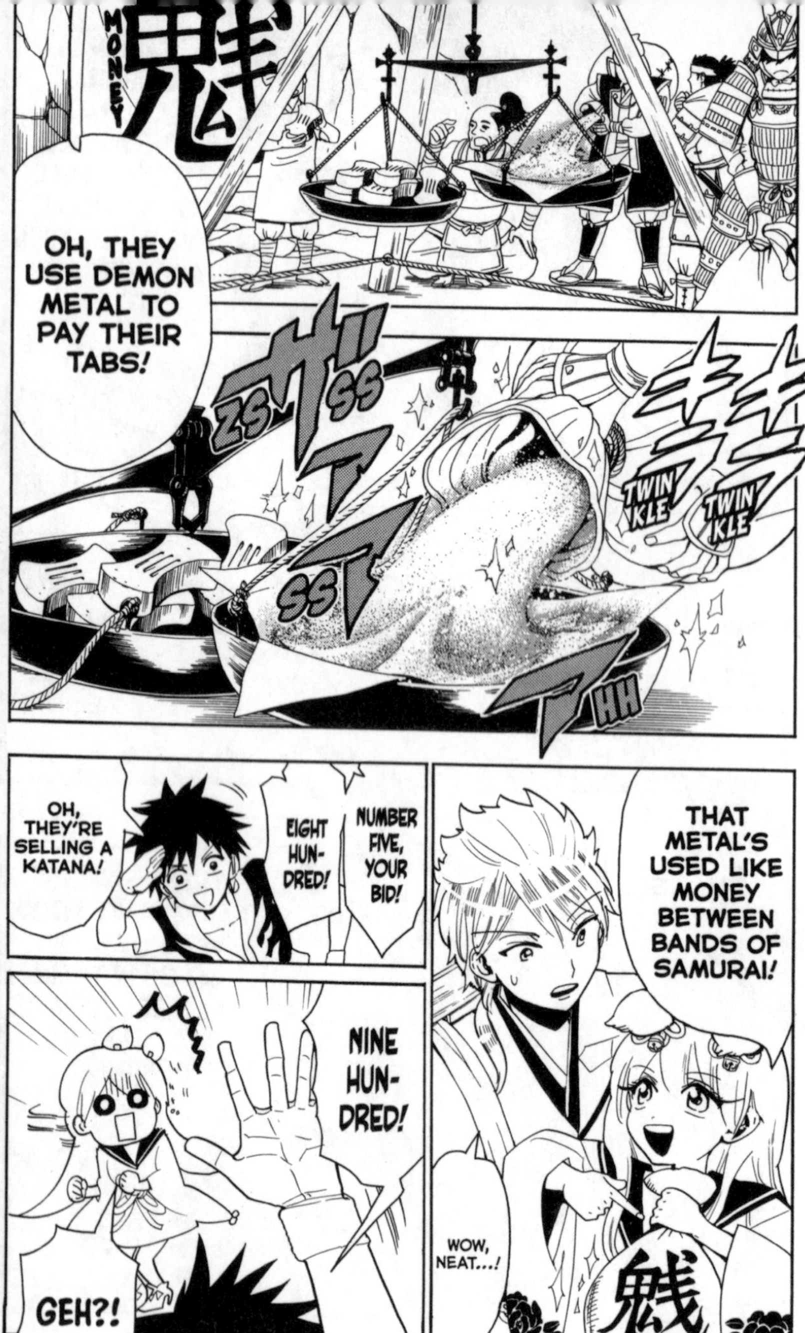

MONEY
OH, THEY USE DEMON METAL TO PAY THEIR TABS!
ZSSSSSHH
TWINKLE TWINKLE
THAT METAL'S USED LIKE MONEY BETWEEN BANDS OF SAMURAI!
WOW, NEAT...!
魁
NUMBER FIVE, YOUR BID!
EIGHT HUNDRED!
OH, THEY'RE SELLING A KATANA!
NINE HUNDRED!
GEH?!

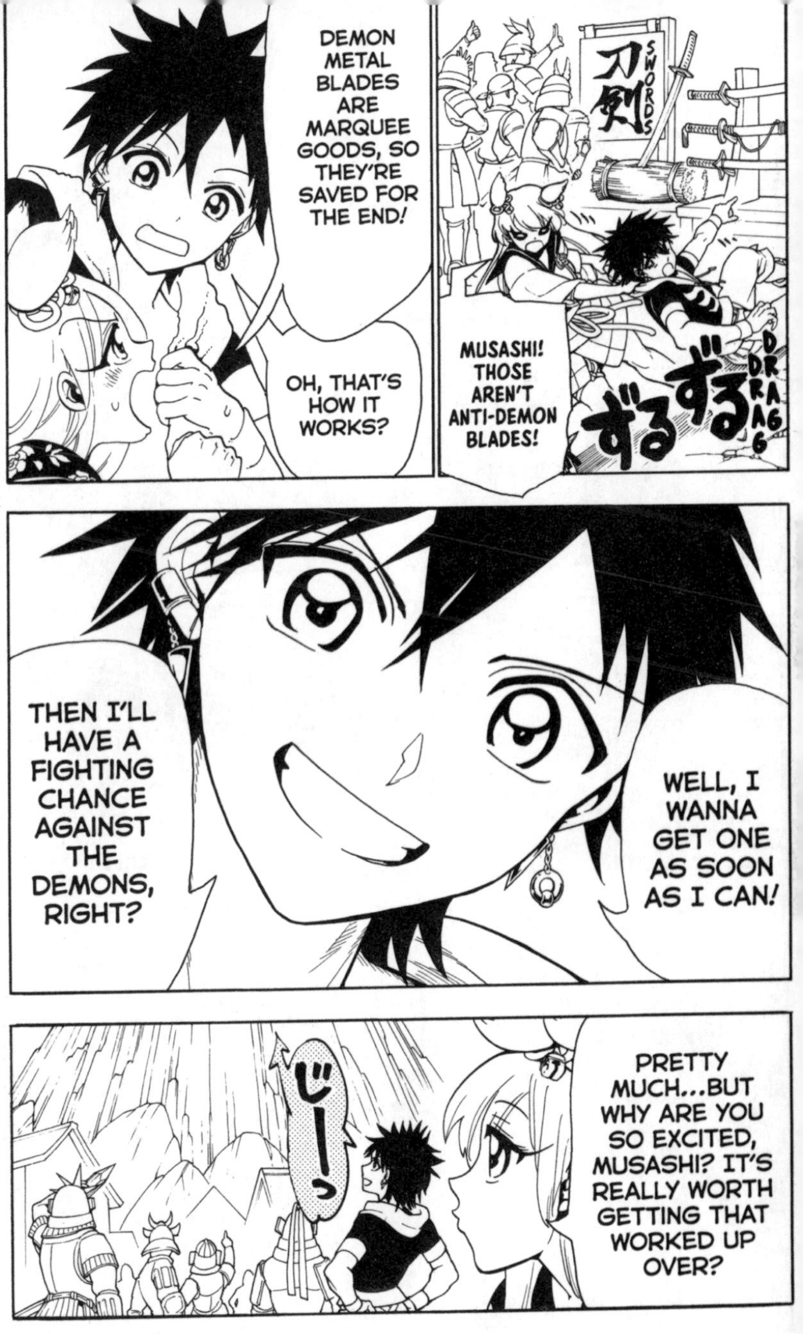
刀剣
SWORDS
MUSASHI! THOSE AREN'T ANTI-DEMON BLADES!
ずるずる
DRAG DRAG
DEMON METAL BLADES ARE MARQUEE GOODS, SO THEY'RE SAVED FOR THE END!
OH, THAT'S HOW IT WORKS?
WELL, I WANNA GET ONE AS SOON AS I CAN!
THEN I'LL HAVE A FIGHTING CHANCE AGAINST THE DEMONS, RIGHT?
PRETTY MUCH...BUT WHY ARE YOU SO EXCITED, MUSASHI? IT'S REALLY WORTH GETTING THAT WORKED UP OVER?
じーっ

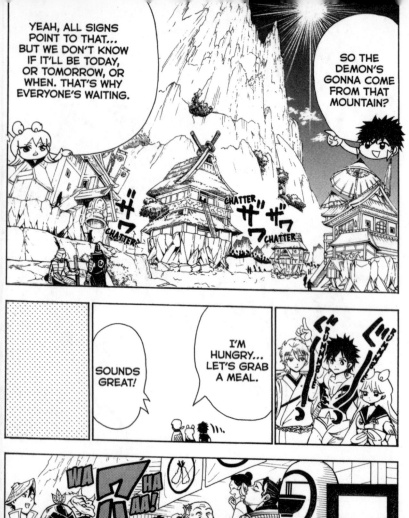

SO THE DEMON'S GONNA COME FROM THAT MOUNTAIN?
YEAH, ALL SIGNS POINT TO THAT... BUT WE DON'T KNOW IF IT'LL BE TODAY, OR TOMORROW, OR WHEN. THAT'S WHY EVERYONE'S WAITING.
CHATTER
CHATTER
CHATTER
I'M HUNGRY... LET'S GRAB A MEAL.
SOUNDS GREAT!
TAVERN
WA HA HAA!

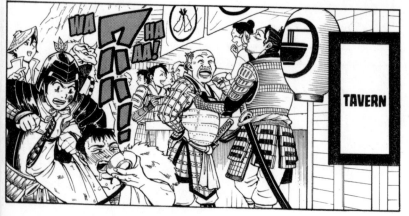

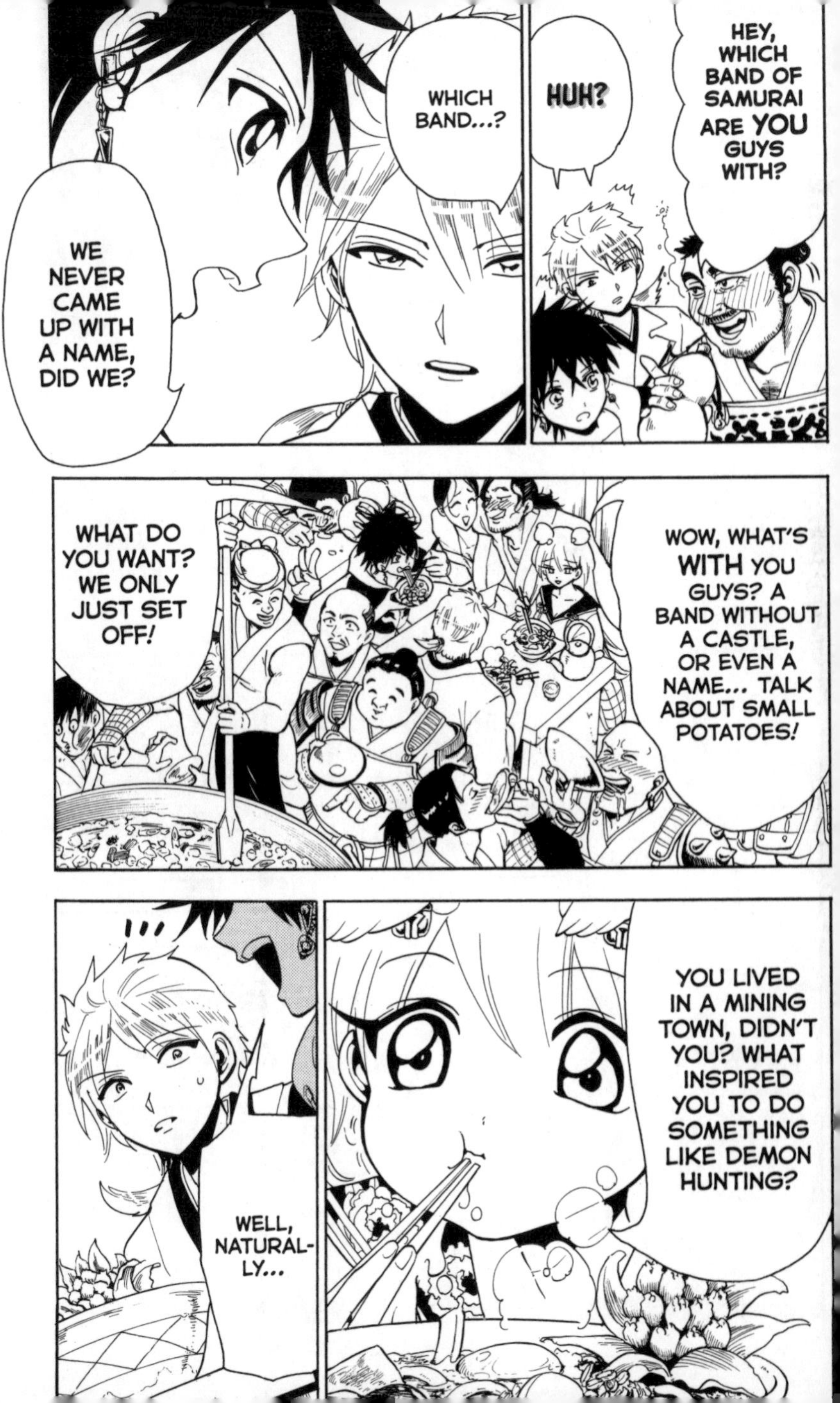
HEY, WHICH BAND OF SAMURAI ARE YOU GUYS WITH?
HUH?
WHICH BAND...?
WE NEVER CAME UP WITH A NAME, DID WE?
WOW, WHAT'S WITH YOU GUYS? A BAND WITHOUT A CASTLE, OR EVEN A NAME... TALK ABOUT SMALL POTATOES!
WHAT DO YOU WANT? WE ONLY JUST SET OFF!
YOU LIVED IN A MINING TOWN, DIDN'T YOU? WHAT INSPIRED YOU TO DO SOMETHING LIKE DEMON HUNTING?
WELL, NATURAL-LY...

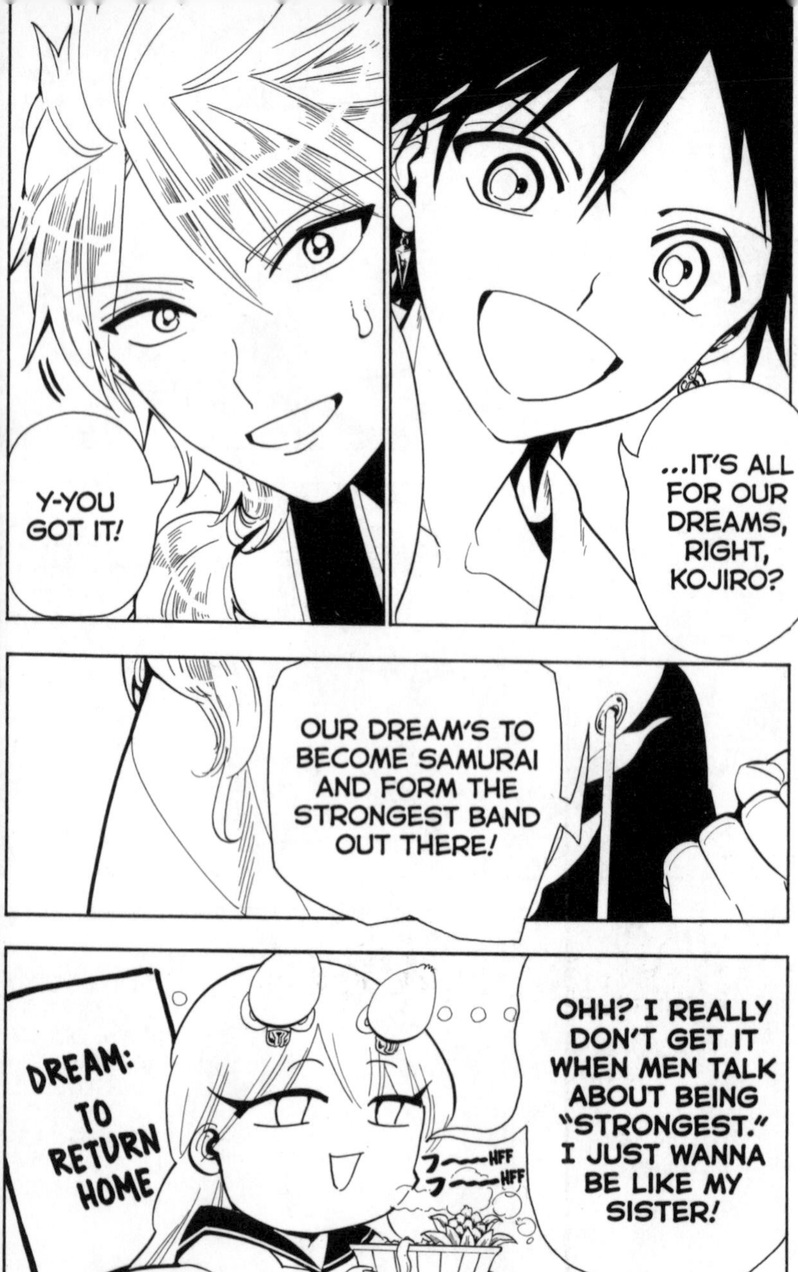
...IT'S ALL FOR OUR DREAMS, RIGHT, KOJIRO?
Y-YOU GOT IT!
OUR DREAM'S TO BECOME SAMURAI AND FORM THE STRONGEST BAND OUT THERE!
OHH? I REALLY DON'T GET IT WHEN MEN TALK ABOUT BEING "STRONGEST." I JUST WANNA BE LIKE MY SISTER!
フ~~~HFF
フ~~~HFF
DREAM: TO RETURN HOME

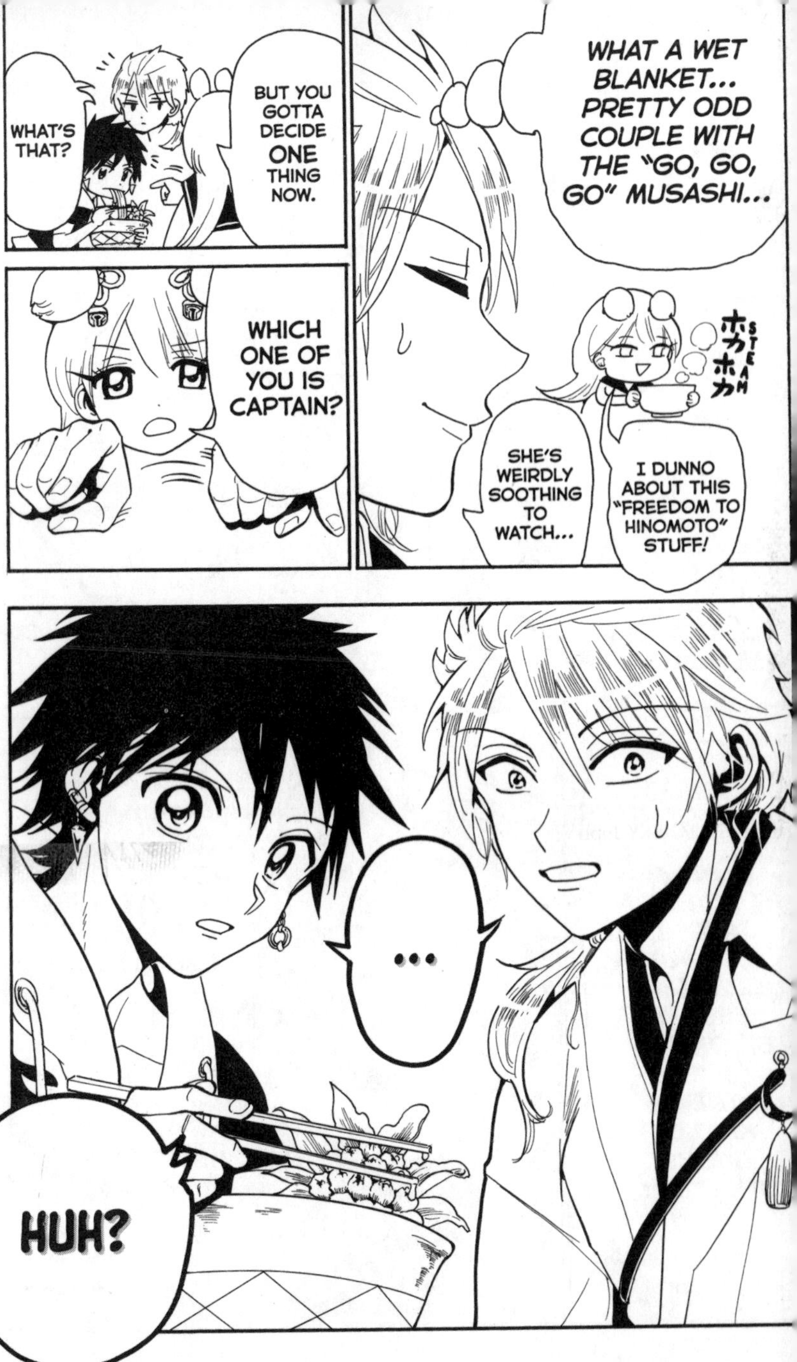
WHAT A WET BLANKET... PRETTY ODD COUPLE WITH THE "GO, GO, GO" MUSASHI...
ホカホカ STEAM
I DUNNO ABOUT THIS "FREEDOM TO HINOMOTO" STUFF!
SHE'S WEIRDLY SOOTHING TO WATCH...
BUT YOU GOTTA DECIDE ONE THING NOW.
WHAT'S THAT?
WHICH ONE OF YOU IS CAPTAIN?
...
HUH?

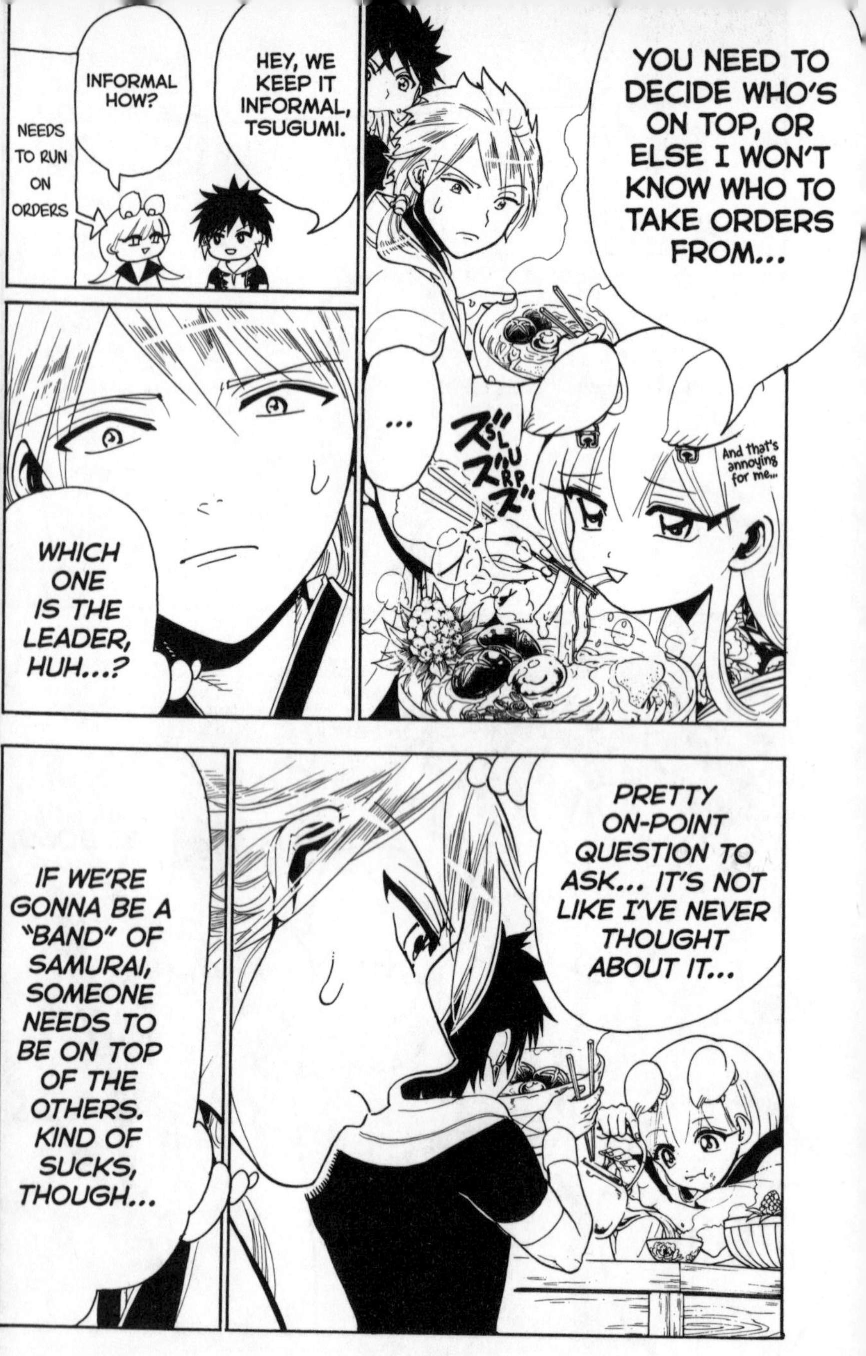
YOU NEED TO DECIDE WHO'S ON TOP, OR ELSE I WON'T KNOW WHO TO TAKE ORDERS FROM...
And that's annoying for me...
SLURP
...
HEY, WE KEEP IT INFORMAL, TSUGUMI.
INFORMAL HOW?
NEEDS TO RUN ON ORDERS
WHICH ONE IS THE LEADER, HUH...?
PRETTY ON-POINT QUESTION TO ASK... IT'S NOT LIKE I'VE NEVER THOUGHT ABOUT IT...
IF WE'RE GONNA BE A "BAND" OF SAMURAI, SOMEONE NEEDS TO BE ON TOP OF THE OTHERS. KIND OF SUCKS, THOUGH...

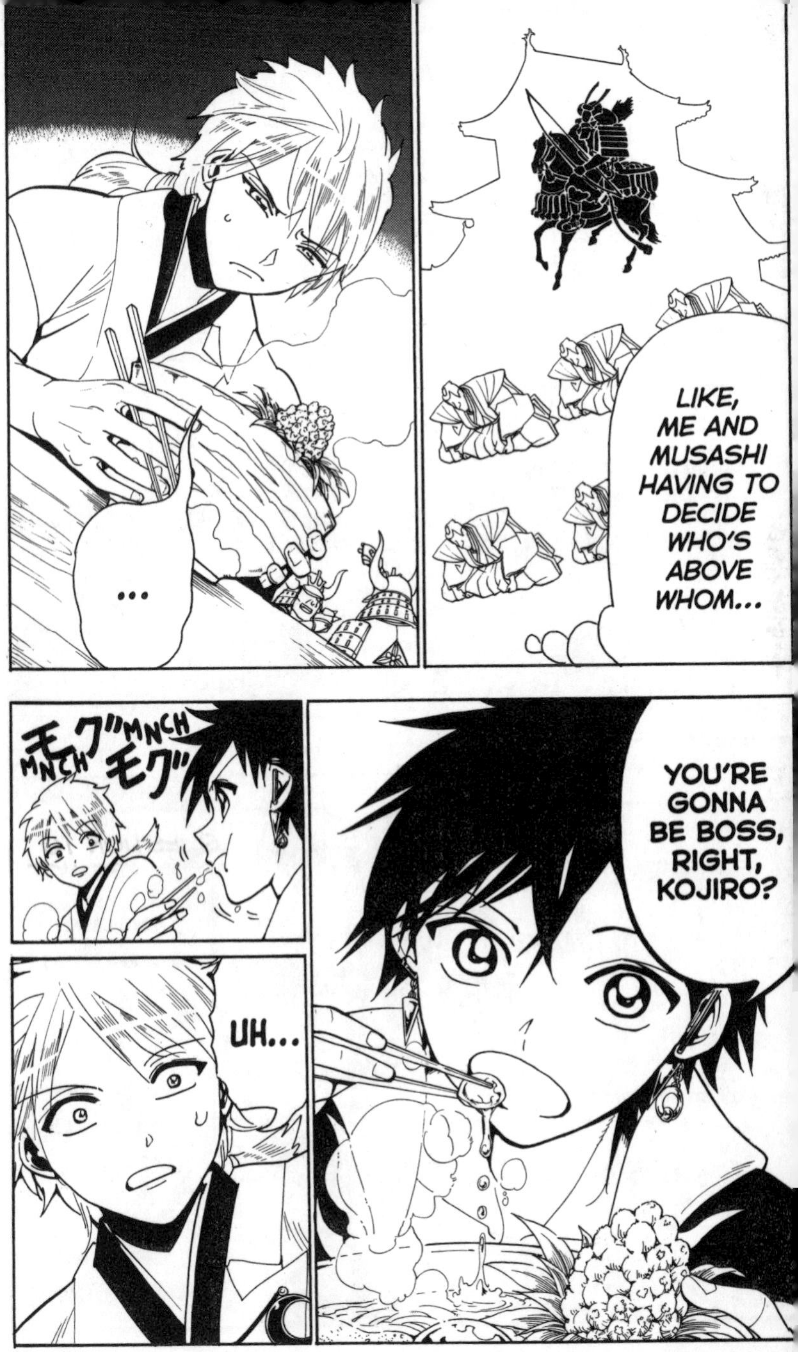
LIKE, ME AND MUSASHI HAVING TO DECIDE WHO'S ABOVE WHOM...
...
YOU'RE GONNA BE BOSS, RIGHT, KOJIRO?
モグ MNCH
モグ MNCH
UH...

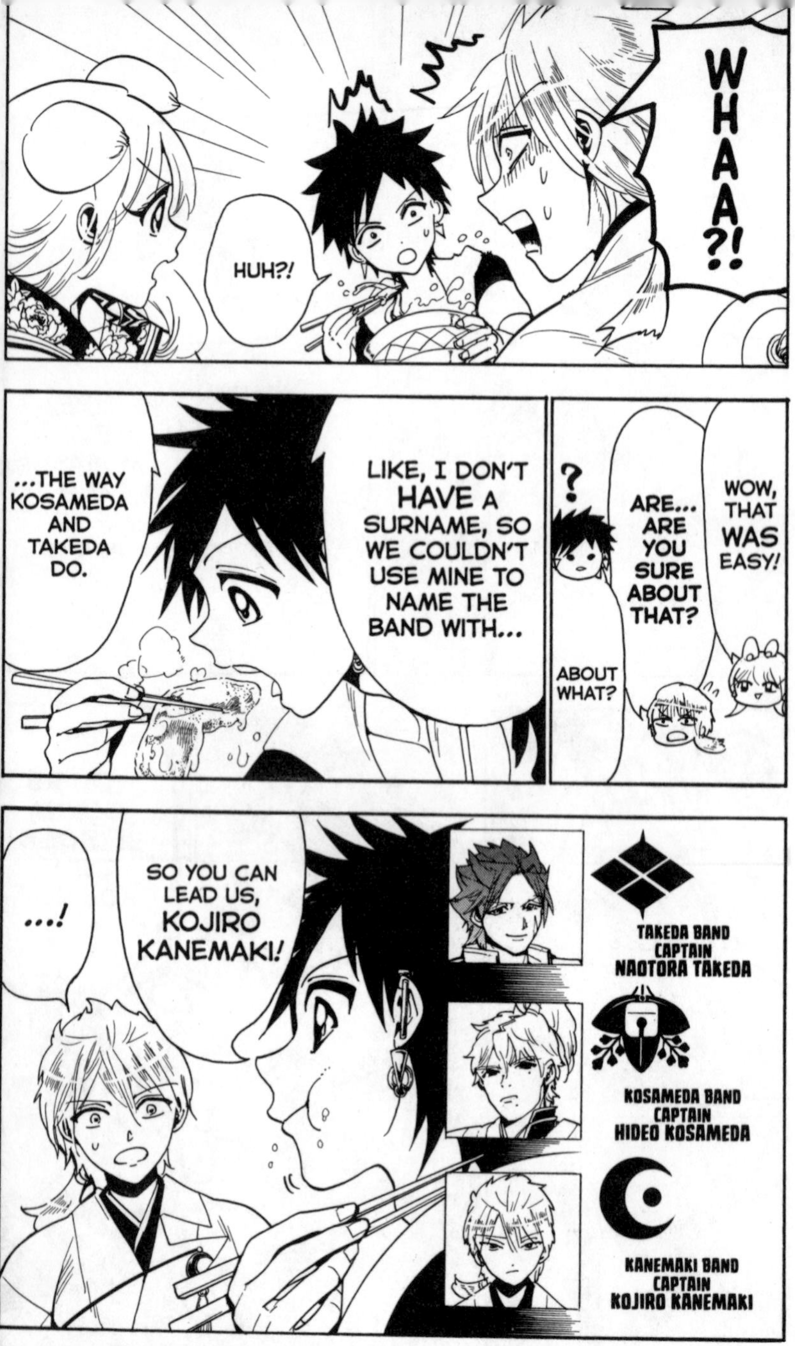
WHAAA?!
HUH?!
WOW, THAT WAS EASY!
ARE... ARE YOU SURE ABOUT THAT?
?
ABOUT WHAT?
LIKE, I DON'T HAVE A SURNAME, SO WE COULDN'T USE MINE TO NAME THE BAND WITH...
...THE WAY KOSAMEDA AND TAKEDA DO.
TAKEDA BAND CAPTAIN NAOTORA TAKEDA
KOSAMEDA BAND CAPTAIN HIDEO KOSAMEDA
KANEMAKI BAND CAPTAIN KOJIRO KANEMAKI
SO YOU CAN LEAD US, KOJIRO KANEMAKI!
...!

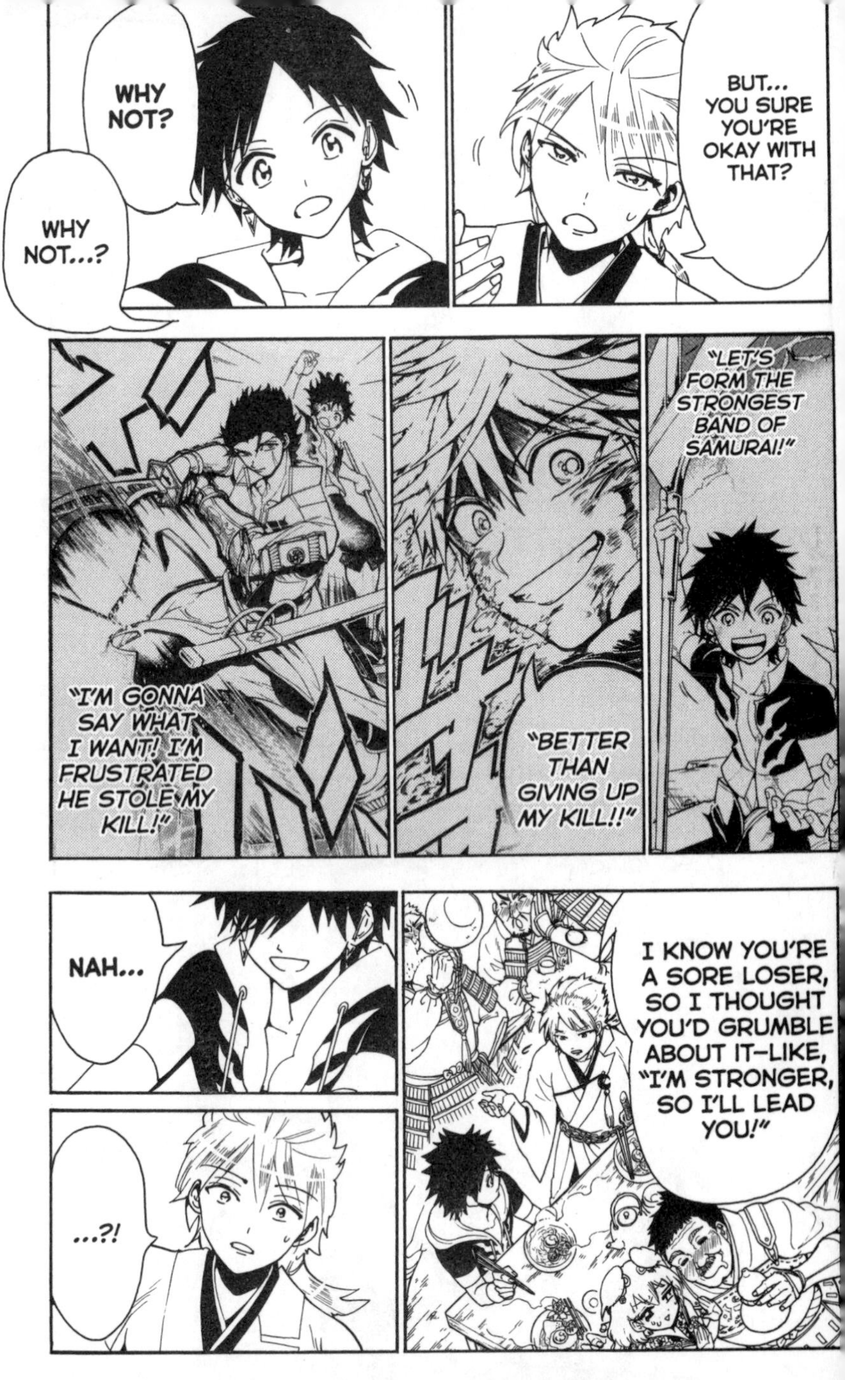
BUT... YOU SURE YOU'RE OKAY WITH THAT?
WHY NOT?
WHY NOT...?
"LET'S FORM THE STRONGEST BAND OF SAMURAI!"
"BETTER THAN GIVING UP MY KILL!!"
"I'M GONNA SAY WHAT I WANT! I'M FRUSTRATED HE STOLE MY KILL!"
I KNOW YOU'RE A SORE LOSER, SO I THOUGHT YOU'D GRUMBLE ABOUT IT–LIKE, "I'M STRONGER, SO I'LL LEAD YOU!"
NAH...
...?!

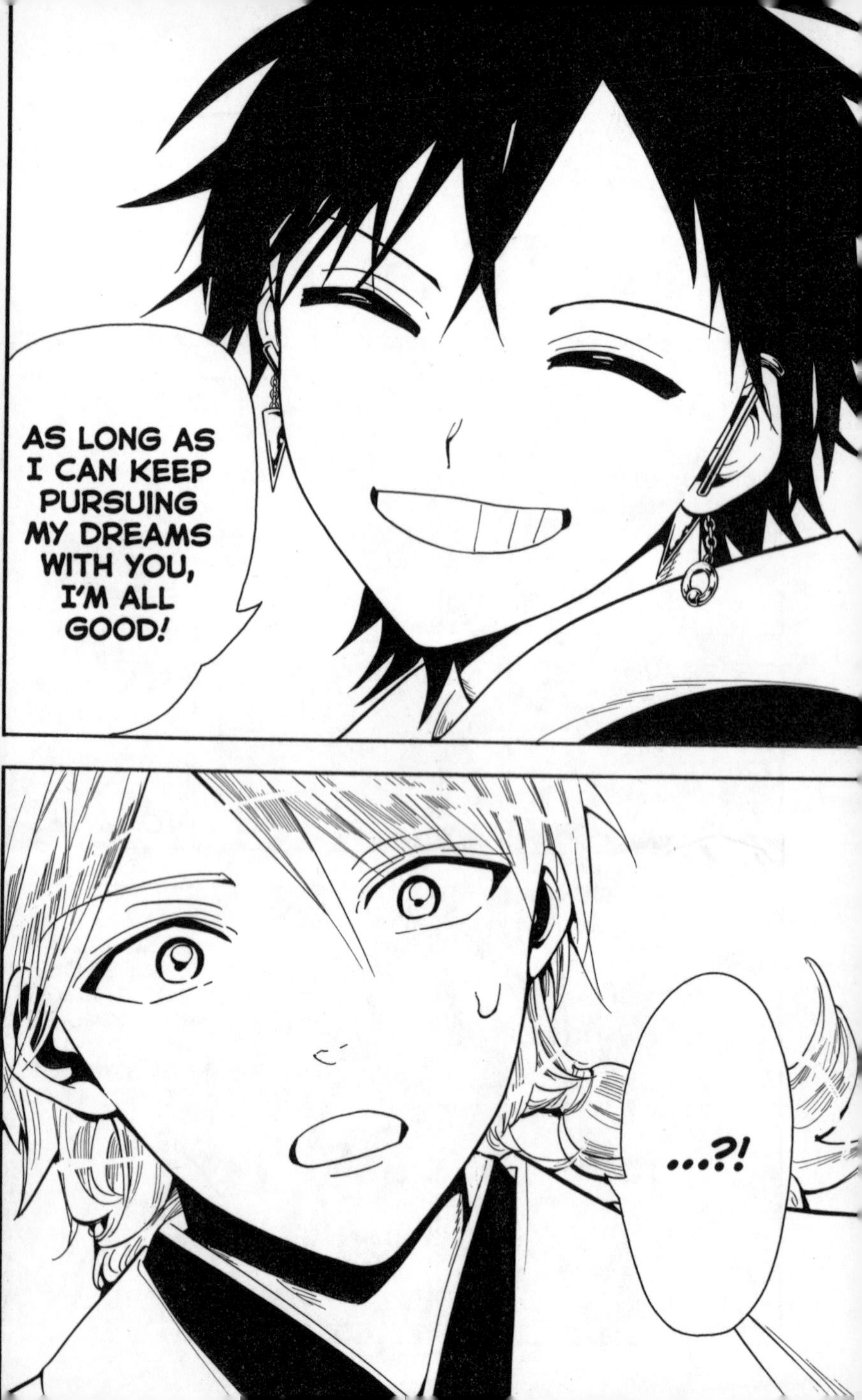
AS LONG AS I CAN KEEP PURSUING MY DREAMS WITH YOU, I'M ALL GOOD!
...?!

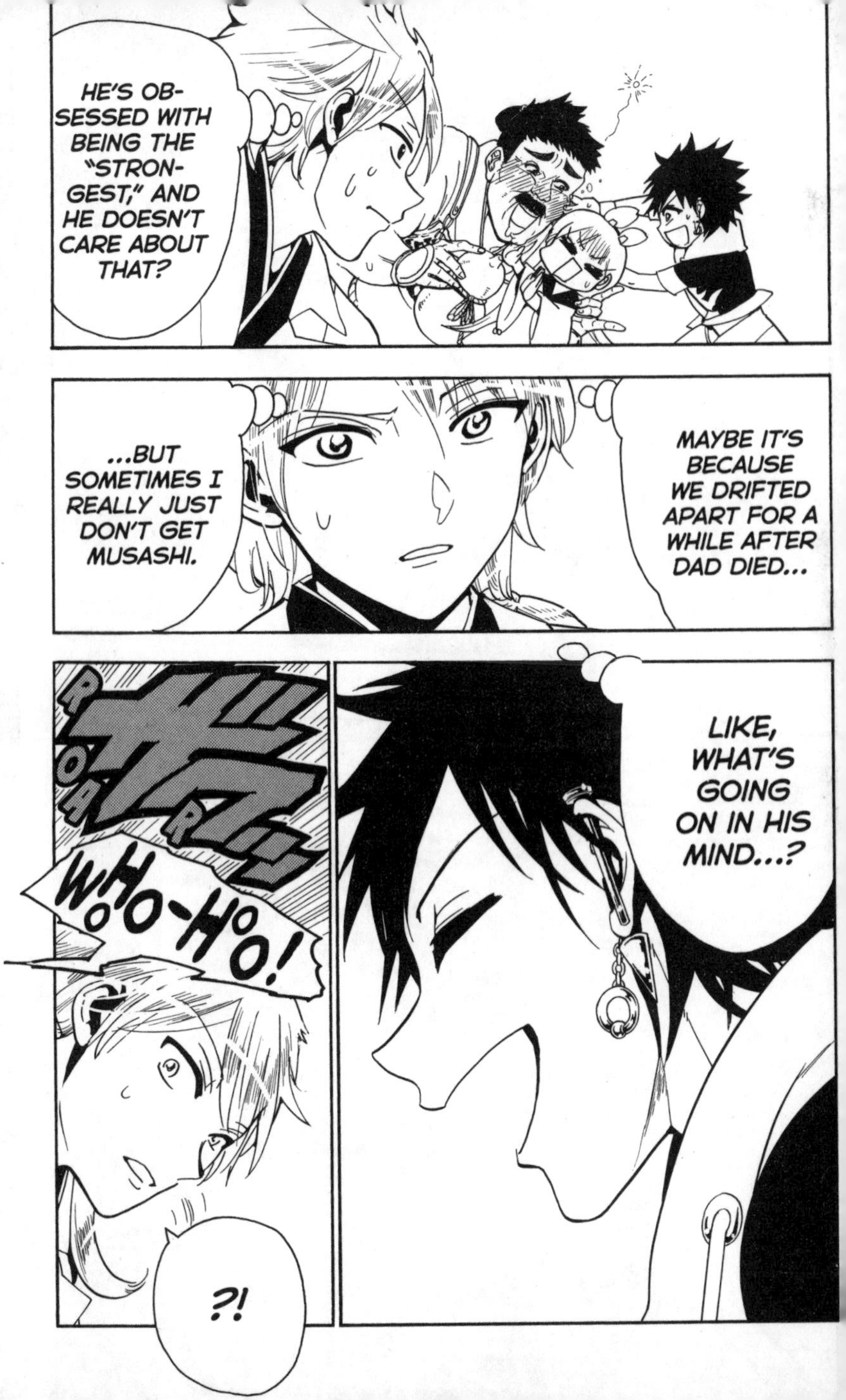
HE'S OB-SESSED WITH BEING THE "STRON-GEST," AND HE DOESN'T CARE ABOUT THAT?
MAYBE IT'S BECAUSE WE DRIFTED APART FOR A WHILE AFTER DAD DIED...
...BUT SOMETIMES I REALLY JUST DON'T GET MUSASHI.
LIKE, WHAT'S GOING ON IN HIS MIND...?
ROAR
WHOO-HO-HO!
?!

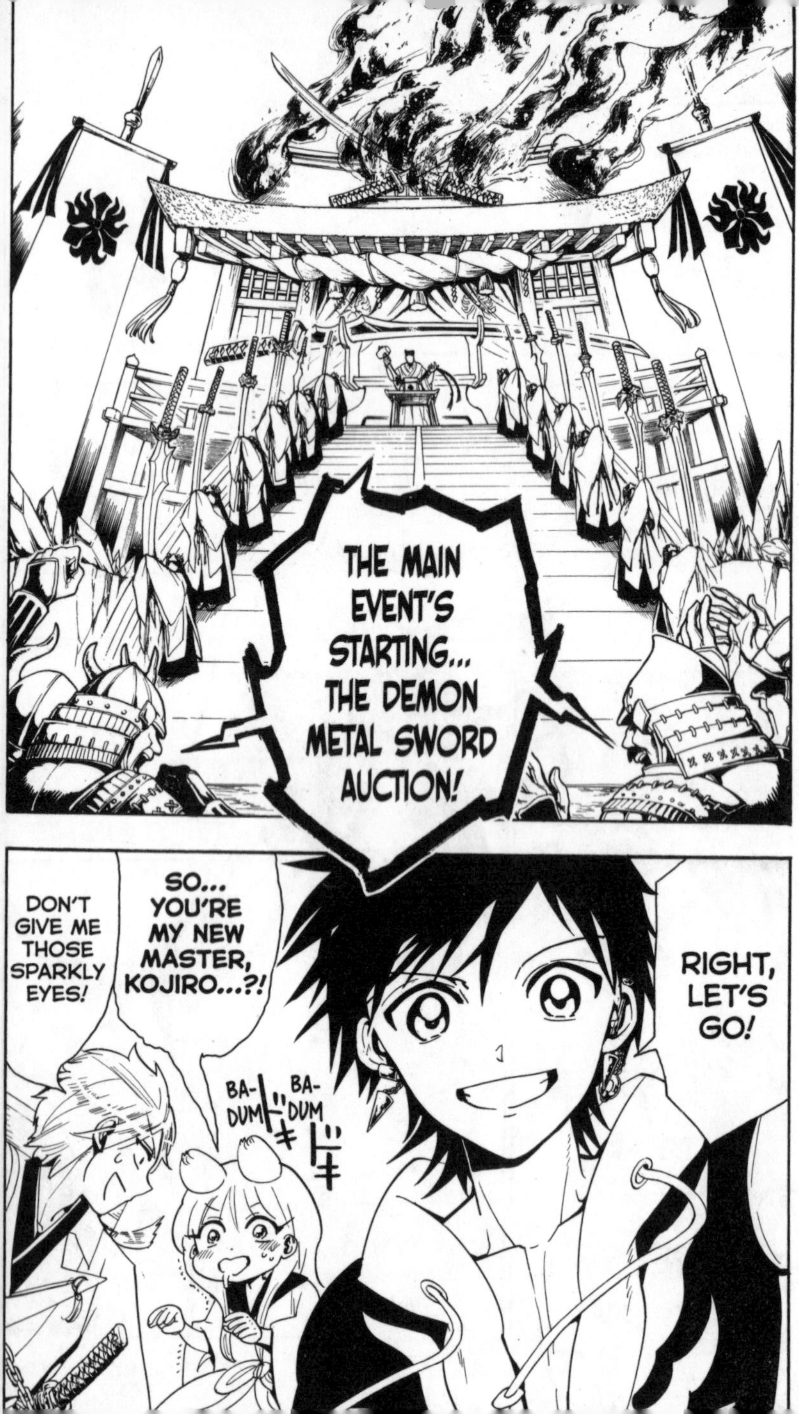
THE MAIN EVENT'S STARTING... THE DEMON METAL SWORD AUCTION!
RIGHT, LET'S GO!
SO... YOU'RE MY NEW MASTER, KOJIRO...?!
DON'T GIVE ME THOSE SPARKLY EYES!
BA-DUM
ドキ
BA-DUM
ドキ

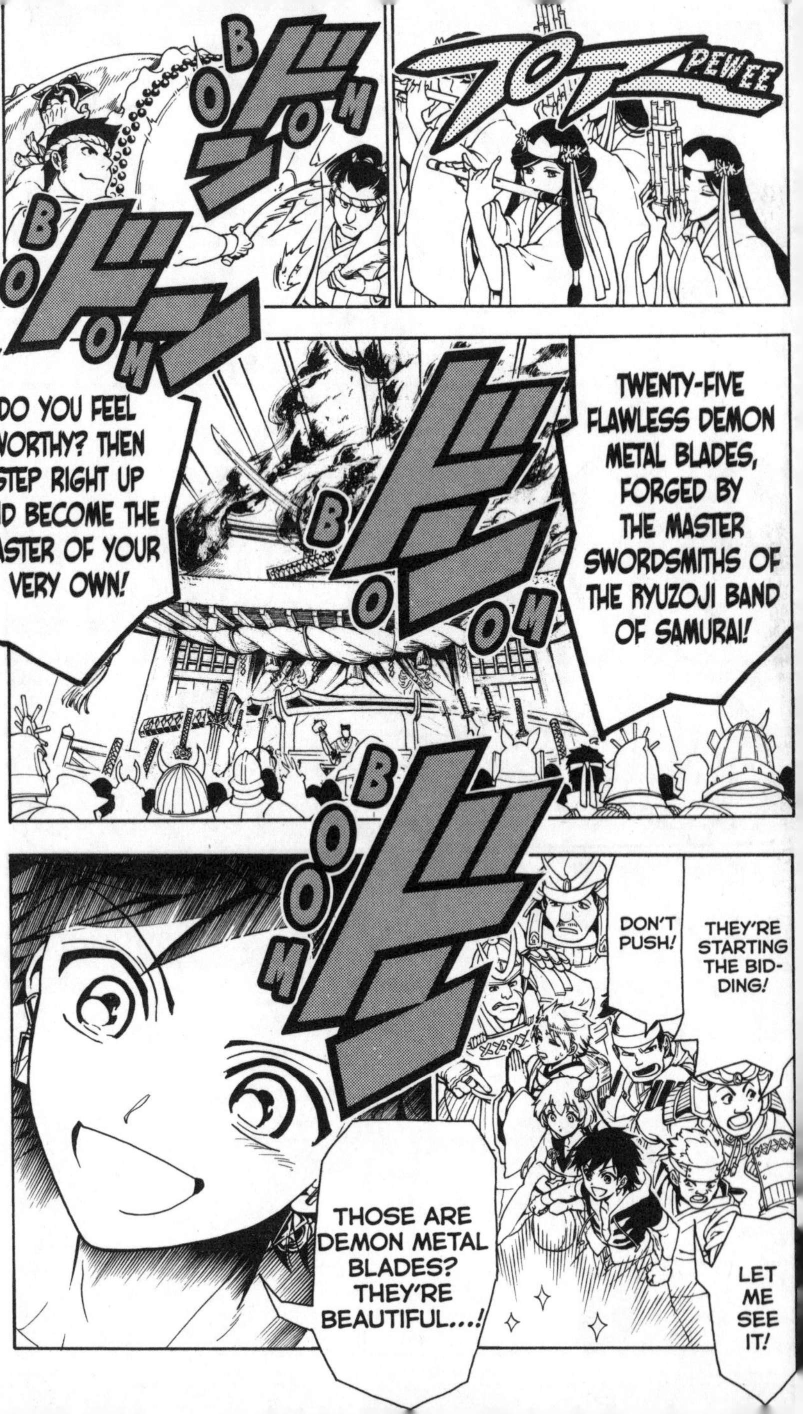
PEWEE
BOOM
BOOM
TWENTY-FIVE FLAWLESS DEMON METAL BLADES, FORGED BY THE MASTER SWORDSMITHS OF THE RYUZOJI BAND OF SAMURAI!
BOOM
DO YOU FEEL WORTHY? THEN STEP RIGHT UP AND BECOME THE MASTER OF YOUR VERY OWN!
BOOM
THEY'RE STARTING THE BID-DING!
DON'T PUSH!
LET ME SEE IT!
THOSE ARE DEMON METAL BLADES? THEY'RE BEAUTIFUL...!

CHAPTER 22: THE BLADE TEST

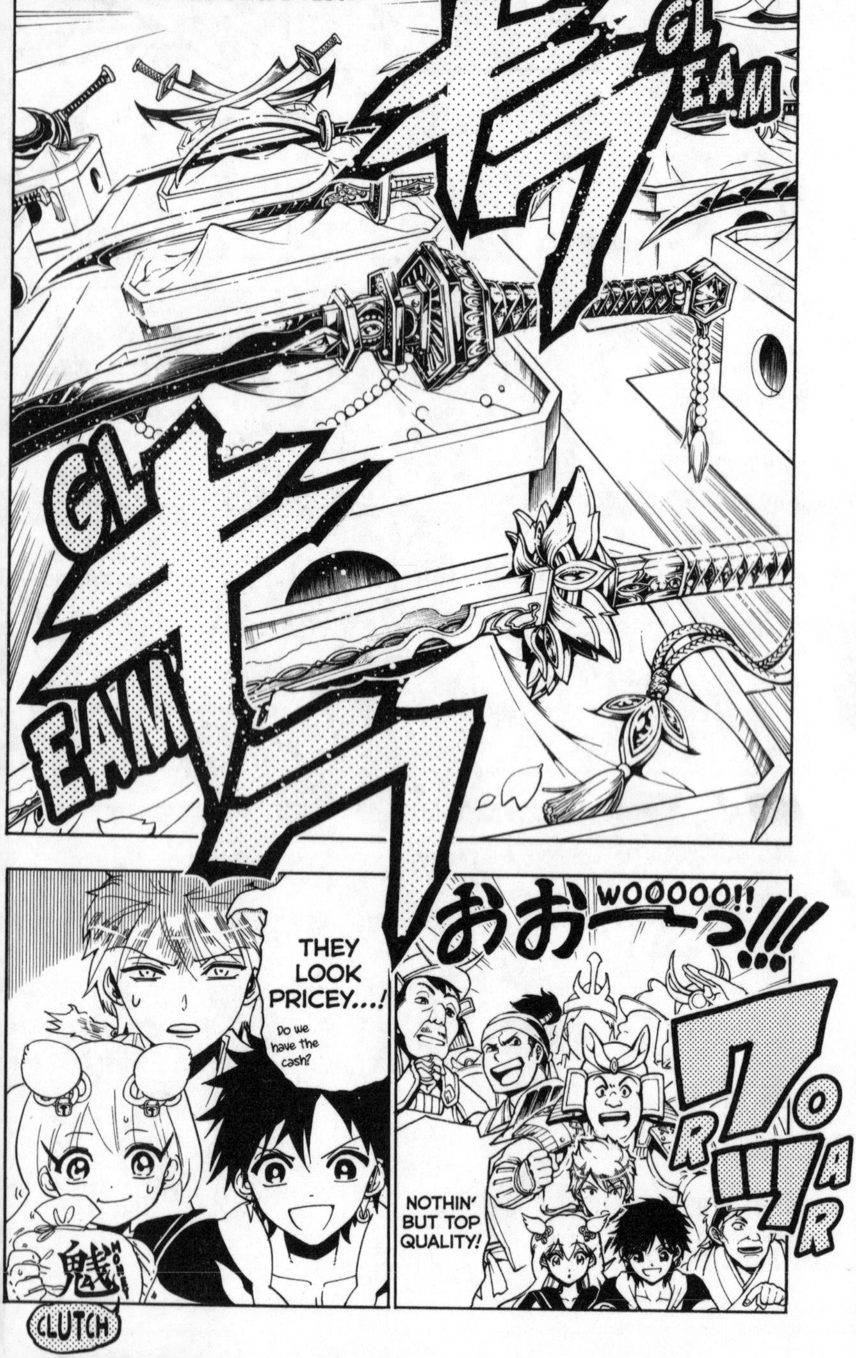

GLEAM
GLEAM
おおーっ!!!
WOOOOO!!
ROAR
NOTHIN' BUT TOP QUALITY!
THEY LOOK PRICEY...!
Do we have the cash?
魁
MONEY
CLUTCH

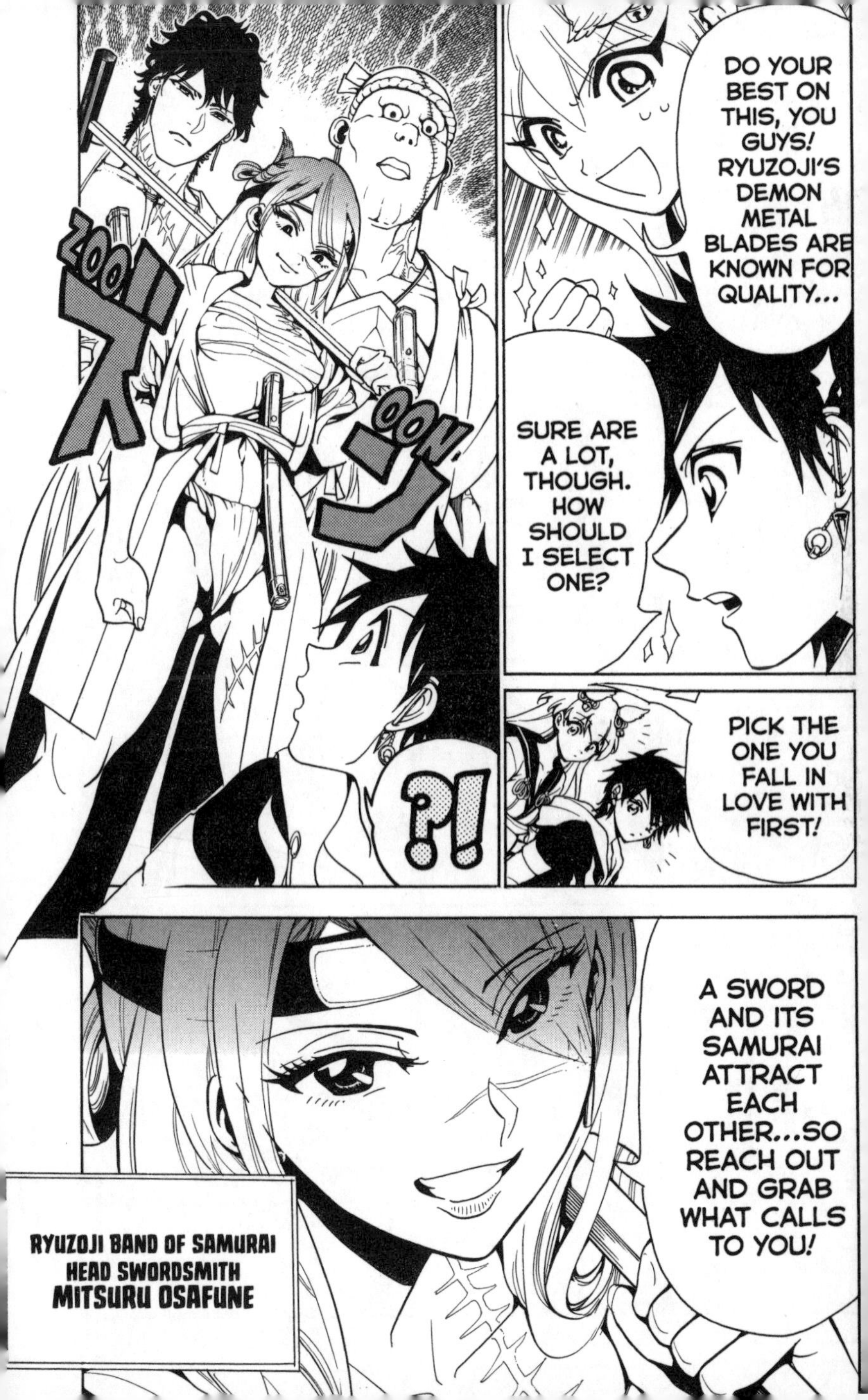
DO YOUR BEST ON THIS, YOU GUYS! RYUZOJI'S DEMON METAL BLADES ARE KNOWN FOR QUALITY...
SURE ARE A LOT, THOUGH. HOW SHOULD I SELECT ONE?
PICK THE ONE YOU FALL IN LOVE WITH FIRST!
ZOO
OON.
?!
A SWORD AND ITS SAMURAI ATTRACT EACH OTHER...SO REACH OUT AND GRAB WHAT CALLS TO YOU!
RYUZOJI BAND OF SAMURAI
HEAD SWORDSMITH
MITSURU OSAFUNE

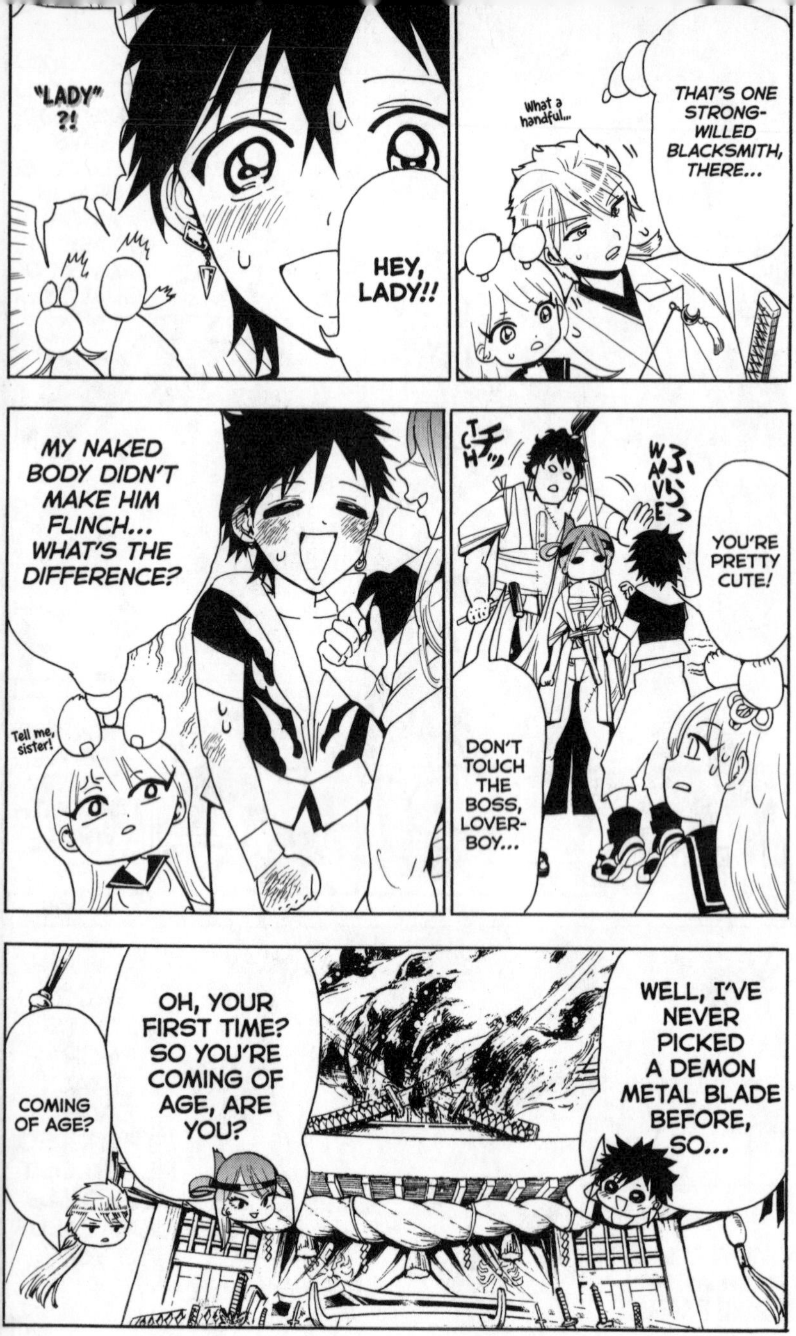

What a handful...
THAT'S ONE STRONG-WILLED BLACKSMITH, THERE...
HEY, LADY!!
"LADY" ?!
TCH
WAVE
YOU'RE PRETTY CUTE!
DON'T TOUCH THE BOSS, LOVER-BOY...
MY NAKED BODY DIDN'T MAKE HIM FLINCH... WHAT'S THE DIFFERENCE?
Tell me, sister!
WELL, I'VE NEVER PICKED A DEMON METAL BLADE BEFORE, SO...
OH, YOUR FIRST TIME? SO YOU'RE COMING OF AGE, ARE YOU?
COMING OF AGE?

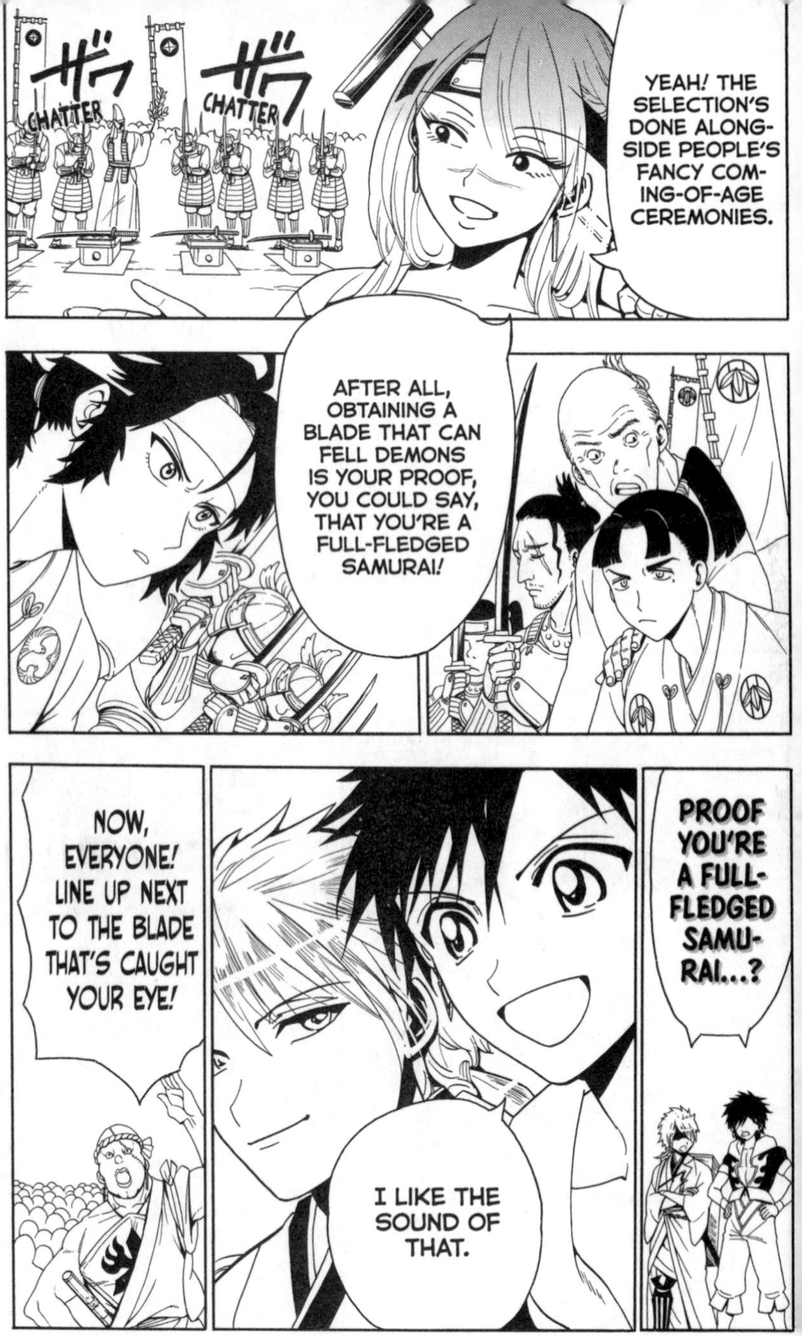
YEAH! THE SELECTION'S DONE ALONG-SIDE PEOPLE'S FANCY COM-ING-OF-AGE CEREMONIES.
ザワ CHATTER
ザワ CHATTER
AFTER ALL, OBTAINING A BLADE THAT CAN FELL DEMONS IS YOUR PROOF, YOU COULD SAY, THAT YOU'RE A FULL-FLEDGED SAMURAI!
PROOF YOU'RE A FULL-FLEDGED SAMU-RAI...?
I LIKE THE SOUND OF THAT.
NOW, EVERYONE! LINE UP NEXT TO THE BLADE THAT'S CAUGHT YOUR EYE!

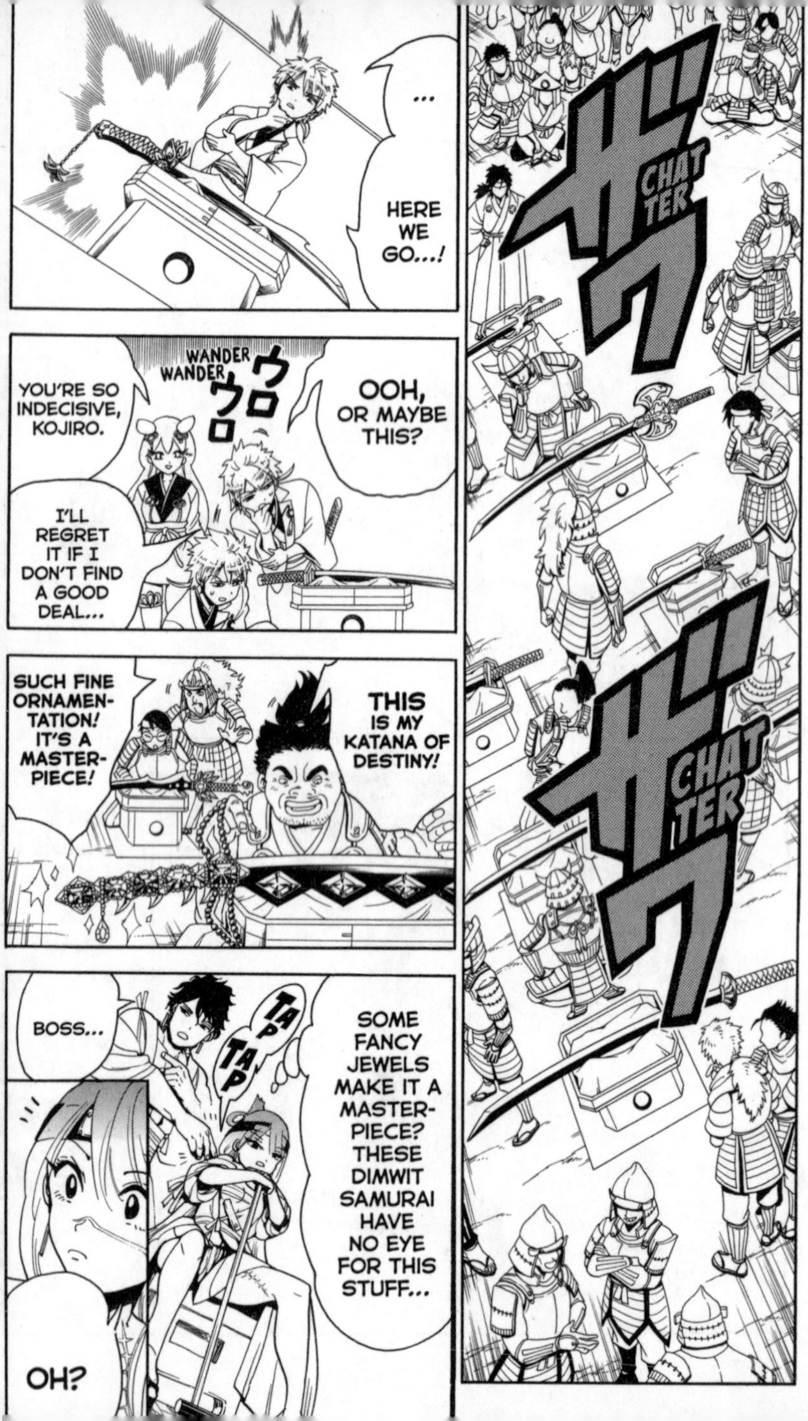
ザワ
CHATTER
ザワ
CHATTER
...
HERE WE GO...!
OOH, OR MAYBE THIS?
WANDER WANDER ウロウロ
YOU'RE SO INDECISIVE, KOJIRO.
I'LL REGRET IT IF I DON'T FIND A GOOD DEAL...
THIS IS MY KATANA OF DESTINY!
SUCH FINE ORNAMENTATION! IT'S A MASTERPIECE!
SOME FANCY JEWELS MAKE IT A MASTERPIECE? THESE DIMWIT SAMURAI HAVE NO EYE FOR THIS STUFF...
TAP TAP
BOSS...
OH?

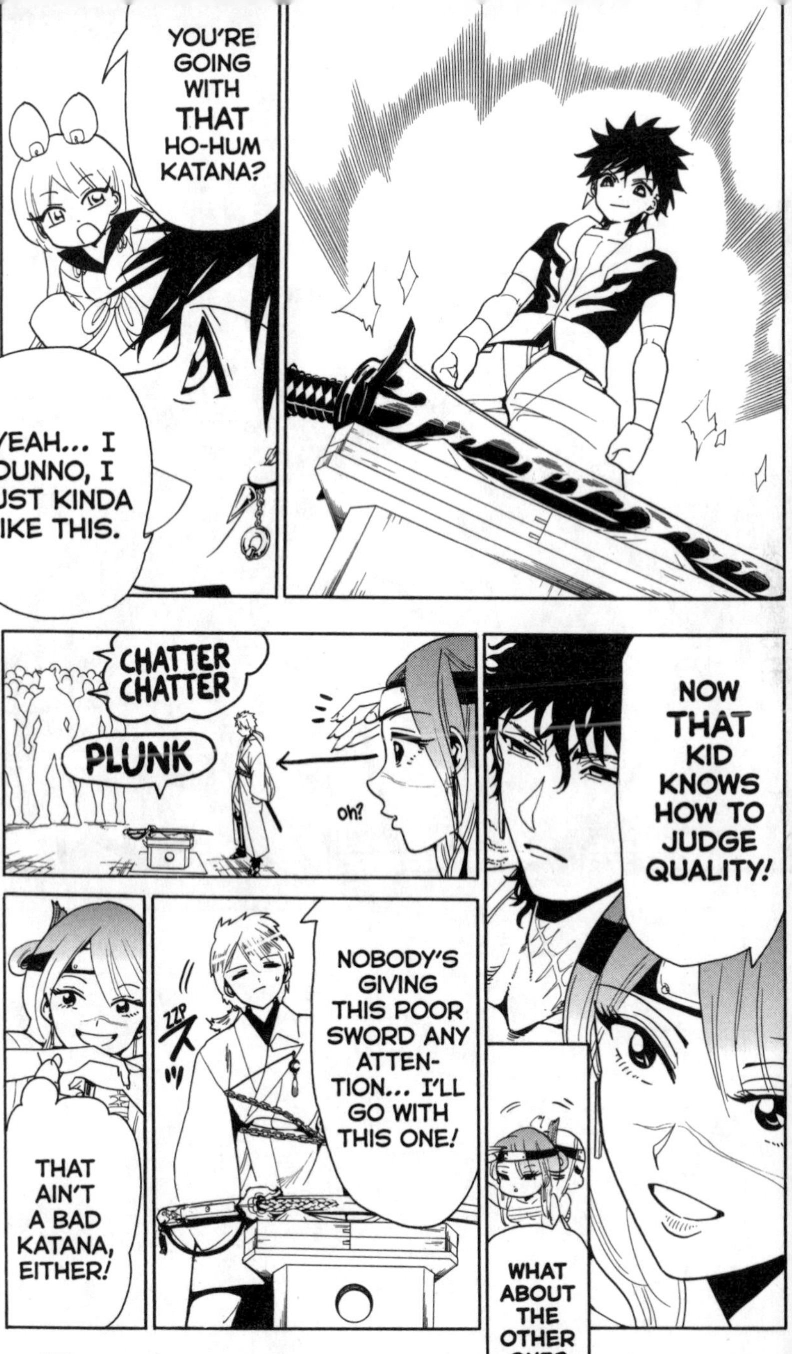
YOU'RE GOING WITH THAT HO-HUM KATANA?
YEAH... I DUNNO, I JUST KINDA LIKE THIS.
NOW THAT KID KNOWS HOW TO JUDGE QUALITY!
WHAT ABOUT THE OTHER ONE?
CHATTER CHATTER
PLUNK
oh?
NOBODY'S GIVING THIS POOR SWORD ANY ATTEN-TION... I'LL GO WITH THIS ONE!
ZZP
THAT AIN'T A BAD KATANA, EITHER!

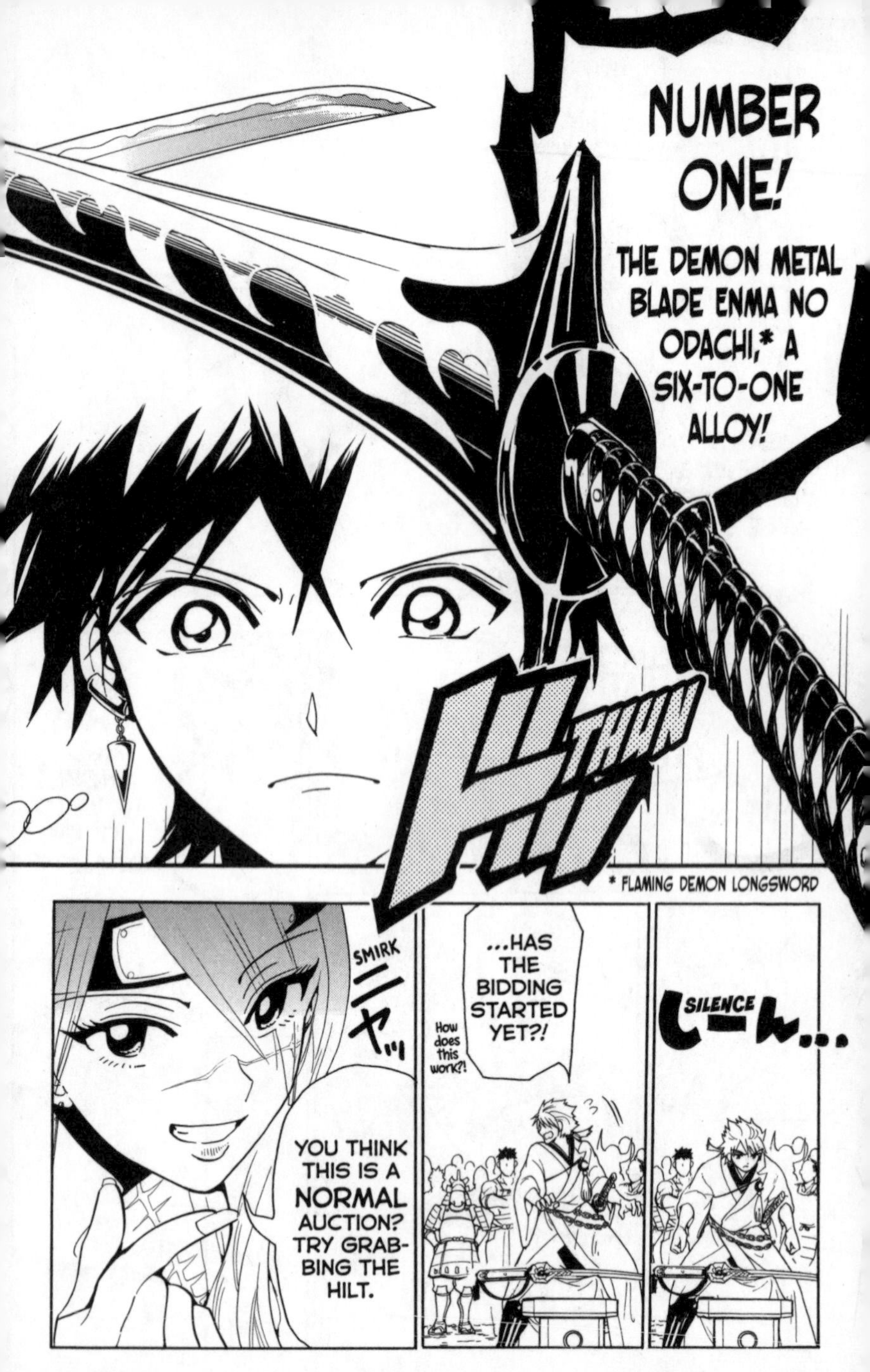
NUMBER ONE!
THE DEMON METAL BLADE ENMA NO ODACHI,* A SIX-TO-ONE ALLOY!
THWUN
* FLAMING DEMON LONGSWORD
SILENCE
...HAS THE BIDDING STARTED YET?!
How does this work?!
SMIRK
YOU THINK THIS IS A NORMAL AUCTION? TRY GRABBING THE HILT.

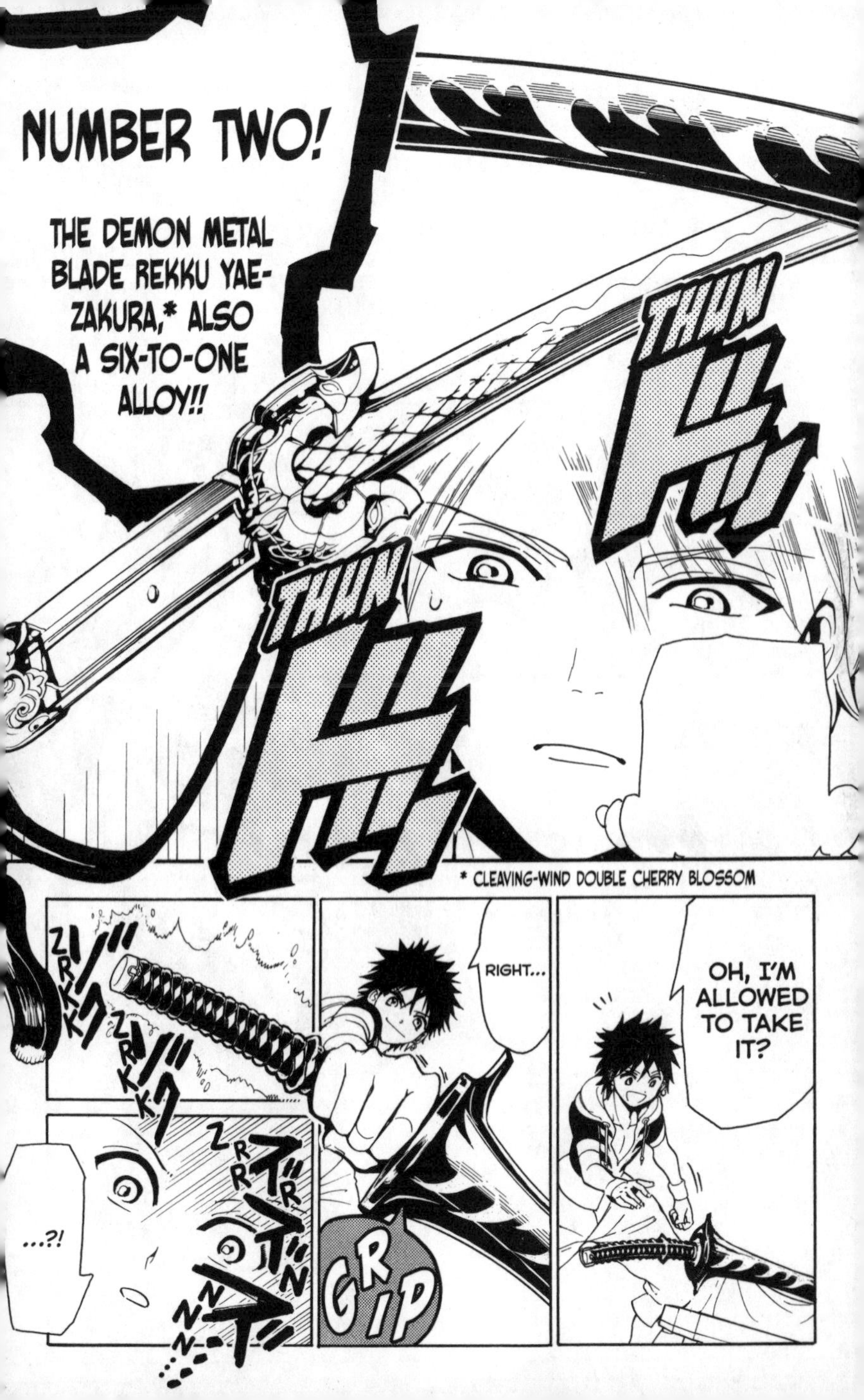
NUMBER TWO!
THE DEMON METAL BLADE REKKU YAE-ZAKURA,* ALSO A SIX-TO-ONE ALLOY!!
THUN
THUN
* CLEAVING-WIND DOUBLE CHERRY BLOSSOM
OH, I'M ALLOWED TO TAKE IT?
RIGHT...
GRIP
ZRKK
ZRKK
...?!
ZRRRT
TNNNN

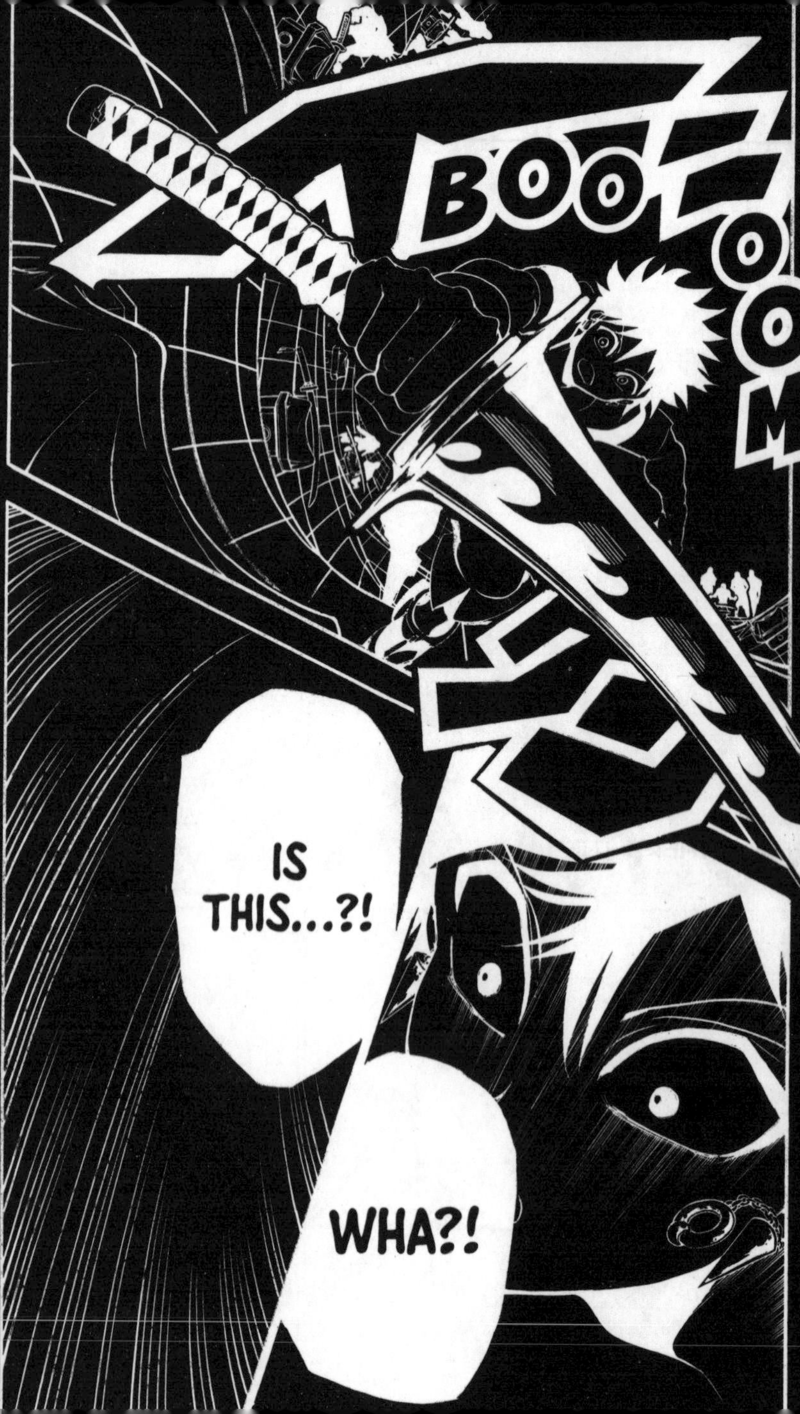
BOOOOM
IS THIS...?!
WHA?!

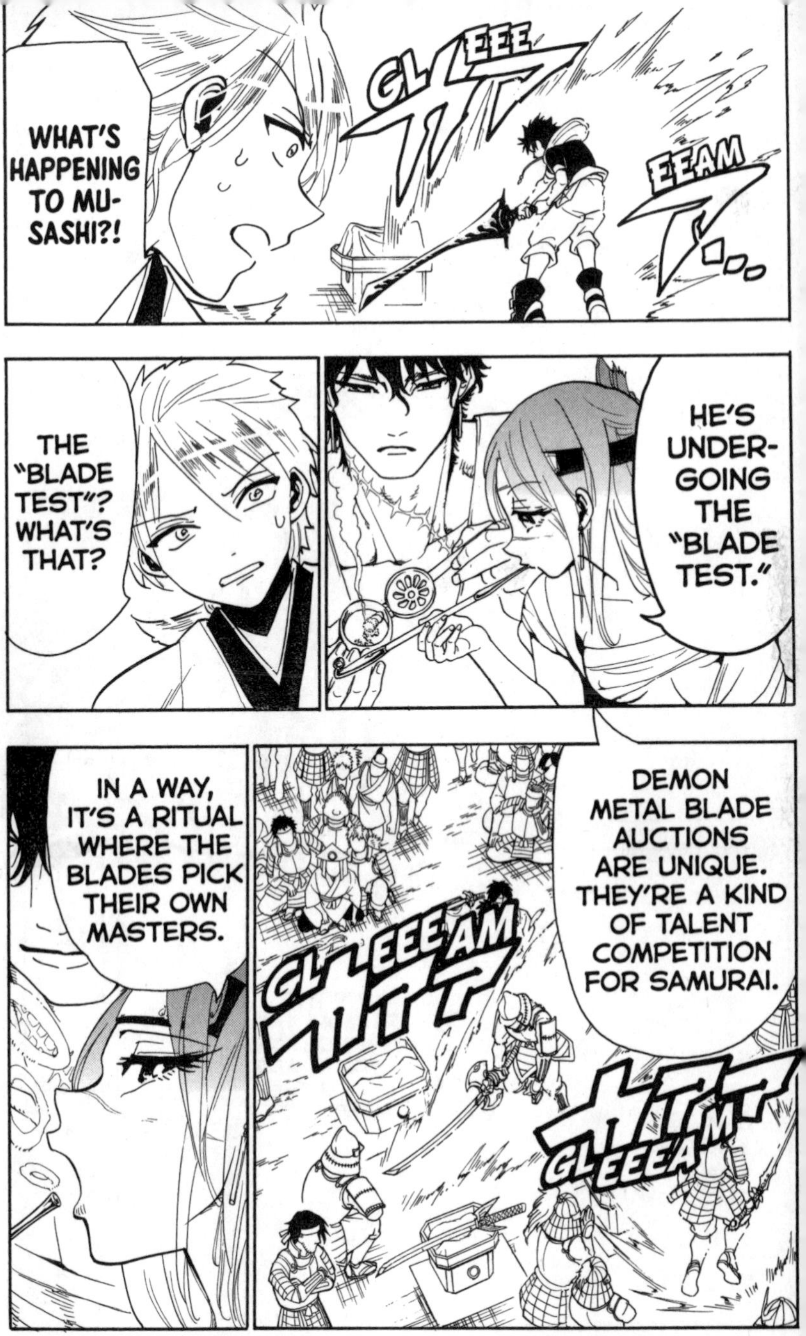
GLEEE
EEAM
WHAT'S HAPPENING TO MU-SASHI?!
HE'S UNDER-GOING THE "BLADE TEST."
THE "BLADE TEST"? WHAT'S THAT?
DEMON METAL BLADE AUCTIONS ARE UNIQUE. THEY'RE A KIND OF TALENT COMPETITION FOR SAMURAI.
GLEEEAM
GLEEEAM
IN A WAY, IT'S A RITUAL WHERE THE BLADES PICK THEIR OWN MASTERS.

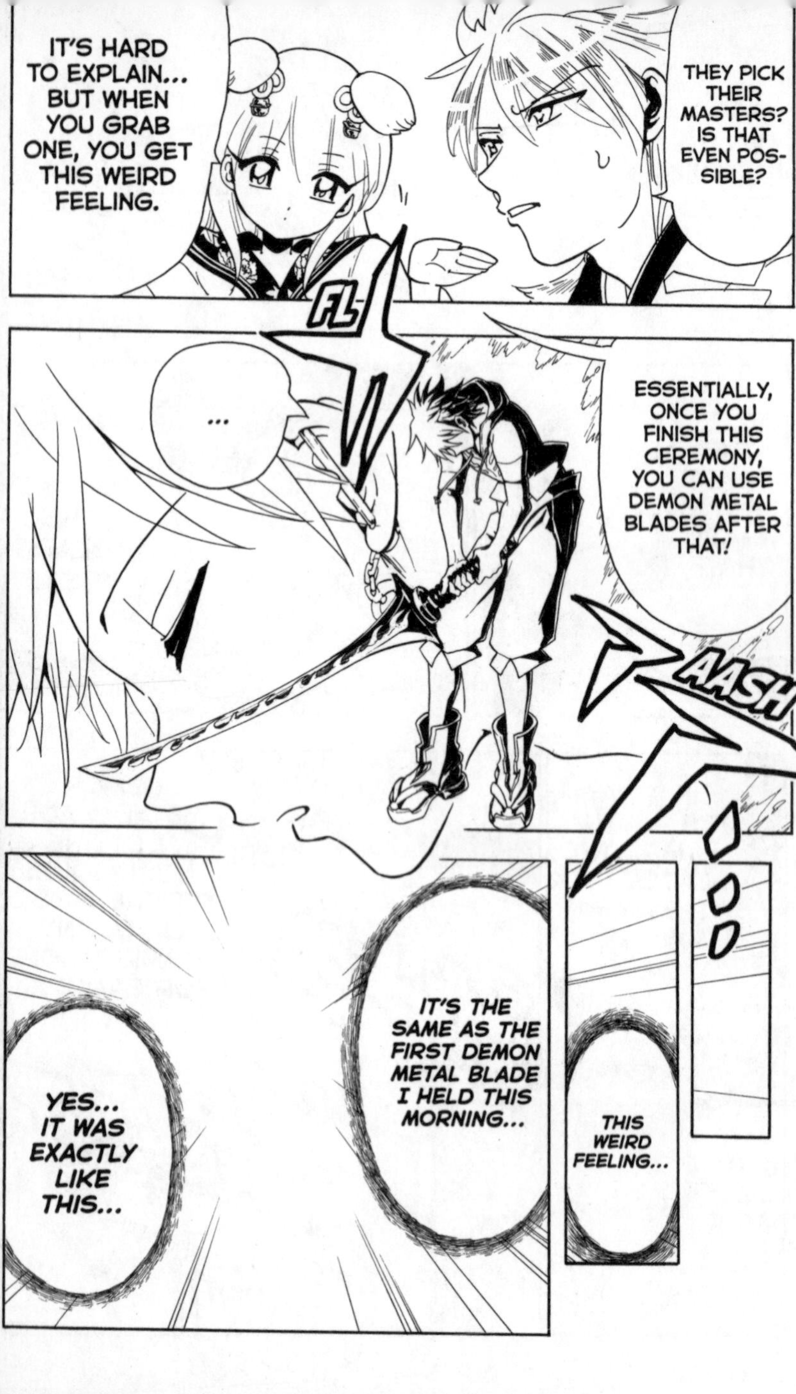
THEY PICK THEIR MASTERS? IS THAT EVEN POSSIBLE?
IT'S HARD TO EXPLAIN... BUT WHEN YOU GRAB ONE, YOU GET THIS WEIRD FEELING.
FL-
ESSENTIALLY, ONCE YOU FINISH THIS CEREMONY, YOU CAN USE DEMON METAL BLADES AFTER THAT!
...
RAASH
THIS WEIRD FEELING...
IT'S THE SAME AS THE FIRST DEMON METAL BLADE I HELD THIS MORNING...
YES... IT WAS EXACTLY LIKE THIS...

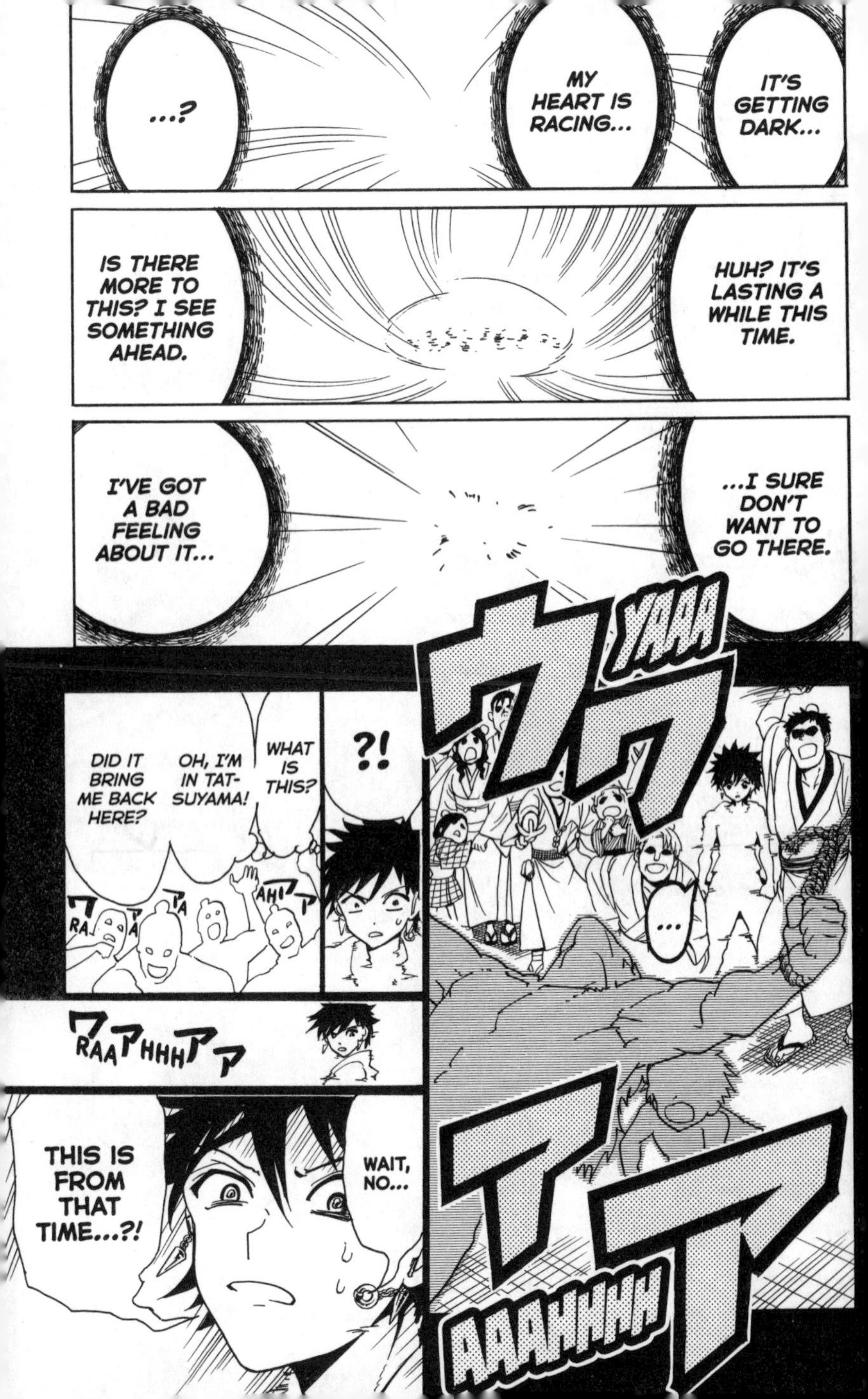

IT'S GETTING DARK...
MY HEART IS RACING...
...?
HUH? IT'S LASTING A WHILE THIS TIME.
IS THERE MORE TO THIS? I SEE SOMETHING AHEAD.
...I SURE DON'T WANT TO GO THERE.
I'VE GOT A BAD FEELING ABOUT IT...
YAAA
...
AAAHHHH
?!
WHAT IS THIS?
OH, I'M IN TAT-SUYAMA!
DID IT BRING ME BACK HERE?
AH
A
A
RA
RAAAHHH
WAIT, NO...
THIS IS FROM THAT TIME...?!

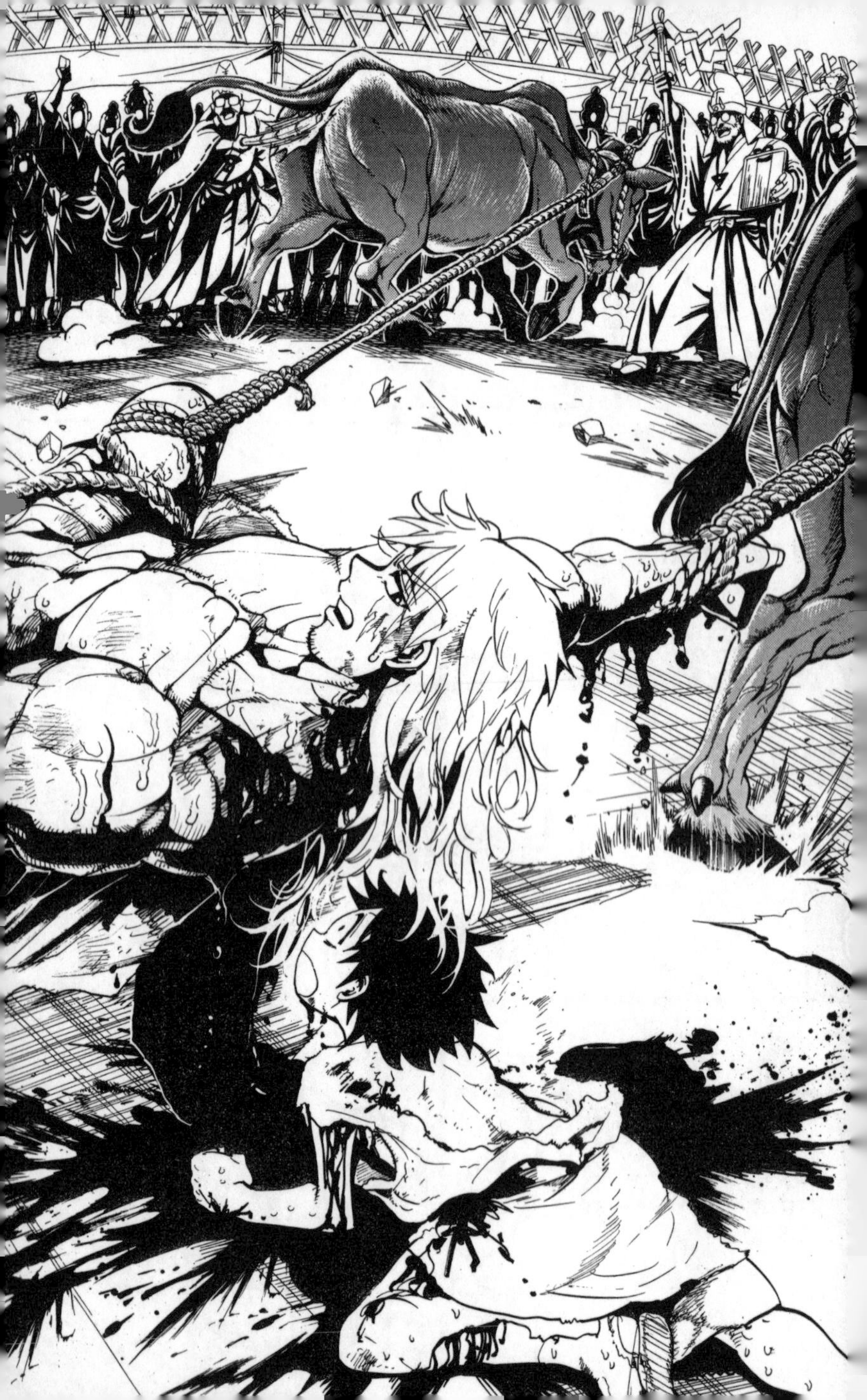

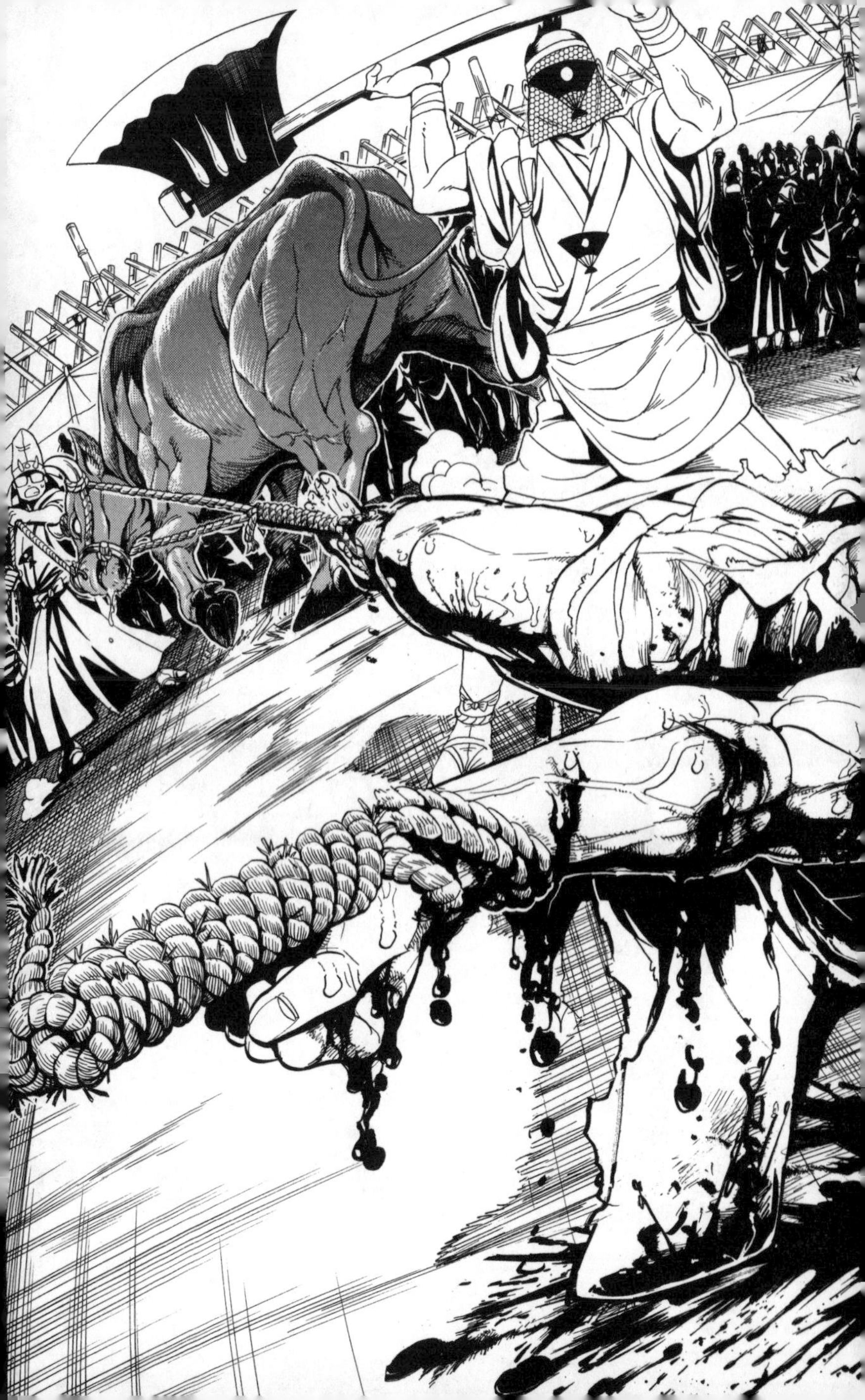

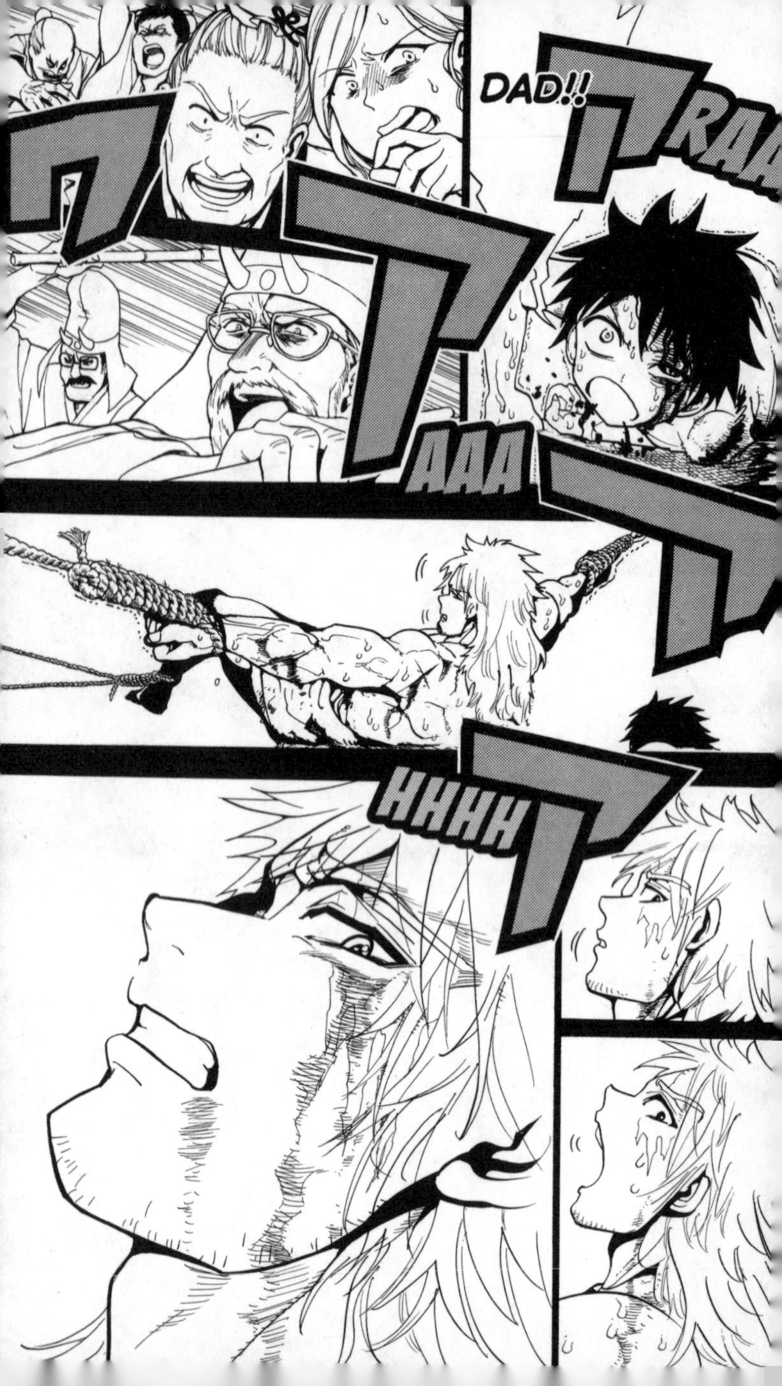
DAD!!
RAA
AAA
HHHH

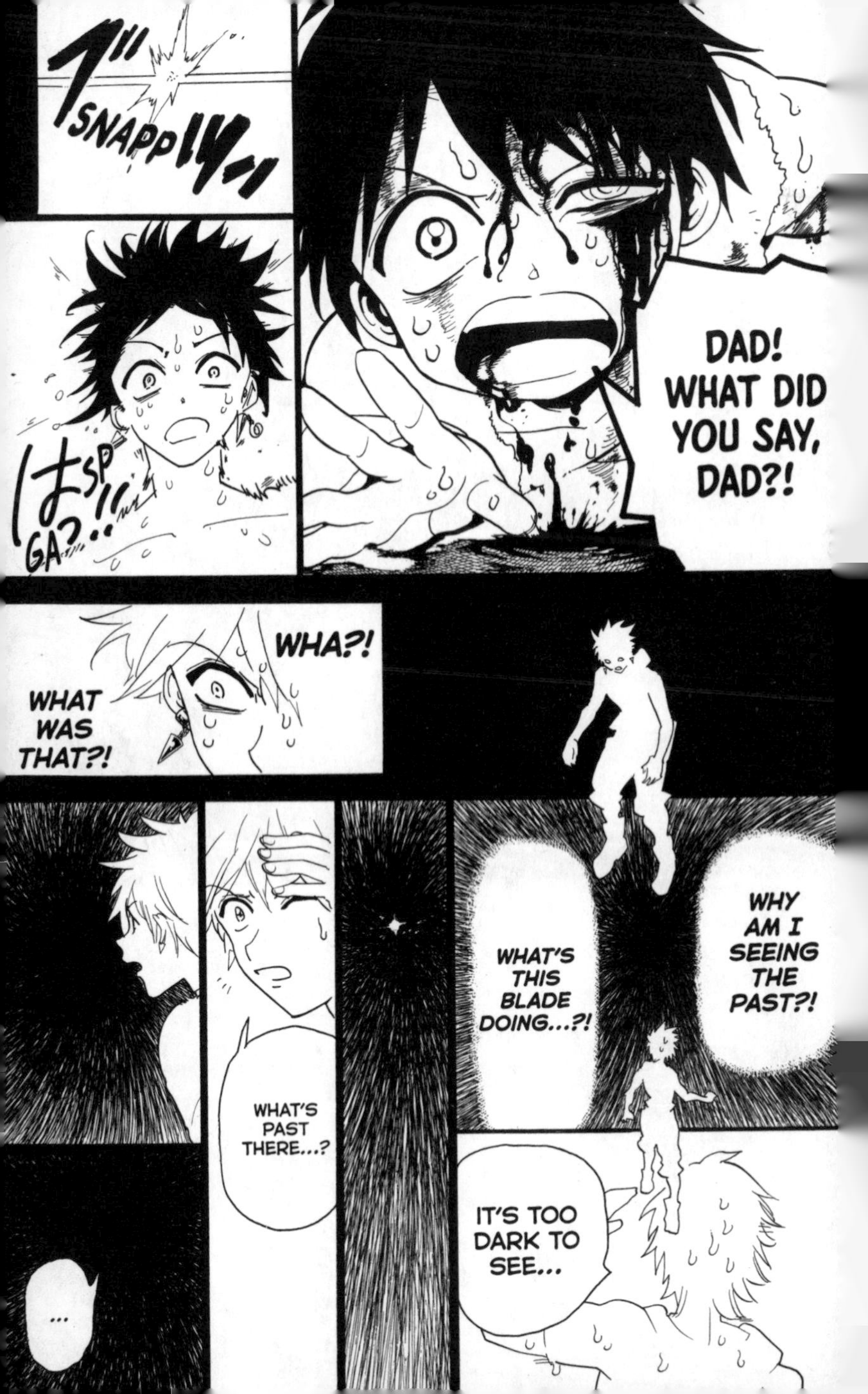
DAD! WHAT DID YOU SAY, DAD?!
SNAPP
GASP?!
WHA?!
WHAT WAS THAT?!
WHY AM I SEEING THE PAST?!
WHAT'S THIS BLADE DOING...?!
IT'S TOO DARK TO SEE...
WHAT'S PAST THERE...?
...

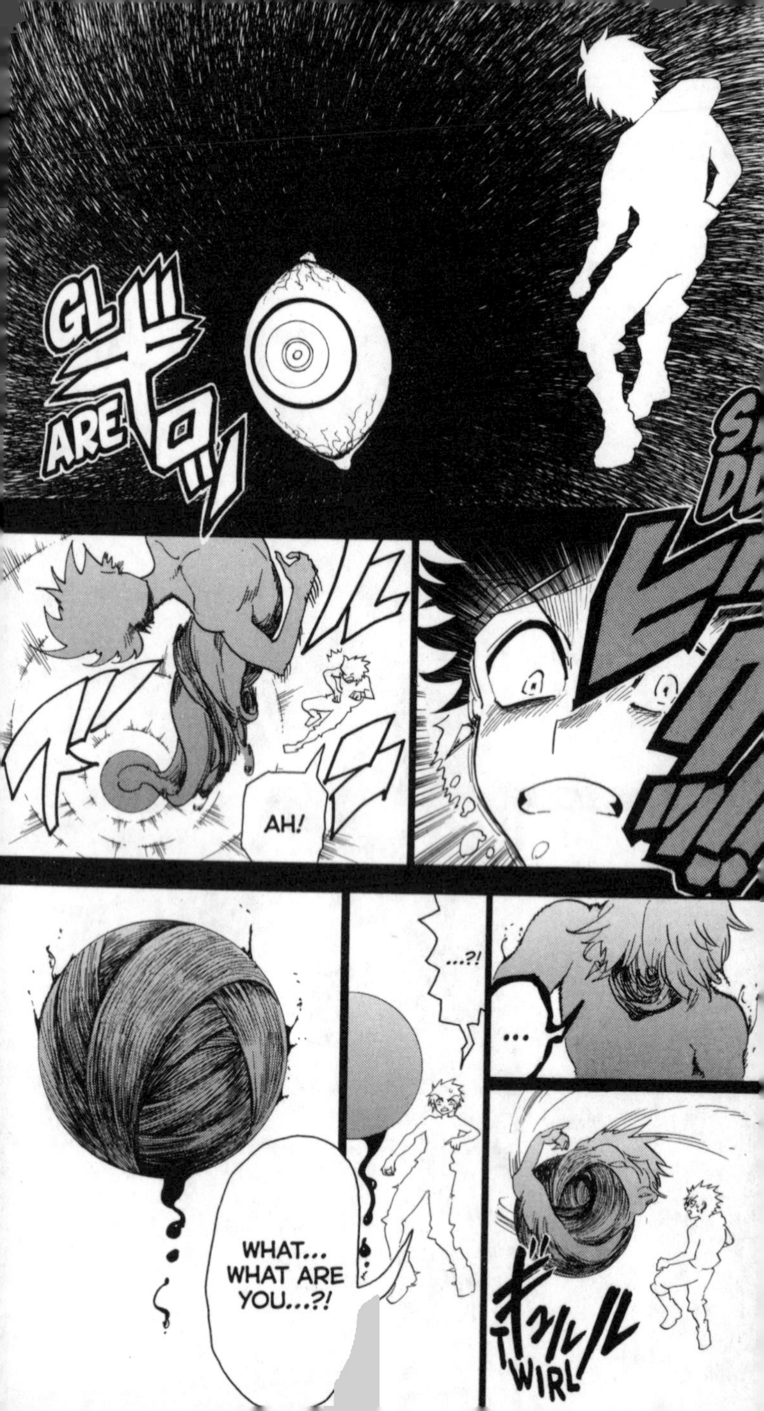
GLARE
AH!
...
TWIRL
...?!
WHAT... WHAT ARE YOU...?!

STAFF

REGULAR ASSISTANTS

舞嶋 大
Maizima Hiro

秋山 有緒子
Yuiko Akiyama

メギ
Megi

吉田 真美
Mami Yoshida

石後 千鳥
Chidori Ishigo

中村 犬彦
Inuhiko Nakamura

EDITORIAL TEAM

詫摩 尚樹
Naoki Takuma

菊地 優斗
Yuto Kikuchi

長塚 雅彦
Masahiko Nagatsuka

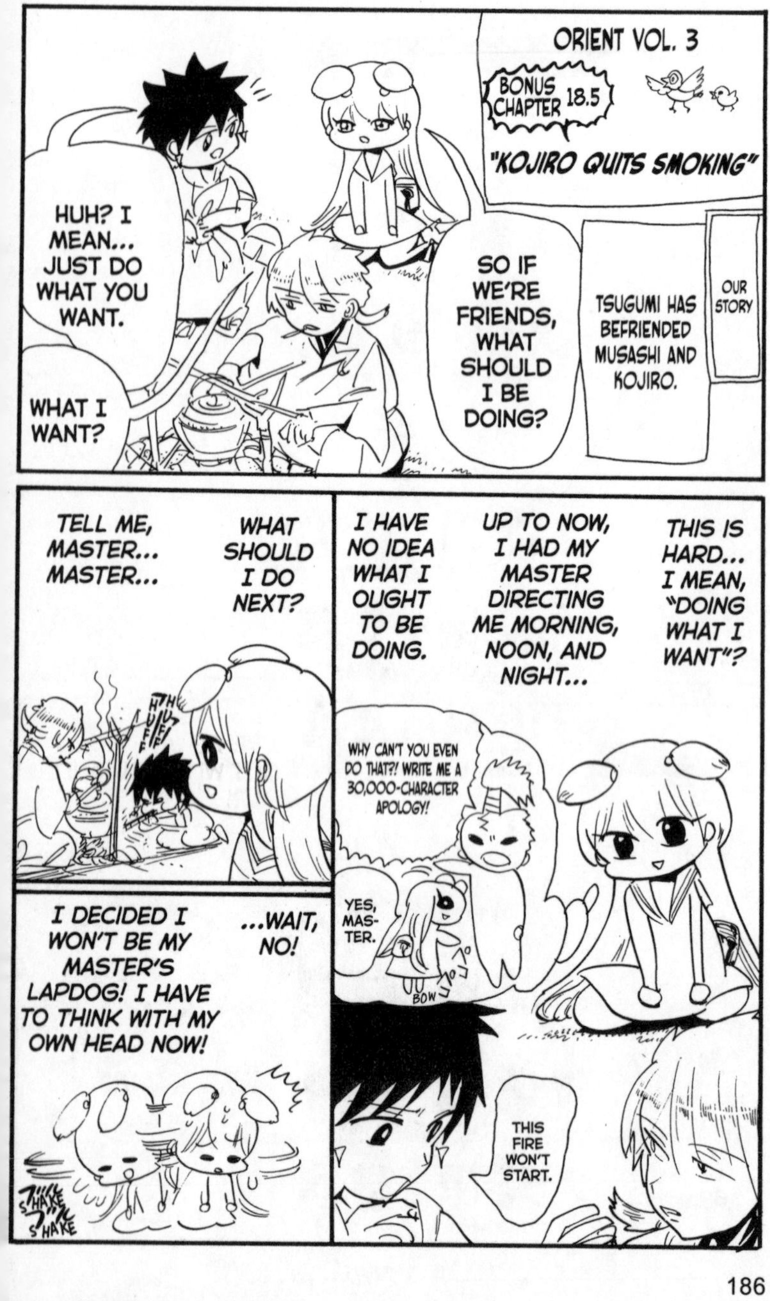
ORIENT VOL. 3
BONUS CHAPTER 18.5
"KOJIRO QUITS SMOKING"
OUR STORY
TSUGUMI HAS BEFRIENDED MUSASHI AND KOJIRO.
SO IF WE'RE FRIENDS, WHAT SHOULD I BE DOING?
HUH? I MEAN... JUST DO WHAT YOU WANT.
WHAT I WANT?
THIS IS HARD... I MEAN, "DOING WHAT I WANT"?
UP TO NOW, I HAD MY MASTER DIRECTING ME MORNING, NOON, AND NIGHT...
I HAVE NO IDEA WHAT I OUGHT TO BE DOING.
WHY CAN'T YOU EVEN DO THAT?! WRITE ME A 30,000-CHARACTER APOLOGY!
YES, MASTER.
BOW
THIS FIRE WON'T START.
WHAT SHOULD I DO NEXT?
TELL ME, MASTER... MASTER...
...WAIT, NO!
I DECIDED I WON'T BE MY MASTER'S LAPDOG! I HAVE TO THINK WITH MY OWN HEAD NOW!
SHAKE
SHAKE

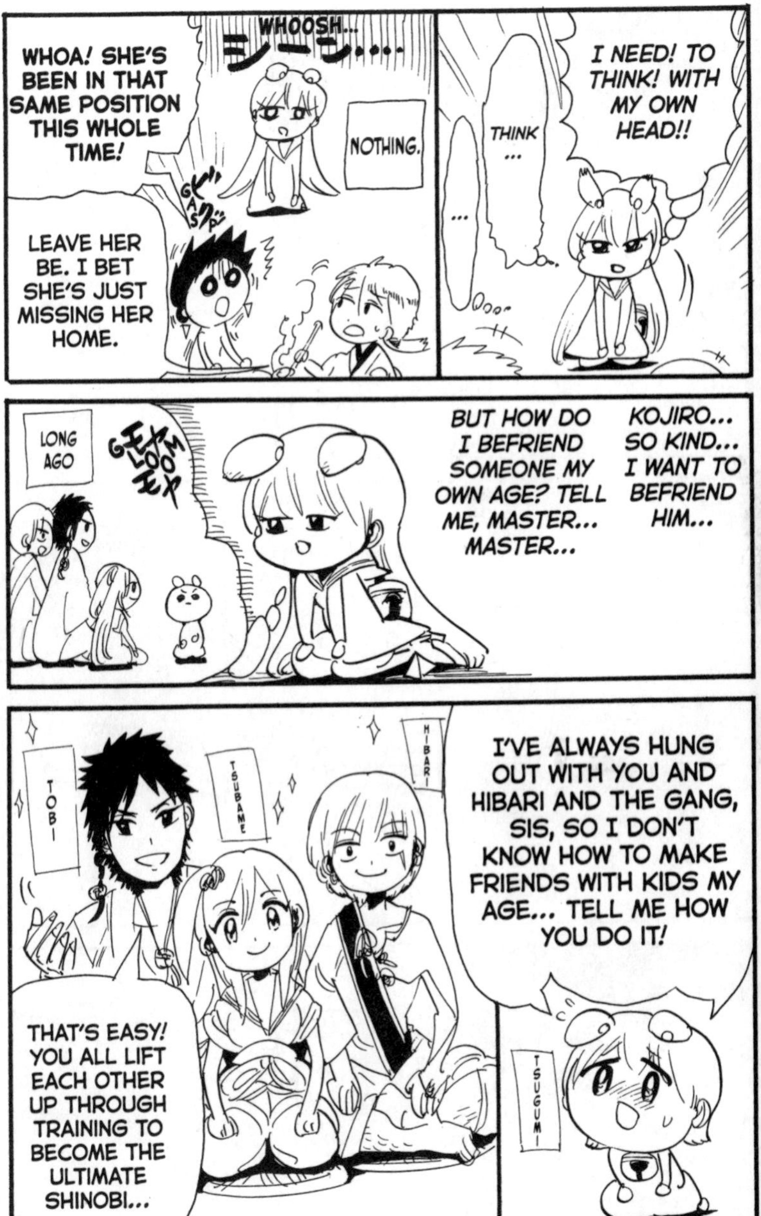
I NEED! TO THINK! WITH MY OWN HEAD!!
THINK ...
...
NOTHING.
WHOOSH...
WHOA! SHE'S BEEN IN THAT SAME POSITION THIS WHOLE TIME!
GASP
LEAVE HER BE. I BET SHE'S JUST MISSING HER HOME.
KOJIRO... SO KIND... I WANT TO BEFRIEND HIM...
BUT HOW DO I BEFRIEND SOMEONE MY OWN AGE? TELL ME, MASTER... MASTER...
GLEAM
LONG AGO
I'VE ALWAYS HUNG OUT WITH YOU AND HIBARI AND THE GANG, SIS, SO I DON'T KNOW HOW TO MAKE FRIENDS WITH KIDS MY AGE... TELL ME HOW YOU DO IT!
HIBARI
TSUBAME
TOBI
TSUGUMI
THAT'S EASY! YOU ALL LIFT EACH OTHER UP THROUGH TRAINING TO BECOME THE ULTIMATE SHINOBI...

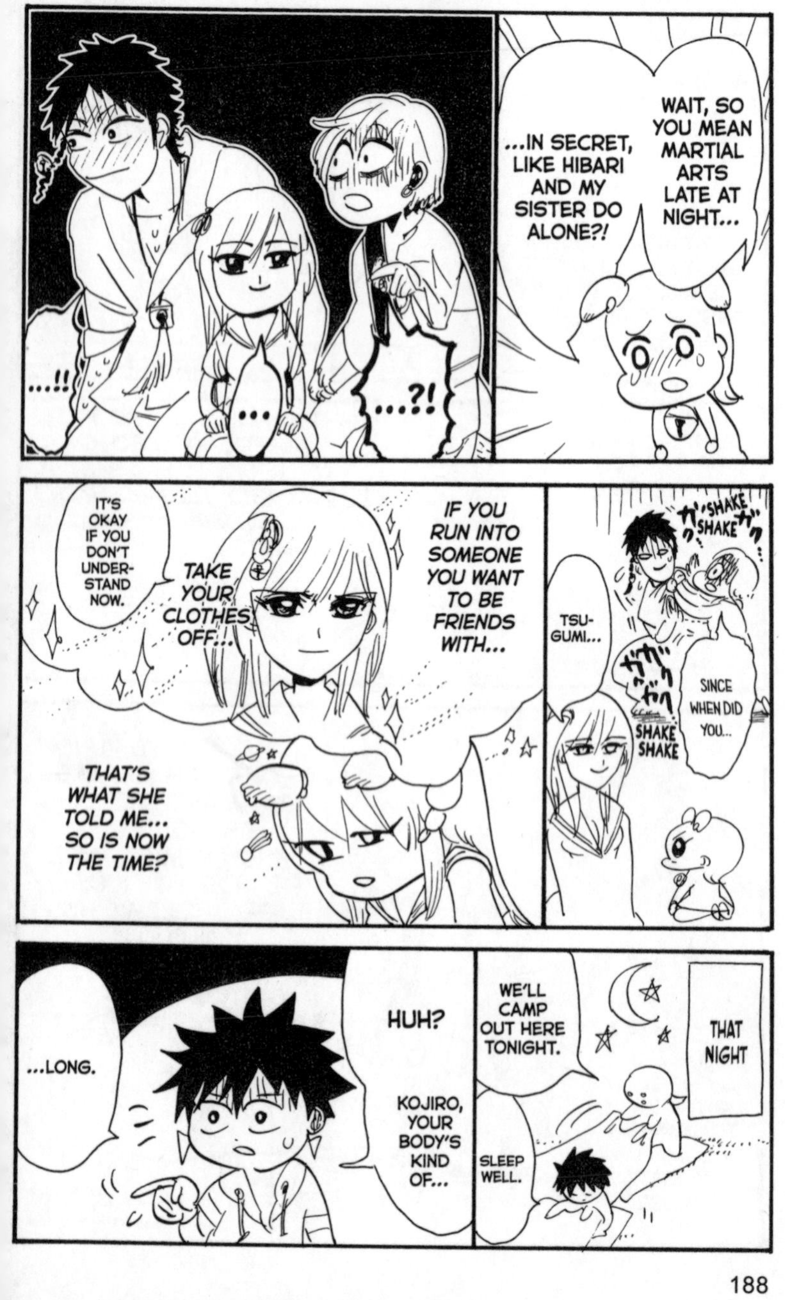
WAIT, SO YOU MEAN MARTIAL ARTS LATE AT NIGHT...
...IN SECRET, LIKE HIBARI AND MY SISTER DO ALONE?!
...?!
...
...!!
SHAKE SHAKE
TSU-GUMI...
SINCE WHEN DID YOU...
SHAKE SHAKE
IF YOU RUN INTO SOMEONE YOU WANT TO BE FRIENDS WITH...
TAKE YOUR CLOTHES OFF...
IT'S OKAY IF YOU DON'T UNDER-STAND NOW.
THAT'S WHAT SHE TOLD ME... SO IS NOW THE TIME?
THAT NIGHT
WE'LL CAMP OUT HERE TONIGHT.
SLEEP WELL.
HUH?
KOJIRO, YOUR BODY'S KIND OF...
...LONG.

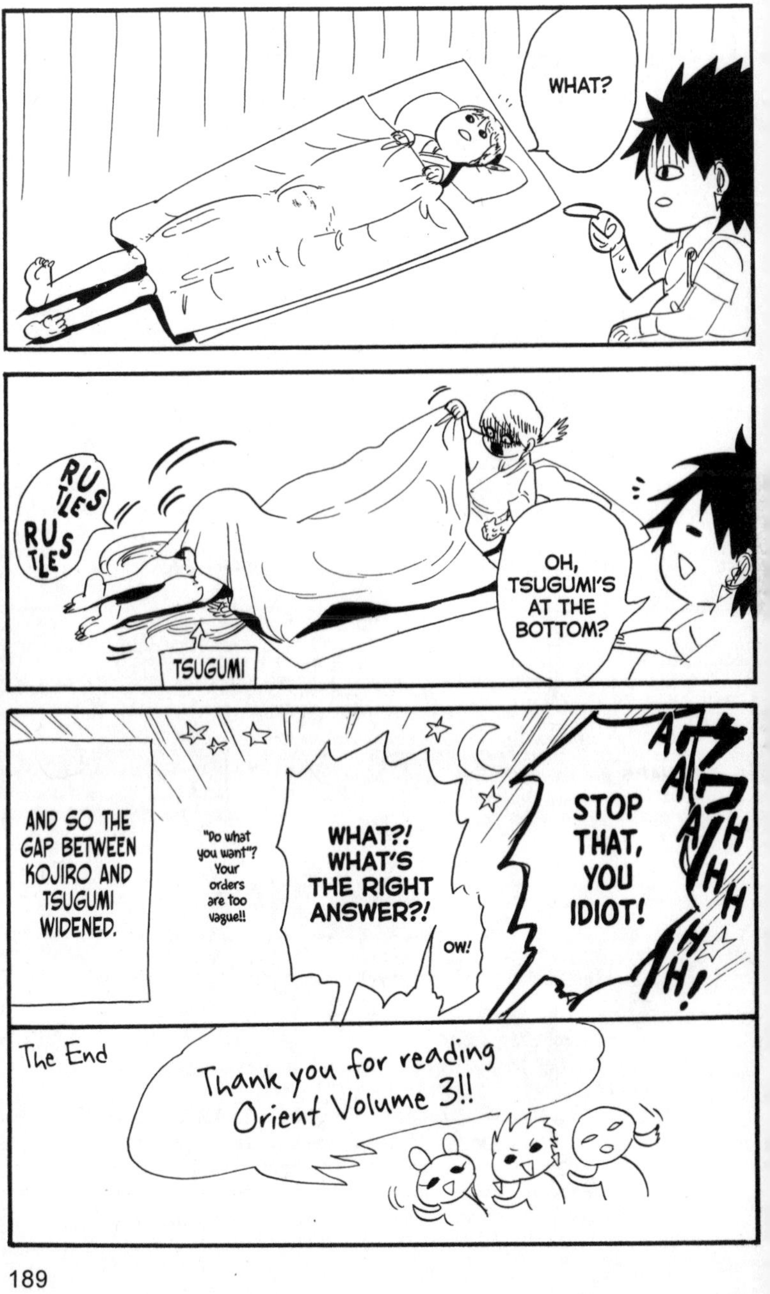
WHAT?
OH, TSUGUMI'S AT THE BOTTOM?
RUSTLE RUSTLE
TSUGUMI
AAAHHHHHH!
STOP THAT, YOU IDIOT!
OW!
WHAT?! WHAT'S THE RIGHT ANSWER?!
"Do what you want"? Your orders are too vague!!
AND SO THE GAP BETWEEN KOJIRO AND TSUGUMI WIDENED.
Thank you for reading Orient Volume 3!!
The End

A Kodansha Comics Trade Paperback Original
Orient 3 copyright © 2018 Shinobu Ohtaka
English translation copyright © 2021 Shinobu Ohtaka

All rights reserved.

Published in the United States by Kodansha Comics, an imprint of
Kodansha USA Publishing, LLC, New York.

Publication rights for this English edition arranged through
Kodansha Ltd., Tokyo.

First published in Japan in 2018 by Kodansha Ltd., Tokyo.

ISBN 978-1-64651-162-4

Printed in the United States of America.

www.kodanshacomics.com

9 8 7 6 5 4 3 2 1
Translation: Kevin Gifford
Lettering: Belynda Ungurath
Kodansha Comics edition cover design by Phil Balsman
YKS Services LLC/SKY Japan, INC.

Publisher: Kiichiro Sugawara

Director of publishing services: Ben Applegate
Associate director of operations: Stephen Pakula
Publishing services managing editors: Alanna Ruse, Madison Salters
Assistant production managers: Emi Lotto, Angela Zurlo
Logo and character art ©Kodansha USA Publishing, LLC